Türing Machine: In 1936 Dr. Turing wrote a paper on the design and the limitations of computing machines. For this reason they are sometimes known by his name. The umlaut is an unearned and undesirable addition, due, presumably, to an impression that anything so incomprehensible must be Teutonic.

— *Faster Than Thought: A Symposium on Digital Computing Machines* (1953)

Credits

Executive Editor
Chris Webb

Development Editor
Christopher J. Rivera

Technical Editor
Peter Bonfanti

Production Editor
Angela Smith

Copy Editor
Sydney Jones

Editorial Manager
Mary Beth Wakefield

Production Manager
Tim Tate

Vice President and Executive Group Publisher
Richard Swadley

Vice President and Executive Publisher
Joseph B. Wikert

Project Coordinator, Cover
Lynsey Stanford

Proofreader
David Fine

Indexer
Melanie Belkin

The Annotated Turing

A Guided Tour through Alan Turing's Historic Paper on Computability and the Turing Machine

Charles Petzold

WILEY

Wiley Publishing, Inc.

The Annotated Turing: A Guided Tour through Alan Turing's Historic Paper on Computability and the Turing Machine

Published by
Wiley Publishing, Inc.
10475 Crosspoint Boulevard
Indianapolis, IN 46256
www.wiley.com

Copyright © 2008 by Wiley Publishing, Inc., Indianapolis, Indiana

Published simultaneously in Canada

ISBN: 978-0-470-22905-7

Manufactured in the United States of America

V10007895_012919

Contents

Introduction

Anyone who has explored the history, technology, or theory of computers has likely encountered the concept of the *Turing Machine*. The Turing Machine is an imaginary — not quite even hypothetical — computer invented in 1936 by English mathematician Alan Turing (1912–1954) to help solve a question in mathematical logic. As a by-product, Turing founded a new field of research known as *computation theory* or *computability*, which is the study of the abilities and limitations of digital computers.

Although the Turing Machine is a rather implausible computer, it benefits from being extremely simple. The basic Turing Machine performs just a few simple operations. If the machine did anything less than what it does, it wouldn't do anything at all. Yet, through combinations of these simple operations, the Turing Machine can perform any computation that can be done on modern digital computers.

By stripping the computer to the raw basics, we can understand better the abilities of digital computers — and just as importantly, their inabilities. Years before anyone had demonstrated what a computer could do, Turing proved what computers could *never* do.

The Turing Machine remains a popular topic for exposition and discussion. (Try the term "Turing Machine" in your favorite Internet search engine.) Yet, I suspect that Alan Turing's original paper describing his invention is rarely read. Perhaps this neglect has something to do with the title: "On Computable Numbers, with an Application to the Entscheidungsproblem." Even if you can say that word — try accenting the second syllable and pronouncing it like "shy" and you won't be far off — and you know what it means ("decision problem"), the suspicion remains that Turing is expecting his reader to have basic knowledge of heavy German mathematical matters. A quick glance through the paper — and its use of a German gothic font to represent machine states — doesn't help allay these fears. Can a reader today take on a paper published 70 years ago in the *Proceedings of the London Mathematical Society* and stay afloat long enough to glean a few insights and even (perhaps) satisfaction?

That's what this book is all about. It contains Turing's original 36-page paper[1] "On Computable Numbers, with an Application to the Entscheidungsproblem" and the follow-up 3-page correction[2] with background chapters and extensive

---

[1] Alan Turing, "On Computable Numbers, with an Application to the Entscheidungsproblem," *Proceedings of the London Mathematical Society*, 2nd series, Vol. 42 (1936), pp. 230–265.
[2] Alan Turing, "On Computable Numbers, with an Application to the Entscheidungsproblem. A Correction," *Proceedings of the London Mathematical Society*, 2nd series, Vol. 43 (1937), pp. 544–546.

annotations. Reading Turing's original paper allows a unique journey inside his fertile and fascinating mind as he constructs the machine that has had such profound implications for computing and, indeed, our understanding of the limitations of mathematics, the workings of the human mind, and perhaps even the nature of the universe. (The term "Turing Machine" doesn't appear in Turing's paper, of course. He called it a "computing machine." But the term "Turing Machine" was used as early as 1937[3] and has remained the standard term ever since.)

In my annotations to Turing's paper, I have found it useful to interrupt his narrative frequently with explanations and elaborations. I have tried (without total success) not to interrupt him in the middle of a sentence. For the most part I retain Turing's own terminology and notation in my discussion, but at times I felt compelled to introduce terms that Turing doesn't use but which I found helpful in explaining his work.

The text of Turing's paper is identified by a shaded background, like so:

> We shall avoid confusion by speaking more often of computable sequences than of computable numbers.

We (meaning my publisher and I) have attempted to preserve the typography and layout of the original paper, except where oddities (such as spaces before colons) cause panicky reactions in modern editors. All original line breaks are retained. Turing's paper has a few typographical errors, mistakes, and omissions. Although I have left these uncorrected, I point them out in my commentary. Turing often refers to early parts of his paper by the page numbers in the original journal. I've left those references alone, but provided help in my commentary for finding the particular page in this book. Occasionally you'll see a number in Turing's text in brackets:

> When the letters are replaced by figures, as in § 5, we shall have a numerical
> [243]
> description of the complete configuration, which may be called its description number.

That's the original page break and the original page number. My footnotes are numbered; Turing's footnotes use symbols, and are also identified by shading.

If you were to remove the pages from this book, cut out and discard everything that doesn't have a shaded background, and then tape the remnants back together, you'd be left with Turing's complete paper, and one sad author. Perhaps a more interesting strategy is to read this book first, and then go back and read Turing's paper by itself without my rude interruptions.

---

[3] Alonzo Church, review of "On Computable Numbers, with an Application to the Entscheidungsproblem," *The Journal of Symbolic Logic*, Vol. 2, No. 1 (Mar. 1937), 42–43.

Turing's paper is spread out between pages 64 and 297 of this book, and the correction appears between pages 309 and 321. Turing's paper is divided into 11 sections (and an appendix) that begin on the following book pages:

Turing's original motivation in writing this paper was to solve a problem formulated by German mathematician David Hilbert (1862–1943). Hilbert asked for a general process to determine the provability of arbitrary statements in mathematical logic. Finding this "general process" was known as the Entscheidungsproblem. Although the Entscheidungsproblem was certainly the motivation for Turing's paper, the bulk of the paper itself is really about computable numbers. In Turing's definition, these are numbers that can be calculated by a machine. Turing's exploration of computable numbers accounts for the first 60 percent of the paper, which can be read and understood without any familiarity with Hilbert's work in mathematical logic or the Entscheidungsproblem.

The distinction between computable numbers and "real numbers" is crucial to Turing's argument. For that reason, the preliminary chapters of this book provide a background into our classification of numbers, encompassing integers, rational numbers, irrational numbers, algebraic numbers, and transcendental numbers, all of which are also categorized as real numbers. I have tried not to rely on any prior knowledge more sophisticated than high-school mathematics. I am aware that several decades may separate some readers from the joys of high school, so I have tried to refresh those memories. I apologize if my pedagogical zeal has resulted in explanations that are condescending or insulting.

Although I suspect that this book will be read mostly by computer science majors, programmers, and other techies, I have tried to make the non-programmer feel welcome by defining chummy jargon and terms of art. Turing's paper is "one of the intellectual landmarks of the last century,"[4] and I hope this book makes that paper accessible to a much broader audience.

---

[4] John P. Burgess, preface in George S. Boolos, John P. Burgess, and Richard C. Jeffrey, *Computability and Logic*, fourth edition (Cambridge University Press, 2002), xi.

To accommodate the needs of different readers, I have divided this book into four parts:

Part I ("Foundations") covers the historical and mathematical background necessary to begin reading Turing's paper.

Part II ("Computable Numbers") contains the bulk of Turing's paper and will be of primary interest to readers interested in the Turing Machine and issues related to computability.

Part III ("Das Entscheidungsproblem") begins with an all-too-brief background in mathematical logic and continues with the remainder of Turing's paper.

Part IV ("And Beyond") discusses how the Turing Machine has come to be an essential tool for understanding computers, human consciousness, and the universe itself.

The mathematical content of Part III is necessarily more difficult than that of earlier chapters, and covered at a faster pace. Those readers not particularly interested in the implications of Turing's paper for mathematical logic might even want to skip the five chapters of Part III and jump right to Part IV.

This book touches on several large areas in mathematics, including computability and mathematical logic. I have picked and chosen only those topics and concepts most relevant to understanding Turing's paper. Many details are omitted, and this book is no substitute for the rigor and depth you'll find in dedicated books on the subjects of computability and logic. Those readers interested in delving further into these fascinating areas of study can consult the bibliography for guidance.

Alan Turing published about 30 papers and articles during his lifetime[5] but never wrote a book. Two of Turing's papers account for most of his continued fame: "On Computable Numbers" is the first, of course. The second is a far less technical article entitled "Computing Machinery and Intelligence" (published in 1950) in which Turing invented what is now called the Turing Test for artificial intelligence. Basically, if a machine can fool us into believing that it's a person, we should probably grant that it's intelligent.

The Turing Machine and the Turing Test are Alan Turing's two bids for lexical and cultural immortality. They may at first seem like two entirely different concepts, but they're not. The Turing Machine is really an attempt to describe in a very mechanistic way what a human being does in carrying out a mathematical algorithm; the Turing Test is a human evaluation of the functioning of a computer. From his earliest mathematical researches through his last, Turing explored the relationship between the human mind and computing machines in a manner that continues to be fascinating and provocative.

---

[5]These and other documents are available in the four volumes of *The Collected Works of A.M. Turing* (Amsterdam: Elsevier, 1992, 2001). Much of the important material has been collected by B. Jack Copeland into *The Essential Turing* (Oxford University Press, 2004) and *Alan Turing's Automatic Computing Engine* (Oxford University Press, 2005). The former book contains articles and papers related to the Turing Machine. The latter book is about the ACE computer project in the mid- to late 1940s.

It is possible to discuss Turing's work without mentioning anything about Turing the man, and many textbooks on computability don't bother with the biographical details. I have not found that to be possible here. Turing's secret work in cryptanalysis during World War II, his involvement in seminal computer projects, his speculations about artificial intelligence, his sexual orientation, his arrest and prosecution for the crime of "gross indecency," and his early death by apparent suicide at the age of 41 all demand attention.

My job of recounting the highlights of Turing's life has been greatly eased by the wonderful biography *Alan Turing: The Enigma* (Simon & Schuster, 1983) by English mathematician Andrew Hodges (b. 1949). Hodges became interested in Turing partly through his own participation in the gay liberation movement of the 1970s. Hodges's biography inspired a play by Hugh Whitemore called *Breaking the Code* (1986). On stage and in a shortened version adapted for television in 1996, the role of Alan Turing was portrayed by Derek Jacobi.

Like the earlier English mathematicians and computer pioneers Charles Babbage (1791–1871) and Ada Lovelace (1815–1852), Turing has become an icon of the computer age. The Turing Award is an annual prize of $100,000 given by the Association for Computing Machinery (ACM) for major contributions to computing. There is a Turing Programming Language (derived from Pascal) and Turing's World software for assembling Turing Machines.

Turing's name has become almost a generic term for computer programming — so much so that A. K. Dewdney can title his "Excursions in Computer Science" as *The Turing Omnibus* (Computer Science Press, 1989). A book about "Western Culture in the Computer Age" by J. David Bolter is called *Turing's Man* (University of North Caroline Press, 1984), and Brian Rotman's critique of traditional mathematical concepts of infinity *Ad Infinitum* (Stanford University Press, 1993) is amusingly subtitled "The Ghost in Turing's Machine."

Alan Turing has also attracted some academic interest outside the mathematics and computer science departments. The collection *Novel Gazing: Queer Readings in Fiction* (Duke University Press, 1997) features an essay by Tyler Curtain entitled "The 'Sinister Fruitiness' of Machines: *Neuromancer*, Internet Sexuality, and the Turing Test." Dr. Curtain's title refers to the famous William Gibson "cyberpunk" novel *Neuromancer* (Ace, 1984) in which the Turing Police help ensure that artificial intelligence entities don't try to augment their own intelligence.

Turing has also shown up in the titles of several novels. Marvin Minsky (the famous M.I.T. researcher into artificial intelligence) collaborated with science-fiction novelist Harry Harrison on *The Turing Option* (Warner Books, 1992), and Berkeley Computer Science professor Christos H. Papadimitriou has weighed in with *Turing (A Novel About Computation)* (MIT Press, 2003).

In *Turing's Delirium* (trans. Lisa Carter, Houghton Mifflin, 2006) by Bolivian novelist Edmundo Paz Soldán, a cryptanalyst nicknamed Turing discovers the dangers of using his skills for a corrupt government. In Janna Levin's *A Madman*

Dreams of Turing Machines (Knopf, 2006), the fictionalized lives of Alan Turing and Kurt Gödel strangely interact through space and time.

Alan Turing is a character in Neal Stephenson's *Cryptonomicon* (Avon, 1999), Robert Harris's *Enigma* (Hutchinson, 1995), John L. Casti's *The Cambridge Quintet: A Work of Scientific Speculation* (Perseus Books, 1998), and, of course, Douglas Hofstadter's *Gödel, Escher, Bach* (Basic Books, 1979). Alan Turing even narrates part of *The Turing Test* (BBC, 2000), a Dr. Who novel by Paul Leonard.

While it's nice to see Alan Turing honored in these many ways, there's a danger that Turing's actual work becomes neglected in the process. Even people who have formally studied computation theory and think they know all about Turing Machines will, I hope, find some surprises in encountering the very first Turing Machine built by the master himself.

* * *

This book was conceived in 1999. I wrote a little then and irregularly over the next five years. The first eleven chapters were mostly completed in 2004 and 2005. I wrote the last seven chapters in 2007 and 2008, interrupting work only to get married (finally!) to my longtime best friend and love of my life, Deirdre Sinnott.

Many thanks to the London Mathematical Society for permission to reprint Alan Turing's paper "On Computable Numbers, with an Application to the Entscheidungsproblem" in its entirety.

Walter Williams and Larry Smith read early drafts of this book, caught a number of errors, and offered several helpful suggestions for improvements.

To the folks at Wiley, I am eternally grateful for their work in turning this pet project of mine into an actual published book. Chris Webb got the book going, Development Editor Christopher Rivera and Production Editor Angela Smith conquered the many structural and typographical challenges, and Technical Editor Peter Bonfanti helped me to be a little more diligent with the technical stuff. Many others at Wiley worked behind the scenes to help make this book as good as possible. Any flaws, imperfections, or hideous errors that remain can only be attributed to the author.

Any author stands on the shoulders of those who have come before. The selected bibliography lists a few of the many books that helped me write this one. I'd also like to thank the staff of the New York Public Library, and especially the Science, Industry, and Business Library (SIBL). I've made extensive use of JSTOR to obtain original papers, and I've found Wikipedia, Google Book Search, and Wolfram MathWorld to be useful as well.

* * *

Information and resources connected with this book can be found on the website www.TheAnnotatedTuring.com.

Charles Petzold
New York City and Roscoe, New York
May, 2008

Foundations

1 This Tomb Holds Diophantus

Many centuries ago, in ancient Alexandria, an old man had to bury his son. Heartbroken, the man distracted himself by assembling a large collection of algebra problems and their solutions in a book he called the *Arithmetica*. That is practically all that is known of Diophantus of Alexandria, and most of it comes from a riddle believed to have been written by a close friend soon after his death[1]:

> This tomb holds Diophantus. Ah, what a marvel! And the tomb tells scientifically the measure of his life. God vouchsafed that he should be a boy for the sixth part of his life; when a twelfth was added, his cheeks acquired a beard; He kindled for him the light of marriage after a seventh, and in the fifth year after his marriage He granted him a son. Alas! late-begotten and miserable child, when he had reached the measure of half his father's life, the chill grave took him. After consoling his grief by this science of numbers for four years, he reached the end of his life.[2]

The epitaph is a bit ambiguous regarding the death of Diophantus's son. He is said to have died at "half his father's life," but does that mean half the father's age at the time of the son's death, or half the age at which Diophantus himself eventually died? You can work it out either way, but the latter assumption — Diophantus's son lived half the number of years that Diophantus eventually did — is the one with the nice, clean solution in whole numbers without fractional years.

Let's represent the total number of years that Diophantus lived as x. Each part of Diophantus's life is either a fraction of his total life (for example, x divided by 6 for the years he spent as a boy) or a whole number of years (for example, 5 years

[1] Thomas L. Heath, *Diophantus of Alexandria: A Study in the History of Greek Algebra*, second edition (Cambridge University Press, 1910; Dover Publications, 1964), 3.
[2] *Greek Mathematical Works II: Aristarchus to Pappus of Alexandria* (Loeb Classical Library No. 362), translated by Ivor Thomas (Harvard University Press, 1941), 512–3.

from the time he was married to the birth of his son). The sum of all these eras of Diophantus's life is equal to x, so the riddle can be expressed in simple algebra as:

$$\frac{x}{6} + \frac{x}{12} + \frac{x}{7} + 5 + \frac{x}{2} + 4 = x$$

The least common multiple of the denominators of these fractions is 84, so multiply all the terms on the left and right of the equal sign by 84:

$$14x + 7x + 12x + 420 + 42x + 336 = 84x$$

Grouping multipliers of x on one side and constants on the other, you get:

$$84x - 14x - 7x - 12x - 42x = 420 + 336$$

Or:

$$9x = 756$$

And the solution is:

$$x = 84$$

So, Diophantus was a boy for 14 years and could finally grow a beard after 7 more years. Twelve years later, at the age of 33, he married, and he had a son 5 years after that. The son died at the age of 42, when Diophantus was 80, and Diophantus died 4 years later.

There's actually a faster method for solving this riddle: If you look deep into the soul of the riddle maker, you'll discover that he doesn't want to distress you with fractional ages. The "twelfth part" and "seventh part" of Diophantus's life must be whole numbers, so the age he died is equally divisible by both 12 and 7 (and, by extension, 6 and 2). Just multiply 12 by 7 to get 84. That seems about right for a ripe old age, so it's probably correct.

Diophantus may have been 84 years old when he died, but the crucial historical question is *when*. At one time, estimates of Diophantus's era ranged from 150 BCE to 280 CE.[3] That's a tantalizing range of dates: It certainly puts Diophantus after early Alexandrian mathematicians such as Euclid (flourished ca. 295 BCE[4]) and Eratosthenes (ca. 276–195 BCE), but might make him contemporaneous with Heron of Alexandria (also known as Hero, flourished 62 CE), who wrote books on mechanics, pneumatics, and automata, and seems to have invented a primitive steam engine. Diophantus might also have known the Alexandrian astronomer Ptolemy (ca. 100–170 CE), remembered mostly for the *Almagest*, which contains the first trigonometry table and established the mathematics for the movement of the heavens that wasn't persuasively refuted until the Copernican revolution of the sixteenth and seventeenth centuries.

[3]Those dates persist in Simon Hornblower and Antony Sprawforth, eds., *Oxford Classical Dictionary*, revised third edition (Oxford University Press, 2003), 483.

[4]All further dates of Alexandrian mathematicians are from Charles Coulston Gillispie, ed., *Dictionary of Scientific Biography* (Scribners, 1970).

Unfortunately, Diophantus probably did not have contact with these other Alexandrian mathematicians and scientists. For the last hundred years or so, the consensus among classical scholars is that Diophantus flourished about 250 CE, and his major extant work, the *Arithmetica*, probably dates from that time. That would put Diophantus's birth at around the time of Ptolemy's death. Paul Tannery, who edited the definitive Greek edition of the *Arithmetica* (published 1893–1895), noted that the work was dedicated to an "esteemed Dionysius." Although a common name, Tannery conjectured that this was the same Dionysius who was head of the Catechist school at Alexandria in 232–247, and then Bishop of Alexandria in 248–265. Thus, Diophantus may have been a Christian.[5] If so, it's a bit ironic that one of the early (but lost) commentaries on the *Arithmetica* was written by Hypatia (ca. 370–415), daughter of Theon and the last of the great Alexandrian mathematicians, who was killed by a Christian mob apparently opposed to her "pagan" philosophies.

Ancient Greek mathematics had traditionally been strongest in the fields of geometry and astronomy. Diophantus was ethnically Greek, but he was unusual in that he assuaged his grief over the death of his son with the "science of numbers," or what we now call *algebra*. He seems to be the source of several innovations in algebra, including the use of symbols and abbreviations in his problems, signifying a transition between word-based problems and modern algebraic notation.

The 6 books of the *Arithmetica* (13 are thought to have originally existed) present increasingly difficult problems, most of which are quite a bit harder than the riddle to determine Diophantus's age. Diophantus's problems frequently have multiple unknowns. Some of his problems are *indeterminate*, which means they have more than one solution. All but one of the problems in *Arithmetica* are abstract in the sense that they are strictly numerical and don't refer to real-world objects.

Another element of abstraction in Diophantus involves powers. Up to that time, mathematicians had been familiar with powers of 2 and 3. Squares were required for calculating areas on the plane, and cubes were needed for the volumes of solids. But Diophantus admitted higher powers to his problems: powers of 4 (which he called a "square-square"), 5 ("square-cube"), and 6 ("cube-cube"). These powers have no physical analogy in the world that Diophantus knew and indicate that Diophantus had little concern for the practicality of his mathematics. This was purely recreational mathematics with no goal but to strengthen the mind.

Here's the first problem from Book IV.[6] Diophantus states it first in general terms:

> To divide a given number into two cubes such that the sum of
> their sides is a given number.

---

[5] Heath, *Diophantus of Alexandria*, 2, note 2. Heath himself seems to be skeptical.
[6] Heath, *Diophantus of Alexandria*, 168.

Then he provides the two numbers:

Given number 370, given sum of sides 10.

Visualized geometrically, he's dealing with two cubes of different sizes. As a modern algebraist, you or I might label the sides of the two cubes x and y:

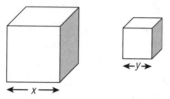

The two sides (x and y) add up to 10. The volumes of the two cubes (x^3 and y^3) sum to 370. Now write down two equations:

$$x + y = 10$$
$$x^3 + y^3 = 370$$

The first equation indicates that y equals $(10 - x)$, so that could be substituted in the second equation:

$$x^3 + (10 - x)^3 = 370$$

Now multiply $(10 - x)$ by $(10 - x)$ by $(10 - x)$ and pray that the cubes eventually disappear:

$$x^3 + (1000 + 30x^2 - 300x - x^3) = 370$$

Fortunately they do, and after a bit of rearranging you get:

$$30x^2 - 300x + 630 = 0$$

Those three numbers on the left have a common factor, so you'll want to divide everything by 30:

$$x^2 - 10x + 21 = 0$$

Now you're almost done. You have two choices. If you remember the quadratic formula,[7] you can use that. Or, if you've had recent practice solving equations of this sort, you can stare at it and ponder it long enough until it magically decomposes itself like so:

$$(x - 7)(x - 3) = 0$$

The lengths of the two sides are thus 7 and 3. Those two sides indeed add up to 10, and their cubes, which are 343 and 27, sum to 370.

Diophantus doesn't solve the problem quite like you or I would. He really can't. Although Diophantus's problems often have multiple unknowns, his notation

---

[7]For $ax^2 + bx + c = 0$, solve $x = \frac{-b \pm \sqrt{b^2 - 4ac}}{2a}$

allows him to represent only a single unknown. He compensates for this limitation in ingenious ways. Rather than labeling the sides of the two cubes as x and y, he says that the two sides are $(5 + x)$ and $(5 - x)$. These two sides are both expressed in terms of the single unknown x, and they indeed add up to 10. He can then cube the two sides and set the sum equal to 370:

$$(5 + x)^3 + (5 - x)^3 = 370$$

Now this looks worse than anything we've yet encountered, but if you actually expand those cubes, terms start dropping out like crazy and you're left with:

$$30x^2 + 250 = 370$$

With some rudimentary rearranging and another division by 30, it further simplifies to:

$$x^2 = 4$$

Or x equals 2. Because the two sides are $(5 + x)$ and $(5 - x)$, the sides are really 7 and 3.

Diophantus's skill in solving this problem with less sweat than the modern student results from his uncanny ability to express the two sides in terms of a single variable in precisely the right way. Will this technique work for the next problem? Maybe. Maybe not. Developing general methods for solving algebraic equations is really *not* what Diophantus is all about. As one mathematician observed, "Every question requires a quite special method, which often will not serve even for the most closely allied problems. It is on that account difficult for a modern mathematician even after studying 100 Diophantine solutions to solve the 101st problem."[8]

Of course, it's obvious that when Diophantus presents the problem of cubes adding to 370 and sides adding to 10, he's not pulling numbers out of thin air. He knows that these assumptions lead to a solution in whole numbers. Indeed, the term *Diophantine equation* has come to mean an algebraic equation in which only whole number solutions are allowed. Diophantine equations can have multiple unknowns, and these unknowns can be raised to powers of whole numbers, but the solutions (if any) are always whole numbers. Although Diophantus often uses subtraction in formulating his problems, his solutions never involve negative numbers. "Of a negative quantity *per se*, *i.e.*, without some positive quantity to subtract it from, Diophantus had apparently no conception."[9] Nor does any problem have zero for a solution. Zero was not considered a number by the ancient Greeks.

---

[8]Hermann Hankel (1874) as quoted in Heath, *Diophantus of Alexandria*, 54–55. Other mathematicians find more explicit patterns in Diophantus's methods. See Isabella Grigoryevna Bashmakova, *Diophantus and Diophantine Equations* (Mathematical Association of America, 1997), ch. 4.
[9]Heath, *Diophantus of Alexandria*, 52–53.

Modern readers of Diophantus — particularly those who are already acquainted with the requirement that Diophantine equations have solutions in whole numbers — can be a bit startled when they encounter *rational numbers* in Diophantus. Rational numbers are so named not because they are logical or reasonable in some way, but because they can be expressed as the *ratio* of two whole numbers. For example,

$$\frac{3}{5}$$

is a rational number.

Rational numbers show up in the only problem in the *Arithmetica* that involves actual real-world objects, in particular those perennial favorites: drink and drachmas. It doesn't seem so in the formulation of the problem, but rational numbers are required in the solution:

> A man buys a certain number of measures of wine, some at 8 drachmas, some at 5 drachmas each. He pays for them a *square* number of drachmas; and if we add 60 to this number, the result is a square, the side of which is equal to the whole number of measures. Find how many he bought at each price.[10]

By a "square number," Diophantus means a result of multiplying some number by itself. For example, 25 is a square number because it equals 5 times 5.

After a page of calculations,[11] it is revealed that the number of 5-drachma measures is the rational number:

$$\frac{79}{12}$$

and the number of 8-drachma measures is the rational number:

$$\frac{59}{12}$$

Let's check these results. (Verifying the solution is much easier than deriving it.) If you multiply 5 drachmas by 79/12, and add to it 8 drachmas times 59/12, you'll discover that the man paid a total of $72\frac{1}{4}$ drachmas. Diophantus says the man pays "a *square* number of drachmas." The amount paid has to be a square of something. Curiously enough, Diophantus considers $72\frac{1}{4}$ to be a square number because it can be expressed as the ratio

$$\frac{289}{4}$$

and both the numerator and denominator of this ratio are squares: of 17 and 2, respectively. So, $72\frac{1}{4}$ is the square of 17/2 or $8\frac{1}{2}$. Diophantus further says that "if

[10]Heath, *Diophantus of Alexandria*, 224.
[11]Heath, *Diophantus of Alexandria*, 225.

we add 60 to this number, the result is a square, the side of which is equal to the whole number of measures." That phrase "whole number of measures" is *not* referring to whole numbers. What Diophantus (or rather, his English translator, Sir Thomas Heath) means is the *total* number of measures. Adding 60 to $72\frac{1}{4}$ is $132\frac{1}{4}$, which is the rational number:

$$\frac{529}{4}$$

Again, Diophantus considers that to be a square because both the numerator and denominator are squares: of 23 and 2, respectively. Thus, the total number of measures purchased is 23/2 or $11\frac{1}{2}$, which can also be calculated by adding 79/12 and 59/12.

Perhaps the most famous problem in the *Arithmetica* is Problem 8 of Book II: "To divide a given square number into two squares," that is, to find x, y, and z such that:

$$x^2 + y^2 = z^2$$

This problem has a geometrical interpretation in the relationship of the sides of a right triangle as described by the Pythagorean Theorem:

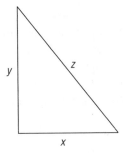

The problem has many solutions in whole numbers, such as x, y, and z equaling 3, 4, and 5, respectively. (The squares 9 and 16 sum to 25.) Such a simple solution apparently doesn't appeal to Diophantus, who sets the "given square number" (that is, z^2) to 16, which makes the other two sides the rational numbers 144/25 and 256/25. To Diophantus, these are both squares, of course. The first is the square of 12/5 and the second the square of 16/5, and the sum is the square of 4:

$$\left(\frac{12}{5}\right)^2 + \left(\frac{16}{5}\right)^2 = 4^2$$

It doesn't really matter that Diophantus allows a solution in rational numbers because the solution is equivalent to one in whole numbers. Simply multiply both sides of the equation by 5^2 or 25:

$$12^2 + 16^2 = 20^2$$

Or, 144 plus 256 equals 400. It's really the same solution because it's only a different way of measuring the sides. In Diophantus's statement of the problem, the hypotenuse is 4. That could be 4 inches, for example. Now use a different ruler that measures in units of a fifth of an inch. With that ruler, the hypotenuse is 20 and the sides are 12 and 16.

Whole numbers came about when people started counting things. Rational numbers probably came about when people started measuring things. If one carrot is as long as the width of three fingers, and another carrot is as long as the width of four fingers, then the first carrot is $\frac{3}{4}$ the length of the second.

Rational numbers are sometimes called *commensurable* numbers because two objects with lengths expressed as rational numbers can always be remeasured with whole numbers. You just need to make your unit of measurement small enough.

Diophantus wrote the *Arithmetica* in Greek. At least parts of the work were translated into Arabic. It was first translated into Latin in 1575 and then into a better edition in 1621, when it began to have an influence on European mathematicians. Pierre de Fermat (1601–1665) owned a copy of the 1621 Latin translation and covered its margins with extensive notes. In 1670, Fermat's son published those notes together with the Latin *Arithmetica*. One such note accompanied the problem just described. Fermat wrote:

> On the other hand it is impossible to separate a cube into two cubes, or a biquadrate [power of 4] into two biquadrates, or generally *any power except a square into two squares with the same exponent*. I have discovered a truly marvelous proof of this, which however the margin is not large enough to contain.[12]

Fermat is asserting, for example, that

$$x^3 + y^3 = z^3$$

has no solutions in whole numbers, and neither does any similar equation with powers of 4, or 5, or 6, and so forth. This is not obvious at all. The equation:

$$x^3 + y^3 + 1 = z^3$$

is very, very close to

$$x^3 + y^3 = z^3$$

and it has many solutions in whole numbers, such as x, y, and z equaling 6, 8, and 9, respectively. The equation

$$x^3 + y^3 - 1 = z^3$$

[12] Heath, *Diophantus of Alexandria*, 144, note 3.

is also quite similar, and it too has many solutions in whole numbers, for example, 9, 10, and 12. Why do these two equations have solutions in whole numbers but

$$x^3 + y^3 = z^3$$

does not?

All the problems that Diophantus presented in *Arithmetica* have solutions, but many Diophantine Equations, such as the ones Fermat described, seemingly have no solutions. It soon became more interesting for mathematicians not necessarily to *solve* Diophantine Equations, but to determine whether a particular Diophantine Equation has a solution in whole numbers at all.

Fermat's nonexistent proof became known as Fermat's Last Theorem (sometimes known as Fermat's Great Theorem), and over the years it was generally acknowledged that whatever proof Fermat *thought* he had, it was probably wrong. Only in 1995 was Fermat's Theorem proved by English mathematician Andrew Wiles (b. 1953), who had been interested in the problem since he was ten years old. (For many special cases, such as when the exponents are 3, it had been determined much earlier that no solutions exist.)

Obviously, proving that some Diophantine Equation has *no* possible solution is more challenging than finding a solution if you know that one exists. If you know that a solution exists to a particular Diophantine Equation, you could simply test all the possibilities. The only allowable solutions are whole numbers, so first you try 1, then 2, and 3, and so forth. If you'd rather not do the grunt work yourself, just write a computer program that tests all the possibilities for you. Sooner or later, your program will find the solution.

But if you don't know that a solution exists, then the brute-force computer approach is not quite adequate. You could start it going, but how do you know when to give up? How can you be sure that the very next series of numbers you test won't be the very ones for which you're searching?

That's the trouble with numbers: They're just too damn *infinite*.

2

The Irrational and the Transcendental

We begin counting 1, 2, 3, and we can go on as long as we want. These are known as the *counting* numbers, the *whole* numbers, the *cardinal* numbers, the *natural* numbers, and they certainly *seem* natural and intuitive enough because the universe contains so many objects that we can count. Natural numbers were likely the first mathematical objects conceived by early humans. Some animals, too, it seems, have a concept of numbers, as long as the numbers don't get too large.

For many centuries, zero was not included among the natural numbers, and even now there is no firm consensus. (Text books on number theory usually tell you on the first page whether the author includes zero among the natural numbers.) On the other side of zero are the negative whole numbers. To refer to all the positive and negative whole numbers as well as zero, the word *integer* does just fine. The integers go off into infinity in two different directions:

$$\ldots \ -3 \ -2 \ -1 \ 0 \ 1 \ 2 \ 3 \ \ldots$$

To refer to only the positive whole numbers starting at 1, the term *positive integers* works well. For positive numbers starting with zero (that is, 0, 1, 2, 3, ...) the term *non-negative integers* is unambiguous and not *too* wordy.

Rational numbers are numbers that can be expressed as ratios of integers, except that a denominator of zero is not allowed. For example,

$$\frac{3}{5}$$

is a rational number, also commonly written in the decimal form:

$$.6$$

Rational numbers also encompass all the integers, because any integer (47, say) can be written as a ratio with 1 on the bottom:

$$\frac{47}{1}$$

Any number with a finite number of decimal places is also a rational number. For example,

$$-23.45678$$

can be represented as the ratio:

$$\frac{-2{,}345{,}678}{100{,}000}$$

Some rational numbers, such as

$$\frac{1}{3}$$

require an infinite number of digits to be represented in a decimal form:

$$0.3333333333\ldots$$

This is still a rational number because it's a ratio. Indeed, any number with a *repeating pattern* of digits somewhere after the decimal point is a rational number. This is a rational number,

$$0.234562345623456\ldots$$

if the digits 23456 keep repeating forever. To demonstrate that it's rational, let x represent the number:

$$x = 0.234562345623456\ldots$$

Now multiply both sides by 100,000:

$$100000x = 23456.23456234562346\ldots$$

It's well known that if you subtract the same value from both sides of an equality, you still have an equality. That means that you can subtract the two values in the first expression from the two values in the second expression: Subtract x from $100000x$ and $0.23456\ldots$ from $23456.23456\ldots$ and the decimals disappear:

$$99999x = 23456$$

So:

$$x = \frac{23{,}456}{99{,}999}$$

That's a ratio, so it's a rational number.

Just offhand, rational numbers seem to be quite complete. If you add two rational numbers, you'll get another rational number. Subtract, multiply, or divide rational numbers, and the result is also rational.

One might assume (as people did for many years) that all numbers are rational, but consider the hypotenuse of this simple right triangle:

According to the Pythagorean Theorem,

$$x^2 = 1^2 + 1^2$$

or

$$x^2 = 2$$

or

$$x = \sqrt{2}$$

Does there exist a ratio of two integers that, when multiplied by itself, equals 2? One can certainly search and find many rational numbers that come very close. Here's one:

$$\frac{53,492}{37,825}$$

This one is just a little bit short. Multiplied by itself it's about 1.99995. Maybe if we keep searching we'll find one that's perfect.

Or are we wasting our time?

It's hard to prove that something doesn't exist, but mathematicians have developed a type of proof that often comes in handy in such circumstances. It's called an *indirect proof* or a *proof by contradiction*, or the Latin *reductio ad absurdum* ("reduction to absurdity"). You begin by making an assumption. Then, you logically follow the implications of that assumption until you run into a contradiction. That contradiction means that your original assumption was incorrect.

Reductio ad absurdum proofs seem roundabout, but they are probably more common in real life than we realize. An alibi is a form of *reductio ad absurdum*. If the defendant were at the scene of the crime *and* at his mother's house, it would mean he was at two different places at the same time. Absurd.

Let's begin by assuming that the square root of 2 is rational. Because it's rational, there exist whole numbers a and b such that:

$$\frac{a}{b} = \sqrt{2}$$

Are a and b both even? If so, divide them both by 2 and use those numbers instead. If they're still both even, divide them both by 2 again, and keep doing this until either a or b (or both) is odd.

Square both sides of the equation:

$$\frac{a^2}{b^2} = 2$$

Or:

$$a^2 = 2b^2$$

Notice that a squared is 2 times b squared. That means that a squared is even, and the only way that a squared can be even is if a is even. Earlier I indicated that a and b can't both be even, so we now know that b is odd.

If a is even, it equals 2 times some number, which we'll call c:

$$(2c)^2 = 2b^2$$

Or:

$$4c^2 = 2b^2$$

Or:

$$2c^2 = b^2$$

That means that b squared is even, which means that b is even, which is contrary to the original requirement that a and b can't both be even.

Hence, the original assumption that the square root of 2 is a rational number is flawed. The square root of 2 is incontrovertibly *irrational*. Expressed as a decimal, the digits keep going with no discernable pattern:

$$1.41421356237309504880168887242097\ldots$$

The number can't be expressed exactly without an infinite supply of paper, pen, and time. Only an approximation is possible, and the ellipsis acknowledges our defeat. The closest you can come to expressing this number finitely is providing an algorithm for its calculation. (I'll do precisely that in Chapter 6.)

There's a reason why the terms that we use — rational and irrational — oddly seem to pass judgment on the mental stability of the numbers. Irrational numbers are also sometimes called *surds*, to which the word *absurd* is related. The ancient Greeks were familiar with irrational numbers but they didn't like them very much. According to legend (but not reliable history), it was Pythagoras's disciple Hippasus who in the sixth century BCE determined that the square root of 2 is irrational. The legend continues to report that this finding was so disturbing to these logical and rational Greeks that Pythagoras and his followers tried to suppress it by tossing Hippasus into the Mediterranean Sea. They would certainly have preferred that irrational numbers didn't exist. Diophantus, in rejecting irrational numbers as solutions to his problems, was carrying on a long tradition in finding irrational numbers not quite to his taste.

With the decimal notation that we have (but the ancient Greeks did not), it's easy to create numbers that are clearly irrational. Just write down something nutty *without* a repeating pattern of digits. For example, here's a number with some kind of crazy pattern in the decimals, but it's certainly not repeating:

$$.00101101110111101111110111111\ldots$$

After the decimal point, there are two 0s and a 1, then a 0 and two 1s, then a 0 and three 1s, and so forth. This is not a rational number! It cannot be represented by a ratio of two integers. It is, therefore, irrational.

The square root of 2 is a solution to the following equation:

$$x^2 - 2 = 0$$

It's the same as an equation I showed earlier except that the 2 has been moved to the other side of the equal sign. The cube root of 17 (which is also an irrational number) is a solution to the following equation:

$$x^3 - 17 = 0$$

Both of those equations are called *algebraic equations*. Here's another algebraic equation:

$$-12x^5 + 27x^4 - 2x^2 + 8x - 4 = 0$$

An algebraic equation has one variable, usually called x. (Algebraic equations are not the same as Diophantine equations because Diophantine equations can have multiple variables.) The algebraic equation has a series of terms — five of them in this last example — that sum to zero. Each term contains the variable raised to a power, which is a whole number or zero. (Because anything to the zero power equals 1, the fifth term can be interpreted as -4 times x to the zero power.) Each variable raised to a power is multiplied by an integer coefficient, in this example, the numbers -12, 27, -2, 8, and -4. These coefficients can be zero, as is the case with the "missing" term of x to the third power.

Algebraic equations tend to show up a lot in real-life problems, so they've come to be considered quite important. The general form of an algebraic equation is:

$$a_N x^N + a_{N-1} x^{N-1} + \cdots + a_2 x^2 + a_1 x + a_0 = 0$$

where N is a positive integer and a_i are integers. It's possible to write this more concisely as a summation:

$$\sum_{i=0}^{N} a_i x^i = 0$$

Here's the example I showed earlier:

$$-12x^5 + 27x^4 - 2x^2 + 8x - 4 = 0$$

In this equation, N (the highest exponent, called the *degree* of the polynomial) is 5, and a_5 equals -12, a_4 equals 27, a_3 equals 0, and so on.

The solutions to an algebraic equation (also called the *roots* of the equation) are called *algebraic numbers*. An N-degree polynomial has at most N unique solutions. In Chapter 1, the algebraic equation

$$x^2 - 10x + 21 = 0$$

came up. That equation has solutions of 3 and 7.

The square root of 2 is one solution of the algebraic equation:

$$x^2 - 2 = 0$$

The negative square root of 2 is the second solution.

The category of algebraic numbers also includes all integers and all rational numbers. For example, the integer 5 is the solution of the algebraic equation

$$x - 5 = 0$$

and 3/7 is the solution of:

$$7x - 3 = 0$$

Some algebraic equations can be solved only with square roots of negative numbers:

$$x^2 + 5 = 0$$

This equation looks insolvable because any number multiplied by itself is a positive quantity, so adding 5 to it won't ever yield zero. Square roots of negative numbers are called *imaginary* numbers. (The square root of -1 is assigned the letter i for convenience.) Despite the name, imaginary numbers are very useful and have actual real-world applications, but imaginary numbers play no role in Turing's paper or this book.

Sometime in the eighteenth century, mathematicians began speaking of *real* numbers in contrast to imaginary numbers. By definition, the category of real numbers includes *everything* except numbers involving square roots of negatives.

Real numbers are also referred to as the *continuum* because real numbers can be visualized as all the points on a continuous line:

Some integers are labeled on this line, but by themselves the integers obviously could not form a continuous line.

But neither can rational numbers. Rational numbers certainly seem very dense on the line. Between any two rational numbers, for example, *a* and *b*, you can insert another rational number which is the average of the two:

$$\frac{a+b}{2}$$

But there still exist gaps between the rational numbers where irrational numbers reside. For example, one such gap corresponds to the square root of 2.

Now, we're coming at the subject of categorizing numbers from two directions. We've defined a category called *algebraic numbers* that are solutions to algebraic equations. This category of numbers includes integers, rational numbers, and many irrational numbers such as square roots and cube roots. We've also defined a category called *real numbers*, which are all numbers that do not involve square roots of negative numbers. The question that now poses itself is this:

Are all real numbers also algebraic numbers? Or are there some real numbers that are not solutions of algebraic equations?

In the 1740s, Leonhard Euler (1707–1783) — the indefatigable Swiss-born mathematician, whose name is pronounced "oiler" — speculated that non-algebraic numbers do indeed exist, and these he called *transcendental* numbers because they transcend the algebraic. Proving that transcendental numbers existed was tough. How do you prove that a particular number is *not* the solution of some extremely long and unspeakably hairy algebraic equation?

The existence of transcendental numbers was an open question until 1844, when French mathematician Joseph Liouville (1809–1882) devised a number that he was able to prove was not algebraic. Displayed with the first 30 decimal places, the number Liouville chose was:

$$.110001000000000000000001000000\ldots$$

But that excerpt doesn't quite reveal the complete pattern. Liouville constructed this crazy number with *factorials*. The factorial of a number is the product of the number and all positive integers less than itself, and is represented by the exclamation point:

$$1! = 1$$
$$2! = 1 \times 2 = 2$$
$$3! = 1 \times 2 \times 3 = 6$$
$$4! = 1 \times 2 \times 3 \times 4 = 24$$
$$5! = 1 \times 2 \times 3 \times 4 \times 5 = 120$$

and so forth. Liouville's Number (as it is sometimes called) contains a 1 in the 1st, 2nd, 6th, 24th, 120th, and so forth, decimal places. Liouville designed this number specifically for proving that it was not the solution of any algebraic equation. The increasing scarcity of nonzero digits is the key to the proof.[1]

---

[1] The proof is discussed in Edward B. Burger and Robert Tubbs, *Making Transcendence Transparent: An Intuitive Approach to Classical Transcendental Number Theory* (Springer, 2004), 9–26.

In 1882, German mathematician Ferdinand Lindemann (1852–1939) proved that one of the most famous irrational numbers of all time was also transcendental. This is π, the ratio of the circumference of a circle to its diameter:

$$\pi = 3.14159265358979323846264338327795\ldots$$

Lindemann showed that π was not the solution to an algebraic equation, and this fact provided an insight into a very old problem: For over two millennia, mathematicians and non-mathematicians alike had been trying to "square the circle." The problem can be stated simply: Given a circle, use a straightedge and compass to construct a square with the same area as the circle. (A similar problem is called the rectification of the circle, and it requires constructing a straight line with a length equal to the circle's circumference.) So fanatically did people try to solve this problem that the ancient Greeks even had a word for the obsessive activity: τετραγωνίζειν, literally, to *tetragonize*.[2]

Using a straightedge and compass to construct geometrical shapes is equivalent to solving certain forms of algebraic equations. Because π is not a solution to an algebraic equation, you cannot represent the number in a geometrical construction. Squaring the circle with a straightedge and compass is impossible.

Another famous transcendental number is symbolized by the letter e (for Euler). If you calculate this number

$$\left(1 + \frac{1}{N}\right)^N$$

for increasingly large values of N, you'll approach e:

$$e = 2.71828182845904523536028747135527\ldots$$

You can also calculate e by this infinite series involving factorials:

$$1 + \frac{1}{1!} + \frac{1}{2!} + \frac{1}{3!} + \frac{1}{4!} + \frac{1}{5!} + \cdots$$

You can calculate it, but it's not a solution to any algebraic equation.

Over the past century many numbers have been shown to be transcendental, but there exists no general process for determining whether a number is transcendental. For example, the jury is still out on:

$$\pi^\pi$$

Turing's paper (and this book) restricts itself to real numbers (not imaginary numbers), and the following diagram summarizes the most important categories within the realm of the reals:

---

[2] E. W. Hobson, *Squaring the Circle: A History of the Problem* (Cambridge University Press, 1913), 3.

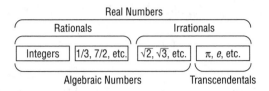

This diagram is not to scale.

Wait: What do I mean by that?

All those categories of numbers are infinite, right? There are an infinite number of integers, an infinite number of fractions, an infinite number of irrationals, right? Infinite is infinite, right? There aren't different *sizes* of infinity, are there? There can't be an infinity that's larger than another infinity, can there?

Right?

Infinity has never been an easy subject, regardless of whether it's approached from a philosophical, theological, or mathematical perspective. In mathematics, however, infinity can scarcely be avoided. We are compelled to examine this concept of infinity with all the bravery we can summon.

The relentless persistence of the natural numbers to get bigger and bigger seems to lie at the very root of our concept of the infinitely large. Whatever number we count to, we can always count one more. Real numbers can get infinitely large as well, of course, but only because they tag along with the natural numbers. Real numbers also allow us to ponder the infinitely small as we divide and subdivide the continuum into smaller and smaller pieces.

Are these two infinities — the infinity of the never-ending natural numbers, and the infinity of the density of the continuum — similar in some way? Or are they completely different?

The following discussion will be a little easier if we're armed with some rudimentary set theory. A *set* is a collection of objects, which are called the *elements* of the set. A set is often symbolized with a pair of curly brackets. For example,

$$\{ 1, 2, 3, 4 \}$$

is the set of the first four positive integers. The elements in a set are unique. Two 4s in the same set isn't allowed, for example. The order of the elements in a set doesn't matter. The set

$$\{ 4, 1, 3, 2 \}$$

is identical to the previous one. The number of elements in a set is called the *cardinal number* of the set, or the set's *cardinality*. The cardinality of the finite set shown above is 4. Sets that have the same cardinality are said to be *equivalent*.

Some sets have a finite cardinality; others have an infinite cardinality. Consider the set of positive integers:

$$\{ 1, 2, 3, \ldots \}$$

The cardinality is certainly infinite. That's also true for the set of *even* positive integers:

$$\{\, 2, \, 4, \, 6, \, \ldots \,\}$$

What is the relationship between the cardinalities of these two sets?

Perhaps our immediate instinct is to say that the first set has *double* the number of elements as the second set because the second set is missing all the odd numbers. That's certainly one way of looking at it, and that would be true if the two sets were finite. But how can we speak of one set having "double the number" of elements of another set when they're both infinite?

Let's try to count the elements of the second set. What does it really mean to *count* something? It means to put the items into correspondence with the natural numbers: "Number 1, number 2, number 3, . . ." we recite, as we touch the noses of our subjects.

We can count the even positive integers in the infinite set by corresponding each of them to the natural numbers:

$$
\begin{array}{ccccccccc}
1 & 2 & 3 & 4 & 5 & 6 & 7 & 8 & \ldots \\
\updownarrow & \updownarrow & \updownarrow & \updownarrow & \updownarrow & \updownarrow & \updownarrow & \updownarrow & \\
2 & 4 & 6 & 8 & 10 & 12 & 14 & 16 & \ldots
\end{array}
$$

For every positive integer, there's a corresponding even number. For every even number, there's a corresponding positive integer. Looking at it this way, now the two sets appear to be exactly the same size, which means that they're equivalent. Is this a paradox or what? (Actually, this peculiar characteristic of infinite collections was noted by Galileo in 1638[3] and is sometimes called Galileo's Paradox.)

Nobody seems to have worried too much about this paradox until Georg Cantor (1845–1918) began wrestling with it. Cantor, the mathematician largely credited with founding set theory, was born in St. Petersburg. His father was a merchant who drove his son to excel in whatever he did. Cantor's mother was a member of the Böhm family of musicians. Cantor himself displayed talents in art as well as music, but at the age of 17 he decided to "devote his life to mathematics."[4] He attended the Polytechnicum in Zurich, and the University of Berlin. In 1869, Cantor got a teaching job at the University of Halle, where he remained for the rest of his life.

In 1873, in a letter to mathematician Richard Dedekind (1831–1916), Cantor pondered correspondences such as the one between natural numbers and even numbers, and wondered whether a similar correspondence could be established

---

[3]Galileo Galilei, *Two New Sciences*, second edition, trans. Stillman Drake (Wall & Emerson, 2000), 40–41. The translation is based on *Opere di Galileo Galilei* (Florence, 1898), VIII, 78–79. Apparently Galileo wasn't the first to notice the paradox: For a list of others, see Stephen Cole Kleene, *Mathematical Logic* (Wiley, 1967; Dover, 2002), pg. 176, footnote 121.

[4]Joseph Warren Dauben, *Georg Cantor: His Mathematics and Philosophy of the Infinite* (Harvard University Press, 1979; Princeton University Press, 1990), 277.

between the natural numbers and *real* numbers. He suspected not, but he couldn't see why. "I cannot find the explanation which I seek; perhaps it is very easy," Cantor wrote.[5] Famous last words.

A set whose elements can be paired off with the natural numbers is now said to be *enumerable* (or sometimes *denumerable* or *countable*). A set is enumerable if we can order the elements or list them in some way, because any list can be numbered — that is, paired off with the natural numbers starting with 1, 2, 3, and so on. All finite sets are enumerable, of course. The real problem involves infinite sets.

For example, consider the integers including negative and positive integers as well as zero. Is this set enumerable? Yes, it is, because we can list all the integers starting at zero:

$$0$$
$$1$$
$$-1$$
$$2$$
$$-2$$
$$3$$
$$-3$$
$$\cdots$$

That's not the way the integers are usually listed, but this particular pattern clearly demonstrates that a single list contains all the integers.

Interestingly enough, the rational numbers are *also* enumerable. Let's begin with positive rational numbers, and let's not worry if we have a few duplicates in the list:

$$1/1$$
$$1/2$$
$$2/1$$
$$1/3$$
$$2/2$$
$$3/1$$
$$1/4$$
$$2/3$$
$$3/2$$
$$4/1$$
$$\cdots$$

---

[5] Georg Cantor, letter of November 29, 1873, in *From Kant to Hilbert: A Source Book in the Foundations of Mathematics* (Oxford University Press, 1996), Vol. II, 844.

Do you see the pattern? With the first item in the list, the numerator and denominator add up to 2. The next two items on the list have numerators and denominators that add up to 3. The next three items on the list have numerators and denominators that add up to 4. And so forth. A list that continues like this contains all the positive rational numbers. We can include negative rational numbers by just alternating between positive and negative. Therefore, the rational numbers are enumerable.

In a paper published in 1874, "On a Property of the Set of Real Algebraic Numbers,"[6] Cantor showed that even the algebraic numbers are enumerable. As you'll recall, algebraic numbers are solutions to algebraic equations, which have the general form

$$a_N x^N + a_{N-1} x^{N-1} + \cdots + a_2 x^2 + a_1 x + a_0 = 0$$

where N is a positive integer and a_i are integers. For any particular algebraic equation, let's add up all of the coefficients (the a_i values) and N itself. Let's call that number the equation's *height*. For a particular height (for example, 5), there are a finite number of algebraic equations. Each equation has at most N solutions. Thus, all the algebraic numbers can be listed in order of their heights and their solutions. The algebraic numbers are therefore enumerable.

What about the transcendentals? Can the transcendental numbers be listed in some manner? It hardly seems likely! There's not even a general procedure for determining whether a particular number is transcendental!

What about the real numbers, which encompass algebraic numbers and transcendental numbers? Can the real numbers be enumerated?

In that same 1874 paper where Cantor demonstrated that the algebraic numbers are enumerable, he also demonstrated that the real numbers are *not* enumerable.

Cantor began his proof by assuming that the real numbers *are* enumerable. He assumes that there exists some way to enumerate the real numbers, and that they've been enumerated in a list like so, symbolized by subscripted omegas:

$$\omega_1 \quad \omega_2 \quad \omega_3 \quad \omega_4 \quad \omega_5 \quad \omega_6 \quad \cdots$$

Cantor is going to show that this list is incomplete — that no matter how this list was made, it simply cannot contain all the real numbers.

Pick any number α (alpha) and a larger number β (beta). You can represent these two numbers on a number line like so:

Now start going through your enumerated list of real numbers until you find the first two real numbers that are between α and β. These two numbers are greater than α and less than β. Call the lesser of these two numbers α' and the greater β':

---

[6]Most conveniently available in *From Kant to Hilbert*, Vol. II, 839–843.

Continue going through your list of real numbers from where you left off until you find two new numbers between α' and β'. Call these two numbers α'' and β''

And again:

It should be obvious that this process must continue forever. You'll always be able to find two more numbers between the last two numbers.

How do you know this? Easy: Suppose you get stuck at this point

where the superscript (v) indicates v prime marks, maybe a million billion trillion or so, but a finite number. Now, no matter how much you continue to search through the list of enumerated real numbers, you can't find another pair of numbers that falls between $\alpha^{(v)}$ and $\beta^{(v)}$. Then it's obvious that your list of real numbers is incomplete. The list is missing every number between $\alpha^{(v)}$ and $\beta^{(v)}$. For example, the number midway between $\alpha^{(v)}$ and $\beta^{(v)}$ is the average of the two, or:

$$\frac{\alpha^{(v)} + \beta^{(v)}}{2}$$

And that's just for starters. Your list is missing lots of numbers.

That's how you know the process must continue forever. The alphas keep getting larger and the betas keep getting smaller, but the largest alpha can't get larger than the smallest beta. (When you find two new numbers that fall between the last alpha and beta, the smaller one is always the alpha and the larger one the beta.) Both the alphas and the betas have a boundary — a *limit* — that Cantor symbolizes using a superscripted infinity sign: α^{∞} and β^{∞}.

Is it possible that α^{∞} is less than β^{∞}? Take a look:

No, that's not possible. If the alphas never get larger than α^{∞} and the betas never get smaller than β^{∞}, then the list of real numbers is missing every number between α^{∞} and β^{∞}, for starters:

$$\frac{\alpha^{\infty} + \beta^{\infty}}{2}$$

It must be that α^∞ is equal to β^∞. Cantor calls this limit η (the Greek letter eta):

$$\alpha \quad \alpha' \quad \alpha'' \quad \alpha''' \qquad \cdots \qquad \eta \qquad \cdots \qquad \beta''' \quad \beta'' \quad \beta' \quad \beta$$

Because this has to be an infinite process (we've already established that it can't stop at some point), the alphas never reach η and neither do the betas. Now, you know what that means, don't you? That means that η is not in the original list of real numbers!

If η *were* in the list, then it would turn up sometime when you were searching for the next alpha and beta, but consider the alpha and beta that turned up in the list right before η:

$$\alpha \quad \alpha' \quad \alpha'' \quad \alpha''' \quad \cdots \quad \alpha^{(v)} \quad \eta \quad \beta^{(v)} \quad \cdots \quad \beta''' \quad \beta'' \quad \beta' \quad \beta$$

Now the list of real numbers is missing every number between $\alpha^{(v)}$ and $\beta^{(v)}$ except η.

We've run out of scenarios here. Nothing works, nothing makes sense, and it's all the fault of the original assumption — the assumption that we were able to enumerate the real numbers. It must be that we can't do that.

Integers are enumerable. Rational numbers are enumerable. Even algebraic numbers are enumerable. Real numbers, however, are not.

Cantor considered the non-enumerability of real numbers to be a new proof of the existence of transcendental numbers. (If transcendental numbers did not exist, real numbers would be the same as algebraic numbers and hence would be enumerable.) What Cantor eventually realized is that there are at least two kinds of infinity: There's an enumerable infinity and a non-enumerable infinity — an infinity of the natural numbers and an infinity of the continuum. Infinite sets of natural numbers, rational numbers, and even algebraic numbers are enumerable. When we throw in the transcendentals, suddenly we're in a whole different universe. We're looking at two different infinite cardinalities: One cardinality applies to natural numbers, rational numbers, and algebraic numbers. The other cardinality is that of the real numbers and the continuum.

Cantor's work was controversial in his day and has never entirely shed that controversy. Since Cantor, however, no mathematician has thought about infinity in quite the same way. Moreover, the distinction between enumerable and non-enumerable infinities has proved to be extremely useful, even if imagining just *one* simple type of infinity boggles the human mind.

In the popular mythology, Cantor himself went mad from contemplating infinity too much. It's true that Cantor spent the last twenty or so years of his life in and out of psychiatric hospitals, but it probably was a form of manic depression that would have manifested itself regardless of his occupation.[7] Still, the worst of Cantor's bouts with mental illness seem to have been triggered by fatigue and stress, and the stress may have been related to problems connected with the acceptance of his unconventional mathematical theories. In recuperation, Cantor pursued interests other than mathematics. He explored philosophy, theology, metaphysics, and the hypothesis that Francis Bacon wrote the plays attributed to William Shakespeare.

Finite sets and infinite sets have quite different characteristics. One big difference involves *proper subsets*, which are subsets that are not the same as the sets themselves. A proper subset of a finite set always has a smaller cardinality than the set itself. That much is obvious. A proper subset of an infinite set can also have a smaller cardinality than the set. (For example, the set of natural numbers is a proper subset of the set of real numbers, and the two cardinalities are different.) In some cases, however, a proper subset of an infinite set has the *same* cardinality as the set itself. This can only be true of infinite sets. The set of natural numbers is a proper subset of the set of integers, which is a proper subset of the set of rational numbers, which is a proper subset of the set of algebraic numbers. All these infinite sets have the *same* cardinality. They are equivalent.

It's also the case that various proper subsets of the real numbers are equivalent to each other. Consider the real numbers between 0 and 1. These can be placed in a one-to-one correspondence with the real numbers greater than 1. Just divide each number into 1. For example, 0.5 corresponds with 2, 0.25 corresponds with 4, 0.1 corresponds with 10, and 0.0001 corresponds with 10,000. This little fact proves to be very useful: It means that we can examine certain properties of real numbers restricted to the range between 0 and 1, and what we find will apply to all the real numbers. (Turing uses this concept in his paper, and Cantor used it as well.)

As Cantor explored infinite sets, he made other astonishing discoveries: He found that he could establish a one-to-one correspondence between the continuum — the real numbers on a line — and the two-dimensional points on a plane, and indeed the points in any N-dimensional space.

For example, let's restrict ourselves to that segment of the plane with x and y coordinates between 0 and 1. Each point on the plane can be expressed as a number pair (x, y), and each of the two numbers contains infinite digits following the decimal point. In the following expression, each digit of x following the decimal point is symbolized by a subscripted a:

$$x = .a_1 \, a_2 \, a_3 \, a_4 \, \ldots$$

Similarly for y:

$$y = .b_1 \, b_2 \, b_3 \, b_4 \, \ldots$$

---

[7] Dauben, *Georg Cantor*, 285.

Now take these digits and interweave them into a single number:

$$.a_1\, b_1\, a_2\, b_2\, a_3\, b_3\, a_4\, b_3\, \ldots$$

That's one real number encapsulating two real numbers. Each two-dimensional point corresponds to a real number on the continuum. Hence, the collection of points on the plane has the same cardinality as the real numbers on a line. Cantor was so astonished by this discovery that German failed him. "*Je le vois, mais je ne le crois pas,*" he wrote to Dedekind.[8] I see it, but I don't believe it.

In 1891, Cantor published another proof of the non-enumerability of real numbers,[9] and this proof has been blowing people's minds ever since. Cantor's proof involved sets rather than numbers and was more general than the example I'm going to show you, but the idea is the same. For reasons that will be very apparent, it's called the *diagonal proof* or the *diagonal process* or the *diagonal argument* or *diagonalization*. Whatever you call it, a diagonal is involved.

Let's restrict our attention to real numbers between 0 and 1. Suppose we have devised some way to list all these real numbers. (As you may be anticipating, this is yet another *reductio ad absurdum* proof.) Suppose the list begins something like this:

.1234567890 ...

.2500000000 ...

.3333333333 ...

.3141592653 ...

.0010110111 ...

.4857290283 ...

.0000000000 ...

.9999999999 ...

.7788778812 ...

.2718281828 ...

...

We seem to be off to a good start. The list includes 0, 1/4, 1/3, $\pi/10$, $e/10$, that weird irrational number I showed earlier with the varying number of 1s, and some others that aren't quite recognizable. Each number has an infinite number of decimal places (even if they're just 0s) and the list has an infinite number of numbers.

Even though this list is infinite, we can persuade ourselves that it's missing something. Let's look at the digits that form a diagonal through the list from

---

[8]Letter of June 29, 1877 in *From Kant to Hilbert*, Vol. II, 860.

[9]Georg Cantor, "On an Elementary Question in the Theory of Manifolds," *From Kant to Hilbert*, Vol. II, 920-922.

upper-left to lower-right. These digits are shown here in bold face:

.**1**234567890...
.2**5**00000000...
.33**3**3333333...
.314**1**592653...
.0101**1**01110...
.48572**9**0283...
.000000**0**000...
.9999999**9**99...
.77887788**1**2...
.271828182**8**...
...

Now, use those bold-face digits to form a number:

.1531190918...

Because the list of real numbers is infinite, and the number of digits in each number is infinite, this number has an infinite number of digits. Now increase each individual digit in this number by 1. If the digit is 9, make it 0:

.26422010259...

Is this new number in the original list? Let's be methodical about it: Is this new number the first number in the list? No, it's not, because the first digit of the first number in the list is 1, and the first digit of the new number is 2.

Is it the second number in the list? No again, because the second digit of the second number in the list is 5, and the second digit of the new number is 6.

Is it the third number in the list? No, because the third digit of the third number in the list is 3, and the third digit of the new number is 4.

And so forth. The new number is not the N-th number in the list because the N-th digit of the N-th number in the list is not equal to the N-th digit of the new number.

Thus, the list is incomplete and our original premise is flawed. It's impossible to list the real numbers between 0 and 1. Once again, we see that the real numbers are not enumerable.

What happens when you perform this same experiment on a list of algebraic numbers? We already know how to list algebraic numbers, so that's not a problem. When you construct a diagonal and change all the digits, the resultant number is not in the list. That means the resultant number is not an algebraic number. The resultant number is transcendental.

You could order your list of algebraic numbers in many different ways; you could create different rules for making the diagonal different from any number in the list; each time, you'll be creating another transcendental number.

In 1895, Cantor chose to represent the cardinality of the enumerable set of natural numbers (and thus, any enumerable infinite set) using the first letter of the Hebrew alphabet with a subscripted zero: $\aleph_0$, pronounced "aleph null." Cantor called this the first *transfinite* number. He combined this with other transfinite numbers ($\aleph_1$, $\aleph_2$, $\aleph_3$, and so on) to create an entire mathematics of the transfinite.

If the cardinality of enumerable sets is $\aleph_0$, what is the cardinality of the non-enumerable set of real numbers? Can we even represent that cardinality?

Perhaps. Let's begin with an example involving finite sets. Here is a set of just three elements:

$$\{ a, b, c \}$$

How many subsets of this set can you construct? (The set of all subsets of a set is called the *power set.*) You can try it manually, but just don't forget the empty set and the set with all three elements:

{ }	{ a, b }
{ a }	{ a, c }
{ b }	{ b, c }
{ c }	{ a, b, c }

There are eight subsets of a set of three elements, and not coincidentally:

$$2^3 = 8$$

The exponent is the number of elements in the original set. The result is the number of subsets of that set. A set of 4 elements has 16 (2 to the 4th power) subsets. A set of 5 elements has 32 subsets.

There's a more methodical way to enumerate these subsets that better reveals this relationship. Let's create a table with a column for each element in the original three-element set. Use 0s and 1s to indicate whether that element is in each particular subset:

a	b	c	Subset
0	0	0	{ }
0	0	1	{ c }
0	1	0	{ b }
0	1	1	{ b, c }
1	0	0	{ a }
1	0	1	{ a, c }
1	1	0	{ a, b }
1	1	1	{ a, b, c }

The successive combinations of 0s and 1s in the three columns are the same as the binary numbers from 0 through 7. Three bits yield 8 binary numbers. The general rule is:

$$\text{Cardinality of a power set} = 2^{\text{cardinality of the original set}}$$

A set of 10 elements has a power set of 1,024 elements. A set of 100 elements has a power set of 1,267,650,600,228,229,401,496,703,205,376 elements.

Now let's look at the natural numbers (including 0 for this purpose):

$$\{ 0, 1, 2, 3, 4, 5, \ldots \}$$

The cardinality of this set is $\aleph_0$. How many subsets does it have? In other words, what is the cardinality of its power set? By analogy, it's

$$2^{\aleph_0}$$

Perhaps further convincing is required. Let's construct a table similar to that for the finite set (except obviously not so complete). At the top of the columns we have all the elements of the set of natural numbers. Each column has a 0 or 1 indicating whether that number is included in each particular subset. The resultant subset is shown at the right:

0	1	2	3	4	5	...	Subset
0	0	0	0	0	0	...	{ }
1	0	0	0	0	0	...	{ 0 }
0	1	0	0	0	0	...	{ 1 }
1	1	0	0	0	0	...	{ 0, 1 }
0	0	1	0	0	0	...	{ 2 }
1	0	1	0	0	0	...	{ 0, 2 }
0	1	1	0	0	0	...	{ 1, 2 }
1	1	1	0	0	0	...	{ 0, 1, 2 }
...	...	...	...	...	...	...	...

What we are actually attempting here is a list of all possible infinite combinations of 0 and 1. Let's put a little period before each of the sequences of numbers in the list:

$$.000000 \ldots$$
$$.100000 \ldots$$
$$.010000 \ldots$$
$$.110000 \ldots$$
$$.001000 \ldots$$
$$.101000 \ldots$$

$$.011000 \ldots$$

$$.111000 \ldots$$

$$\ldots$$

These are binary numbers between 0 and 1, and (judging from the way we created these numbers) *all* the binary numbers between 0 and 1, and hence all the real numbers between 0 and 1.[10] I showed earlier how the real numbers between 0 and 1 can be put into a correspondence with the totality of real numbers, which means that the real numbers can be put into a correspondence with the members of the power set of the natural numbers. This power set therefore has the same cardinality as the continuum.

The cardinality of the continuum is thus

$$2^{\aleph_0}$$

where $\aleph_0$ is the cardinality of the natural numbers.

Cantor proved that it is not possible for the members of any nonempty set to be put into a one-to-one correspondence with the members of its power set, a fact that's obvious for finite sets but not so obvious for infinite ones. This is now known as Cantor's Theorem, and it was the primary result of the 1891 paper that introduced the diagonalization technique. Just as a set can have a power set, a power set can have its own power set, and so on. All these sets have different cardinalities.

Cantor speculated that the cardinality of the continuum was the next higher transfinite number after $\aleph_0$, which is the transfinite number he called $\aleph_1$. This speculation is called Cantor's *continuum hypothesis*, and it can be expressed mathematically like this:

$$\aleph_1 = 2^{\aleph_0}$$

Cantor struggled to prove his hypothesis, but was never able to do so. The problem is that there could be some other transfinite number between $\aleph_0$ and the cardinality of the continuum.

Regardless, the profound implication of all this is that the cardinality of enumerable sets is not only smaller than the cardinality of the continuum

$$\aleph_0 < 2^{\aleph_0}$$

but much, much, much, much, much smaller:

$$\aleph_0 <<<<<<<<<<<<<<<<<<<<<<<<<<<< 2^{\aleph_0}$$

---

[10]It may also seem as if we've stumbled on a method to enumerate all the real numbers between 0 and 1. The pattern is already evident — the first digit after the period alternates between 0 and 1, the second digit alternates at half the speed, and so on — and we could easily continue this list as long as we want. The fallacy, however, is that the list will never contain a transcendental number. Every number in the list has a finite number of non-zero digits after the period.

The only difference between the continuum and enumerable sets is the inclusion of transcendental numbers. We are compelled to conclude that transcendental numbers — which were not even proved to exist before 1844 — really account for the vast majority of all possible numbers — indeed, *virtually all* possible numbers.

For millennia, our ideas about numbers have been completely skewed and distorted. As humans we value neatness, order, and patterns, and we live in a world of compromise and approximation. We're interested only in numbers that have meaning to us. From counting farm animals, we have invented the natural numbers. From measurement, we have invented the rational numbers, and from higher mathematics, we have invented the algebraic numbers. We have plucked all these numbers from the continuum while ignoring the vast depths in which they swim like microscopic bacteria in the ocean. We live under the comforting illusion that rational numbers are more common than irrational numbers, and algebraic numbers are more numerous than transcendental numbers, and certainly they are in our manufactured lives. In the realm of the continuum, however, virtually every number is transcendental.

What are all these transcendental numbers? Most of them are just sequences of random digits, without rhyme, reason, or meaning. Indeed, any sequence of random digits is almost assuredly transcendental.

Toss a dart at a dart board. Now measure the distance between the dart and the exact center of the bull's eye using progressively higher magnification and finer rulers. First measure to the whole number of inches, and then to the whole number of tenths of an inch, and then to the whole number of hundredths of an inch, and you'll be going on forever. The probability that the distance is a rational number — 1.437 inches exactly, for example — is negligible.

Of course, at some point when measuring the dart we're going to have to deal with the real world. It's not like the dart is going to split an atom! No, the dart will wedge between discrete molecules of cork, and as our magnification gets into the realm of these molecules, we see that they're vibrating too much for an accurate measurement, and there are visual distortions due to the finite wavelength of light, and at some point the Heisenberg Uncertainty Principle kicks in, and then we can't really be sure of anything any more.

At those magnifications, the whole idea of a "continuum" seems hopelessly quaint, and we may even be tempted to look outwards from the molecules to the universe at large, and speculate whether infinity exists at all in the real world — particularly considering that the Big Bang very likely unleashed only a *finite* amount of matter and energy at a point in time in a *finite* past to create a universe seemingly characterized by a discrete rather than continuous structure.

We might wonder, too, if Cantor's exploration into enumerable and non-enumerable sets is just some highly abstract (and still somewhat suspect) area of speculative mathematics, or if there's actually some utility in this exercise.

Although it's hard to find infinity in the real world, there is still much usefulness in the mathematical concepts of infinity. It turns out that certain mathematical proofs that have actual real-life implications — including the one in Turing's paper — hinge on the difference between enumerable sets and non-enumerable sets, as illustrated by this diagram:

The tools we have.

$$\aleph_0 <<<<<<<<<<<<<<<<<<<<<<<<<<<<<< 2^{\aleph_0}$$

The jobs we need to do.

You see the problem?

3 Centuries of Progress

A s the seconds ticked down to midnight on Friday, December 31, 1999, the festivities that normally accompany any new year were tempered by anxiety and fear. At the stroke of midnight, it was possible — some even thought inevitable — that major technological crashes and shutdowns would ripple through the world's interconnected computer systems. This crisis wouldn't be an act of global terrorism, but instead the momentous result of a simple little shortcut used by computer programmers for nearly half a century. In programs written for a variety of different applications on multitudes of different systems, programmers had saved valuable computer storage space by representing years by only their last two digits, for example, 75 rather than 1975. At midnight, that two-digit year would roll over from 99 to 00, suddenly getting much smaller rather than larger. What had once been an innocent shortcut had become a treacherous bug referred to by the high-tech nickname Y2K.

Programmers themselves, of course, had known of the impending problem for decades. Alarmist warnings to the general public began around 1998 with books such as *Y2K: The Day the World Shut Down; Deadline Y2K; Y2K: It's Already Too Late; Y2K: An Action Plan to Protect Yourself, Your Family, Your Assets, and Your Community on January 1, 2000; 101 Ways to Survive the Y2K Crisis; Y2K for Women: How to Protect Your Home and Family in the Coming Crisis; Crisis Investing for the Year 2000: How to Profit from the Coming Y2K Computer Crash; Y2K: A Reasoned Response to Mass Hysteria; Spiritual Survival During the Y2K Crisis; Y2K: The Millennium Bug — A Balanced Christian Response; Awakening: The Upside of Y2K*; and, for children, *Y2K-9: The Dog Who Saved the World*. Television news features and magazines soon joined in. The April 1999 issue of *Wired* magazine featured an ominously black cover with the big words "Lights Out" and the smaller text "Learning to Love Y2K."[1]

We were informed that computers were embedded in nearly all of our electronic technologies, and the disaster scenarios ranged from massive electrical blackouts

---

[1] *Wired*, Volume 7, Issue 4 (April, 1999), archived at www.wired.com/wired/archive/7.04

and water cutoffs, to planes falling out of the sky and automobiles going haywire, to recalcitrant microwave ovens and videocassette recorders.

The twentieth century had been an era of enormous scientific and technological progress, and now this technology was about to take a big bite out of our complacent posteriors.

No such fears accompanied the previous turn of the century. The nineteenth century had been an era of enormous scientific and technological progress, but nothing was due to blow up at midnight and the new century was greeted with optimism. Scientists were on the verge of total knowledge. Prominent physicists such as Lord Kelvin (1824–1907) predicted imminent solutions to the last few remaining riddles of the physical universe, including the nature of the ether that pervaded all space and provided a medium for the propagation of light and other electromagnetic radiation.

In mathematics — perhaps the nineteenth-century discipline closest to computer science — great progress had been made as well, and more was anticipated. A potential crisis had been weathered gracefully, and mathematics seemed stronger than ever.

The potential mathematical crisis in the nineteenth century involved a field that dated from about 300 BCE: geometry as defined by Euclid. (Although Euler's name is pronounced "oiler," Euclid's is pronounced "yoo-clid.")

Euclid's *Elements* begins with a series of definitions followed by five *postulates* and some common notions (also known as *axioms*). From these few basic assumptions, Euclid derives hundreds of theorems.

Euclid's first four postulates are so obvious it seems barely necessary to spell them out. In Sir Thomas Health's translation, the first three state that it is possible to draw lines and circles using a straightedge and compass and the fourth is equally simple:

1. To draw a straight line from any point to any point.
2. To produce a finite straight line continuously in a straight line.
3. To describe a circle with any centre and distance.
4. That all right angles are equal to one another.

Compared to the brevity and self-evidence of the first four postulates, the fifth is notoriously lengthy and awkward:

5. That, if a straight line falling on two straight lines make the interior angles on the same side less than two right angles, the two straight lines, if produced indefinitely, meet on that side on which are the angles less than the two right angles.[2]

This postulate defines the conditions under which lines are not parallel.

---

[2]Thomas L. Heath, *The Thirteen Books of Euclid's Elements*, second edition (Cambridge University Press, 1926; Dover Publications, 1956), Vol. 1, 154–155.

Beginning with the very earliest commentaries on Euclid's *Elements*, that fifth postulate was controversial. Some mathematicians thought that the fifth postulate was superfluous or redundant, and that it could actually be derived from the first four, but all attempts to derive the fifth postulate failed. The only successes occurred when implicit assumptions were made that were equivalent to the fifth postulate.

In the early nineteenth century, some mathematicians began exploring another approach: Suppose you assume something *contrary* to the fifth postulate. Perhaps two straight lines always meet regardless of the angle they form with the other line. Perhaps two straight lines never meet. If Euclid's fifth postulate were truly superfluous, then a contradiction would turn up somewhere down the road, and the fifth postulate would be proved by *reductio ad absurdum*.

It didn't quite work out that way. In Germany, Hungary, and Russia, Carl Friedrich Gauss (1777–1855), Johann Bolyai (1802–1860), and Nicolai Ivanovitch Lobachevsky (1792–1856), all working independently, discovered that alternatives to Euclid's fifth postulate didn't result in contradictions, but instead led to the creation of strange — but entirely consistent — geometric universes.

In a less sophisticated era, mathematicians might have rejected these non-Euclidean geometries as abominations, or despaired that basic geometry had been rendered invalid by these absurd constructions. Instead, mathematicians accepted these alternatives to Euclid and learned a major lesson about the nature of mathematics.

Euclid had been right to include the windy fifth postulate among his basic assumptions. That postulate was necessary to distinguish Euclid's geometry as the geometry of the plane, but that postulate wasn't the only possibility. Replacing it with something else yielded geometries that were just as legitimate as Euclid's and just as interesting (if not more so). Did these non-Euclidean geometries have anything to do with what we so blithely call "the real world"? Sometimes, certainly. One non-Euclidean geometry describes the surface of a sphere, and in some respects a sphere is more "real world" than the plane is.

Nineteenth-century mathematicians also developed a new and deeper appreciation of the *axiomatic method* that Euclid had employed in his *Elements*. (Although Euclid and Aristotle distinguished between postulates and axioms,[3] that difference has largely disappeared in modern times.) A mathematical system begins with particular axioms and continues by proving implications of those axioms. Depending on our mood, those axioms may or may not coincide with our intuitive notions of the real world. For two millennia, the idea of mimicking the real world had actually imprisoned geometry. If the axioms could be liberated from the real word

---

[3] See Thomas Heath, *Mathematics in Aristotle* (Oxford University Press, 1949; Thoemmes Press, 1998), 50–57 or Howard Eves, *Foundations and Fundamental Concepts of Mathematics*, 3rd edition (PWS-Kent, 1990; Dover, 1997), 29–32.

and made sufficiently abstract, then mathematics itself could be freed, as well, to explore new vistas. The axioms and the mathematics that result must be treated abstractly without any implicit assumptions.

Or as a young mathematics instructor once pondered, "One must be able to say at all times — instead of points, straight lines, and planes — tables, chairs, and beer mugs."[4]

That young mathematics instructor was David Hilbert (1862–1943), who was then on his way to becoming one of the preeminent mathematicians of his age. Hilbert was born near Königsberg, a port city on the Baltic Sea and at the time the capital of East Prussia. In mathematical lore, Königsberg was already a famous city by the time Hilbert was born. It was the city where the seven bridges that crossed the Pregel River found their way into a topological puzzle solved by Leonhard Euler.

Königsberg was also home to the University of Königsberg, where philosopher Immanuel Kant (1724–1804) studied and taught. Hilbert also attended that university and briefly taught there as well, but in 1895 a position opened up at the University of Göttingen; Hilbert accepted it. Hilbert had first visited Göttingen nine years earlier, "and he found himself charmed by the little town and the pretty, hilly countryside, so different from the bustling city of Königsberg and the flat meadows beyond it."[5]

The University of Göttingen was also famous before Hilbert arrived. There, in 1833, Gauss and physicist Wilhelm Weber (1804–1891) had collaborated on an electromagnetic telegraph. With a mathematics department run by Hilbert and Felix Klein (1849–1925), Göttingen was about to become a mecca for mathematicians around the world.

In his early years, Hilbert had made a name for himself by tackling unsolved problems in the areas of algebraic invariants and number fields, but in the 1898–1899 school year, his interests took an unusual turn. Hilbert taught a class on geometry — a subject not usually taught on the university level — to students who had already received a full dose of Euclid in their elementary education.

Hilbert's geometry was familiar in structure to Euclid's — it began with axioms (actually, several *groups* of axioms) and from these axioms many theorems were derived — but the level of rigor was unsurpassed. Hilbert had entirely rethought and re-axiomatized geometry. It was a Euclid for the modern age with all the knowledge of non-Euclidean geometries entering into its conception. In 1899, Hilbert published his geometry lectures in the book *Grundlagen der Geometrie* (*Foundations of Geometry*), which became an instant classic of mathematics. (The second English edition based on the tenth German edition was published by Open Court Press in 1971 and remains in print.)

Hilbert's book wasn't called the *elements* of geometry like Euclid's; it was the *Grundlagen* — the *groundwork* or *foundations* — of geometry. Putting geometry

---

[4]Constance Reid, *Hilbert* (Springer-Verlag, 1970, 1996), 57.
[5]Reid, *Hilbert*, 25.

on a firm axiomatic foundation was more important to Hilbert than solving the theorems. Part of establishing a foundation for geometry was demonstrating that the axioms were consistent — that they could never lead to contradictions. Hilbert did this by constructing an analogue of his geometry on the real-number plane. This was basically analytic geometry within the Cartesian coordinate system. The consistency of Hilbert's geometry then became a problem in the consistency of real-number arithmetic.

Hilbert wasn't the only mathematician interested at the time in establishing foundations in mathematics. In 1889 Giuseppe Peano (1858–1932) had applied the axiomatic method to an area where few non-mathematicians would think it was needed — the formulation of the arithmetic of natural numbers. Less well known at the time (but highly regarded now) was Gottlob Frege (1848–1925), who had reconceived mathematical logic with a radical new notation that he described in an 1879 pamphlet called *Begriffschrift* (roughly "concept script").[6] Frege had written a *Grundlagen* of his own, the *Grundlagen der Arithmetik* (1884), in which he attempted to establish a foundation for real-number arithmetic through mathematical logic. Frege then elaborated on this system in a larger work, and in 1893 published the first volume of his *Grundgesetze* (or Basic Laws) *der Arithmetik*, in which set theory and mathematical logic were combined to establish the legitimacy of the real numbers.

With these foundations being nailed into place shortly before the turn of the century, mathematics seemed to be on a good track, and David Hilbert was invited to give a major address at the Second International Congress of Mathematicians to be held in Paris in August 1900. The address would kick off the new century of mathematics, and Hilbert was unsure what to say.

Hilbert turned to his good friend from the University of Königsberg, the Lithuanian-born mathematician Hermann Minkowski (1864–1909) for advice. Minkowski suggested that Hilbert's address look forward rather than back:

> Most alluring would be the attempt at a look into the future and
> a listing of the problems on which mathematicians should try
> themselves during the coming century. With such a subject you
> could have people talking about your lecture decades later.[7]

So, on August 8, 1900, Hilbert began his address fashioned just as Minkowski had suggested:

> Who of us would not be glad to lift the veil behind which the
> future lies hidden; to cast a glance at the next advances of our

---

[6] An English translation is available in Jean van Heijenoort, ed., *From Frege to Gödel: A Source Book in Mathematical Logic, 1879–1931* (Harvard University Press, 1967), 1–82.

[7] Reid, *Hilbert*, 69.

science and at the secrets of its development during future centuries? What particular goals will there be toward which the
leading mathematical spirits of coming generations will strive?
What new methods and new facts in the wide and rich field of
mathematical thought will the new centuries disclose?[8]

Hilbert then discussed rather generally some of the problems that would require
solutions by the mathematicians of the new century. He assured his audience that
these problems were just waiting to be solved:

However unapproachable these problems may seem to us and
however helpless we stand before them, we have, nevertheless,
the firm conviction that their solution must follow by a finite
number of purely logical processes. . . . This conviction of the
solvability of every mathematical problem is a powerful incentive
to the worker. We hear within us the perpetual call: There is the
problem. Seek its solution. You can find it by pure reason, for in
mathematics there is no *ignorabimus*.[9]

Although a rather unusual Latin word, the mathematicians in Hilbert's audience
could easily decode the verb and tense as "We shall not know." Some of Hilbert's
listeners possibly also made a connection with a famous 1876 lecture in which
physiologist Emil du Bois-Reymond (1818–1896) had pessimistically concluded
that "concerning the riddle of matter and force . . . the scientist must concur once
and for all with the much harder verdict that is delivered: Ignorabimus."[10]

To du Bois-Reymond, the nature of matter and energy would forever be
unknown. Hilbert's optimism just couldn't tolerate such an attitude. In mathematics, he made clear, there is no "We shall not know."

Hilbert then challenged his colleagues to solve 23 outstanding problems in
several fields of mathematics. (Due to time constraints, only 10 were mentioned
in the spoken address; all 23 problems appeared in the published version.) While
some of the problems were quite esoteric, others were fundamental in their
scope.

Number 1 concerned "Cantor's Problem of the Cardinal Number of the
Continuum" — whether the cardinality of the continuum represented the next

---

[8]As quoted in Ben H. Yandell, *The Honors Class: Hilbert's Problems and Their Solvers* (A. K. Peters, 2002),
389. The English version of the address was originally printed in the *Bulletin of the American
Mathematical Society*, Vol. 8 (July 1902) in a translation by Dr. Mary Winston Newson. A slightly revised
version appears in Jeremy J. Gray, *The Hilbert Challenge* (Oxford University Press, 2000), 240.
[9]As quoted in Yandell, *The Honors Class*, 395.
[10]As quoted in Gray, *The Hilbert Challenge*, 58.

transfinite number after the cardinality of the natural numbers, or whether there were other transfinite numbers between those to be considered. Georg Cantor's work had become less controversial by this time, and Hilbert was one of Cantor's biggest proponents.

Problem 2 focused on "The Compatibility of the Arithmetical Axioms." Hilbert had based the consistency of his geometry on the consistency of the real number system and arithmetic. Now the real numbers needed axiomatization and "*To prove that they are not contradictory, that is, that a finite number of logical steps based upon them can never lead to contradictory results.*"[11]

Problem 10 in Hilbert's German read:

> Entscheidung der Lösbarkeit einer diophantischen Gleichung.

Take note of that word *Entscheidung*. It's a very important word in this book. It means *decision, decidability, determination*. Hilbert's 10th problem read in its entirety:

> 10. Determination of the Solvability of a Diophantine Equation
>
> Given a diophantine equation with any number of unknown quantities and with rational integral numerical coefficients: *To devise a process according to which it can be determined by a finite number of operations whether the equation is solvable in rational integers.*[12]

Yes, it was 1,650 years after Diophantus's *Arithmetica*, and mathematicians were still wrestling with Diophantine equations. While some mathematicians worked with specific forms of Diophantine equations, Hilbert asked for a *general* decision process. Notice that he's not asking for a general method to *solve* all Diophantine equations. What he wants is a *determination* of the solvability. Consider an arbitrary Diophantine equation: Is it solvable? Does it have a solution? Hilbert wants a process, and there doesn't seem to be the slightest doubt in his mind that such a process exists. It only has to be found.

The words that Hilbert uses in defining this problem will set the tone for this particular *Entscheidung* problem and other *Entscheidung* problems in the years ahead. Hilbert wants a *process* with a *finite number of operations*. In short, Hilbert wants an *algorithm*, but that word (either in English or the German *Algorithmus*)

---

[11] Yandell, *The Honors Class*, 397.

[12] Yandell, *The Honors Class*, 406. It's translated as "Decidability of solvability of Diophantine equations" in Ivor Grattan-Guinness, "A Sideways Look at Hilbert's Twenty-three Problems of 1900," *Notices of the American Mathematical Society*, Vol. 47, No. 7 (August 2000), 752–757. The term "rational integers" means the regular integers with which we're familiar.

was not used at the time, at least not in its modern sense. The modern usage of the word only became common in the 1960s in literature about computers.[13]

In that 1900 address, Hilbert invited his audience to "lift the veil" behind which the twentieth century lay hidden. Neither he nor anyone else could have imagined quite the spectacle they would have seen. If physicists believed they were on the verge of total knowledge, those hopes were dashed in 1905, the year now known as the *annus mirabilis* of physicist Albert Einstein (1879–1955). In a single year, Einstein published a doctoral thesis and four other papers that established the basic principles of relativity and quantum mechanics.

No longer was there any sense that the universe was linear, Euclidean, and fully deterministic. Space and time lost their moorings in a relativistic universe. In a famous 1907 paper on relativity, Hilbert's friend Hermann Minkowski would coin the word *Zaumreit* or *spacetime*. (Minkowski had come to Göttingen in 1902, but died suddenly of appendicitis in 1909.) Eventually, the century's best known result of quantum mechanics would be something known as the Uncertainty Principle (1927).

Perhaps in response to this new displacement and uncertainty, modern art and music went in startling and provocative directions. Visual forms and objects were broken apart and reassembled in cubist paintings and sculptures. As the real-world "objective" universe became less reliable, surrealists looked inward to their subconscious lives and irrational dreams.

In music, the chromaticism of late romantics like Wagner and Debussy seemed almost tame as it gave way to the harsh dissonances and jagged new rhythms of Igor Stravinsky's *Rite of Spring*, which incited riots at its 1913 Paris premiere. In the early 1920s, Austrian composer Arnold Schönberg's development of twelve-tone music represented nothing less than a re-axiomatization of the principles of musical harmony to create a non-Euclidean music.

Twentieth-century mathematics was not immune to these upsets. The first jarring notes sounded in 1902.

Gottlob Frege, born in Wismar, Germany, in 1848, had received his Ph.D. at Göttingen two decades before Hilbert arrived there, and then began teaching at the University of Jena, where he would remain for 44 years. The first volume of his life's work, the *Grundgesetze der Arithmetik*, was published in 1893, and attempted a systematic development of all of mathematics beginning with mathematical logic — a program now known as *logicism*. This first volume sold so poorly that the publisher didn't want to hear about the second volume, so in 1902 Frege was attempting to publish it at his own expense.

---

[13]See *Oxford English Dictionary*, 2nd edition, I, 313. Also see the opening pages of Donald E. Knuth, *The Art of Computer Programming, Volume 1, Fundamental Algorithms*, 3rd edition (Addison-Wesley, 1997). The most famous algorithm of them all is Euclid's method to find the greatest common divisor of two numbers, but the first known usages of the term "Euclid's Algorithm" seem to date only from the early twentieth century.

Meanwhile, the first volume of *Grundgesetze der Arithmetik* had acquired an important new reader.

This was Bertrand Russell (1872–1970), an extraordinary figure whose first mathematics papers were published in the reign of Victoria but who lived long enough to protest the Vietnam War. Russell was born into an aristocratic and intellectual family. His grandfather, John Russell (1792–1878), had been Prime Minister of England; his godfather was the utilitarian philosopher John Stuart Mill (1806–1873). Russell's interest in mathematics started early:

> At the age of eleven, I began Euclid, with my brother as my tutor.
> This was one of the great events of my life, as dazzling as first
> love. I had not imagined that there was anything so delicious in
> the world. After I learned the fifth proposition, my brother told
> me that it was generally considered difficult, but I had found no
> difficulty whatever. This was the first time it had dawned upon
> me that I might have some intelligence.[14]

In 1902, Russell was working on his book *The Principles of Mathematics* (to be published the next year) and had discovered a problem in the set theories of both Peano and Frege.

Sets can have other sets as members, and sets can even contain *themselves* as members. Russell pondered: What about the set that contains all sets that do not contain themselves? Does that set contain itself? If it doesn't, then it's a set that does not contain itself, so it needs to contain itself, but if it does contain itself, then it's no longer a set that doesn't contain itself.

This is now known as the Russell Paradox, and became the latest of several paradoxes that have plagued mathematicians for at least two millennia. Russell later made an analogy with a town barber who shaves all those who do not shave themselves. Who shaves the barber?

Russell wrote a letter to Frege inquiring about the set that contains all sets that do not contain themselves,[15] and Frege was devastated. He quickly wrote an appendix to the second volume of *Grundgesetze der Arithmetik*, but the problem could not be fixed. The paradox was a basic flaw that rippled through Frege's major life's work.

The paradox that Bertrand Russell had discovered resulted from the ability of sets to contain themselves as members. If this sort of self-referentiality were removed, set theory might be made free from the risks of paradox. Russell began to develop a *theory of types* that he discussed a bit in *The Principles of Mathematics*

---

[14]Bertrand Russell, *The Autobiography of Bertrand Russell, 1872–1914* (George Allen and Unwin Ltd, 1967), 36.
[15]*From Frege to Gödel*, 124–125.

and then in more detail in a 1908 paper.[16] Russell constructed a hierarchy of sets. At the bottom of the hierarchy, a Type 1 set could contain only individuals (for example, numbers). Type 1 sets can only belong to sets of Type 2. Type 2 sets can only belong to sets of Type 3, and so on.

By the time Russell published that 1908 paper, something much larger was in the works. Russell had been ready to commence work on a second volume of the *Principles of Mathematics*, and Russell's former teacher and mentor, Alfred North Whitehead (1861–1947), was also preparing to write a second volume to *his* earlier book, *A Treatise on Universal Algebra* (1898). Russell and Whitehead realized that their goals overlapped and about 1906 had begun collaborating on what was to become the most important book on logic since Aristotle.

The almost 2,000 pages of *Principia Mathematica* by A. N. Whitehead and Bertrand Russell were published in three volumes in 1910, 1912, and 1913. Unlike an earlier *Principia Mathematica* — the title under which Isaac Newton's 1687 *Philosophiæ Naturalis Principia Mathematica* is sometimes known — only the title of Whitehead and Russell's work is Latin. Perhaps their choice of title was also influenced by the much shorter *Principia Ethica* (1903) by their Cambridge colleague George Edward Moore (1873–1958).[17] Whitehead, Russell, and Moore were all members of the Cambridge Apostles, the elite secret society devoted to the presentation of philosophical papers and the consumption of sardines on toast.

Although *Principia Mathematica* wasn't written in Latin, it isn't exactly English either. Much of the book consists of dense lists of formulas that cover the pages "like hen-tracks on the barnyard snow of a winter morning," in the words of one early reader.[18]

Principia Mathematica incorporated a theory of types and a mathematical logic largely based on Peano and Frege but with Peano's notation rather than Frege's idiosyncratic graphics. The *Principia Mathematica* carries on Frege's work in logicism, and one of the climaxes comes when Whitehead and Russell prove:

$$1 + 1 = 2$$

It's harder than it looks![19]

Until this time, David Hilbert's interest in logicism was rather spotty. In 1904, Hilbert had addressed the Third International Congress of Mathematicians (held

---

[16]Bertrand Russell, "The Theory of Types" in *From Frege to Gödel*, 150–182.

[17]I. Grattan-Guinness, *The Search for Mathematical Roots, 1870–1940: Logics, Set Theories and the Foundations of Mathematics from Cantor through Russell to Gödel* (Princeton University Press, 2000), 380.

[18]Grattan-Guinness, *The Search for Mathematical Roots*, 454.

[19]The preliminary result is in section *54·43: "From this proposition it will follow, when arithmetical addition has been defined, that $1 + 1 = 2$," most conveniently found in the abridgement: Alfred North Whitehead and Bertrand Russell, *Principia Mathematica to *56* (Cambridge University Press, 1997), 360. Only in *110.643 in Volume II is the proof actually completed with the modest observation, "The above proposition is occasionally useful."

in Heidelberg) "On the Foundations of Logic and Arithmetic" in which he hinted about some possible approaches, but the publication of *Principia Mathematica* threw the whole issue of logicism into center stage.

It would certainly have been interesting for Hilbert and Russell to begin collaborating on logic and mathematics following the publication of *Principia Mathematica*, but world events interceded. On August 4, 1914, Great Britain declared war on Germany, which had days earlier declared war on Russia and France. The Great War was to last until 1918.

Neither Russell nor Hilbert was a militarist. In 1914 the German government asked prominent scientists and artists to sign a declaration refuting the "lies and slanders of the enemy." Hilbert could not determine whether these statements made about Germany were true (a rather political *Entscheidung* problem), so he refused to sign.[20] Russell, who was to be a lifelong activist against war, engaged in more public protests, and was dismissed from his position at Trinity College in 1916 and later imprisoned for five months.[21]

Hilbert actually invited Russell to lecture at Göttingen in 1917. Even if Russell's passport had not been confiscated by the British government, it is hard to imagine such a visit occurring while the countries were still at war.[22]

On September 11, 1917, Hilbert again publicly ventured into the field of mathematical foundations with an address to the Swiss Mathematical Society in Zurich on the subject of "Axiomatic Thought." (Although the war was still going on, Hilbert was able to meet with mathematicians from other countries in Zurich because Switzerland had maintained neutrality.) In this address we can hear the origins of what became known in the early 1920s as the *Hilbert Program*, which veered away from logicism but sought as its goal the rigorous axiomatization of all of mathematics. For analyzing axiomatic systems Hilbert conceived a "metamathematics" and "proof theory" that would use mathematical logic to draw conclusions about the structure of other mathematical systems.

This is an approach in mathematics known as *formalism*. In Hilbert's conception, the construction of a formal mathematical system begins with definitions, axioms, and rules for constructing theorems from the axioms. Ideally, the resultant system should exhibit four interrelated qualities:

- Independence
- Consistency
- Completeness
- Decidability

---

[20] Reid, *Hilbert*, 137.

[21] Mathematician G.H. Hardy later wrote a pamphlet describing these events, which was published by Cambridge University Press in 1942 and privately circulated. It was republished as G.H. Hardy, *Bertrand Russell and Trinity: A College Controversy of the Last War* (Cambridge University Press, 1970).

[22] Grattan-Guinness, *Search for Mathematical Roots*, 471, footnote 28.

Independence means that there aren't any superfluous axioms — there's no axiom that can be derived from the other axioms. Independence is what mathematicians suspected that Euclid's five postulates did *not* exhibit. That's why they attempted to derive the fifth postulate from the other four. It was later established that Euclid's postulates were indeed independent.

Consistency is by far the most important characteristic of any axiomatic system. It must not be possible to derive two theorems that contradict each other!

For example, suppose you devise some new mathematical system. This system contains symbols, axioms, and rules that you use to develop theorems from the axioms. That is mostly what you do: You use the axioms to derive theorems. These are your proofs, but the rules also imply the syntax of a well-formed formula (often called a wff, pronounced "woof") that is possible within the system. You can assemble a well-formed formula without first deriving it from your system, and then you can attempt to show that it's a consequence of the axioms by applying the axioms and rules in a proof.

I'm going to show you two well-formed formulas in a hypothetical mathematical system. Here's the first formula, which we'll call *A*:

$$\text{gobbledygook} = \text{yadda-yadda-yadda}$$

The equal sign means that the two expressions on either side are considered to be equivalent in some way. Here's formula *B*:

$$\text{gobbledygook} \neq \text{yadda-yadda-yadda}$$

It's the same as formula *A* except a not-equal sign has replaced the equal sign. Formula *B* is the negation, or contradiction, of *A*.

Formulas *A* and *B* are opposites. Only one or the other can be true. Now the concept of "truth" is often as slippery in mathematical logic as it is in real life. I have no desire to get into a metaphysical discussion here, so I'll merely define truth as roughly meaning "harmonious with the axiomatic assumptions."

If you can derive *both* formulas *A* and *B* from the axioms, then the axiomatic system is inconsistent, and not only is it inconsistent — it's *worthless*. It's worthless because the inconsistency ripples throughout the entire system and makes everything equally false and true at the same time, a logical disaster traditionally known as *ex falso quodlibet* (from the false everything follows).

That's consistency.

Completeness is the ability to derive *all* true formulas from the axioms. You derive true formulas using proofs. If you can't derive *either* formula *A* or *B* from the axioms (that is, neither *A* nor *B* is provable), then the axiomatic system is said to be incomplete. Which is true? Maybe you don't know at all, or maybe you have a good idea which is true, but you simply can't provide a proof.

The distinction between truth and provability can be tricky: If something is not provable we usually can't know for certain that it's true, but that doesn't stop us from asserting truth without the corresponding proof. For example, almost everyone believes that Goldbach's Conjecture is true: Every even integer greater than 2 is the sum of two prime numbers. Nevertheless, it is called a "conjecture" because it remains one of the great unproven mathematical problems of all time.

(I'm rather simplifying the distinction between "proof" and "truth" for this discussion. Provability is a *syntactic* concept; it's based on the axioms of the system and the rules used to derive theorems. Truth, however, is a *semantic* concept that depends on the actual meaning we give to the symbols in the system. I'll have more to say about these issues in Part III of this book.)

Also important to Hilbert was *decidability* or *Entscheidung*. He wanted a *decision procedure* — a general method to determine the provability of any given well-formed formula.

If a mathematical system is revealed to be incomplete, does that also imply that a decision procedure does not exist? Not necessarily. Suppose neither formula *A* nor *B* can be proved. The system is incomplete, but there might be a decision procedure that would analyze both formulas *A* and *B* and come to precisely the same conclusion — that neither can be proved. The decision procedure would exist even though the system was not complete.

Of course, a better, stronger decision procedure would be one that determined not provability, but truth. Such a decision procedure would identify either *A* or *B* as true even if neither could be proved in the sense of being derivable from the axioms.

Hilbert had first suggested the idea of a decision procedure in his 1900 Paris address in connection with Diophantine problems. Hilbert's 1917 Zurich address on "Axiomatic Thought" also touched on "the problem of the *decidability* of a mathematical question in a finite number of operations." Of all the aspects of axiomatic systems, he said, decidability "is the best-known and the most discussed; for it goes to the essence of mathematical thought."[23] (Of course, it's likely that when Hilbert says something is "best-known and the most discussed," he is referring to the core of *his* mathematical world — namely, himself, his colleagues, and his students in Göttingen. In *Principia Mathematica*, Whitehead and Russell weren't concerned at all with either completeness or decidability.)

Perhaps Hilbert was the first person to concatenate the words *Entscheidung* and *Problem*, but the first recorded use of the five-syllable composite is by one of Hilbert's assistants, Heinrich Behmann (1891–1970), in a talk to the Göttingen Mathematical Society on May 10, 1921, entitled "Entscheidungsproblem und Algebra der Logik." In retrospect, Behmann's description of the hypothetical

---

[23]William Ewald, ed., *From Kant to Hilbert: A Source Book in the Foundations of Mathematics* (Oxford University Press, 1996), Vol. II, 1113.

decision procedure is jaw-droppingly astonishing. (The italics are in the original German from an unpublished document in the Behmann Archives):

> It is of fundamental importance for the character of this problem that *only mechanical calculations* according to given instructions, without any thought activity in the stricter sense, are admitted as tools for the proof. One could, if one wanted to, speak of *mechanical* or *machinelike* thought (Perhaps one could later let the procedure be carried out by a machine).[24]

If Behmann had pursued this concept to its logical conclusions, we might today be talking about Behmann Machines rather than Turing Machines!

In the 1922–23 school year, Hilbert taught a course on Logical Foundations of Mathematics, and also began using the word Entscheidungsproblem,[25] but the Entscheidungsproblem really emerged from Göttingen into the larger mathematical world in 1928. That was the year that Hilbert's assistant Wilhelm Ackermann (1896–1962) helped assemble class lectures by Hilbert (some going back to the 1917–1918 school year) into a slim book published under the title *Grundzüge der Theoretischen Logik*[26] (translated as *Principles of Mathematical Logic*), a book that is now known as "Hilbert & Ackermann."

Hilbert & Ackermann came nowhere close to the scope and ambition of *Principia Mathematica*. The book covered only the basics of mathematical logic apart from any set theory or logicism. In its own way, however, Hilbert & Ackermann proved to be quite influential beyond the modesty of its 120 pages. At the core of the book was an explication of *engere Funktionenkalkül* or "restricted functional calculus," better known today under the term "first-order predicate logic," that included questions concerning completeness and decidability.

One early reader of Hilbert & Ackermann was an Austrian mathematics student in Vienna named Kurt Gödel (1906–1978). About first-order predicate logic Gödel read:

> Whether the axiom system is complete, at least in the sense that all logical formulas that are correct for *every* domain of individuals can be derived from it, is still an unresolved question.[27]

[24]As quoted in Paolo Mancosu, "Between Russell and Hilbert: Behmann on the Foundations of Mathematics," *The Bulletin of Symbolic Logic*, Vol. 5, No. 3 (Sept. 1999), 321.

[25]Wilfried Sieg, "Hilbert's Programs: 1917-1922," *The Bulletin of Symbolic Logic*, Vol. 5, No. 1 (March 1999), 22.

[26]D. Hilbert and W. Ackermann, *Grundzüge der Theoretischen Logik* (Verlag von Julius Springer, 1928). A second edition was published in 1938 reflecting additional research over the past decade, and an English translation of the second German edition was published in 1950 by Chelsea Publishing Company. There is no English translation of the first German edition.

[27]Hilbert & Ackermann, *Grundzüge der Theoretischen Logik*, 68.

The passage is referring to formulas in first-order logic that are true regardless of the interpretation of the propositional functions (today known as predicates) and the domain of these functions. Can all these "universally valid" formulas — as they were called — be derived from the axioms? Gödel took up the challenge, and his 1929 doctoral thesis showed that first-order predicate logic was complete in this sense. This is known as the Gödel Completeness Theorem, and if proving completeness was the extent of Gödel's contribution to mathematical logic, he probably wouldn't be remembered much today. But Gödel was only getting started.

The completeness of first-order predicate logic was an important although expected result. It showed that the axioms and proof mechanisms were adequate for deriving all universally valid statements. Mathematical logic does not exist in a vacuum, however. One of the primary purposes of predicate logic was providing a firm framework and foundation for numbers and arithmetic. Doing so requires adding axioms to the logical system for establishing number theory. That was the primary purpose of *Principia Arithmetica*. After adding these axioms, is first-order predicate logic complete in a much stronger sense, in that every statement or its negation is provable? This is sometimes known as "negation completeness," and it's a much more difficult goal. This was the problem Gödel tackled next.

In the spring of 1930, David Hilbert retired from teaching. He was 68 years old. Later that year, he was awarded an honorary citizenship of Königsberg, his birthplace. Hilbert was as optimistic as ever as he delivered an address on "Logic and the Knowledge of Nature."[28] It had been 30 years since he told his Paris audience that there was no "We shall not know" for the mathematician and now he repeated that claim: "For the mathematician there is no *ignorabimus*, nor, in my opinion, for any part of natural science." Hilbert tells how the philosopher Auguste Comte once said that we would never know the compositions of distant stars, and how that problem was solved just a few years later:

> The real reason why Comte was unable to find an unsolvable
> problem is, in my opinion, that there are absolutely no unsolv-
> able problems. Instead of the foolish *ignorabimus*, our answer is
> on the contrary:
>
> We must know.
> We shall know.

Wir müssen wissen. Wir werden wissen.

On the day before Hilbert was made an honorary citizen of Königsberg, Gödel was also visiting Königsberg, attending a conference on mathematics.

---

[28] *From Kant to Hilbert*, Vol. II, 1157–1165.

On September 7, 1930, Gödel announced that he had shown that axioms added to first-order predicate logic that allowed the derivation of arithmetic (including addition and multiplication) rendered the system incomplete. He had derived from within this system a formula and its negation. If arithmetic is consistent, then one of these statements must be true. Neither, however, could be proved.

Through a technique later called Gödel Numbering, Gödel had used the arithmetic developed within the system to associate every formula and every proof with a number. He was then able to develop a formula that asserted its own unprovability. This sounds like a mathematical form of the Liar's Paradox ("Everything I say is a lie, including this statement"), but it's really not. The formula asserts nothing about its truth or falsehood, but instead that it's *unprovable*. If arithmetic is consistent, then this formula can't be false, because that would lead to a contradiction. The formula must be true — but true only in a metamathematical sense because truth is not a concept of the logical system itself — which means that it really is unprovable.

Gödel's paper was published the following year under the title "On Formally Undecidable Propositions of *Principia Mathematica* and Related Systems I."[29] The Roman numeral I indicated that Gödel intended to follow up his paper with additional demonstrations, but the paper had such an immediate impact that a second part wasn't required.

One crucial premise for the Incompleteness Theorem is that arithmetic is consistent. As a corollary, Gödel also showed that a consistency proof for arithmetic within the system was impossible. Because certain formulas could not be proved or disproved, it was possible that these formulas were inconsistent. (Does this mean that arithmetic and elementary number theory is inconsistent? It's hardly likely, and nobody believes that to be so. The problem is that the consistency cannot be proved within the system itself.)

Upon hearing of Gödel's Incompleteness Theorem, David Hilbert had a rather strange reaction for a mathematician. He was "somewhat angry,"[30] but eventually he began to incorporate Gödel's findings in his program.

---

[29]Actually, the title was "Über formal unentscheidbare Sätze der Principia mathematica und verwandter Systeme I" and it was published in the *Monatshefte für Mathematik und Physik*, Vol. 38 (1931), 173–198. The first published English translation was by Bernard Meltzer of the University of Edinburg and appeared in the book Kurt Gödel, *On Formally Undecidable Propositions of Principia Mathematica and Related Systems* (Basic Books, 1962; Dover Publications, 1992). A second translation by Professor Elliott Mendelson of Queens College, New York City, appeared in Martin Davis, ed. *The Undecidable: Basic Papers on Undecidable Propositions, Unsolvable Problems and Computable Functions* (Raven Press, 1965), 5–38. A third translation by Jean van Heijenoort (with input from Gödel) appears in his book *From Frege to Gödel*, 596–616. This is also the translation used in Kurt Gödel, *Collected Works, Volume I, 1929–1936* (Oxford University Press, 1986), 144–195. The paper is often referred to as "Gödel 1931."

[30]Reid, *Hilbert*, 198.

Other mathematicians simply lost interest in mathematical logic. Bertrand Russell seemed to suffer permanent burnout from the experience of writing *Principia Mathematica*:

> [I]n the end the work was finished, but my intellect never quite recovered from the strain. I have been ever since definitely less capable of dealing with difficult abstractions than I was before. This is part, though by no means the whole, of the reason for the change in the nature of my work.[31]

Russell began pursuing other interests, such as writing about philosophy, politics, and social issues. He won the Nobel Prize for Literature in 1950 "in recognition of his varied and significant writings in which he champions humanitarian ideals and freedom of thought."[32] By that time many people had forgotten that he was originally a mathematician.

Hungarian mathematician John von Neumann (1903–1957), who had been at Göttingen in the mid-1920s, also abandoned logic after Gödel (or so he said) but was later instrumental in applying principles of mathematical logic to the development of digital computers.

Gödel's Incompleteness Theorem was certainly not the worst problem at Göttingen. In 1933, the Nazi party ordered the removal of all Jews from teaching positions in German universities. For Göttingen, where for decades the sole criterion was intellectual excellence, the edict was devastating. Richard Courant (1888–1972) left for the United States, where he found a position at New York University. (Today, the Courant Institute of Mathematical Sciences occupies a building on West 4th Street in Manhattan.) Hermann Weyl (1885–1955) wasn't Jewish, but his wife was. Like Albert Einstein, Weyl went to the Institute for Advanced Study in Princeton, New Jersey. Paul Bernays (1888–1977) lost his teaching job but kept his position as Hilbert's most loyal assistant until leaving for Zurich. Bernays is largely credited with writing the two volumes of *Grundlagen der Mathematik* (1934, 1939) although the books were published under both Hilbert's and Bernay's names.

At a banquet, Hilbert found himself sitting next to the Minister of Education. "And how is mathematics at Göttingen now that it has been freed of the Jewish influences?" Hilbert was asked. He replied, "Mathematics at Göttingen? There is really none anymore."[33]

For those mathematicians who continued to explore mathematical logic — now increasingly not at Göttingen — problems still remained to be solved. As the

---

[31] *The Autobiography of Bertrand Russell, 1872–1914*, 153.

[32] http://nobelprize.org/nobel_prizes/literature/laureates/1950

[33] Reid, *Hilbert*, 205.

1928 edition of Hilbert & Ackermann asserted with well-deserved italics, the "*Entscheidungsproblem muß als das Hauptproblem der mathematischen Logik bezeichnet werden.*" "The decision problem must be called the main problem of mathematical logic."[34] Gödel's Incompleteness Theorem didn't imply that a decision process couldn't exist, but it did mean that such a decision process could not determine the *truth* of any arbitrary formula. It could at best determine the provability of a formula.

Nine pages of Hilbert & Ackermann were devoted to the *Entscheidungsproblem* in first-order predicate logic, and nearly half of those pages discussed "Solutions of the Decision Problem for Special Cases." For several standard (and common) types of formulas in mathematical logic, decision processes had already been developed. It didn't seem so unlikely that a general decision process was also possible.

It was not to be. In 1936, American mathematician Alonzo Church (1903–1995) concluded (again with well-deserved italics) that "*The general case of the Entscheidungsproblem of the engere Funktionenkalkül* [first-order predicate logic] *is unsolvable.*"[35]

Working independently of Church and using a completely different methodology, Alan Turing came to the same conclusion, that "the Hilbertian Entscheidungsproblem can have no solution,"[36] as he states at the beginning of his paper, and towards the end in conclusion, "Hence the Entscheidungsproblem cannot be solved."[37]

By the time Church and Turing had published their works, Hilbert was 74. Even Hilbert himself had come under suspicion by the Nazis, who wondered about his first name of *David*.[38] Hilbert's final years were spent in loneliness and senility. He died in 1943. On Hilbert's tombstone in Göttingen are the words

> Wir müssen wissen.
> Wir werden wissen.

We must know. We shall know. Except that now when people read Hilbert's words, all they can think about is Gödel and Church and Turing, incompleteness and undecidability.

Hilbert's home town of Königsberg was largely destroyed by British bombing during the war. It fell to the Russians in 1945 and became part of Russia following the war. Königsberg was renamed Kaliningrad in 1946 after a Soviet president.

---

[34] Hilbert & Ackermann, *Grundzüge der Theoretischen Logik*, 77.

[35] Alonzo Church, "A Note on the Entscheidungsproblem," *The Journal of Symbolic Logic*, Vol. 1 No. 1 (March 1936), 41.

[36] Alan Turing, "On Computable Numbers, with an Application to the Entscheidungsproblem," *Proceedings of the London Mathematical Society*, 2nd Series, Vol. 42 (1936), 231. (Page 67 of this book.)

[37] Ibid, 262. (Page 277 of this book.)

[38] Reid, *Hilbert*, 209.

The Russians who moved there were intent on destroying all remnants of German culture, and the Germans who stayed were victims of Stalinist atrocities. The location of the city on the Baltic Sea made it ideal for a military naval base. For decades it was closed to visitors.

Following the breakup of the Soviet Union, Kaliningrad remained part of Russia but on an enclave separated from the rest of the country, tucked between Lithuania and Poland, and known largely for its high crime rate.

The Y2K problem — which some had predicted would add a final crowning catastrophe to the horrors of the twentieth century — didn't turn out so badly. As the front page of the *New York Times* exhaled on the first morning of the year 2000:

1/1/00:
Technology and 2000

Momentous Relief;
Computers Prevail
in First Hours of '00

Computer programmers hadn't really embedded time bombs in lots of crucial systems. Programmers are generally much smarter than that! Moreover, they had put in some hard work and long hours to locate many of the potential problems. Changing computer programs is often fairly easy. That's why it's called *soft*ware.

Computer programs begin life and are maintained as text files called *source code*. These text files can themselves be read and analyzed by other programs. Programmers were able to write special programs to examine existing source code to locate possible problem areas. Such programs, for example, could search for variable names that include the letters "year" or "yr" and then a human programmer might examine how the program treated calendar years.

As these potential Y2K bugs were being hunted down and extinguished, it must have occurred to someone to ponder an even more ambitious scheme: Could one write a program that analyzed other programs and located other bugs? Such a program would be enormously difficult, of course, but after the program was finished, it could be used to debug any other program, and that would be extremely valuable.

Yes, it would be hard, but is it theoretically *possible*?

And the answer is *No*. A generalized bug-finding algorithm is *not* possible. That, too, is one of the unsettling implications of Alan Turing's paper on computable numbers and the Entscheidungsproblem.

Computable Numbers

4 The Education of Alan Turing

W hen Alan Turing was 10 years old, someone gave him a book by Edwin Tenney Brewster entitled *Natural Wonders Every Child Should Know*. This book opened the young man's eyes to science, Turing later said,[1] and perhaps had an even more profound influence on his conception of the relationship between human beings and machines. "For, of course, the body is a machine," the book asserted:

> It is a vastly complex machine, many, many times more complicated than any machine ever made with hands; but still after all a machine. It has been likened to a steam engine. But that was before we knew as much about the way it works as we know now. It really is a gas engine; like the engine of an automobile, a motor boat, or a flying machine.[2]

By the early twentieth century, the idea that human beings are machines had become so innocent a concept that it could now be discussed in a children's book. This was not always so. Two centuries separated the life of Alan Turing from that of Julien Offray de La Mettrie (1709–1751), the French doctor and philosopher whose scandalous 1747 work *L'Homme Machine* (*Machine Man*)[3] had uncompromisingly portrayed man's body and even mind as the workings of a machine. Alan Turing grew up with the recognition that his body was a machine; he would be remembered most for exploring the connections between machines and the human mind.

[1] Andrew Hodges, *Alan Turing: The Enigma* (Simon & Schuster, 1983), 11. All biographical information about Turing comes from this book.
[2] Quoted in Hodges, *Alan Turing*, 13.
[3] Julien Offray de La Mettrie, *Machine Man and Other Writings*, translated and edited by Ann Thomson (Cambridge University Press, 1996).

Alan Mathison Turing was born on June 23, 1912, in a nursing home in Paddington, a borough of London. His father served the British Empire in the Indian Civil Service; his mother had been born in Madras, the daughter of an engineer who had made a fortune in India building bridges and railways. Turing's parents met on a ship from India to England in 1907 and married later that year in Dublin. They returned to India in early 1908. Alan, the second of two boys, was conceived in India in 1911 but born in England.

During much of their early childhood, Alan and his older brother John were left in England in the care of a retired couple while their parents lived in India — a not uncommon practice at the time. In 1922, Alan began attending Hazelhurst, a prep school in Kent. His primary interests were maps, chess, and chemistry.[4] In 1926 he was accepted by Sherborne, one of the oldest of the English public schools. On the first day of Turing's first term at Sherborne, a general strike prevented him from taking the rail to the school. Alan decided instead to bicycle the 60 miles to the school, a feat that was reported in the local newspaper.[5]

Alan didn't mix well with the other boys at Sherborne. He was always shy and solitary, and seemed to be perpetually disheveled and ink-stained. "All his characteristics lent themselves to easy mockery, especially his shy, hesitant, high-pitched voice — not exactly stuttering, but hesitating, as if waiting for some laborious process to translate his thoughts into the form of human speech."[6] He might have redeemed himself by excelling in his studies, but that was not the case. Only in mathematics did he show some inkling of authentic intellectual talent.

By 1929, Alan became entranced by *The Nature of the Physical World* (1928), a popular and influential book by Cambridge astronomer Sir Arthur Eddington that explored the implications of the new sciences of relativity and quantum theory. Alan also became entranced by a schoolmate named Christopher Morcom who shared Alan's interests in science and mathematics, and who came from a much more interesting, scientific family than Turing's own. Christopher's maternal grandfather was Sir Joseph Swan, who had invented the incandescent light bulb, in 1879, independently of Edison.

In retrospect, it seems likely that Alan Turing was discovering his homosexuality at this time, and that Christopher was his first love. There is no indication that anything physical occurred between the two teenagers, however. Together they performed chemistry experiments, exchanged mathematical equations, and explored the new astronomy and physics in books by Eddington and Sir James Jeans, another Cambridge professor of astronomy.

---

[4]Hodges, *Alan Turing*, 17.
[5]Hodges, *Alan Turing*, 21
[6]Hodges, *Alan Turing*, 24.

Cambridge was the place to go for aspiring English scientists, and the Cambridge college with the best reputation for science and mathematics was Trinity. In December 1929, Alan and Christopher journeyed to Cambridge for a week to take scholarship examinations and to bask in the alma mater of Francis Bacon, Isaac Newton, and James Clerk Maxwell. The exam results were published in *The Times* a week after they returned to Sherborne. Alan didn't make it, but Christopher did. Christopher would be going to Trinity, and the best that Alan could hope for was to try again for Trinity next year, or perhaps one of the other Cambridge colleges.

Two months later, Christopher became suddenly ill and died within the week, a consequence of the bovine tuberculosis he had contracted as a child. One of their classmates at Sherborne wrote in a letter, "Poor old Turing is nearly knocked out by the shock. They must have been awfully good friends."[7] While Alan Turing was to have other, more sexual relationships with men, apparently nothing ever came close to the love and adulation he had for Christopher Morcom.

In December 1930, Turing tried again for a Trinity scholarship and again didn't make it. His second choice was King's. By this time he had decided to concentrate on mathematics, and prepared himself by plowing into G.H. Hardy's classic, *A Course in Pure Mathematics*, at the time in its fifth edition. Alan Turing began his education at King's College, Cambridge, in the fall of 1931.

By the next year Turing was tackling a recent book on the mathematical foundations of quantum mechanics, *Mathematische Grundlagen der Quantenmechanik* by the young Hungarian mathematician John von Neumann, whose last name is pronounced "noy-man." Von Neumann had spent the mid-1920s working with David Hilbert in Göttingen, the site of much of the early research on the mathematics of quantum mechanics. He had immigrated to the United States in 1930 to teach at Princeton, and had been among the first mathematicians recruited by the Institute for Advanced Studies in 1933. Now the lives of John von Neumann and Alan Turing would begin to intersect in several interesting ways.

Turing probably first met von Neumann in the summer of 1935 when von Neumann took a break from his current post at Princeton University to lecture at Cambridge on the subject of almost-periodic functions. Turing already knew the subject and von Neumann's work in it: Just that spring Turing had published his first paper, a two-pager on the "Equivalence of Left and Right Almost Periodicity" (*Journal of the London Mathematical Society*, 1935) that expanded on a paper by von Neumann published the previous year.

Neither man could possibly have guessed that they would meet again the following year in Princeton, New Jersey.

---

[7]Hodges, *Alan Turing*, 46.

Turing's interest in the rarefied world of mathematical logic might have begun in 1933 when he read Bertrand Russell's 1919 work *Introduction to Mathematical Philosophy*, which ends:

> If any student is led into a serious study of mathematical logic by this little book, it will have served the chief purpose for which it has been written.[8]

In the spring term of 1935, Turing took a Foundations of Mathematics course given by Maxwell Herman Alexander Newman (1897–1984), generally known by the initials M.H.A. Newman and familiarly as Max. Max Newman's reputation was for his work in combinatorial topology, but he was also probably the person at Cambridge most knowledgeable about mathematical logic. The climax of Newman's course was the proof of Gödel's Incompleteness Theorem. (Graduate-level introductions to mathematical logic are still structured similarly.)

Also covered in Newman's course was the unresolved Entscheidungsproblem. "Was there a definite method, or as Newman put it, a *mechanical process* which could be applied to a mathematical statement, and which would come up with the answer as to whether it was provable?"[9] By "mechanical process" Newman didn't mean a machine, of course. Machines may be able to perform simple arithmetic, but they can hardly do actual mathematics. No, Newman was alluding to a type of process that would eventually be called an *algorithm* — a set of precise (but basically "mindless") instructions for solving a problem. It's likely that Turing began working on the decision problem in the early summer of 1935.[10] By this time he had been awarded a Cambridge fellowship, which paid £300 a year. Turing later said that the main idea for approaching the Entscheidungsproblem came to him while lying in Grantchester meadows, a popular recreational spot for Cambridge students about two miles from King's College.

By April 1936, Turing was able to give Max Newman a draft of his paper "On Computable Numbers, with an Application to the Entscheidungsproblem."[11]

Turing's paper takes an unusual approach for a mathematical proof: He begins by describing a fictional computing machine capable of a few simple operations. Despite the simplicity of this machine, Turing asserts that it

[8]Bertrand Russell, *Introduction to Mathematical Philosophy*, second edition (George Allen & Unwin Ltd, 1920; Dover Publications, 1993), 206.

[9]Hodges, *Alan Turing*, 93.

[10]Hodges, *Alan Turing*, 96.

[11]Hodges, *Alan Turing*, 109.

is functionally equivalent to a human being performing mathematical oper-ations. He sets these machines to work computing numbers. Turing's first example machine computes the number 1/3 in binary form (.010101...). The second computes an irrational number that is probably also transcenden-tal (.001011011101111...). He persuades us that machines can also be defined to calculate π, e, and other well-known mathematical constants. Turing even creates a Universal Machine that can simulate the operation of any other computing machine.

Yet, Turing Machines — as these imaginary devices came to be called — cannot calculate *every* real number. The machines he designed have a finite number of operations, and by representing these operations with numbers, he is able to show that each machine can be uniquely described by a single integer called a Description Number. Turing Machines are thus enumerable. The computable numbers — the numbers that Turing Machines are capable of computing — must also be enumerable, but real numbers (we know from Cantor's proofs) are not enumerable. The computable numbers certainly include the algebraic numbers, and they also include such transcendental numbers as π and e, but because the computable numbers are enumerable, they simply cannot encompass all real numbers.

Turing Machines are not infallible. It is possible to define a Turing Machine that simply doesn't work right or that doesn't do anything worthwhile. Turing divides his machines into "satisfactory" machines and "unsatisfactory" machines.

Because Turing Machines are entirely defined by a Description Number, it might be possible to create a Turing Machine that analyzes these Description Numbers to determine whether a particular machine is satisfactory or unsatis-factory. Turing proves that this is *not* the case: There is no general process to determine whether a Turing Machine is satisfactory. The only way one Turing Machine can analyze another is to trace through the operation of the machine step by step. In short, you must actually run a machine to determine what it's going to do.

What goes for Turing Machines also applies to computer programs: In general, it's not possible for one computer program to analyze another except by simulating that program step by step.

Turing also proves that no Turing Machine can be defined to do something that seems very straightforward — for example, to determine whether another machine ever prints the digit 0. In the final section of his paper (which is discussed in Part III of this book), Turing constructs a statement in mathe-matical logic equivalent to determining whether a particular Turing Machine ever prints the digit 0. Since he's already established that this determination is not possible, this statement in logic is not provable, and hence, "the Entschei-dungsproblem cannot be solved" (page 262 of Turing's paper and page 277 of this book).

Around the same time that Max Newman was reading a draft of Turing's paper, he received an offprint of a short paper by American mathematician Alonzo Church entitled "A Note on the Entscheidungsproblem."[12] Building upon a paper published earlier,[13] Church's paper also concluded that the Entscheidungsproblem "is unsolvable."

Turing had been scooped. That would normally imply that his paper was unpublishable and doomed to oblivion, but Max Newman realized that Turing's approach was innovative and considerably different from Church's. He recommended that Turing submit his paper to the London Mathematical Society for publication anyway. (The published paper indicates that the Society received it on May 28, 1936.) Turing explained the situation in a letter to his mother on May 29:

> Meanwhile a paper has appeared in America, written by Alonzo Church, doing the same things in a different way. Mr Newman and I decided however that the method is sufficiently different to warrant the publication of my paper too. Alonzo Church lives at Princeton so I have decided quite definitely about going there.[14]

On May 31, Max Newman wrote letters to both Alonzo Church and the secretary of the London Mathematical Society. To Church he wrote:

> An offprint which you kindly sent me recently of your paper in which you define 'calculable numbers', and shew that the Entscheidungsproblem for Hilbert logic is insoluble, had a rather painful interest for a young man, A.M. Turing, here, who was just about to send in for publication a paper in which he had used a definition of 'Computable numbers' for the same purpose. His treatment — which consists in describing a machine which will grind out any computable sequence — is rather different from yours, but seems to be of great merit, and I think it of great importance that he should come and work with you next year if that is at all possible.[15]

---

[12]Alonzo Church, "A Note on the Entschiedungsproblem," *The Journal of Symbolic Logic*, Vol. 1, No. 1 (Mar. 1936), 40–41.

[13]Alonzo Church, "An Unsolvable Problem of Elementary Number Theory," *American Journal of Mathematics*, Vol. 58, No. 2 (Apr. 1936), 345–363. Both of Church's papers appear in Martin Davis, ed., *The Undecidable* (Raven Press, 1965).

[14]Hodges, *Alan Turing*, 113.

[15]Hodges, *Alan Turing*, 112.

To F. P. White, the secretary of the London Mathematical Society, Max Newman wrote,

> I think you know the history of Turing's paper on Computable numbers. Just as it was reaching its final state an offprint arrived, from Alonzo Church of Princeton, of a paper anticipating Turing's results to a large extent.
>
> I hope it will nevertheless be possible to publish the paper. The methods are to a large extent different, and the result is so important that different treatments of it should be of interest. The main result of both Turing and Church is that the Entscheidungsproblem on which Hilbert's disciples have been working for a good many years — i.e., the problem of finding a mechanical way of deciding whether a given row of symbols is the enunciation of a theorem provable from the Hilbert axioms — is insoluble in its general form.[16]

Turing now needed to add an appendix to his paper showing that his concept of computability and Church's notion of "effective calculability" were equivalent. This appendix was received by the London Mathematical Society on August 28, 1936.

Turing's paper was published in the *Proceedings of the London Mathematical Society* in November and December, 1936.[17] A three-page Correction was published in December 1937.[18] A four-paragraph review of the paper by Alonzo Church in the March 1937 *Journal of Symbolic Logic* includes the statement, "a human calculator, provided with pencil and paper and explicit instructions, can be regarded as a type of Turing machine,"[19] which is the first known occurrence of the term "Turing machine" in print.

Turing's paper is divided into eleven sections and the appendix. It begins with an introduction that launches right into a description of this new category of numbers that Turing has conceived.

---

[16] Hodges, *Alan Turing*, 113.

[17] The paper was split between two monthly installments (called "parts") of the *Proceedings*: The first 11 pages appeared in Volume 42, Part 3 (dated November 30, 1936) and the remainder in Volume 42, Part 4 (dated December 23, 1936). In 1937, parts published from October 1936 through April 1937 were collectively published as 2nd Series, Volume 42. This is why the publication date of Turing's paper is variously given as 1936 (the year the individual parts were published), 1937 (which is when the completed Volume 42 was published) or 1936–1937 (which are the dates of *all* the parts included in Volume 42).

[18] Specifically, Volume 43, Part 7 (issued December 30, 1937), which then appeared in 2nd Series, Volume 43, which includes parts issued from May through December 1937.

[19] Alonzo Church, Review of "On Computable Numbers, with an Application to the Entscheidungsproblem," *The Journal of Symbolic Logic*, Vol. 2, No. 1 (Mar. 1937), 42–43.

[230]

ON COMPUTABLE NUMBERS, WITH AN APPLICATION TO THE ENTSCHEIDUNGSPROBLEM

By A. M. Turing.

[Received 28 May, 1936. — Read 12 November, 1936.]

The "computable" numbers may be described briefly as the real numbers whose expressions as a decimal are calculable by finite means.

Turing limits consideration here to real numbers, and he implies that the computable numbers are a *subset* of the reals, which means there are some real numbers that are not computable. This is certainly not immediately obvious.

By "expressions as a decimal" Turing means that 1/3 is to be expressed as 0.33333..., and π is to be calculated as 3.14159..., which immediately seems to conflict with his notion of "finite means." Obviously we can never really finish calculating the decimals of 1/3 or π. In Turing's paper, however, "means" refers not to the actual process of determining the digits but to the *method*. A method that says, "The next digit is 4. The next digit is 7. The next digit is 0..." can obviously be used to compute any real number, but it's not a finite method. Both 1/3 and π are calculable by algorithms (one less complex than the other), and the means by which we calculate them (a long division or something messier) involve a finite number of rules.

Although the subject of this paper is ostensibly the computable *numbers*, it is almost equally easy to define and investigate computable functions of an integral variable or a real or computable variable, computable predicates, and so forth. The fundamental problems involved are, however, the same in each case, and I have chosen the computable numbers for explicit treatment as involving the least cumbrous technique. I hope shortly to give an account of the relations of the computable numbers, functions, and so forth to one another. This will include a development of the theory of functions of a real variable expressed in terms of computable numbers.

Turing never followed up on his paper in this way. Gödel also intended to write a follow-up to his famous paper on incompleteness, and even included the Roman numeral I in its title in anticipation. Gödel never wrote the sequel because the results of his paper were accepted more quickly than he anticipated. Turing, on the other hand, got interested in other matters.

Turing concludes the first paragraph of his paper with the statement:

> According to my definition, a number is computable if its decimal can be written down by a machine.

This was rather a strange thing to say in 1936 because at the time no machine had ever been built that could do what Turing required in a general way.

Turing probably knew about the work of Charles Babbage (1791–1871), the English mathematician who had designed a Difference Engine to calculate pages of logarithmic tables, and then abandoned that project sometime around 1833 to work on an Analytical Engine that was more like a general-purpose computer. Babbage had also attended Cambridge and parts of Babbage's uncompleted machines were on display at the Science Museum in Kensington. Nevertheless, Turing doesn't seem influenced at all by Babbage's conceptions or terminology.

Turing may or may not have known about the Differential Analyzer constructed by Vannevar Bush (1890–1974) and his students at MIT starting in 1927, but this was an analog computer that solved differential equations with mostly engineering applications. Turing might have been interested in such a machine from a mathematical or engineering perspective, but it wouldn't have been much help with this particular problem.

It is hard to imagine how Turing could possibly have been aware of other early computer projects in the mid-1930s. Turing certainly didn't know that engineering student Konrad Zuse (1910–1995) had in 1935 begun building a computer in the living room of his parents' apartment in Berlin. It wasn't until 1937, after Turing's paper was published, that George Stibitz (1904–1995) took home some telephone relays from his workplace at Bell Telephone Laboratories and started wiring up binary adders. It was in 1937, as well, that Harvard graduate student Howard Aiken (1900–1973) began exploring automated computing, leading to a collaboration between Harvard and IBM in the creation of the Harvard Mark I.[20]

In attacking problems of calculability and Hilbert's Entscheidungsproblem at this particular time, Turing was part of a trend that included Alonzo Church, Emil Post (1897–1954), and Stephen Kleene (1909–1994),[21] but Turing can also be counted among those in the mid-1930s who were thinking about automated computing.

---

[20] An excellent introduction to these early computers is Paul E. Ceruzzi, *Reckoners: The Prehistory of the Digital Computer, from Relays to the Stored Program Concept, 1935–1945* (Greenwood Press, 1983).

[21] Robin Gandy, "The Confluence of Ideas in 1936," in Rolf Herken, ed., *The Universal Turing Machine: A Half-Century Survey* (Oxford University Press, 1988), 55-111; second edition (Springer-Verlag, 1995), 49–102.

Turing summarizes some of his conclusions that will appear in the later sections of this paper:

> In §§ 9, 10 I give some arguments with the intention of showing that the computable numbers include all numbers which could naturally be regarded as computable. In particular, I show that certain large classes of numbers are computable. They include, for instance, the real parts of all algebraic numbers, the real parts of the zeros of the Bessel functions, the numbers π, e, etc.

Those "numbers which could naturally be regarded as computable" are numbers that people have actually computed, and for which algorithms exist. Turing doesn't even bother to mention that all rational numbers are computable. That's obvious. He quickly adds algebraic numbers to the computable list as well. (He qualifies algebraic numbers to the *real* parts because solutions to algebraic equations can have real and imaginary parts, and he's already restricted himself to real numbers.)

With his assertion that algebraic numbers are computable, Turing has now thrown this discussion into the realm of the transcendentals. Yet, he says, some transcendental numbers are computable. Bessel functions are solutions to particular forms of differential equations. The zeros are values where the functions equal zero. These were once published in tables so they would be considered computable. (They are now generally calculated by computer programs when needed.) Turing doesn't mention them, but trigonometric and logarithmic functions generally have transcendental values, and these are computable as well. So are the constants π and e.

What Turing does not claim is that all transcendental numbers are computable. Otherwise the computable numbers would be the same as the real numbers.

> The computable numbers do not, however, include all definable numbers, and an example is given of a definable number which is not computable.

So let that be a lure. Turing will define a number that neither he (nor this machine of his) can compute.

Now Turing comes to the crux of the difference between real numbers and computable numbers:

> Although the class of computable numbers is so great, and in many ways similar to the class of real numbers, it is nevertheless enumerable.

Computable numbers are enumerable. The enumerability of computable numbers implies that they are not the same as real numbers, because the real numbers are not enumerable.

> In § 8 I examine certain arguments which would seem to prove the contrary. By the correct application of one of these arguments, conclusions are reached which are superficially similar to those of Gödel†.

> † Gödel, "Über formal unentscheidbare Sätze der Principia Mathematica und verwandter Systeme, I", *Monatshefte Math. Phys.*, 38 (1931), 173–198.

That's the famous Gödel Incompleteness Theorem. Notice that Turing's footnote refers to the German title of Gödel's paper. An English translation wouldn't be published until 1962.

> These results
>
> [231]
>
> have valuable applications. In particular, it is shown (§ 11) that the Hilbertian Entscheidungsproblem can have no solution.

This is the last mention of Hilbert for the next 18 pages of the paper.

Turing needed to add an appendix to the paper after he had learned about Alonzo Church's proof and had determined that the two approaches were equivalent. The last paragraph of the introduction was added at the same time.

> In a recent paper Alonzo Church† has introduced an idea of "effective calculability", which is equivalent to my "computability", but is very differently defined. Church also reaches similar conclusions about the Entscheidungsproblem‡. The proof of equivalence between "computability" and "effective calculability" is outlined in an appendix to the present paper.

> † Alonzo Church, "An unsolvable problem of elementary number theory", *American J. of Math.*, 58 (1936), 345–363.
> ‡ Alonzo Church, "A note on the Entscheidungsproblem", *J. of Symbolic Logic*, 1 (1936), 40–41.

That's the last mention of the Entscheidungsproblem for almost the next 28 pages of Turing's paper. According to the *Oxford English Dictionary* (second edition), that paragraph contains the first known use of the word "computability" other than an 1889 dictionary. There have since been well over 30 books published with the word "computability" in the title; the first was Martin Davis's *Computability and Unsolvability*, published by McGraw-Hill in 1958.

The first of eleven sections in Turing's paper now begins.

1. *Computing machines.*

We have said that the computable numbers are those whose decimals are calculable by finite means. This requires rather more explicit definition. No real attempt will be made to justify the definitions given until we reach § 9. For the present I shall only say that the justification lies in the fact that the human memory is necessarily limited.

Turing has said that computable numbers are those that can be written down by a machine, but now he justifies the "finite means" part of the definition by the limitation of human memory. This casual association of machine and human is characteristic of Turing's work.

When Turing originally said that a computable number was calculable by finite means, it sounded reasonable, but now that he justifies it by the limitations of the human mind, he's raising certain issues about the nature of mathematical reality. We call the real numbers "real" despite the fact that the vast majority of them have never been seen by anyone. Moreover, Turing will show in this paper that the vast majority of real numbers can't even be calculated by finite algorithms. In what sense do real numbers exist? That is a philosophical question that Turing touches upon only obliquely in the correction to his paper (Chapter 16 of this book).

Turing next links a human being with a machine in terms of discrete states of mind:

We may compare a man in the process of computing a real number to a machine which is only capable of a finite number of conditions $q_1, q_2, \ldots, q_R$ which will be called "*m*-configurations".

The *m* stands for *machine*. A machine has a finite number of configurations and does something different depending on its current configuration. A more modern term is *state*, and later Turing makes reference to "states of mind" that are analogous to these machine states. A simple washing machine, for example, has states called fill, wash, rinse, and spin. Performing a long division likewise involves a number of different mental configurations or states of mind: "Now I need to multiply." "Now I need to subtract." "Now I need to borrow." A machine operates by switching between different configurations, often in a repetitive manner.

> The machine is supplied with a "tape" (the analogue of paper) running through it, and divided into sections (called "squares") each capable of bearing a "symbol".

Turing calls this tape "the analogue of paper" because paper is what a person would use to compute a number. The tape in the Turing machine is often visualized as a paper tape, but if a Turing machine were actually built, the tape would probably be magnetic or simply a block of computer memory.

Humans generally use a two-dimensional sheet of paper, but Turing is limiting his machine to a one-dimensional tape divided into squares. The symbols in these squares could be the decimal digits 0 through 9, or they could include all the letters of the alphabet, or the 95 symbols available from your computer keyboard. (As you'll see, Turing even allows a "symbol" to consist of multiple characters.)

To represent these symbols in this section of the paper, Turing uses a capital S (standing for "symbol") in a gothic German font, so it looks like this: $\mathfrak{S}$. This is not the last you'll see of that font.

> At any moment there is just one square, say the r-th, bearing the symbol $\mathfrak{S}(r)$ which is "in the machine".

Here Turing is assuming that the squares of the tape can be numbered for identification. For example, $\mathfrak{S}(3451)$ would refer to the symbol on square number 3451. If that square contained the character 'A' then $\mathfrak{S}(3451)$ would be 'A'. Strictly speaking, however, the squares on the tape are *not* numbered, and the machine does not refer to a particular square using its number. (In other words, a square has no explicit address.)

At any time, Turing says, just one square of the tape is "in the machine" and can be examined by the machine.

> We may call this square the "scanned square". The symbol on the scanned square may be called the "scanned symbol". The "scanned symbol" is the only one of which the machine is, so to speak, "directly aware".

The machine can't "see" the whole tape at once. It can only "look at" one square at a time.

> However, by altering its m-configu-ration the machine can effectively remember some of the symbols which it has "seen" (scanned) previously.

A machine switches from one m-configuration to another depending on the scanned symbol. For example, in the particular m-configuration q_{34}, if the scanned symbol is 'A', it could switch to m-configuration q_{17}. If the scanned symbol were 'B', it could switch to m-configuration q_{123}. Thus m-configuration q_{17} "knows" that the last scanned symbol was an 'A' and m-configuration q_{123} knows that the last scanned symbol was a 'B'. (This is not *entirely* true; other configurations could have switched to q_{17} and q_{123} as well, but presumably the design of the machine implies that q_{17} and q_{123} know enough of what happened prior to carry out a job.)

> The possible behaviour of the machine at any moment is determined by the m-configuration q_n and the scanned symbol $\mathfrak{S}(r)$. This pair q_n, $\mathfrak{S}(r)$ will be called the "configuration": thus the configuration determines the possible behaviour of the machine.

The m-configurations are q_1, q_2, and so on. When an m-configuration is paired with a scanned symbol, Turing calls it simply the *configuration*.

Turing has already implied that the machine switches from one m-configuration to another depending on the scanned symbol. What else can the machine actually do? Not much:

> In some of the configurations in which the scanned square is blank (*i.e.* bears no symbol) the machine writes down a new symbol on the scanned square: in other configurations it erases the scanned symbol. The machine may also change the square which is being scanned, but only by shifting it one place to right or left.

I don't think I'm betraying Turing's conception if I refer to the mechanism that reads and writes symbols as the machine's *head*. Just like in a tape recorder or a camcorder, the head is in contact with the tape at only one point. The head in Turing's machine can read a symbol from the tape, or erase a symbol from the tape, or write a new symbol to the tape. It can also move one square left or right. (Although the head is probably stationary and the tape is moving through the machine, it's best to think of the head as moving relative to the tape.)

> In addition to any of these operations the *m*-configuration may be changed. Some of the symbols written down
>
> [232]
>
> will form the sequence of figures which is the decimal of the real number which is being computed. The others are just rough notes to "assist the memory". It will only be these rough notes which will be liable to erasure.

Because Turing wants his machine to compute a number, the machine will need to print figures (or digits), and in general, an *infinite* sequence of digits. To assist itself in this process, the machine may need to use part of the tape as a type of scratch pad.

What does a Turing machine look like? You can certainly imagine some crazy looking machine,[22] but a better approach is to look in a mirror. To paraphrase the climax of a famous science fiction movie,[23] "Turing Machines are people" — but *living* people carrying out an algorithm in a very limited but precise manner.

> It is my contention that these operations include all those which are used in the computation of a number.

That is, a computation by a *human being*. If you think that this machine is missing some basic arithmetical operations such as addition and subtraction, you're absolutely right. Addition and subtraction are not built into the Turing Machine. Instead, a Turing Machine can perform arithmetical operations if it has the right configurations.

> The defence of this contention will be easier when the theory of the machines is familiar to the reader. In the next section I therefore proceed with the development of the theory and assume that it is understood what is meant by "machine", "tape", "scanned", etc.

We are probably ready to begin looking at some actual machines, but Turing won't gratify us yet. He wants to throw out some definitions first.

---

[22] One of the best — complete with bells and whistles — accompanies the article Gregory J. Chaitin, "Computers, Paradoxes and the Foundations of Mathematics," *American Scientist*, Vol. 90 (March–April 2002), 168. See http://www.cs.auckland.ac.nz/CDMTCS/chaitin/amsci.pdf for an online version.

[23] *Soylent Green* (1973).

> ### 2. *Definitions.*
>
> *Automatic machines.*
>
> If at each stage the motion of a machine (in the sense of § 1) is *completely* determined by the configuration, we shall call the machine an "automatic machine" (or *a*-machine).
>
> For some purposes we might use machines (choice machines or *c*-machines) whose motion is only partially determined by the configuration (hence the use of the word "possible" in § 1).

When describing how a machine's behavior is determined by the configuration (page 70) Turing used the expression "possible behaviour of the machine." The behavior had to be qualified because in some machines it can be altered somewhat by some human interaction — an external "operator" of the machine:

> When such a machine reaches one of these ambiguous configurations, it cannot go on until some arbitrary choice has been made by an external operator. This would be the case if we were using machines to deal with axiomatic systems. In this paper I deal only with automatic machines, and will therefore often omit the prefix *a*-.

Turing's distinction between automatic machines and choice machines is somewhat reminiscent of the traditional separation of programming into batch processing and interactive computing. So much of our computing experience is interactive today that we may forget there are still many computer programs that run without heeding a user's every keystroke and mouse click.

While choice machines may be interesting, they play almost a negligible role in Turing's paper. The behavior of the automatic machines in Turing's paper will be completely determined by the machines' configurations.

> *Computing machines.*
>
> If an *a*-machine prints two kinds of symbols, of which the first kind (called figures) consists entirely of 0 and 1 (the others being called symbols of the second kind), then the machine will be called a computing machine.

Before he even begins showing us sample machines, Turing has decided to restrict the machines to printing figures of 0 and 1, the two digits needed for representing binary numbers.[24] Using binary numbers is a smart move, but it probably wouldn't have been as obvious to most 1937 readers as it is to us. Claude E. Shannon (1916–2001), whose 1937 MIT Master's thesis *A Symbolic Analysis of Relay and Switching Circuits* demonstrated the equivalence between circuits and Boolean algebra, certainly would have appreciated the choice, but the use of binary numbers in early computers was certainly not universal: Although Zuse used binary numbers, Eiken's and Stibitz's machines were decimal based. The ENIAC (1943–1945) was also a decimal computer. The word "bit" (which is short for "binary digit") did not appear in print until 1948 in a later Shannon paper.[25]

Turing doesn't attempt to justify the use of binary numbers for his machines. The advantage really only becomes apparent on page 245 of his paper (page 159 of this book), but just to put all doubts to rest I'll show a comparison of simple binary and decimal machines in the next chapter.

> If the machine is supplied with a blank tape and set in motion, starting from the correct initial *m*-configuration, the subsequence of the symbols printed by it which are of the first kind will be called the *sequence computed by the machine*.

A machine is set in motion with a blank tape. The machine prints 0s and 1s (symbols of the first kind) and other symbols (of the second kind). The 0s and 1s constitute the computed sequence. Turing differentiates between this computed *sequence* and the computed *number*.

> The real number whose expression as a binary decimal is obtained by prefacing this sequence by a decimal point is called the *number computed by the machine*.

That sentence is somewhat painful to read because the terminology is not quite right. We must, however, forgive Turing's confusion because people at that time were simply not accustomed to discussing binary numbers. Even today, people who are fluent in binary are often not entirely comfortable with binary fractions.

---

[24] An overview of binary numbers can be found in Charles Petzold, *Code: The Hidden Language of Computer Hardware and Software* (Microsoft Press, 1999).

[25] Claude E. Shannon, "A Mathematical Theory of Communication," *The Bell System Technical Journal*, Vol. 27 (July, October 1948). Shannon credits the coining of the word to American mathematician J. W. Tukey. The word got a bad review from Lancelot Hogben in *The Vocabulary of Science* (Stein and Day, 1970), 146: "The introduction by Tukey of *bits* for binary digits has nothing but irresponsible vulgarity to commend it." I disagree: Bits are so common in our modern life that a tiny word is ideal, rather like the things themselves.

Even the Windows Calculator in Scientific mode is no help: It simply truncates fractions when converting to binary.

The word "decimal" derives from the Latin for "ten" and the use of this word should be restricted to numbers based on ten. These are decimal fractions:

.25
.5
.75

The decimal point separates the integer part (if any) from the fractional part. Those same three values are represented in binary as:

.01
.1
.11

But that dot is not a decimal point. It really must be called a *binary point*.

Just as the individual digits of binary integers represent powers of 2, fractional binary numbers represent negative powers of 2:

.1 is the binary equivalent of 2^{-1} or the decimal ratio 1/2
.01 is the equivalent of 2^{-2} or 1/4
.001 is 2^{-3} or 1/8
.0001 is 2^{-4} or 1/16
.00001 is 2^{-5} or 1/32

and so forth. The binary number .10101 is

$$1 \cdot 2^{-1} + 0 \cdot 2^{-2} + 1 \cdot 2^{-3} + 0 \cdot 2^{-4} + 1 \cdot 2^{-5}$$

or perhaps visually clearer,

$$\frac{1}{2} + \frac{0}{4} + \frac{1}{8} + \frac{0}{16} + \frac{1}{32}$$

The decimal equivalent is 21/32 or .65625. Just as in decimal, many binary fractional numbers have repeating patterns of digits. Here's 1/3 in binary:

.01010101 ...

And this is 2/3:

.10101010 ...

Similarly:

1/5 is .001100110011 ...
2/5 is .011001100110 ...

3/5 is .100110011001 . . .
4/5 is .110011001100 . . .

Turing's statement is more correctly worded: "The real number whose expression as a binary fraction is obtained by prefacing this sequence with a binary point is called the number computed by the machine."

While we're at it, let's rework the sentence even further: "The number computed by the machine is the binary fraction obtained by prefacing this sequence with a binary point."

For example, if one of Turing's computing machine prints a 0 and a 1 and nothing more, then the "sequence computed by the machine" is:

0 1

The "number computed by the machine" is obtained by prefacing this sequence with a binary point:

.01

That's the binary equivalent of 1/4.

Because a binary point is always assumed to precede the computed sequence, Turing's machines will compute only binary numbers between 0 and 1, but this short range should be fine for any insights into enumerability that might be needed.

> At any stage of the motion of the machine, the number of the scanned square, the complete sequence of all symbols on the tape, and the *m*-configuration will be said to describe the *complete configuration* at that stage.

This is Turing's third use of the word *configuration* in discussing aspects of these machines, and it will be important to keep them straight:

- The *m-configuration* is one of the states of the machine.
- The *configuration* is a combination of an *m*-configuration and a scanned symbol.
- The *complete configuration* is basically a "snapshot" of the entire tape at some point in time, plus the current *m*-configuration and the position of the head.

> The changes of the machine and tape between successive complete configurations will be called the *moves* of the machine.

The next two definitions are not used until somewhat later in the paper:

[233]

Circular and circle-free machines.

If a computing machine never writes down more than a finite number of symbols of the first kind, it will be called *circular*. Otherwise it is said to be *circle-free*.

A machine will be circular if it reaches a configuration from which there is no possible move, or if it goes on moving, and possibly printing symbols of the second kind, but cannot print any more symbols of the first kind. The significance of the term "circular" will be explained in § 8.

Earlier I mentioned a machine that prints 0 and 1 and then nothing more. That's a finite number of figures, so it falls under Turing's definition of a *circular* machine. The machine is stuck somewhere and can't print any more numbers. This is no good. Turing wants his machines to keep printing digits *forever*.

The circle-free machines are the good machines. A machine that prints just 0 and 1 and nothing else is not a circle-free machine. If the machine really wants to compute the binary equivalent of 1/4, it should print 0 and 1 and then continue printing 0s forever.

Although Turing hasn't addressed the issue, he seems to be implying that his computing machines print digits from left to right, just as we would read the digits following the binary point.

Computable sequences and numbers.

A sequence is said to be computable if it can be computed by a circle-free machine. A number is computable if it differs by an integer from the number computed by a circle-free machine.

Turing is making a distinction between sequences and numbers. A computable sequence is:

010000 . . .

The corresponding computable number is:

.010000 . . .

The number

1.010000 . . .

is also considered to be computable because it differs by an integer from the number computed by the machine. So is

10.01000 . . .

and negatives as well.

We shall avoid confusion by speaking more often of computable sequences than of computable numbers.

Turing undoubtedly realized that the introduction of an imaginary computing machine into a mathematical paper was both novel and daring. Like a good mathematician, he has provided definitions and a formal description of these machines. It's not necessary for him to show any examples, but I imagine he knew that his readers wouldn't be satisfied with the merely abstract. They needed something concrete. He will now satisfy that craving.

3. *Examples of computing machines.*

I. A machine can be constructed to compute the sequence 010101 . . . .

The machine prints a tape that looks like this:

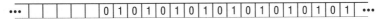

Well, not exactly. As Turing will later explain, he prefers his machines to use only alternate squares for printing numeric sequences. The first example machine will actually print a tape like this:

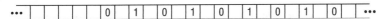

To denote the *m*-configurations of his machines, Turing uses lower-case letters of a German gothic font. These may take some getting used to, so I'll take care to point out potentially troublesome characters. The letters that Turing uses for this first machine are b, c, k, and e. (Watch out: The German k looks like an f.)

The machine is to have the four *m*-configurations "b", "c", "f", "e" and is capable of printing "0" and "1". The behaviour of the machine is described in the following table in which "*R*" means "the machine moves so that it scans the square immediately on the right of the one it was scanning previously". Similarly for "*L*". "*E*" means "the scanned symbol is erased" and "*P*" stands for "prints".

A *P* in these tables is always followed by the particular symbol to be printed. For example, *P*0 means print a 0, *P*1 means print a 1, and *Px* means print an *x*.

This table (and all succeeding tables of the same kind) is to be understood to mean that for a configuration described in the first two columns the operations in the third column are carried out successively, and the machine then goes over into the *m*-configuration described in the last column.

The table has four columns, separated into two pairs:

Configuration   *Behaviour*

m-config.   *symbol*   *operations*   *final m-config.*

What the machine does depends on the configuration, which is the combination of the *m*-configuration and the symbol in the scanned square. The third column contains operations (which can only be *P*, *E*, *L*, and *R*) and the fourth column is the next *m*-configuration.

Often the second column explicitly indicates a particular scanned symbol, such as 0 or 1, but Turing also uses the word "Any", which means any symbol, or "None" to mean no symbol, that is, a blank square. (This may be just a little confusing to modern programmers who are accustomed to treating a blank space as a symbol much like any other. When Turing uses the word "Any" he usually means "any non-blank" symbol.) The case for any symbol *including* blank squares is handled this way:

When the second column is left blank, it is understood that the behaviour of the third and fourth columns applies for any symbol and for no symbol.

Fortunately, the potential ambiguity is minimal.

The machine starts in the *m*-configuration b with a blank tape.

Turing's machines always start in *m*-configuration b (for *begin*, or rather, begin).
Here's the long-awaited machine:

Configuration		Behaviour	
m-config.	*symbol*	*operations*	*final m-config.*
b	None	*P*0, *R*	c
c	None	*R*	e
e	None	*P*1, *R*	f
f	None	*R*	b

These lines can be read like so: "For *m*-configuration b, when the scanned
square is blank (the symbol "None"), print 0, move the head right, and change to
m-configuration c."

Let's crank up this machine and watch it work. We begin in *m*-configuration
b with a blank tape. Although the tape is theoretically infinite in both directions,
the machines that Turing describes in this paper require only that the tape extend
infinitely towards the right because that's where the digits of the computable
sequences are printed:

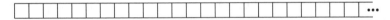

The read/write head can be symbolized in many ways. I've chosen a thick
border around the current scanned square. The head can initially be positioned
anywhere on the tape:

There is no symbol in that square. The table tells us that for *m*-configuration b and
no symbol, print 0 and move to the right:

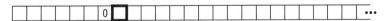

The new *m*-configuration is c. If the square is blank, move to the right and go into
m-configuration e:

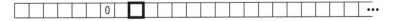

For *m*-configuration e, if there's no symbol, print 1 and move right:

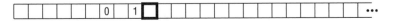

Now we're in *m*-configuration f. Move right:

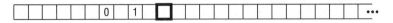

The machine is now in *m*-configuration b — back to the first state, and the cycle begins again. In this way, the machine prints an infinite sequence of 0s and 1s.

It is tempting to refer to each of the four lines of the table as an *instruction*, and indeed, Turing later adopts that terminology. Recognize, however, that these lines are not instructions *to* the machine; they instead represent a description *of* the machine. That's why a better term is *state*. If we think of these lines as instructions, then we're implying that we can replace them with something else and the same machine would perform differently, but that would mean that the machine is interpreting these instructions, and that's just not so. (Not yet, anyway.) This machine is performing a specific task. It doesn't matter how the machine actually works; what's important is that we can denote the working of the machine in a standard way based on configurations, symbols, and operations.

Can this machine be built? This particular machine could be built in a variety of ways. It could have a revolving wheel with self-inking rubber stamps on its circumference that print alternating 0s and 1s. Building a Turing Machine that works in the same way it's described — a machine that actually scans characters and interprets them — probably requires more sophisticated computer logic internally than the machine exhibits externally. Turing Machines are most commonly "built" as computer simulations.

Turing Machines jump around from *m*-configuration to *m*-configuration depending on the scanned character. This "conditional branching" (as it's known in computer science) is something that early computers of this era didn't do well. Konrad Zuse coded his machine instructions by punching holes in old 35-millimeter film stock. In his first machine, the Z1, the instructions had to be executed sequentially. The Z3 machine could branch but conditional branches were awkward. It wasn't until computers began storing programs in memory (the "stored program computer") that branching became easy and routine.

The *symbol* column of this particular table always indicates "None", which means that the configuration applies only when the square is blank. If this particular machine happened to scan a square in which a symbol were actually present, the machine would not know what to do. It might grind to a halt. It might crash. It might burst into flames. It might reformat your hard drive. We don't know. Whatever happens, such a machine would not be considered a "circle-free" machine. As long as this particular machine begins with a blank tape, however, that's not a problem.

Because Turing has defined a machine to print the sequence

01010101...

he has shown that this is a computable sequence. This sequence can be converted into a computable number by prefacing it with a period:

.01010101...

Now it's clear that the machine is calculating the binary equivalent of the rational number 1/3. If you switched the order (1 first then 0), the machine would compute the binary number

.10101010...

which is 2/3.

Let me show you a machine that computes 1/4, which in binary is:

.01000000...

This machine complies with Turing's conventions and uses German letters b, c, d, e, and f for the *m*-configurations:

Configuration		*Behaviour*	
m-config.	*symbol*	*operations*	*final m-config.*
b	None	P0, R	c
c	None	R	d
d	None	P1, R	e
e	None	R	f
f	None	P0, R	e

In particular, notice the last two *m*-configurations, e and f. These just alternate so the machine ends up printing an infinite series of 0s. Continuing to print 0s is necessary for the machine to comply with Turing's definition of "circle-free."

It should be very, very obvious that similar computing machines can be defined to compute *any rational number*. The rational numbers are not the issue here.

Earlier (in the second paragraph of Section 1) Turing said, "The machine may also change the square which is being scanned, but only by shifting it one place to right or left." Now he wants to be a little more flexible.

[234]

If (contrary to the description in § 1) we allow the letters L, R to appear more than once in the operations column we can simplify the table considerably.

m-config.	symbol	operations	final m-config.
	None	$P0$	b
b	0	$R, R, P1$	b
	1	$R, R, P0$	b

(Turing will also soon allow a configuration to have multiple P operations.) Now, the table has only one m-configuration, and everything depends on the scanned symbol. If the scanned square is blank (which only happens when the machine first starts up), then the machine simply prints a 0:

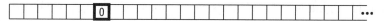

The head does not move. The machine remains in the same m-configuration, but now the scanned symbol is 0. The machine moves two squares right and prints 1:

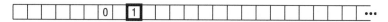

Now the scanned symbol is a 1, so the machine moves two places right and prints 0:

Once again, this machine prints 0 and 1 on alternate squares.

The important lesson is that any particular sequence can be computed by a variety of different machines. However, a particular automatic machine starting with a blank tape always computes the same sequence. (I'm referring to *automatic* machines here, of course, because choice machines allow a human operator to intervene, and thus can create different sequences, but Turing barely considers choice machines in this paper.) There is no way to insert any indeterminacy or randomness into one of Turing's automatic machines, or to obtain information (such as the date and time, or longitude and latitude, or a Web page) from the "outside world."

Using multiple *L*, *R*, and *P* operations in a single configuration can simplify machines considerably, but keep in mind that these simplified tables can always be converted back into the more rigid style that allows only one *L*, *R*, or *P* operation per state. This may seem like a trivial distinction now, but it becomes important later on.

> II. As a slightly more difficult example we can construct a machine to compute the sequence 001011011101111011111....

Slightly more difficult? Notice what Turing is proposing here. The sequence contains increasingly longer runs of 1s separated by 0s. First one 1, then two 1s then three 1s, and so on. Turing is obviously already bored with computing rational numbers. What he wants to tackle now is an irrational number, and one that very likely is also transcendental.

When this new machine is printing a run of 1s, it must somehow "remember" how many 1s it printed in the previous run, and then print one more. By scanning back and forth, the machine always has access to the previous run so it can use that information to build the next run. It will be interesting to study Turing's strategy for accomplishing this feat.

Again, Turing uses lower-case letters of a German font for his *m*-configurations, in this case the letters o, q, p, f, and b.

> The machine is to be capable of five *m*-configurations, viz. "o", "q", "p", "f", "b" and of printing "ə", "x", "0", "1". The first three symbols on the tape will be "əə0"; the other figures follow on alternate squares.

This is where Turing first mentions printing the figures (0s and 1s, or symbols of the first kind) on alternate squares. Assuming that the leftmost symbols appear on the left edge of the tape, he's proposing that the tape end up like this:

| ə | ə | 0 | | 0 | | 1 | | 0 | | 1 | | 1 | | 0 | | 1 | | 1 | | 1 | | 0 | | ••• |

Of course, the tape will never "end up" as anything because the machine goes on forever. It has to print forever to qualify as "circle-free."

The ə character is known in phonetics and linguistics circles as a *schwa*. Turing uses the schwa for what programmers call a *sentinel*. It's a special character that, in this case, indicates the boundary of the number. The machine can move its head to the very beginning of the tape by moving left whenever the scanned square is *not* the schwa. (Why are there two schwas? Only one is required in this example, but Turing later creates a machine that requires two schwas for a sentinel. Perhaps he added a second schwa in this example just for consistency.)

In the first example machine, the blank squares between the 0 and 1 digits served no purpose. Here they will play an important role.

> On the inter-
> mediate squares we never print anything but "*x*". These letters serve to "keep the place" for us and are erased when we have finished with them.

Turing is dividing the squares of his tape into two categories. The machine prints the 0s and 1s on every other square. With the exception of the sentinel, no other symbols appear on these squares. Turing uses the intermediate squares as a temporary scratchpad of sorts. We can thus refer to "numeric squares" that contain 0s and 1s and "non-numeric squares" that can contain other symbols. (Turing later calls these *F*-squares and *E*-squares for *figures* and *erasable*.)

> We also arrange that in the sequence of figures on alternate squares there shall be no blanks.

As the machine progressively computes the 0s and 1s, it prints them sequentially from left to right. Every new figure that the machine computes is printed on the next available blank numeric square. No numeric squares are skipped. These restrictions are a collection of rules (some explicit and some implied) that Emil Post later called a "Turing convention-machine,"[1] which is a little more restrictive than the generalized "Turing Machine." A Turing convention-machine never erases a numeric square, or writes over an existing figure on a numeric square with a different figure. These implicit rules become important later on.

Here's Turing's table for the machine to compute the irrational number he's defined:

---

[1]In an appendix to the paper Emil Post, "Recursive Unsolvability of a Problem of Thue," *The Journal of Symbolic Logic*, Vol. 12, No. 1 (Mar. 1947), 1–11. The entire paper is reprinted in Martin Davis, ed., *The Undecidable* (Raven Press, 1965), 293–303. The appendix is reprinted in B. Jack Copeland, ed., *The Essential Turing* (Oxford University Press, 2004), 97–101.

| Configuration | | Behaviour | |
m-config.	symbol	operations	final m-config.
ƀ		$P\partial, R, P\partial, R, P0, R, R, P0, L, L$	ᴏ
ᴏ	1	R, Px, L, L, L	ᴏ
	0		q
q	Any (0 or 1)	R, R	q
	None	$P1, L$	ᴩ
ᴩ	x	E, R	q
	ә	R	ſ
	None	L, L	ᴩ
ſ	Any	R, R	ſ
	None	$P0, L, L$	ᴏ

As usual, the machine begins in *m*-configuration ƀ. It prints two schwas and two zeros. The tape looks like this:

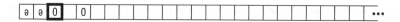

The *m*-configuration ƀ performs duties that a programmer might call *initialization*. The machine never goes into *m*-configuration ƀ again.

Before we get all greasy exploring the innards of this machine, let's get a general feel for what the other *m*-configurations do. In several configurations (q, ᴩ, and ſ, specifically), the *operations* column shows movement of two squares at a time: *R*, *R* or *L*, *L*. In these cases, the machine is effectively moving along numeric squares (in the cases of q and ſ) or non-numeric squares (ᴩ).

All the *m*-configurations except ƀ also circle back on themselves depending on the scanned symbol. Programmers often call such an operation a *loop*. Loops perform repetitive tasks, even those as simple as searching for a particular symbol.

The *m*-configuration ᴏ moves from right to left through a run of 1s on the numeric squares. For every 1 it finds, it prints an *x* to the right of the 1 and then goes left to check the next numeric square. When it's finished, it switches to *m*-configuration q.

The *m*-configuration q moves from left to right along numeric squares until it encounters a blank. That's the end of the current sequence. It then prints a 1, moves left (to a non-numeric square) and switches to ᴩ.

Similarly, the *m*-configuration f also moves rightward along numeric squares until it encounters a blank. It then prints a 0, moves 2 squares left and switches to ɒ.

The *m*-configuration p is a dispatcher of sorts. It spends most of its time moving leftward on non-numeric squares searching for *x* symbols. When it finds an *x*, it erases it, moves right, and switches to q. If it reaches the sentinel, it moves right and switches to f.

Turing uses the *x* symbols in a very clever manner. When constructing a new run of 1s, the machine begins by printing an *x* after each 1 in the previous run. The machine prints a 1 at the end of the existing sequence, and then prints another 1 for each *x*, thus increasing the run by one.

Although it's possible to illustrate what the tape looks like after each and every operation, for this example it might be best to view the tape after each configuration has completed.

From the *m*-configuration b, the machine goes to ɒ; however, for a scanned symbol of 0, ɒ does nothing and zips right into *m*-configuration q. For *m*-configuration q, if the scanned symbol is 0 or 1, the head moves two squares right and remains in the same *m*-configuration. When a blank square is encountered, however, it prints 1 and moves left. Overall, *m*-configuration q moves right along numeric squares until it encounters a blank. It then prints a 1 and moves left.

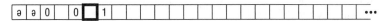

The next *m*-configuration is p, which generally moves along non-numeric squares. It moves two squares left until it encounters a non-numeric square with either an *x* or a schwa. In this case, it'll be a schwa. It moves right:

| ə | ə | 0 | | 0 | | 1 | | | | | | | | | | | | | | | | | | | ••• |

The *m*-configuration f moves the head along numeric squares. It keeps moving two squares right until a blank is scanned. Then it prints a 0 and moves two squares left:

| ə | ə | 0 | | 0 | | 1 | | 0 | | | | | | | | | | | | | | | | | ••• |

That's how a 0 is printed between each run of 1s.

We're now in *m*-configuration ɒ. This *m*-configuration always begins at the rightmost 1 in a run of 1s. Its job is to print an *x* after every 1. It ends up at the 0 to the left of the run of 1s:

| ə | ə | 0 | | 0 | | 1 | x | 0 | | | | | | | | | | | | | | | | ••• |

Back to *m*-configuration q. This one moves right on numeric squares until a blank is encountered. Then it prints a 1 and moves left.

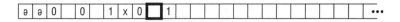

The *m*-configuration 𝔭 moves left on non-numeric squares until it encounters an *x* or a schwa. When it hits an *x*, it will erase it and move right:

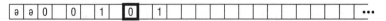

Back to *m*-configuration q again. Move right on numeric squares until a blank, then print 1 and move left:

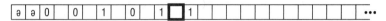

Now we're in *m*-configuration 𝔭. Move left on non-numeric squares until the schwa is scanned. Then move right:

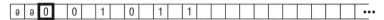

The *m*-configuration 𝔣 then moves right on numeric squares until it finds a blank. It then prints a 0 and moves two squares left:

This seems to be working. We now have a run of one 1 and a run of two 1s. Let's see if it continues to do what we want it to do.

The *m*-configuration 𝔬 has the job of printing an *x* after every 1 in the last run of 1s.

The *m*-configuration q moves right along numeric squares until it scans a blank. It then prints 1 and moves left:

Now notice there are two *x*'s and two remaining 1s for this run. For every *x* that will be erased, another 1 will be printed. The *m*-configuration 𝔭 moves left on non-numeric squares until it finds an *x*. It erases it and moves right:

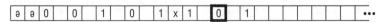

The *m*-configuration q moves right on numeric squares until it finds a blank. Then it prints a 1 and moves left:

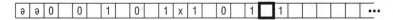

Back to *m*-configuration 𝔭, which moves left until it hits the *x*. It erases it and moves right.

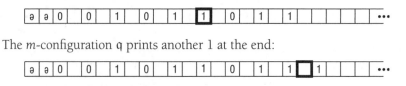

The *m*-configuration q prints another 1 at the end:

Now the *m*-configuration p moves the head left until it encounters the schwa:

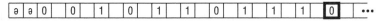

The *m*-configuration f̄ moves right on numeric squares until it gets to the end and prints a 0:

Now the machine has successfully printed a run of three 1s and another 0.

How did Turing develop the technique used by this machine? I suspect he tried computing the sequence by hand while resisting the temptation to count. He might have found himself keeping track of the runs of 1s using little check marks above the digits. These check marks became the *x* characters that the machine prints in the non-numeric squares.

The diagrams of the tape do not appear in Turing's paper. He is not interested in providing such a blatantly "realistic" visual representation of the machine or its operations. Instead, he has a different idea for notating the workings of the machine.

In Section 2 of his paper (page 75 of this book) Turing said, "At any stage of the motion of the machine, the number of the scanned square, the complete sequence of all symbols on the tape, and the *m*-configuration will be said to describe the *complete configuration* at that stage." Although Turing's reference to "the number of the scanned square" seems a little peculiar because the squares are not explicitly numbered, a tape that is infinite in only one direction has an implicit numbering.

Turing is about to show a method for notating the workings of the machine using these complete configurations — essentially snapshots of the tape together with the current *m*-configuration and scanned square.

> To illustrate the working of this machine a table is given below of the first few complete configurations. These complete configurations are described by writing down the sequence of symbols which are on the tape,
>
> [235]
>
> with the *m*-configuration written below the scanned symbol. The successive complete configurations are separated by colons.

What follows in the paper are four entries of a "table" with two lines each that at first glance looks rather like complete gibberish. Here's the first of the four entries:

: əə0	0:əə0	0:əə0	0:əə0	0	:əə0	0 1:
b	ɒ	q		q		q	p

Heed the colons! Between each pair of colons are successive snapshots of the tape. Some of the spacing between the 0s and (later) between the 0s and 1s is a little wider than the regular space. This wider space represents a blank square. Taken together with the m-configuration shown under the tape, these constitute the first six complete configurations of this machine, showing all the symbols printed on the tape so far.

The first b indicates the starting configuration. The tape is initially blank. That configuration prints the sequence between the first two colons, shown earlier as:

| ə | ə | 0 | | 0 | | | | | | | | | | | | | | | | | | | | | | | | | ... |

Instead of using a heavy box to show the position of the head at the next scanned symbol, Turing indicates the next m-configuration *under* the next scanned symbol:

:əə0 0:
ɒ

Because m-configuration ɒ doesn't do anything when the scanned symbol is 0, the next snapshot of the tape is the same, but now the m-configuration is q:

:əə0 0:
q

When m-configuration q scans a 0, the head moves two squares right, and the next configuration is also q:

:əə0 0:
q

The scanned square is 0 again. The head moves two squares right, and the m-configuration is still q:

:əə0 0   :
q

Notice how the tape seems to become wider as the head moves beyond the last printed number. Now, the scanned square is blank, so the machine prints 1, moves one square to the left, and switches to configuration p:

:əə0 0 1:
p

While less visually satisfying than the physical tape, Turing's notation provides more information, in particular by indicating the next m-configuration at the current position of the head. These successive complete configurations show a complete history of the machine's operations. It's easy to look at any one of these complete configurations, match the m-configuration and scanned symbol to the machine's states, and come up with the next complete configuration.

The next sequence that Turing provides shows m-configuration p searching backward until it finds the schwa, then switching to configuration f, which searches forward looking for a blank:

> әә0 0 1:әә0 0 1:әә0 0 1:әә0 0 1:
>   p   p   f   f

Next entry: Still in m-configuration f, the machine finds a blank numeric square (notice how the space between the colons is widened again), prints a 0, moves two squares left, and switches to configuration o.

> әә0 0   1:әә0   0 1   :әә0   0 1 0:
>   f   f   o

The m-configuration o responds to a scanned 1 by moving right, printing an x, then moving three squares left:

> әә0 0   1x0: ....
>   o

That's all that Turing shows, but if this representation of the tape's history isn't concise enough for you, Turing proposes an alternative:

> **This table could also be written in the form**
>
> $$b:әә o\ 0\quad 0:әә q\ 0\quad 0:\ ...\ ,\qquad\qquad (C)$$
>
> **in which a space has been made on the left of the scanned symbol and the m-configuration written in this space.**

Turing has flagged this format with the letter C (for "configuration"). He will refer to it in Section 6. The complete configuration shown previously as:

> :әә0   0:
>   o

now becomes:

: ɘ ɘ ɒ 0   0 :

Now, we see at least one reason why Turing used German letters for the
m-configurations: In this format the *m*-configurations might not be so easily
distinguished from the symbols printed by the machine. The sequence of characters
between each pair of colons is no longer exactly like the tape because an extra
space is required for the next *m*-configuration. Even Turing admits it's a bit
awkward.

> This form is less easy to follow, but
> we shall make use of it later for theoretical purposes.

Actually, in a still more modified form, it will become *essential*. Turing is
already gearing up for a major presentation: He will unveil a Universal Computing Machine — today commonly termed the Universal Turing Machine or
UTM — that is a functional (if not exactly commercial) equivalent of a modern
computer.

Try to notice what's *good* about this final format: The entire history of the
operation of a machine has been arranged into a single stream of characters, a
format much beloved by programmers. When reading or writing files or engaging
in digital communications, the ideal approach is reading or writing a stream of
characters, one after another from beginning to end without skipping forward or
backward.

Also, notice that Turing has slipped the next *m*-configuration *in front of* the
next scanned character. These two items in combination were defined by Turing
as a *configuration*, and this pair of items occurs in the complete configuration in
the same order as they occur in the first two columns of a machine table. You
can take that *m*-configuration and symbol pair and scan through the *m-config* and
symbol columns of a machine table looking for a match. (Obviously, this works
better when the machine contains actual symbols in the *symbol* column rather than
"Any" or "None" or blanks.) Turing will actually automate this searching process
when constructing his Universal Machine.

Turing next discusses his choice to print the numeric sequence on alternate
squares:

> The convention of writing the figures only on alternate squares is very
> useful: I shall always make use of it. I shall call the one sequence of alter-

nate squares *F*-squares and the other sequence *E*-squares. The symbols on *E*-squares will be liable to erasure. The symbols on *F*-squares form a continuous sequence. There are no blanks until the end is reached.

Earlier I referred to these as numeric squares and non-numeric squares. You can remember which is which by the words *figures* (meaning 0s and 1s) and *erasable*. The comment about "no blanks until the end is reached" refers only to the *F*-squares. The digits of a computable sequence are always printed sequentially from left to right, never skipping an *F*-square and never rewriting a figure on an *F*-square. These rules are required for Turing's Universal Machine.

The *E*-squares are a type of scratchpad, perhaps equivalent somehow to human memory.

There is no need to have more than one *E*-square between each pair of *F*-squares: an apparent need of more *E*-squares can be satisfied by having a sufficiently rich variety of symbols capable of being printed on *E*-squares.

Turing's second machine used a technique of identifying characters by printing *x* symbols in the *E*-squares. This is a general technique he'll exploit often so he'll give it a name.

If a symbol *β* is on an *F*-square *S* and a symbol *α* is on the *E*-square next on the right of *S*, then *S* and *β* will be said to be *marked* with *α*. The process of printing this *α* will be called marking *β* (or *S*) with *α*.

This 0 (on an *F*-square) is said to be *marked* with *x*:

These markers turn out to be very handy, and are one of Turing's best inventions.

However, markers are not strictly needed. It is possible to define machines that use only two symbols, or which differentiate solely between a blank square and a marked square. Such an approach was explored by mathematician Emil Post in an interesting paper[2] that independently described a configuration similar to

---

[2]Emil L. Post, "Finite Combinatory Processes. Formulation I.," *The Journal of Symbolic Logic*, Vol. I, No. 3 (Sep. 1936), 103–105. Reprinted in Martin Davis, ed., *The Undecidable*, 289–291. Although Post's paper was published prior to Turing's, Post's paper was received by *The Journal of Symbolic Logic* on October 7, 1936; the *Proceedings of the London Mathematical Society* received Turing's paper on May 28, 1936.

Turing's. Post has a "worker" with a collection of "boxes" arranged in a sequence. The worker is capable of:

(a) *Marking the box he is in (assumed empty)*,
(b) *Erasing the mark in the box he is in (assumed marked)*,
(c) *Moving to the box on his right*,
(d) *Moving to the box on his left*,
(e) *Determining whether the box he is in, is or is not marked*.

Post doesn't actually show his worker performing real applications. Working with squares or boxes that can be only marked or unmarked is obviously much more laborious than Turing's shortcut.

6

Addition and Multiplication

As early as May 1935 Alan Turing had considered attending Princeton University, and had applied for a visiting Fellowship.[1] A year later, when he discovered that Princeton mathematics professor Alonzo Church had also published a paper on the Entscheidungsproblem, Turing "decided quite definitely"[2] that he wanted to go there.

Max Newman helped. In the same letter in which Newman informed Church of Turing's work (page 62), he also pleaded for help in getting Turing a scholarship:

> I should mention that Turing's work is entirely independent: he
> has been working without any supervision or criticism from any-
> one. This makes it all the more important that he should come
> into contact as soon as possible with the leading workers on this
> line, so that he should not develop into a confirmed solitary.[3]

The tendency to work alone without outside influences was actually one of Turing's big problems. Earlier in his life, Turing had reinvented the binomial theory and developed his own notation for calculus. In attacking the Entscheidungsproblem, perhaps it was best that he wasn't familiar with the earlier work of Church and his colleagues, or he might not have developed such an interesting solution. In general, however, knowing what's going on in the rest of the world is essential, and for the field of mathematical logic, Princeton was the place to be. Turing failed to get the Procter Fellowship he applied for, but he was able to get by on his King's College fellowship.

The intellectual aura around the town of Princeton, New Jersey, had recently grown even brighter with the establishment of the Institute for Advanced Study. The IAS was founded with a $5,000,000 endowment from Louis Bamberger, who

---

[1] Andrew Hodges, *Alan Turing: The Enigma* (Simon & Schuster, 1983), 95.

[2] Hodges, *Alan Turing*, 113.

[3] Ibid.

had previously created the Bamberger's department store chain and then sold it to Macy's right before the 1929 stock market crash.

From the very beginning, the Institute for Advanced Study was intended as a place to foster scientific and historical research. In the early years, the IAS School of Mathematics shared a building with the Mathematics Department at Princeton University, so there was considerable cross-fertilization between the two institutions. The IAS quickly became a mecca for talented scientists and mathematicians, some of them fleeing the increasingly dangerous atmosphere of Europe. The most famous of these was Albert Einstein, who came to the IAS in 1933 and stayed there for the rest of his life.

When Turing arrived in Princeton in September 1936, he was very much interested in meeting Kurt Gödel. Gödel had also been at the IAS the year before, and he would later return, but he and Turing never met.

John von Neumann, whom Turing had met in Cambridge, was at the IAS, and so was G.H. Hardy from Cambridge. Both Richard Courant and Hermann Weyl were at the IAS as well, having fled Göttingen a few years earlier.

Turing stayed two years at Princeton University, and got the Procter Fellowship (a sum of $2,000) for his second year. Church became Turing's thesis advisor, and under Church's supervision Turing wrote a thesis[4] and received his Ph.D. on June 21, 1938. He was back in England a month later, having turned down an offer from John von Neumann to be his assistant at the IAS with a salary of $1,500 a year.

In the spring of 1939, Alan Turing returned to Cambridge to teach a Foundations of Mathematics course. Four years earlier, Turing had taken Foundations of Mathematics with Max Newman and had learned about the Entscheidungsproblem. Now Turing was able to ask a question on the final exam about the unprovability of the Entscheidungsproblem based on his own work on computable numbers.[5]

In his paper, Turing is asking for a little faith from his readers that these machines of his can actually calculate nontrivial numeric sequences. So far, we haven't really seen anything we would call *calculation*. The machine in Turing's first example ostensibly printed the binary equivalent of 1/3, but it did it by just stupidly alternating 0s and 1s. Surely it's not dividing 3 into 1. Nor does the machine implement a general process for computing any rational number by dividing the numerator by the denominator.

Even programmers who work at the low levels of processor machine code are accustomed to computer hardware that performs the basic mathematical operations

---

[4]Alan Turing, "Systems of Logic Based on Ordinals," *Proceedings of the London Mathematical Society*, 2nd Series, Volume 45 (1939), 161–228. Republished in Alan Turing, *Collected Works of A. M. Turing: Mathematical Logic* (Elsevier, 2001), 161–228, and B. Jack Copeland, ed., *The Essential Turing* (Oxford University Press, 2004) 146–204.

[5]Hodges, *Alan Turing*, 152.

of addition and subtraction. For that reason we may be skeptical — and even a bit frightened — of a machine in which even addition has to be accomplished through the definition of configurations and operations.

Let's confront our fears head on by building machines that transcend the trivial. Let's convince ourselves that Turing Machines can indeed add and multiply (and hence, also subtract, divide, calculate powers, and perhaps even write poetry).

The first example is a small Turing Machine that calculates all the positive integers in sequence. This machine does *not* comply with Turing's conventions because it writes each new number over the previous one. It doesn't skip any squares when printing the results, and it replaces each result with the next highest number. Also, given that these are integers, I have designed the machine to print the digits as we would normally write integers — with the more significant digits extending to the left of the tape rather than the right. Despite noncompliance with Turing's conventions, this machine *does* show how a number can be incremented by adding 1 to it, which is at least one basic feat we require of a modern computer.

Rather than using German letters in my examples, I've chosen descriptive words in boldface, and (in later examples) sometimes more than one word joined by dashes. As Turing did, I use the word "none" to refer to a blank square. As Turing did not, I use the word "else" to indicate that a configuration is to apply to all other characters not explicitly listed. This particular machine begins with configuration **begin** and has just three *m*-configurations:

m-config.	symbol	operations	*final m-config.*
begin	none	P0	**increment**
increment	0	P1	**rewind**
	1	P0,L	**increment**
	none	P1	**rewind**
rewind	none	L	**increment**
	else	R	**rewind**

The *m*-configuration **begin** simply prints a single 0 and then switches to **increment**. The *m*-configuration **increment** reads a digit. If it's a 0, then **increment** changes that to a 1. It has then finished incrementing the entire integer. If it reads a 1, then **increment** changes it to a 0 and moves left for the carry. It must now increment the next highest digit. The *m*-configuration **rewind** moves the head right to the least significant digit of the number in preparation for the next increment.

Once you start writing machines that do arithmetic, it becomes obvious why binary numbers are so convenient. Here's the equivalent machine that generates all the positive integers in decimal rather than in binary:

m-config.	symbol	operations	final m-config.
begin	none	P0	**increment**
	0	P1	**rewind**
	1	P2	**rewind**
	2	P3	**rewind**
	3	P4	**rewind**
	4	P5	**rewind**
increment	5	P6	**rewind**
	6	P7	**rewind**
	7	P8	**rewind**
	8	P9	**rewind**
	9	P0, L	**increment**
	none	P1	**rewind**
rewind	none	L	**increment**
	else	R	**rewind**

You see the problem. The machine needs to handle every decimal digit explicitly. The binary number system is simpler because it has fewer options. The binary addition and multiplication tables are tiny:

+	0	1
0	0	1
1	1	10

and

×	0	1
0	0	0
1	0	1

I'll make use of these addition and multiplication rules in the second example in this chapter. This is a machine that adheres to Turing's conventions and calculates the square root of 2 in binary. Actually, if the binary point is assumed to precede all the digits, the machine calculates

$$\frac{\sqrt{2}}{2}$$

which in decimal is 0.70710678.... In describing the machine, I'll assume it's calculating $\sqrt{2}$ for the sake of clarity and familiarity.

The algorithm implemented by the machine calculates one binary digit at a time. Suppose the machine has been running awhile and has already determined the first four digits. The first four digits of $\sqrt{2}$ in binary are 1.011, equivalent to $1\frac{3}{8}$ in decimal or 1.375. What is the next digit? The machine's strategy is always to assume that the next digit is 1. To test whether this is correct, multiply 1.0111 by itself:

$$
\begin{array}{r}
1.0111 \\
\times\ 1.0111 \\
\hline
10111 \\
10111 \\
10111 \\
00000 \\
10111 \\
\hline
10.00010001
\end{array}
$$

The product exceeds 2, so that assumption was incorrect. The fifth digit is instead 0, so the first five digits are 1.0110. Let's determine the sixth digit similarly. Assume that the sixth digit is 1 and multiply 1.01101 by itself:

$$
\begin{array}{r}
1.01101 \\
\times\ 1.01101 \\
\hline
101101 \\
000000 \\
101101 \\
101101 \\
000000 \\
101101 \\
\hline
1.1111101001
\end{array}
$$

That result is less than 2, so the assumption was good. We now have six digits: 1.01101, which in decimal is $1\frac{3}{32}$ or 1.40625.

Obviously, the square-root-of-2 machine needs to multiply. In general, a multiplication of two multidigit numbers requires that each digit of one number be multiplied by each digit of the other number. If one number has n digits, and the other number m digits, the total number of digit-times-digit multiplications is $(n \times m)$.

When doing multiplication by hand, we generally multiply a single digit of one number by the whole other number, yielding n or m partial products, which are then added together. The machine I'll show does the multiplication a little differently — by maintaining a running total during the multiplication. The result of each bit-by-bit multiplication is added to this running total. What makes this particular addition tricky is that each bit-by-bit product is generally *not* added to the least significant bit of the running total, but somewhere in the middle of it.

For example, consider the multiplication of 1.01101 by itself. Each of the six bits must be multiplied by itself and by the other five bits, so 36 bit-by-bit multiplications are required. The multiplications themselves are trivial: When multiplying 1 times 1, the result is 1; otherwise, the result is 0. Where this result is deposited in the running total depends on the placement of the bits within the number. If the third bit from the right is multiplied by the fourth bit from the right, the result is added to the sixth place from the right in the running total. (This makes more sense when you number the bits beginning with zero: The third bit from the right is bit 2; the fourth bit from the right is bit 3; the sum is 5, and that's the bit position where the product goes.)

In determining the binary square root of 2, we're always multiplying an n-bit number by itself. If the result has $(2n - 1)$ bits, that means the product is less than 2 and the assumption that the new last digit is indeed 1 was correct. If the result has $2n$ bits, the product exceeds 2, so the new last digit must be 0. The machine will make use of this fact to determine whether each new digit is a 0 or 1.

The machine I'll be showing adheres to Turing's conventions, which means that the only things it prints in the F-squares are the successive digits of the square root of 2 as they are being calculated. Everything else — including maintaining the running total of the multiplication — is done on E-squares.

The machine begins in m-configuration **begin**. The machine uses an *at* sign (@) rather than a schwa for the sentinel. (Let's just say it's an easier symbol on today's computers.) The machine begins by printing the sentinel and the digit 1:

m-config.	*symbol*	*operations*	*final m-config.*
begin	none	P@, R, P1	**new**

Thus, the only initial assumption the machine makes is that the square root of 2 is at least 1 but less than 2.

The machine always comes back to the m-configuration **new** when it's ready to calculate a new digit. The configuration moves the head to the leftmost digit:

	@	R	**mark-digits**
new			
	else	L	**new**

The rest of the machine will be easier to understand if we look at what it does after it's already calculated a few digits. Here's the tape with the first three digits already computed, which is the binary equivalent of 1.25. The machine will print the fourth digit (which I'll refer to as the "unknown" digit) in the square marked with the question mark:

@	1		0		1		?																			•••

That question mark is for our benefit only; it does not actually appear on the tape and is not used by the machine!

In preparation for the multiplication, the machine marks the digits of the number. (Recall that Turing defined "marking" as printing a symbol to the right of a figure.) The machine uses multiple x markers in a manner similar to Turing's Example II (page 85) machine. The m-configuration **mark-digits** marks all the known digits with x, the unknown digit with a z (which I'll explain shortly) and prints one r in the least significant place of the running total:

mark-digits	0	R, Px, R	**mark-digits**
	1	R, Px, R	**mark-digits**
	none	R, Pz, R, R, Pr	**find-x**

The tape is now:

@	1	x	0	x	1	x	?	z		r															•••

That r is the least significant digit of the running total and should be interpreted as a 0. The next section prints two more r's for every x, erasing the x markers in the process.

find-x	x	E	**first-r**
	@	N	**find-digits**
	else	L, L	**find-x**
first-r	r	R, R	**last-r**
	else	R, R	**first-r**
last-r	r	R, R	**last-r**
	none	Pr, R, R, Pr	**find-x**

The tape now has a 7-digit running total symbolizing an initial value of 0000000:

@	1		0		1		?	z		r		r		r		r		r		r		r		•••

The bit order of the running total is reversed from that of the calculated number. The least significant bit of the running total is on the left. The seven initialized digits of the running total are sufficient if the assumption is correct that the unknown digit is a 1. If an eighth digit is required, then the unknown digit is 0.

The number the machine must multiply by itself consists of the number computed already (101 in this example) and a new digit assumed to be 1, so the number is actually 1011. To keep track of what digits are being multiplied by each other, the machine marks the digits with x, y, and z characters. At any time during the multiplication, only one digit is marked with x and one digit with y, and the digit marked x is multiplied by the digit marked y. If the x and y markers happen to coincide, the character z is used, so any digit marked z is multiplied by itself.

That's why the unknown digit (assumed to be 1) is initially marked with a z. The first multiplication involves that unknown digit times itself; however, it will help in the analysis of the following configurations to keep in mind that during the multiplication, any digit could be marked with x and any digit with y, or just one digit with z.

We're now ready for the first bit-by-bit multiplication. The machine multiplies either the two digits marked x and y by each other, or the single digit marked z by itself. The m-configuration **find-digits** first goes back to the sentinel and then goes to **find-1st-digit** to find the left-most digit marked x, y, or z.

find-digits	@	R, R	**find-1st-digit**
	else	L, L	**find-digits**
find-1st-digit	x	L	**found-1st-digit**
	y	L	**found-1st-digit**
	z	L	**found-2nd-digit**
	none	R, R	**find-1st-digit**

If **find-1st-digit** detects an x, y, or z, it positions the head over the digit. Depending on the letter, the machine goes to **found-1st-digit** or **found-2nd-digit**.

If the first marked digit is 0, the second digit isn't required because the product will be 0 anyway. So we can add 0 to the running total by going to **add-zero**:

found-1st-digit	0	R	**add-zero**
	1	R, R, R	**find-2nd-digit**

If the first digit is a 1, the second digit must be found. The machine searches for the second digit marked x or y:

find-2nd-digit	x	L	**found-2nd-digit**
	y	L	**found-2nd-digit**
	none	R, R	**find-2nd-digit**

The second digit determines what must be added to the running total:

found-2nd-digit	0	R	**add-zero**
	1	R	**add-one**
	none	R	**add-one**

Notice that a blank F-square is the unknown digit, which is assumed to be 1. In our example, the digit marked z is the unknown digit, so **add-one** will be used to add a 1 to the running total.

Adding a 0 onto the running total normally wouldn't affect it; however, this machine must perform some maintenance of the running total regardless of what's added to it.

When I described how the running total is initialized on the E-squares to the right, I indicated that the letter r symbolizes 0. The letters s and t also symbolize 0, and the letters u, v, and w all represent 1. This multitude of letters is required to keep track of the bit position where the bit-times-bit product is added to the running total.

The *m*-configuration **add-zero** changes the first *r* it finds to an *s*, or the first *u* to a *v*:

$$
\textbf{add-zero} \quad \left\{
\begin{array}{lll}
\text{r} & \text{Ps} & \textbf{add-finished} \\
\text{u} & \text{Pv} & \textbf{add-finished} \\
\text{else} & \text{R, R} & \textbf{add-zero}
\end{array}
\right.
$$

The change of the *r* (meaning 0) to an *s* (meaning 0) and the *u* (meaning 1) to a *v* (also meaning 1) ensures that the next time a digit is added to the running total, it gets added one place over.

Adding a 1 to the running total is more involved. The first *r* (meaning 0) is changed to a *v* (meaning 1), or the first *u* (meaning 1) is changed to an *s* (meaning 0). For the latter case, a carry is also required:

$$
\textbf{add-one} \quad \left\{
\begin{array}{lll}
\text{r} & \text{Pv} & \textbf{add-finished} \\
\text{u} & \text{Ps, R, R} & \textbf{carry} \\
\text{else} & \text{R, R} & \textbf{add-one}
\end{array}
\right.
$$

If the carry results in a digit being written into a blank square, then the running total has exceeded 2, so the configuration becomes **new-digit-is-zero**:

$$
\textbf{carry} \quad \left\{
\begin{array}{lll}
\text{r} & \text{Pu} & \textbf{add-finished} \\
\text{none} & \text{Pu} & \textbf{new-digit-is-zero} \\
\text{u} & \text{Pr, R, R} & \textbf{carry}
\end{array}
\right.
$$

After the first bit-by-bit multiplication and addition to the running total, the tape is:

@	1		0		1		?	z		v		r		r		r		r		r		r	•••

Notice the first *r* has been changed to a *v* (meaning 1).

Now the *x*, *y*, and *z* markers must be shifted around to indicate the next pair of bits to be multiplied. In general, the *x* marker is moved left one character. (A *z* marker, you'll recall, simply indicates that the *x* and *y* markers coincide, so a *z* marker becomes a *y* marker and an *x* marker is printed one digit to the left.) But when the *x* marker gets to the end (past the most significant bit), the *y* marker is moved left one character and the *x* marker is moved back to the rightmost digit. When the *y* marker gets to the end, the multiplication is complete.

First the head is moved to the sentinel:

$$
\textbf{add-finished} \quad \left\{
\begin{array}{lll}
@ & \text{R, R} & \textbf{erase-old-x} \\
\text{else} & \text{L, L} & \textbf{add-finished}
\end{array}
\right.
$$

If **erase-old-x** finds an x, it erases it; if it finds a z, it is replaced with a y. In either case, the head moves to the next E-square to the left:

$$\textbf{erase-old-x} \quad \begin{cases} x & \text{E, L, L} & \textbf{print-new-x} \\ z & \text{Py, L, L} & \textbf{print-new-x} \\ \text{else} & \text{R, R} & \textbf{erase-old-x} \end{cases}$$

The next x marker can now be printed:

$$\textbf{print-new-x} \quad \begin{cases} @ & \text{R, R} & \textbf{erase-old-y} \\ y & \text{Pz} & \textbf{find-digits} \\ \text{none} & \text{Px} & \textbf{find-digits} \end{cases}$$

Our example tape is now ready to go back to **find-digits** for the next bit-by-bit multiplication:

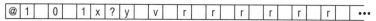

That multiplication will result in another 1 being added to the running total, but this time, it will be added one place over because it's always added to the leftmost r or u:

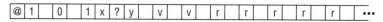

The machine then shifts the x marker one place over to the left:

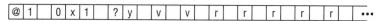

This multiplication results in a 0 being added to the running total. The value of the total doesn't change, but the leftmost r is changed to an s:

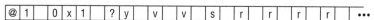

Again, the x marker is shifted left:

@ | 1 | x | 0 | | 1 | | ? | y | | v | | v | | s | | r | | r | | r | | r | | ...

Another bit-by-bit multiplication results in the leftmost r being changed to v:

@ | 1 | x | 0 | | 1 | | ? | y | | v | | v | | s | | v | | r | | r | | r | | ...

Now the x is about to be shifted into the sentinel. That case is handled by **erase-old-y** and **print-new-y**:

$$\textbf{erase-old-y} \quad \begin{cases} y & \text{E, L, L} & \textbf{print-new-y} \\ \text{else} & \text{R, R} & \textbf{erase-old-y} \end{cases}$$

$$\textbf{print-new-y} \quad \begin{cases} @ & \text{R} & \textbf{new-digit-is-one} \\ \text{else} & \text{Py, R} & \textbf{reset-new-x} \end{cases}$$

Notice that if the y marker is about to be shifted into the sentinel, then the entire multiplication has concluded without the running total spilling over beyond the area allotted for it. We now know that the unknown digit is a 1.

Otherwise, the x marker must be reset to the least significant bit of the number, which is the unknown digit:

reset-new-x	none	R, Px	**flag-result-digits**
	else	R, R	**reset-new-x**

The example tape now has the x and y markers set like this:

```
@ 1 | 0 | 1 y ? x | v | v | s | v | r | r | r | ...
```

More still needs to be done. The next bit-by-bit product should be added to the second digit of the running total. To accomplish this feat, the first s or v in the running total is changed to a t or w (respectively):

flag-result-digits	s	Pt, R, R	**unflag-result-digits**
	v	Pw, R, R	**unflag-result-digits**
	else	R, R	**flag-result-digits**

The remaining s and v markers are changed to r and u (respectively):

unflag-result-digits	s	Pr, R, R	**unflag-result-digits**
	v	Pu, R, R	**unflag-result-digits**
	else	N	**find-digits**

This process ensures that the next bit-by-bit multiplication is added to the running total in the correct spot.

The tape is truly ready for the next bit-by-bit multiplication, the result of which will be added to the running total at the first r or u.

```
@ 1 | 0 | 1 y ? x | w | u | r | u | r | r | r | ...
```

The multiplication completes in one of two ways, both of which you've already seen. If the machine attempts a carry from the running total into a blank square, then the result is known to exceed 2, the unknown digit is known to be 0, and the configuration becomes **new-digit-is-zero**. Otherwise, if the next destination for the y marker is the sentinel, then the entire multiplication has completed without the running total exceeding 2, and **new-digit-is-one** takes over.

These two sections are essentially the same. First, the machine goes back to the sentinel:

new-digit-is-zero	@	R	**print-zero-digit**
	else	L	**new-digit-is-zero**

Now the machine can locate the blank square, and print the 0 there. In moving through all the digits, it can erase any markers still left:

	0	R, E, R	**print-zero-digit**
print-zero-digit	1	R, E, R	**print-zero-digit**
	none	P0, R ,R, R	**cleanup**

Similarly, the *m*-configuration **new-digit-is-one** prints a 1 as the new digit and also goes into **cleanup** mode:

new-digit-is-one	@	R	**print-one-digit**
	else	L	**new-digit-is-one**

	0	R, E, R	**print-one-digit**
print-one-digit	1	R, E, R	**print-one-digit**
	none	P1, R ,R, R	**cleanup**

After the new digit has been printed, the *m*-configuration **cleanup** removes the running total and then goes to **new** for the next digit.

	none	N	**new**
cleanup			
	else	E, R, R	**cleanup**

The example tape has a new fourth digit and is ready for the fifth:

@	1		0		1		1		?															•••

Obviously, the Turing Machine is not a programmer-friendly medium. Most programming languages have functions called *sqrt* (or something similar) that calculate square roots not only of 2 but of any other number.

Yet, these square-root functions are often limited in precision. Most computer languages these days store floating-point numbers in a format that complies with standards set by the Institute of Electrical and Electronics Engineers (IEEE). A double-precision floating-point number stores numbers accurate to 52 bits or approximately 15 to 16 decimal digits. Until fairly recently (when special collections of math functions with greater precision became available), if you wanted something more precise than that, you'd be pretty much on your own. In duplicating the power of the Turing Machine to perform calculations to an arbitrary number of digits, you might find yourself doing it much like the process I've just described.

On a real computer, you'd at least have the convenience of addition and multiplication. If you were faced with the job of implementing several different types of functions on a Turing Machine, you might consider assembling a collection of common machine tables that you could then use as building blocks in implementing more complex tables.

This is precisely what Turing does next, although his real goal is a Universal Machine that can simulate any other machine.

7

Also Known as Subroutines

Every programmer knows that certain types of tasks are frequently encountered in almost all programming jobs. Sometimes the tasks are identical; more often they turn up with some variations. Even within the square-root-of-2 machine, several *m*-configurations were rather similar. For example, look at these three:

new	@	R	**mark-digits**
	else	L	**new**

new-digit-is-zero	@	R	**print-zero-digit**
	else	L	**new-digit-is-zero**

new-digit-is-one	@	R	**print-one-digit**
	else	L	**new-digit-is-one**

These *m*-configurations all move the head left in a loop until the sentinel is encountered. Then the head is moved one place right (over the leftmost digit), and the machine switches to another *m*-configuration.

It might be advantageous to determine beforehand that certain similar *m*-configurations will be required in a machine, and to predefine special *m*-configurations just for those chores. Doing so might help clarify certain strategies used in programming a Turing Machine, and to make the final job easier.

Let's call the *m*-configuration that moves the head back to the sentinel **goto-sentinel**. Then, when we're writing the states for a particular machine, and we want the head to be positioned over the figure to the right of the sentinel, we just specify **goto-sentinel** and we don't have to figure out how to do it all over again. Not only would it make the machine description a bit smaller, but (in theory) it would help anyone who had to look at the machine understand it.

We might define **goto-sentinel** on its own like so:

$$
\text{goto-sentinel} \quad \begin{cases} @ & R & ????? \\ \text{else} & L & \text{goto-sentinel} \end{cases}
$$

and immediately we see a problem indicated by that insistent squad of question marks. After the machine finds the sentinel, it must go into some other *m*-configuration, but that isn't known until we actually need to use **goto-sentinel** in a machine. We need some way to specify the final *m*-configuration in a general way so that **goto-sentinel** remains flexible.

The solution is to define **goto-sentinel** much like a mathematical function, where the final destination is an argument to the function:

$$
\text{goto-sentinel(A)} \quad \begin{cases} @ & R & A \\ \text{else} & L & \text{goto-sentinel(A)} \end{cases}
$$

The **new, new-digit-is-zero** and **new-digit-is-one** *m*-configurations can now be eliminated. At the beginning of the square-root machine, instead of having **begin** go to **new**, and **new** go to **mark-digits**, we can specify:

begin	none	P@, R, P1	goto-sentinel(mark-digits)

Instead of defining **carry** to go to **new-digit-is-zero**, like this

$$
\text{carry} \quad \begin{cases} r & Pu & \text{add-finished} \\ \text{none} & Pu & \text{new-digit-is-zero} \\ u & Pr, R, R & \text{carry} \end{cases}
$$

it can instead refer to **goto-sentinel** to go back to the sentinel and then switch to **print-zero-digit**:

$$
\text{carry} \quad \begin{cases} r & Pu & \text{add-finished} \\ \text{none} & Pu & \text{goto-sentinel(print-zero-digit)} \\ u & Pr, R, R & \text{carry} \end{cases}
$$

Speaking of **print-zero-digit**, did you notice that it's functionally identical to **print-one-digit** except for the digit it prints? We can profitably define a generalized **print-digit** function. The argument for this function is the character to print:

$$
\text{print-digit(a)} \quad \begin{cases} 0 & R, E, R & \text{print-digit(a)} \\ 1 & R, E, R & \text{print-digit(a)} \\ \text{none} & Pa, R, R, R & \text{cleanup} \end{cases}
$$

Notice the "Pa" operation in the last line indicating that the character to be printed is the argument to **print-digit**. Now the *m*-configuration **carry** becomes:

carry	r	Pu	**add-finished**
	none	Pu	**goto-sentinel(print-digit(0))**
	u	Pr, R, R	**carry**

The *m*-configuration **print-new-y** (which was responsible for detecting when it's time for **new-digit-is-one**) now becomes:

print-new-y	@	R	**goto-sentinel(print-digit(1))**
	else	Py, R	**reset-new-x**

Today's programmers will recognize this concept immediately. Although different programming languages provide this facility in the form of *procedures* or *functions* or *methods*, the most general term is *subroutine*. For decades, subroutines have been the most universal structural element of computer programs.

Programmers reading this book might want to exercise a little caution in applying *too* much of what they know about subroutines to these configurations with arguments. These configurations exist primarily to clarify the structure of Turing Machines and to make them easier to write. There's no concept of "calling" one of these configurations or of "returning" from a configuration.

Turing calls these configurations with arguments "skeleton tables" before settling on the better term "*m*-function." A machine table that makes use of skeleton tables he calls an "abbreviated table."

> ### 4. *Abbreviated tables.*
>
> There are certain types of process used by nearly all machines, and these, in some machines, are used in many connections. These processes include copying down sequences of symbols, comparing sequences, erasing all symbols of a given form, etc. Where such processes are concerned we can abbreviate the tables for the *m*-configurations considerably by the use of "skeleton tables". In skeleton tables there appear capital German letters and small Greek letters.

Astonishingly, the capital German letters are even more difficult to read than the lower-case letters are. Fortunately, Turing doesn't go beyond the letter E, but it might be helpful to get familiar with them in large-type versions:

A B C D E
𝔄 𝔅 ℭ 𝔇 𝔈

Notice, in particular, that the A looks more like a U, and take heed of the subtle difference between the C and the E. The Greek letters that Turing uses in this section are italicized versions of alpha, beta, and gamma: α, β, and γ.

> These are of the nature of "variables".
> By replacing each capital German letter throughout by an m-configuration
>
> [236]
>
> and each small Greek letter by a symbol, we obtain the table for an m-configuration.

Where I used a capital Latin letter in my example to represent an m-config-uration, Turing uses a capital German letter. Where I used a small Latin letter to represent a symbol, Turing uses a small Greek letter. Turing's examples often have multiple arguments.

These days subroutines (such as *sqrt*) are stored in files called *libraries* that allow programmers to use them by just specifying their names. It could even be said that entire operating systems — such as Unix, Microsoft Windows, or the Apple Mac OS — consist primarily of subroutines made available to applications that run under them.

For Turing, however, the skeleton tables exist solely to make his larger machines easier to construct (from his perspective) and easier to read and understand (from our perspective).

> The skeleton tables are to be regarded as nothing but abbreviations: they are not essential. So long as the reader understands how to obtain the complete tables from the skeleton tables, there is no need to give any exact definitions in this connection.

The skeleton tables are not essential, he says, and that's true. If the skeleton tables were presented solely as a matter of interest and restricted only to this section of the paper, they could easily be skipped. However, Turing is setting the stage for his Universal Machine, which makes *extensive* use of the skeleton tables presented in this section. Without these tables, the Universal Machine would be much longer and more complex than it is.

For that reason, knowing a little about Turing's ultimate intentions can help make these tables just a bit more comprehensible. As he will discuss in Section 7, the Universal Machine interprets a tape that contains a computing machine encoded as a series of letters. At the far left is a schwa sentinel. The tape alternates between F-squares and E-squares. The E-squares are, as usual, erasable. In the Universal Machine, the F-squares contain mostly letters rather than digits. Even so, the machine always prints the F-squares sequentially from left to right, and without erasing a previous symbol. For that reason, two blank squares in a row indicate that no F-squares exist to the right of that point.

Let us consider an example:

m-config.	Symbol	Behaviour	Final m-config.	
$\mathfrak{f}(\mathfrak{C}, \mathfrak{B}, \alpha)$	ə	L	$\mathfrak{f}_1(\mathfrak{C}, \mathfrak{B}, \alpha)$	From the m-configuration
	not ə	L	$\mathfrak{f}(\mathfrak{C}, \mathfrak{B}, \alpha)$	$\mathfrak{f}(\mathfrak{C}, \mathfrak{B}, \alpha)$ the machine finds the
				symbol of form α which is far-
	α		$\mathfrak{C}$	thest to the left (the "first α")
$\mathfrak{f}_1(\mathfrak{C}, \mathfrak{B}, \alpha)$	not α	R	$\mathfrak{f}_1(\mathfrak{C}, \mathfrak{B}, \alpha)$	and the m-configuration then becomes $\mathfrak{C}$. If there is no α
	None	R	$\mathfrak{f}_2(\mathfrak{C}, \mathfrak{B}, \alpha)$	then the m-configuration be-
				comes $\mathfrak{B}$.
	α		$\mathfrak{C}$	
$\mathfrak{f}_2(\mathfrak{C}, \mathfrak{B}, \alpha)$	not α	R	$\mathfrak{f}_1(\mathfrak{C}, \mathfrak{B}, \alpha)$	
	None	R	$\mathfrak{B}$	

Well, he might also have started with a simpler example, but this one has the advantage of showing off all the features. Turing's explanation appears to the right of the table. (Turing will also put explanations to the right of his tables when defining the Universal Machine.)

Although Turing is really defining a function named $\mathfrak{f}$, the function requires two other functions named $\mathfrak{f}_1$ and $\mathfrak{f}_2$. They all have the same three arguments: two m-configurations and one symbol. The m-configuration $\mathfrak{f}$ moves the head left until it encounters a schwa. The m-configuration becomes $\mathfrak{f}_1$. That m-configuration moves right whenever the square is not an α. (Notice that α is the third argument to $\mathfrak{f}$.) If it encounters an α, it goes to m-configuration $\mathfrak{C}$, the first argument to $\mathfrak{f}$. The m-configurations $\mathfrak{f}_1$ and $\mathfrak{f}_2$ are very similar. Together, they effectively search for two blanks in a row. Whenever $\mathfrak{f}_1$ encounters a blank, it switches to $\mathfrak{f}_2$. If the next character is not a blank, it switches back to $\mathfrak{f}_1$. Only when $\mathfrak{f}_2$ encounters a blank — which must be the second blank in a row — does it give up and go to m-configuration $\mathfrak{B}$, the second argument to $\mathfrak{f}$. The α character was not found in this case.

So, $\mathfrak{f}$ stands for *find*. If it finds an α, it goes to m-configuration $\mathfrak{C}$, and the head will be sitting on the first (leftmost) α. If it can't find an α, then it goes to m-configuration $\mathfrak{B}$.

There's actually a little confusion in this table. In the two m-configurations $\mathfrak{f}_1$ and $\mathfrak{f}_2$, the terms "not α" seem to mean "any non-blank square that's not α"

because another configuration takes care of the "None" or blank square; however, the first *m*-configuration does not have a "None" case and, to be consistent, it should. The None case should be the same as "not ə."[1]

In a table for a complete machine, this skeleton table would be referred to by an entry in the *final m-config* column that looks something like this:

m-config. symbol operations final m-config.

$$\mathfrak{f}(\mathfrak{q}, \mathfrak{r}, x)$$

The *m*-configurations q and r would be defined elsewhere in the machine, and *x* would be a symbol used by the machine.

> If we were to replace $\mathfrak{C}$ throughout by q (say), $\mathfrak{B}$ by r, and α by x, we should have a complete table for the *m*-configuration $\mathfrak{f}(\mathfrak{q}, \mathfrak{r}, x)$.

In the context of the complete machine, this skeleton table effectively expands into this table:

m-config.	symbol	operations	final m-config.
$\mathfrak{f}$	ə	L	$\mathfrak{f}_1$
	not ə	L	$\mathfrak{f}$
$\mathfrak{f}_1$	x		q
	not x	R	$\mathfrak{f}_1$
	None	R	$\mathfrak{f}_2$
$\mathfrak{f}_2$	x		q
	not x	R	$\mathfrak{f}_1$
	None	R	r

Because the $\mathfrak{f}$ function may be used several times in the same machine, the expanded versions of the *m*-configurations $\mathfrak{f}$, $\mathfrak{f}_1$, and $\mathfrak{f}_2$ would all need different names each time they're used.

> $\mathfrak{f}$ is called an "*m*-configuration function" or "*m*-function".

---

[1] This is one of several corrections identified in a footnote to the appendix of the paper Emil Post, "Recursive Unsolvability of a Problem of Thue," *The Journal of Symbolic Logic*, Vol. 12, No. 1 (Mar. 1947), 1–11. The entire paper is reprinted in Martin Davis, ed., *The Undecidable* (Raven Press, 1965), 293–303. The appendix (with the footnote incorporated into the text) is reprinted in B. Jack Copeland, ed., *The Essential Turing* (Oxford University Press, 2004), 97–101.

That's a much better name than "skeleton table." I hope there's no confusion if I generally refer to them simply as *functions*.

> The only expressions which are admissible for substitution in an m-function are the m-configurations and symbols of the machine. These have to be enumerated more or less explicitly: they may include expressions such as $\mathfrak{p}(\mathfrak{e}, x)$; indeed they must if there are any m-functions used at all.

If an m-function named $\mathfrak{p}$ has been defined, and if a machine refers to this m-function in its *final m-config* column, then $\mathfrak{p}$ must be considered to be an m-configuration of the machine.

Turing is a little nervous here because arguments to m-functions can be other m-functions. In other words, m-functions can be *nested*. (Don't worry: You'll see *plenty* of examples.) The problem results from implicitly allowing infinite recursion — that is, a function referring to itself, or referring to a second function which in turn refers to the first. If infinite recursion is allowed, then a machine could end up with an infinite number of m-configurations, and that's in violation of Turing's original definition of a computing machine.

> If we did not insist on this explicit enumeration, but simply stated that the machine had certain m-configurations (enumerated) and all m-configurations obtainable by substitution of m-configurations in certain m-functions, we should usually get an infinity of m-configurations; *e.g.*, we might say that the machine was to have the m-configuration $\mathfrak{q}$ and all m-configurations obtainable by substituting an m-configuration for $\mathfrak{C}$ in $\mathfrak{p}(\mathfrak{C})$. Then it would have $\mathfrak{q}, \mathfrak{p}(\mathfrak{q}), \mathfrak{p}(\mathfrak{p}(\mathfrak{q})), \mathfrak{p}\left(\mathfrak{p}(\mathfrak{p}(\mathfrak{q}))\right), \ldots$ as m-configurations.

We must ensure that after substituting all the m-functions into the machine, we still have a finite number of m-configurations.

> Our interpretation rule then is this. We are given the names of the m-configurations of the machine, mostly expressed in terms of m-functions.

Again, Turing is looking ahead to his Universal Machine, which will indeed be expressed mostly in terms of m-functions defined in this section.

> We are also given skeleton tables. All we want is the complete table for the m-configurations of the machine. This is obtained by repeated substitution in the skeleton tables.

Perhaps at this point, he's being a little *too* paranoid. We don't usually need to enumerate all of the *m*-configurations of a machine explicitly. We really just need to know that there's a finite number of them.

[237]

Further examples.
(In the explanations the symbol "→" is used to signify "the machine goes into the *m*-configuration. . . .")

By "explanations," Turing means the often cryptic descriptions that appear to the right of the skeleton tables. The columns of these tables are rather smushed together, and there are no column headings. Some tables contain only *m*-configurations and final *m*-configurations. Others contain columns for scanned characters and operations that must be differentiated based on their contents.

Turing's next example shows an *m*-function that appears as an argument to another *m*-function:

$e(\mathfrak{C}, \mathfrak{B}, \alpha)$	$\mathfrak{f}\big(e_1(\mathfrak{C}, \mathfrak{B}, \alpha), \mathfrak{B}, \alpha\big)$	From $e(\mathfrak{C}, \mathfrak{B}, \alpha)$ the first α is
		erased and $\rightarrow \mathfrak{C}$. If there is no
$e_1(\mathfrak{C}, \mathfrak{B}, \alpha)$ $\quad E$	$\mathfrak{C}$	$\alpha \rightarrow \mathfrak{B}$.

The e stands for "erase." This function starts by using $\mathfrak{f}$ to search for the first (leftmost) occurrence of α, which will leave the head positioned over the character. Notice how the first argument of $\mathfrak{f}$ is the function e_1. What that means is that when $\mathfrak{f}$ finds the character α, it will then go to e_1, which simply erases the character and goes to *m*-configuration $\mathfrak{C}$. If $\mathfrak{f}$ doesn't find the character α, then it goes to $\mathfrak{B}$.

If you're really examining these things and not just accepting Turing's word that they work, you may question why e_1 needs so many arguments. It does not. It could be defined more simply as $e_1(\mathfrak{C})$.

Programmers, be warned: You may know too much to interpret nested *m*-functions correctly. Resist the almost irresistible inclination to believe that e_1 must be "evaluated" in some way before it is passed to $\mathfrak{f}$. Instead, think of the first argument to $\mathfrak{f}$ as a *reference* to $\mathfrak{f}$'s eventual destination after it finds the character α.

Turing defines a second version of the e function with two arguments rather than three:

$e(\mathfrak{B}, \alpha)$	$e(e(\mathfrak{B}, \alpha), \mathfrak{B}, \alpha)$	From $e(\mathfrak{B}, \alpha)$ all letters α are
		erased and $\rightarrow \mathfrak{B}$.

The definition of two different functions with the same name but distinguished by a different number of arguments is a rather advanced programming technique (called function overloading) that is not allowed in many older programming languages.

This two-argument version of e makes use of the three-argument version to erase the first α, but notice that it specifies the two-argument e as the first argument to the three-argument version! When the three-argument e has successfully located and erased the first α, it then goes to the two-argument version, which proceeds to use the three-argument version again to erase the next α. This continues until all the α characters have been erased.

Very clever. Turing has now effectively used nesting and recursion to symbolize the implementation of repetitive tasks.

Nevertheless, the use of the two-argument e as an argument to the three-argument e to implement the two-argument e seems to invoke the dreaded specter of infinite nesting of m-configurations.

> The last example seems somewhat more difficult to interpret than most. Let us suppose that in the list of m-configurations of some machine there appears $e(b, x)$ $(= q,$ say$)$.

The m-function e can only play a role in a machine only if it appears somewhere in the machine's *final m-config* column, for example, as $e(b, x)$, where b is an m-configuration used in the machine. We can now say that $e(b, x)$ is another m-configuration of the machine and — as long as we haven't used q to represent any other m-configuration in the machine — we can also refer to this new m-configuration as q.

By using $e(b, x)$ in the *final m-config* column of the machine, we've essentially added another state to the machine, which Turing gives in two different forms:

		The table is
	$e(b, x)$	$e(e(b, x), b, x)$
or	q	$e(q, b, x).$

(The period at the end of the last line is there because it's considered part of a sentence that begins "The table is.") This table implies that the m-configuration $e(q, b, x)$ is also another m-configuration of the machine, as well as $e_1(q, b, x)$, as shown by the following expansion:

Or, in greater detail:

q		$e(q, b, x)$
$e(q, b, x)$		$f(e_1(q, b, x), b, x)$
$e_1(q, b, x)$	E	$q.$

(Again, a period follows the q on the last line because this table is considered part of a sentence.) Notice that after erasing the character, e_1 goes back to q, which is already an m-configuration of the machine, so there's no infinite generation of m-configurations.

In this we could replace $e_1(q, b, x)$ by q' and then give the table for f (with the right substitutions) and eventually reach a table in which no m-functions appeared.

Just as Turing used q to represent the configuration $e(b, x)$, he can use q' to represent the configuration $e_1(q, b, x)$, and additional configurations to represent e_1 and f.

Now that we've got the hang of these functions (*yeah, right*), Turing relentlessly piles them on. I know that it's hard right now to see how these will all fit together. To construct his Universal Machine, Turing requires several common types of functions useful in manipulating individual characters and strings of characters. You've already seen find and erase functions. He essentially needs cut, copy, and paste as well, and some standard printing routines.

The $\mathfrak{pe}$ function stands for "print at the end." It prints the symbol represented by β in the first blank F-square.

$\mathfrak{pe}(\mathfrak{C}, \beta)$			$f(\mathfrak{pe}_1(\mathfrak{C}, \beta), \mathfrak{C}, \mathfrak{d})$	From $\mathfrak{pe}(\mathfrak{C}, \beta)$ the machine
$\mathfrak{pe}_1(\mathfrak{C}, \beta)$	$\begin{cases} \text{Any} & R, R \\ \text{None} & P\beta \end{cases}$		$\mathfrak{pe}_1(\mathfrak{C}, \beta)$ $\mathfrak{C}$	prints β at the end of the sequence of symbols and $\rightarrow \mathfrak{C}$.

Some implicit assumptions hide inside this function. The f function normally finds the leftmost occurrence of its third argument, but here that argument is a schwa, which is the same symbol f looks for to get to the far left of the sequence. The $\mathfrak{pe}$ function is therefore assuming there are *two* schwas in a row, just as in Turing's second machine example on page 85. The m-function f first finds the rightmost of the two schwas (the one on an *E*-square) and then moves the head left to be positioned on the left schwa, which is on an *F*-square. The pe_1 function then moves right along *F*-squares until it finds a blank. It prints a β, which for most computing machines will be either a 0 or 1.

These next examples are cute. Turing first defines functions named l (for left) and r (for right) and then uses them in conjunction with f to create two more functions f' and f'' that move the head left or right after finding the desired character.

$l(\mathfrak{C})$	L	$\mathfrak{C}$	From $f'(\mathfrak{C}, \mathfrak{B}, \alpha)$ it does the
$r(\mathfrak{C})$	R	$\mathfrak{C}$	same as for $f(\mathfrak{C}, \mathfrak{B}, \alpha)$ but moves to the left before $\to \mathfrak{C}$.
$f'(\mathfrak{C}, \mathfrak{B}, \alpha)$		$f(l(\mathfrak{C}), \mathfrak{B}, \alpha)$	
$f''(\mathfrak{C}, \mathfrak{B}, \alpha)$		$f(r(\mathfrak{C}), \mathfrak{B}, \alpha)$	

I would have called them fl and fr rather than f' and f'', but that's me.

The Universal Machine will require moving characters from one location to another on the tape. The c function performs a "copy." The character α is likely to be a marker. The function obtains the character in the *F*-square to the left of that marker and uses pe to copy it to the first empty *F*-square at the end.

$c(\mathfrak{C}, \mathfrak{B}, \alpha)$		$f'(c_1(\mathfrak{C}), \mathfrak{B}, \alpha)$	$c(\mathfrak{C}, \mathfrak{B}, \alpha)$. The machine
$c_1(\mathfrak{C})$	β	$pe(\mathfrak{C}, \beta)$	writes at the end the first symbol marked α and $\to \mathfrak{C}$.

Notice the function uses f' to find the α character, so that the head ends up to the left of the marker, which is the figure that the marker marks.

The c_1 function has an unusual syntax: The scanned character becomes the second argument to pe. Turing says:

[238]
The last line stands for the totality of lines obtainable from it by replacing β by any symbol which may occur on the tape of the machine concerned.

If, for example, the c function were to be used only for copying 0s and 1s, then c_1 would actually be defined like:

$$c_1(\mathfrak{C}) \begin{cases} 0 & pe(\mathfrak{C}, 0) \\ 1 & pe(\mathfrak{C}, 1) \end{cases}$$

The ce function stands for "copy and erase." It exists in two-argument and three-argument versions.

$ce(\mathfrak{C}, \mathfrak{B}, \alpha)$	$c(e(\mathfrak{C}, \mathfrak{B}, \alpha), \mathfrak{B}, \alpha)$	$ce(\mathfrak{B}, \alpha)$. The machine copies down in order at the end all symbols marked α and erases the letters α; $\rightarrow \mathfrak{B}$.
$ce(\mathfrak{B}, \alpha)$	$ce(ce(\mathfrak{B}, \alpha), \mathfrak{B}, \alpha)$	

The three-argument ce first uses c to copy the leftmost figure marked with α, and then uses e to erase that marker. The two-argument version of ce uses the three-argument version to copy the first figure and erase the marker, but then goes back to the two-character version. In effect, all symbols marked with α are copied to the end of the tape in the first available F-squares. (Turing's second example on page 87 could have used this function to copy a run of 1s to the end of the tape.)

Now might be a good time to raise the ugly issue of *efficiency*. Turing is defining functions that look nice and compact, but that actually hide an enormous amount of activity. To perform each copy-and-erase, the c function uses f to find the marker (and remember that f backtracks all the way to the sentinel) and then goes to the e function, which uses f again to find the same marker so it can be erased. A more efficient scheme has ce erasing the marker when it's first located and before it copies the character. (In honor of the notorious inefficiency of Turing Machines, the term *Turing tar-pit* describes excessively generalized computer routines that spend much more time flapping their wings than flying.)

But Turing is not interested in mundane issues of efficiency. The machine is, after all, imaginary. If he wants, he can run it at a million zettahertz and nobody will realize how much needless activity is going on.

The re function is "replace." The α and β arguments are assumed to be markers. The function finds the leftmost α and replaces it with β. (We know that α and β are markers because Turing doesn't allow replacing figures already marked on F-squares.)

$re(\mathfrak{C}, \mathfrak{B}, \alpha, \beta)$	$f(re_1(\mathfrak{C}, \mathfrak{B}, \alpha, \beta), \mathfrak{B}, \alpha)$	$re(\mathfrak{C}, \mathfrak{B}, \alpha, \beta)$. The machine replaces the first α by β and $\rightarrow \mathfrak{C} \rightarrow \mathfrak{B}$ if there is no α.
$re_1(\mathfrak{C}, \mathfrak{B}, \alpha, \beta)$ $E, P\beta$	$\mathfrak{C}$	

The three argument version replaces all α markers with β:

$re(\mathfrak{B}, \alpha, \beta)$	$re(re(\mathfrak{B}, \alpha, \beta), \mathfrak{B}, \alpha, \beta)$	$re(\mathfrak{B}, \alpha, \beta)$. The machine replaces all letters α by β; $\rightarrow \mathfrak{B}$.

For consistency, that explanation at the right should have its first line indented.

If you've got the hang of Turing's methodology and naming scheme, you'll know that the $\mathfrak{cr}$ function is "copy and replace":

$\mathfrak{cr}(\mathfrak{C}, \mathfrak{B}, \alpha)$	$\mathfrak{c}(\mathfrak{re}(\mathfrak{C}, \mathfrak{B}, \alpha, \alpha), \mathfrak{B}, \alpha)$	$\mathfrak{cr}(\mathfrak{B}, \alpha)$ differs from $\mathfrak{ce}(\mathfrak{B}, \alpha)$ only in that the letters α are not erased. The m-configuration $\mathfrak{cr}(\mathfrak{B}, \alpha)$ is taken up when no letters "α" are on the tape.
$\mathfrak{cr}(\mathfrak{B}, \alpha)$	$\mathfrak{cr}(\mathfrak{cr}(\mathfrak{B}, \alpha), \mathfrak{re}(\mathfrak{B}, \alpha, \alpha), \alpha)$	

These functions are not used elsewhere in Turing's paper.

The Universal Machine requires a facility to "search and replace," and Turing next presents half a page of functions that begin with the letters $\mathfrak{cp}$ ("compare") and $\mathfrak{cpe}$ ("compare and erase"). The final m-configurations in these functions are so long that Turing's explanations appear under each table instead of at the right. (There's a typo in the first line. In the *final m-config* column the subscripted 1 on the $\mathfrak{C}$ should be a comma. Also, some periods appear in the *final m-config* column where they serve no purpose.)

$\mathfrak{cp}(\mathfrak{C}, \mathfrak{A}, \mathfrak{E}, \alpha, \beta)$		$\mathfrak{f}'(\mathfrak{cp}_1(\mathfrak{C}_1 \mathfrak{A}, \beta), \mathfrak{f}(\mathfrak{A}, \mathfrak{E}, \beta), \alpha)$
$\mathfrak{cp}_1(\mathfrak{C}, \mathfrak{A}, \beta)$	γ	$\mathfrak{f}'(\mathfrak{cp}_2(\mathfrak{C}, \mathfrak{A}, \gamma), \mathfrak{A}, \beta)$
$\mathfrak{cp}_2(\mathfrak{C}, \mathfrak{A}, \gamma) \left\{ \begin{array}{l} \gamma \\ \text{not } \gamma \end{array} \right.$		$\mathfrak{C}$ $\mathfrak{A}.$

The first symbol marked α and the first marked β are compared. If there is neither α nor β, $\rightarrow \mathfrak{E}$. If there are both and the symbols are alike, $\rightarrow \mathfrak{C}$. Otherwise $\rightarrow \mathfrak{A}$.

$\mathfrak{cpe}(\mathfrak{C}, \mathfrak{A}, \mathfrak{E}, \alpha, \beta)$	$\mathfrak{cp}(\mathfrak{e}(\mathfrak{e}(\mathfrak{C}, \mathfrak{C}, \beta), \mathfrak{C}, \alpha), \mathfrak{A}, \mathfrak{E}, \alpha, \beta)$

$\mathfrak{cpe}(\mathfrak{C}, \mathfrak{A}, \mathfrak{E}, \alpha, \beta)$ differs from $\mathfrak{cp}(\mathfrak{C}, \mathfrak{A}, \mathfrak{E}, \alpha, \beta)$ in that in the case when there is similarity the first α and β are erased.

$\mathfrak{cpe}(\mathfrak{A}, \mathfrak{E}, \alpha, \beta)$	$\mathfrak{cpe}(\mathfrak{cpe}(\mathfrak{A}, \mathfrak{E}, \alpha, \beta), \mathfrak{A}, \mathfrak{E}, \alpha, \beta).$

$\mathfrak{cpe}(\mathfrak{A}, \mathfrak{E}, \alpha, \beta)$. The sequence of symbols marked α is compared with the sequence marked β. $\rightarrow \mathfrak{C}$ if they are similar. Otherwise $\rightarrow \mathfrak{A}$. Some of the symbols α and β are erased.

By "similar" Turing means "identical."

Turing has now exhausted his supply of mnemonic function names, for he names the next one simply q, which unfortunately is the same letter he will shortly use to represent m-configurations in general. What's worse is that he later refers to this function as g.

I believe that Turing meant for this function to be named g rather than q. Just as the f function finds the first (that is, leftmost) occurrence of a particular symbol, this function finds the last (rightmost) occurrence of a symbol. It makes a bit of sense that the related f and g functions should be represented by consecutive letters. For that reason, although the following table describes the function q, I'll refer to it as g.

The single-argument version of g moves to the right until it finds two blanks in a row. That is assumed to be the rightmost end of the tape. The two-argument version of g first uses the one-argument g and then moves left looking for the character α.

[239]

$q(\mathfrak{C})$ {	Any	R	$q(\mathfrak{C})$	$q(\mathfrak{C}, \alpha)$. The machine finds the last symbol of form α. → $\mathfrak{C}$.
	None	R	$q_1(\mathfrak{C})$	
$q_1(\mathfrak{C})$ {	Any	R	$q(\mathfrak{C})$	
	None		$\mathfrak{C}$	
$q(\mathfrak{C}, \alpha)$			$q(q_1(\mathfrak{C}, \alpha))$	
$q_1(\mathfrak{C}, \alpha)$ {	α		$\mathfrak{C}$	
	not α	L	$q_1(\mathfrak{C}, \alpha)$	

Turing finishes this section with a few miscellaneous functions with familiar names.

You'll recall the pe function that printed a character in the last F-square. The pe_2 function prints two characters in the last two F-squares:

$pe_2(\mathfrak{C}, \alpha, \beta)$	$pe(pe(\mathfrak{C}, \beta), \alpha)$	$pe_2(\mathfrak{C}, \alpha, \beta)$. The machine prints $\alpha \beta$ at the end.

Similarly, the ce function copied characters marked with α to the end. The ce_2 function copies symbols marked with α and β, while ce_3 copies characters marked $\alpha, \beta,$ and γ.

$ce_2(\mathfrak{B}, \alpha, \beta)$	$ce(ce(\mathfrak{B}, \beta), \alpha)$	$ce_3(\mathfrak{B}, \alpha, \beta, \gamma)$. The mach-
$ce_3(\mathfrak{B}, \alpha, \beta, \gamma)$	$ce(ce_2(\mathfrak{B}, \beta, \gamma), \alpha)$	ine copies down at the end first the symbols marked α, then those marked β, and finally those marked γ; it erases the symbols α, β, γ.

These copies are performed sequentially: First, all the symbols marked with α are copied, then the symbols marked with β, and so on. Later on, Turing uses a function called ce_5 with six arguments that he's never described, but the operation of it should be obvious.

Finally, a single-argument e function erases all markers.

$e(\mathfrak{C})$	$\begin{cases} \vphantom{x} \\ \vphantom{x} \end{cases}$	ə	R	$e_1(\mathfrak{C})$	From $e(\mathfrak{C})$ the marks are erased from all marked sym-
		Not ə	L	$e(\mathfrak{C})$	bols. $\rightarrow \mathfrak{C}$.
$e_1(\mathfrak{C})$	$\begin{cases} \vphantom{x} \\ \vphantom{x} \end{cases}$	Any	R, E, R	$e_1(\mathfrak{C})$	
		None		$\mathfrak{C}$	

Programmers of a certain age may remember a book by Niklaus Wirth (b. 1934), inventor of the Pascal programming language, with the wonderful title *Algorithms + Data Structures = Programs* (Prentice-Hall, 1975). As the title indicates, a computer program requires both code (algorithms) and some data for the code to crunch. Turing has now presented many of the algorithms that his Universal Computing Machine will require, but he hasn't yet described how he will transform an arbitrary computing machine into crunchable data. That's next.

8 Everything Is a Number

I n this digital age of ours we have grown accustomed to representing all forms of information as numbers. Text, drawings, photographs, sound, music, movies — everything goes into the digitization mill and gets stored on our computers and other devices in ever more complex arrangements of 0s and 1s.

In the 1930s, however, only numbers were numbers, and if somebody was turning text into numbers, it was for purposes of deception and intrigue.

In the fall of 1937, Alan Turing began his second year at Princeton amidst heightened fears that England and Germany would soon be at war. He was working on his doctoral thesis, of course, but he had also developed an interest in cryptology — the science and mathematics of creating secret codes or ciphers (cryptography) and breaking codes invented by others (cryptanalysis).[1] Turing believed that messages during wartime could be best encrypted by converting words to binary digits and then multiplying them by large numbers. Decrypting the messages without knowledge of that large number would then involve a difficult factoring problem. This idea of Turing's was rather prescient, for it is the way that most computer encryption works now.

Unlike most mathematicians, Turing liked to get his hands dirty building things. To implement an automatic code machine he began building a binary multiplier using electromagnetic relays, which were the primary building blocks of computers before vacuum tubes were demonstrated to be sufficiently reliable. Turing even built his own relays in a machine shop and wound the electromagnets himself.

The German Army and Navy were already using quite a different encrypting device. The *Enigma* was invented by a German electrical engineer named Arthur Scherbius (1878–1929). After Scherbius had unsuccessfully attempted to persuade the German Navy to use the machine in 1918, it had gone on sale for commercial

---

[1] Andrew Hodges, *Alan Turing: The Enigma* (Simon & Schuster, 1983), 138.

purposes in 1923. The Navy became interested soon after that, eventually followed by the rest of the German military.[2]

The Enigma had a rudimentary 26-key keyboard arranged like a typewriter but without numbers, punctuation, or shift keys. Above the keyboard were 26 light bulbs arranged in the same pattern. Messages were encrypted by typing them on the keyboard. As each letter was pressed, a different letter would light up. These lighted letters were manually transcribed and then sent to the recipient. (The encrypted message could be hand delivered or sent by mail; later, encrypted messages were sent by radio using Morse code.) The person receiving the message had his own Enigma machine, and would type the encrypted message on the keyboard. The flashing lights would then spell out the original text.

The keys of the keyboard were electrically connected to the lights through a series of rotors. Each rotor was a small disk with 26 contacts on each side representing the letters of the alphabet. Inside the rotor, these contacts were connected symmetrically: If contact A on one side connected to contact T on the other, then T on the first side would connect to A on the other. This symmetry is what allowed the machine to be used for both encrypting and decrypting.

The standard Enigma had three connected rotors, each of which was wired differently, and each of which could be set to one of 26 positions. The three rotors on the encrypting and decrypting machines had to be set identically. The three-letter keys to set the rotors could, for example, be changed on a daily basis in accordance with a list known only to the Enigma operators.

So far, nothing I've described about the Enigma makes it capable of anything more than a simple letter-substitution code, easily breakable by even the most amateur cryptanalysts. It's even simpler than most letter-substitution codes because it's symmetrical: If D is encoded as S then S is also encoded as D.

Here's the kicker: As the user of the Enigma pressed the keys on the keyboard, the rotors *moved*. With each keystroke, the first rotor moved ahead one position. If a string of 26 A's were typed, for example, each successive A would be encoded differently as the rotor went through its 26 positions. When the first rotor had completed a full turn, it would move the second rotor ahead one position. Now another series of 26 A's would encode to a different sequence of letters. When the second rotor finished a revolution, it would bump the third rotor up a notch. A fourth stationary rotor routed the electrical signal back through the rotors in reverse order. Only after 17,576 keystrokes (that's 26 to the third power) would the encryption pattern repeat.

But wait, it gets worse: The rotors were replaceable. The basic machine was supplied with five different rotors, which could be used in any of the three rotor

---

[2]David Kahn, *Seizing the Enigma: The Race to Break the German U-Boat Codes, 1939–1943* (Houghton-Mifflin, 1991), ch. 3.

slots. Another enhancement involved a plug-board that added another layer of letter scrambling.

In 1932, three Polish mathematicians began developing methods to decode Enigma messages.[3] They determined that they needed to build devices that simulated the Enigma in an automated manner. The first "bombs" (as they were called) became operational in 1938 and searched through possible rotor settings. One of these mathematicians was Marian Rejewski (1905–1980), who had spent a year at Göttingen after graduation. He wrote that the machines were called bombs "for lack of a better name"[4] but it's possible the name was suggested by the ticking sound they made, or by a particular ice cream sundae enjoyed by the mathematicians.[5]

Traditionally, the British government had employed classics scholars for breaking codes under the reasonable assumption that these were the people best trained to decode difficult languages. As the war approached, it became evident that for analyzing sophisticated encoding devices like the Enigma, the Government Code and Cypher School (GC & CS) would require mathematicians as well.

When Alan Turing returned from Princeton to England in the summer of 1938, he was invited to take a course at the GC & CS headquarters. It's possible the government was in touch with him as early as 1936.[6] In 1939, the GC & CS purchased a large estate with a Victorian mansion called Bletchley Park 50 miles northeast of London. In a sense, Bletchley Park was the intellectual focal point of England — where the rail line between Oxford and Cambridge connected with the rail south to London.

On September 1, 1939, Germany invaded Poland. Two days later, Great Britain declared war on Germany, and on September 4, Alan Turing reported for duty at Bletchley Park. Eventually about ten thousand people would be working there intercepting and decoding covert communications. To accommodate everyone, huts were built around the grounds. Turing was in charge of Hut 8, dedicated to the decryption of codes used by the German Navy. The Germans used these codes to communicate with submarines, which were a particular threat to convoys in the Atlantic between the United States and Great Britain.

Earlier in 1939, the British had met with the Polish mathematicians to learn about the Enigma and the bombs. Soon after Turing started at Bletchley Park, he began redesigning and improving the devices, now known by the French spelling *bombe*. The first Turing Bombe (as they are sometimes called) became operational

---

[3] Marian Rejewski, "How Polish Mathematicians Deciphered the Enigma," *Annals of the History of Computing*, Vol. 3, No. 3 (July 1981), 213–234. See also Elisabeth Rakus-Andersson, "The Polish Brains Behind the Breaking of the Enigma Code Before and During the Second World War," in Christof Teuscher, ed., *Alan Turing: Life and Legacy of a Great Thinker* (Springer, 2004), 419–439.

[4] Rejewski, "How Polish Mathematicians Deciphered the Enigma," 226.

[5] Kahn, *Seizing the Enigma*, 73.

[6] Hodges, *Alan Turing*, 148.

in 1940. It weighed a ton and could simulate 30 Enigma machines working in parallel.[7]

Prior to attacking the message with the Turing Bombe, it was necessary to narrow down the possibilities. The cryptanalysts searched for "cribs," which were common words or phrases that often appeared in the encoded messages. These would establish the initial position of the first rotor. Much valued were cases where the same message was transmitted using two encodings: These were known as "kisses." Another technique used heavy white paper in various widths and printed with multiple rows of the alphabet, much like punched cards later used in computers. The analysts would punch holes in the paper corresponding to the letters of the encoded messages. Different messages from the same day (which would all be based on the same settings of the Enigma) could then be compared by overlapping the sheets. Because the paper used for this came from a nearby town named Banbury, the procedure was called "banburismus."

These varieties of techniques were refined to a point where, by mid-1941, the successes achieved in decoding Enigma communications had greatly decreased naval losses.[8] Many people working at Bletchley Park deserve some credit for this success, although Alan Turing's work played a significant role.

Even in the unusual assemblage of mathematicians and classics scholars at Bletchley Park, Turing established a certain reputation for eccentricity:

> In the first week of June each year [Turing] would get a bad attack of hay fever, and he would cycle to the office wearing a service gas mask to screen the pollen. His bicycle had a fault: the chain would come off at regular intervals. Instead of having it mended he would count the number of times the pedals went round and would get off the bicycle in time to adjust the chain by hand.[9]

In the spring of 1941, Alan Turing made a proposal of marriage to Joan Clarke, one of the rare women at Bletchley Park who wasn't relegated to a mindless clerical job. Joan Clarke had been studying mathematics at Cambridge when she was recruited for code-breaking. A few days after the proposal Turing confessed to her that he had "homosexual tendencies"[10] but the engagement continued for several more months before he felt he had to call it off.

---

[7] Stephen Budiansky, *Battle of Wits: The Complete Story of Codebreaking in World War II* (Free Press, 2000), 155. See also Jack Gray and Keith Thrower, *How the Turing Bombe Smashed the Enigma Code* (Speedwell, 2001).

[8] Hodges, *Alan Turing*, 218–9.

[9] I. J. Good, "Early Work on Computers at Bletchley," *Annals of the History of Computing*, Vol. 1, No. 1 (July 1979), 41.

[10] Hodges, *Alan Turing*, 206.

In November 1942, Turing was sent on a mission to Washington, D.C., to help coordinate code-breaking activities between England and the United States. Following that assignment, he spent the first two months of 1943 at Bell Laboratories, at the time located on West Street in New York City. There he met Harry Nyquist (1889–1976), who pioneered the theory of digital sampling, and Claude Elwood Shannon (1916–2001), whose paper "A Mathematical Theory of Communication" (1948) would found the field of information theory and introduce the word "bit" to the world.

For Turing the primary object of interest at Bell Labs was a speech-scrambling device that was intended to secure telephone communications over the Atlantic. Sound waves were separated into various frequency ranges, digitized, and then encrypted by modular addition, which is addition that wraps around a particular value (such as the value 60 when adding seconds and minutes). On the receiving end, the numbers were decrypted and then reconstituted as speech.

In Nyquist's research and Shannon's work, and in the speech-encryption device, we can see the origin of ideas that would later result in the technologies used for digitizing images in JPEG files and sound in MP3 files, but these particular innovations required decades to come to fruition. The earliest digital computers, on the other hand, did little but emit numbers. Even Babbage's original Difference Engine was conceived solely to print error-free tables of logarithms. In this context, it's not surprising that Turing Machines also generate numbers rather than, for instance, implement generalized functions.

Turing is about to take the paper in a more unusual direction by using numbers to encode other forms of information. The next section of Turing's paper demonstrates how numbers can represent not photographs or songs, but the machines themselves.

Yes, everything is a number. Even Turing Machines are numbers.

> ## 5. *Enumeration of computable sequences.*
>
> A computable sequence γ is determined by a description of a machine which computes γ. Thus the sequence 001011011101111... is determined by the table on p. 234, and, in fact, any computable sequence is capable of being described in terms of such a table.

That's the Example II machine on page 87 of this book.

> It will be useful to put these tables into a kind of standard form.

Turing actually started out with a standard form that he described in Section 1 (page 70 of this book). He indicated that a particular operation can cause the machine to print or erase a symbol, and to move one square to the left or right.

After showing one machine in this format (Example I on page 81, the example that Turing will also soon mention), Turing quickly abandoned his own rules. He allowed printing multiple symbols and moving multiple squares in single operations. This was done solely so the machine tables didn't go on for pages and pages. Now he'd like to return to his original restrictions.

> In the first place let us suppose that the table is given in the same form as the first table, for example, I on p. 233. That is to say, that the entry in the operations column is always of one of the forms E: E, R: E, L: $P\alpha$: $P\alpha$, R: $P\alpha$, L: R: L: or no entry at all.

Turing uses colons to separate the nine different possibilities. These possibilities result from the three types of printing (erase, print a character, or neither) in combination with the three kinds of movement (left, right, or none).

> The table can always be put into this form by introducing more m-configurations.

For example, the table for Example II (page 87) began with configuration $\mathfrak{b}$:

Configuration		Behaviour	
m-config.	symbol	operations	final m-config.
$\mathfrak{b}$		$P\mathfrak{d}, R, P\mathfrak{d}, R, P0, R, R, P0, L, L$	$\mathfrak{o}$

To adhere to Turing's original (and reinstated) restrictions, this single configuration must be split into six simple configurations. For the additional configuration I'll use the German lower-case letters for c, d, e, g, and h (f was already used in the original table).

Configuration		Behaviour	
m-config.	symbol	operations	final m-config.
$\mathfrak{b}$		$P\mathfrak{d}, R$	$\mathfrak{c}$
$\mathfrak{c}$		$P\mathfrak{d}, R$	$\mathfrak{d}$
$\mathfrak{d}$		$P0, R$	$\mathfrak{e}$
$\mathfrak{e}$		R	$\mathfrak{g}$
$\mathfrak{g}$		$P0, L$	$\mathfrak{h}$
$\mathfrak{h}$		L	$\mathfrak{o}$

Now each operation consists solely of a printing operation (or not) followed by possible left or right movement by one square.

> Now let us give numbers to the m-configurations, calling them $q_1, \ldots, q_R$, as in § 1. The initial m-configuration is always to be called q_1.

If there happen to be 237 different m-configurations in a machine, they are now to be labeled q_1 through q_{237}.

For the revised beginning of Example II, the first six m-configurations can be renamed q_1 through q_6. The initial m-configuration that Turing always named b becomes q_1. The table is now:

Configuration		Behaviour	
m-config.	*symbol*	*operations*	*final m-config.*
q_1		Pə, R	q_2
q_2		Pə, R	q_3
q_3		P0, R	q_4
q_4		R	q_5
q_5		P0, L	q_6
q_6		L	q_7

> We also give numbers to the symbols $S_1, \ldots, S_m$
>
> [240]
>
> and, in particular, blank $= S_0, 0 = S_1, 1 = S_2$.

It's a little confusing that a subscripted 1 means the symbol 0 and a subscripted 2 means the symbol 1, but we'll have to live with it. The Example II machine also needs to print ə and x, so the following equivalencies would be defined for this machine:

S_0 means a blank,
S_1 means 0,
S_2 means 1,
S_3 means ə, and
S_4 means x.

The machine that computes the square root of 2 requires symbols up to S_{14}.

The first six configurations of the Example II machine are now:

Configuration		Behaviour	
m-config.	symbol	operations	final m-config.
q_1		PS_3, R	q_2
q_2		PS_3, R	q_3
q_3		PS_1, R	q_4
q_4		R	q_5
q_5		PS_1, L	q_6
q_6		L	q_7

The imposition of a uniform naming system has resulted in these lines taking on very similar patterns. In the general case, Turing identifies three different standard forms:

The lines of the table are now of form

m-config.	Symbol	Operations	Final m-config.	
q_i	S_j	PS_k, L	q_m	(N_1)
q_i	S_j	PS_k, R	q_m	(N_2)
q_i	S_j	PS_k	q_m	(N_3)

At the far right, Turing has labeled these three standard forms N_1, N_2, and N_3. All three print something; the only difference is whether the head moves Left, Right, or not at all.

What about erasures? Because Turing defined S_0 as a blank symbol, erasures can be performed by printing simply S_0:

Lines such as

q_i	S_j	E, R	q_m

are to be written as

q_i	S_j	PS_0, R	q_m

Operations that consist of a Right or Left shift without printing anything can be written to reprint the scanned symbol:

and lines such as

q_i	S_j	R	q_m

to be written as

q_i	S_j	PS_j, R	q_m

In this way we reduce each line of the table to a line of one of the forms $(N_1), (N_2), (N_3)$.

To illustrate the process of standardizing the table, I've been using the first configuration of the Example II table, but that first configuration doesn't even have anything in its *symbol* column because the configuration does the same thing regardless of the symbol. A machine starts with a blank tape so we know that the symbol it reads is a blank. The first configuration of the Example II table converted to standard form becomes:

Configuration		Behaviour	
m-config.	*symbol*	*operations*	*final m-config.*
q_1	S_0	PS_3, R	q_2
q_2	S_0	PS_3, R	q_3
q_3	S_0	PS_1, R	q_4
q_4	S_0	PS_0, R	q_5
q_5	S_0	PS_1, L	q_6
q_6	S_0	PS_0, L	q_7

That's easy enough, but let's take a look at the second *m*-configuration of the Example II machine:

$\mathfrak{o}$	$\left\{ \begin{array}{l} 1 \\ 0 \end{array} \right.$	R, Px, L, L, L	$\mathfrak{o}$
			$\mathfrak{q}$

The *m*-configuration $\mathfrak{o}$ will become the numbered configuration q_7. When the scanned character is 1, the head must move right once, and then left three times.

These three left-shifts will require three more m-configurations, q_8, q_9, and q_{10}. The m-configuration q then becomes q_{11}. Here's m-configuration q_7:

Configuration		Behaviour	
m-config.	symbol	operations	final m-config.
q_7	S_2	PS_2, R	q_8
q_7	S_1	PS_1	q_{11}

In both cases, the machine prints the scanned character. Here are m-configurations q_8, q_9, and q_{10}:

q_8	S_0	PS_4, L	q_9
q_9	S_2	PS_2, L	q_{10}
q_{10}	S_0	PS_0, L	q_7

The problem is the *symbol* column. To fill it in correctly you really have to know what the machine will be encountering. For q_8, the machine is scanning a blank square and printing an x. Once it moves left, what's the next scanned character? It's the 1 that was scanned in q_7, but in other cases it might not be so obvious. The words "Any" or "Not" or "Else" don't work with this scheme, and in some cases you may have to add specific configurations for every single character the machine is using.

It's a mess, but there are always a finite number of characters involved, so it can definitely be done. Let's assume that we have converted all the configurations of a particular machine into the standard forms that Turing denotes as (N_1), (N_2), and (N_3). When we're finished, and we dispose of the original table, have we lost any information? Yes, we have lost a little bit. We know that S_0 is a blank, S_1 is a 0, and S_2 is a 1, but we no longer know the exact characters meant by S_3, S_4, and so on. This shouldn't matter. The machines use these characters internally. All that matters is that they're unique. We're really only interested in the 0s and 1s that the machine prints, and not what it uses as a scratchpad.

Instead of a table, we can express each configuration with a combination of the m-configurations, symbols, L, and R.

From each line of form (N_1) let us form an expression $q_i\, S_j\, S_k\, L\, q_m$;

This form is sometimes known as a *quintuple* because it's composed of five elements. Despite its cryptic nature, it's still readable: "In m-configuration q_i, when character S_j is scanned, print character S_k, move Left, and switch to m-configuration q_m." Similarly for N_2 and N_3:

from each line of form (N_2) we form an expression $q_i\,S_j\,S_k\,R\,q_m$; and from each line of form (N_3) we form an expression $q_i\,S_j\,S_k\,N\,q_m$.

Notice that when the head is not to be moved, the letter is N (meaning No move).

Let us write down all expressions so formed from the table for the machine and separate them by semi-colons. In this way we obtain a complete description of the machine.

Turing will show an example shortly. Each configuration is a quintuple, and an entire machine is now expressed as a stream of quintuples. (Interestingly enough, the quintuples don't have to be in any specific order. It's like a programming language where each statement begins with a label and ends with a *goto*.)

The next substitution is a radical one. It gets rid of all those subscripts and turns the machine into a stream of capital letters:

In this description we shall replace q_i by the letter "D" followed by the letter "A" repeated i times, and S_j by "D" followed by "C" repeated j times.

For example, q_1 is replaced by DA and q_5 is replaced by $DAAAAA$. (Remember that the first configuration is q_1. There is no q_0.) As for the symbols, S_0 (the blank) is now denoted by D, S_1 (the symbol 0) is DC, and S_2 (the symbol 1) is DCC. Other symbols are assigned to S_3 and greater and become $DCCC$ and so on.

This new description of the machine may be called the *standard description* (S.D.). It is made up entirely from the letters "A", "C", "D", "L", "R", "N", and from ";".

The L, R, and N indicate the moves. Semicolons separate each configuration.

If finally we replace "A" by "1", "C" by "2", "D" by "3", "L" by "4", "R" by "5", "N" by "6", and ";" by "7" we shall have a description of the machine in the form of an arabic numeral.

This is an important step. Turing has standardized his machines to such an extent that he can now uniquely identify a machine by an integer, and this integer encodes all the states of the machine. Turing was undoubtedly inspired by the approach Gödel took in his Incompleteness Theorem in converting every mathematical expression into a unique number.

> The integer represented by this numeral may be called a *description number* (D.N) of the machine. The D.N determine the S.D and the structure of the
>
> [241]
>
> machine uniquely. The machine whose D.N is n may be described as $\mathcal{M}(n)$.

Turing has now introduced another font. He will use this script font for representing entire machines.

> To each computable sequence there corresponds at least one description number, while to no description number does there correspond more than one computable sequence.

Since the order of the quintuples doesn't matter, the quintuples can be scrambled without any effect on the sequence the machine computes. It is very clear, then, that multiple description numbers are associated with each computable sequence, but each description number defines a machine that generates only one computable sequence (at least when beginning with a blank tape).

Without much fanfare Turing concludes with a result he mentioned in the very beginning of the article:

> The computable sequences and numbers are therefore enumerable.

You can enumerate the computable sequences by listing all possible description numbers, since these are just integers. The unstated implication is that the computable numbers are only an enumerable subset of the real numbers. Because the computable numbers are enumerable and the real numbers are not, there are many real numbers that are not computable. This, however, is a subject that will be explored more in later sections.

> Let us find a description number for the machine I of § 3.

That machine was originally defined by this table:

Configuration		Behaviour	
m-config.	*symbol*	*operations*	*final m-config.*
b	None	P0, R	c
c	None	R	e
e	None	P1, R	f
f	None	R	b

When we rename the *m*-configurations its table becomes:

q_1	S_0	PS_1, R	q_2
q_2	S_0	PS_0, R	q_3
q_3	S_0	PS_2, R	q_4
q_4	S_0	PS_0, R	q_1

This is a very straightforward translation.

Other tables could be obtained by adding irrelevant lines such as

q_1	S_1	PS_1, R	q_2

That is, *other tables that produce the same computable sequence* could be obtained by adding lines that never come into play. If the tape is blank when the machine begins, and it always shifts right when a square is printed, the machine will never scan the digit 0.

Our first standard form would be

$$q_1\, S_0\, S_1\, R\, q_2;\ q_2\, S_0\, S_0\, R\, q_3;\ q_3\, S_0\, S_2\, R\, q_4;\ q_4\, S_0\, S_0\, R\, q_1\, ;.$$

That's just taking the four-line table and separating the configurations with semicolons. Converting this to the Standard Description form requires replacing q_i with D followed by a quantity of i A's (one or more) and replacing S_j with D followed by j C's (zero or more).

> The standard description is
>
> *DADDCRDAA ;DAADDRDAAA ;*
>
> *DAAADDCCRDAAAA ;DAAAADDRDA ;*

The Standard Description can be hard to read, but it's used a lot so you should try to get accustomed to it. To decode it into its components, begin by taking note of each *D*. Each *D* represents either a configuration or a symbol.

- If the *D* is followed by one or more *A*'s, it's a configuration. The configuration number is the number of *A*'s.
- If the *D* is *not* followed by any *A*'s, it's a symbol. The *D* in this case is followed by 0 or more *C*'s. *D* by itself is a blank, *DC* is a 0, *DCC* is a 1, and more *C*'s indicate other symbols.

Turing does not use the Description Number as much as the Standard Description. The Description Number exists more in abstract; Turing doesn't perform any calculations with the number. For the example Turing is showing, you can replace *A* with 1, *C* with 2, *D* with 3, *R* with 5 and the semicolon with 7 to create a description number:

> A description number is
>
> 31332531173113353111731113322531111731111335317
>
> and so is
>
> 3133253117311335311173111332253111173111133531731323253117

The second of those numbers is the same as the first except it has extra digits at the end (31323253117) corresponding to the "irrelevant" configuration $q_1 S_1 S_1 R q_2$ that Turing defined. The point is this: These two numbers define two different machines, but the two machines both compute exactly the same number, which (as you'll recall) is the binary version of 1/3. A machine with its configurations rearranged still calculates the same number, but its Description Number is different.

These numbers are huge! Turing obviously doesn't care how large the numbers are. To represent q_{35}, for example, he might have figured out some way to embed the number 35 in the Description Number, but no. To represent q_{35}, the Standard Description uses:

DAAAAAAAAAAAAAAAAAAAAAAAAAAAAAAAAAAAA

and the Description Number includes the digits

3111111111111111111111111111111111111111

not only once, but at least twice!

The accomplishment here is quite interesting. Consider a Turing Machine that calculates π. Normally, we indicate the digits of π with an infinite sequence:

$$\pi = 3.14159265358979323846264338327795\ldots$$

Now we can represent π with a *finite* integer — the Description Number of the Turing Machine that calculates the digits. Which is the better representation of π? The first 32 digits followed by an ellipsis? Or the Description Number of the Turing Machine that can generate as many digits as our patience will allow? In a sense, the Description Number is a more fundamental numerical representation of π because it describes the algorithm of calculating the number.

By reducing each machine to a number, Turing has also made it possible, in effect, to generate machines just by enumerating the positive integers. Not every positive integer is a valid Description Number of a Turing Machine, and many valid Description Numbers do not describe circle-free machines, but this enumeration certainly includes all circle-free Turing Machines, each of which corresponds to a computable number. Therefore, computable numbers are enumerable.

That's an important finding, although possibly a disturbing one, for it implies that most — nay, from what we know about the extent of the real numbers, *virtually all* — real numbers are not computable.

This revelation, combined with some mathematical paradoxes and investigations into quantum gravity, have prompted mathematician Gregory Chaitin to ask "How Real are Real Numbers?"[11] The evidence of the existence of real numbers is slim indeed.

To modern programmers it is natural to think of computer programs being represented by numbers, because a program's executable file is simply a collection of consecutive bytes. We don't normally think of these bytes as forming a single number, but they certainly could. For example, the Microsoft Word 2003 executable is the file WinWord.exe, and that file is 12,047,560 bytes in size. That's about 96 million bits, or 29 million decimal digits, so the number representing WinWord.exe is somewhere in the region of $10^{29,000,000}$. That's certainly a big number. In a book of about 50 lines per page and 50 digits per line, that number would stretch out over more than 11,000 pages. That's a much larger number than the famed googol (10^{100}), but it's still a finite integer. WinWord.exe is one of many possible executables that — like all the possible Turing Machines — turn up in

---

[11] Gregory J. Chaitin, "How Real are Real Numbers?", *International Journal of Bifurcation and Chaos*, Vol. 16 (2006), 1841–1848. Reprinted in Gregory J. Chaitin, *Thinking About Gödel and Turing: Essays on Complexity, 1970–2007* (World Scientific, 2007), 267–280.

an enumeration of the integers, along with every other word processing program, even those that haven't yet been written.

For future use, Turing finishes this section with a definition.

A number which is a description number of a circle-free machine will be called a *satisfactory* number. In § 8 it is shown that there can be no general process for determining whether a given number is satisfactory or not.

It's easy to determine whether a particular integer is a well-formed Description Number, but Turing is now asserting that there's no general process to determine whether a particular Description Number represents a circle-free machine and prints a continuing series of 0s and 1s like it's supposed to. There's no general process for determining whether the machine might scan a character it's not expecting, or gets into an infinite loop printing blanks, whether it crashes, burns, goes belly up, or ascends to the great bit bucket in the sky.

9 The Universal Machine

The machine that Turing describes in the next section of his paper is known today as the Universal Turing Machine, so called because it's the only machine we need. The individual computing machines presented earlier were not guaranteed to be implemented similarly or even to have interchangeable parts. This Universal Machine, however, can simulate other machines when supplied with their Standard Descriptions. The Universal Machine is, we would say today, *programmable*.

> ## 6. *The universal computing machine.*
>
> It is possible to invent a single machine which can be used to compute any computable sequence. If this machine $\mathcal{U}$ is supplied with a tape on the beginning of which is written the S.D of some computing machine $\mathcal{M}$,
>
> [242]
>
> then $\mathcal{U}$ will compute the same sequence as $\mathcal{M}$. In this section I explain in outline the behaviour of the machine. The next section is devoted to giving the complete table for $\mathcal{U}$.

There's that script font again. Turing uses $\mathcal{M}$ for an arbitrary machine and $\mathcal{U}$ for the Universal Machine.

When speaking of computer programs, it's common to refer to *input* and *output*. A program reads input and writes output. The machines described so far basically have no input because they begin with a blank tape. The machines generate output in the form of a sequence of 0s and 1s, temporarily interspersed, perhaps, with some other characters used as markers or a scratchpad.

In contrast, the Universal Machine $\mathcal{U}$ requires actual input, specifically a tape that contains the Standard Description of $\mathcal{M}$ — the sequences of letters A, C, D, L, N, and R that describe all the configurations of $\mathcal{M}$. The $\mathcal{U}$ machine reads and interprets that Standard Description and prints the same output that $\mathcal{M}$ would print.

But that's not entirely true: The output of U will *not* be identical to the output of M. In the general case, there is no way that U can perfectly mimic M. Machine M probably begins with a blank tape, but machine U doesn't get a blank tape — it gets a tape with the Standard Description of M already on it. What happens if M doesn't quite follow Turing's conventions but instead writes output in both directions? Any attempt to emulate M precisely could easily result in writing over that Standard Description.

Turing says that U is supplied with a tape "on the beginning of which" is a Standard Description of machine M. A tape that is infinite in both directions does not have a "beginning." Turing is implicitly restricting the output of U to that part of the tape after the Standard Description.

If we limit our consideration to machines that print in only one direction (which is Turing's convention anyway), can we write a Universal Machine that reads the Standard Description of the machine located at the beginning of a tape, and then exactly duplicates the output of the machine in the infinite blank area of the tape beyond that Standard Description?

That doesn't seem likely either. Certainly this Universal Machine would require its own scratchpad area, so its output will be different from the machine that it's trying to emulate. Even if we require only that the Universal Machine duplicate the M machine's F-squares, that Universal Machine would probably be significantly more complex than the one that Turing describes.

Turing doesn't guarantee that his Universal Machine will faithfully duplicate the output of the machine that it is emulating. He says only that "U will compute the same sequence as M." In reality, U prints a lot of extra output *in addition to* this sequence.

Turing approaches the design of the Universal Machine from a rather odd direction.

> Let us first suppose that we have a machine M' which will write down on the F-squares the successive complete configurations of M.

As you'll recall, a complete configuration is a "snapshot" of the tape after an operation has completed, together with the position of the head and the next m-configuration. The successive complete configurations provide an entire history of the operations of the machine.

> These might be expressed in the same form as on p. 235, using the second description, (C), with all symbols on one line.

That's page 92 of this book, in the form that shows the information in a single stream:

$$\mathfrak{b} : \mathfrak{d} \mathfrak{d} \mathfrak{d} \, 0 \quad 0 : \mathfrak{d} \mathfrak{d} \mathfrak{q} \, 0 \quad 0 : \dots$$

In this notation the successive complete configurations are separated by colons. Within each complete configuration, the German letter representing the next *m*-configuration precedes the next scanned symbol.

> Or, better, we could transform this description (as in §5) by replacing each *m*-configuration by "*D*" followed by "*A*" repeated the appropriate number of times, and by replacing each symbol by "*D*" followed by "*C*" repeated the appropriate number of times. The numbers of letters "*A*" and "*C*" are to agree with the numbers chosen in §5, so that, in particular, "0" is replaced by "*DC*", "1" by "*DCC*", and the blanks by "*D*".

Turing devised this Standard Description (as he called it) to encode the states of a machine. Now he is proposing to use it to represent the complete configurations.

> These substitutions are to be made after the complete configurations have been put together, as in (C). Difficulties arise if we do the substitution first.

I think what Turing means here is that *m*-configurations and symbols will now be represented with multiple symbols (for example a 1 becomes *DCC*), so care must be taken to slip in the next *m*-configuration so that it doesn't break up the code for a symbol.

> In each complete configuration the blanks would all have to be replaced by "*D*", so that the complete configuration would not be expressed as a finite sequence of symbols.

The letter *D* represents a blank square. Turing doesn't want any breaks to appear in the complete configurations. He wants each complete configuration to be an unbroken series of letters. Turing's phrase, "so that the complete configuration would not be expressed as a finite sequence of letters," is not quite clear. I suggest the word "not" should be "now." Certainly he doesn't want an infinite series of *D* symbols to represent a blank tape. Each complete configuration is finite.

> If in the description of the machine II of §3 we replace "ɔ" by "*DAA*",
> "ǝ" by "*DCCC*", "q" by "*DAAA*", then the sequence (C) becomes:
>
> *DA : DCCCDCCCDAADCDDC : DCCCDCCCDAAADCDDC* : ... (C₁)
>
> (This is the sequence of symbols on *F*-squares.)

Turing's not mentioning *all* the substitutions he's making. He's also replacing b
with *DA*, blanks with *D*, and 0s with *DC*.

The parenthetical comment refers to the output of the $\mathcal{M}'$ machine that Turing
is proposing. The normal $\mathcal{M}$ machine prints 0s and 1s on *F*-squares and uses the
E-squares for other symbols to help it in computing the 0s and 1s. The $\mathcal{M}'$ machine
prints the successive complete configurations of $\mathcal{M}$ on *F*-squares and uses the
E-squares to aid itself in constructing these successive complete configurations.

The complete configurations represented in this way can be hard to read. As I've
said before, it helps to take note of each *D*, which represents either a configuration
or a symbol.

- If the *D* is followed by one or more *A*'s, it's a configuration. The configuration number is the number of *A*'s.
- If the *D* is *not* followed by any *A*'s, it's a symbol. The *D* in this case is followed by zero or more *C*'s. *D* by itself is a blank, *DC* is a 0, *DCC* is a 1, and
  more *C*'s indicate other symbols.

> It is not difficult to see that if $\mathcal{M}$ can be constructed, then so can $\mathcal{M}'$.
> The manner of operation of $\mathcal{M}'$ could be made to depend on having the rules
> of operation (*i.e.*, the S.D) of $\mathcal{M}$ written somewhere within itself (*i.e.* within
> $\mathcal{M}'$); each step could be carried out by referring to these rules.

This idea of $\mathcal{M}'$ having the Standard Description of $\mathcal{M}$ "written somewhere
within itself" is an entirely new concept. Where is it written? How is it accessed?
Turing is pursuing this $\mathcal{M}'$ machine in a way that's distracting from his goal,
although it does seem reasonable that $\mathcal{M}'$ could be constructed.

> We have
> only to regard the rules as being capable of being taken out and ex-
> changed for others and we have something very akin to the universal
> machine.

Ahh, now it becomes a little clearer. Turing said at the outset of this section that $\mathcal{U}$ is supplied with a tape containing the Standard Description of $\mathcal{M}$. That's what "capable of being taken out and exchanged for others" means. We can give $\mathcal{U}$ a tape containing the Standard Description of whatever machine we want $\mathcal{U}$ to emulate.

Conceptually, $\mathcal{U}$ now seems almost, well, not *exactly* straightforward, but much less difficult. $\mathcal{U}$ starts with a tape on which the Standard Description of $\mathcal{M}$ is printed. It is responsible for printing the successive complete configurations of $\mathcal{M}$. The Standard Description and the complete configurations use the same encoding: Each complete configuration contains a sequence of letters, mostly indicating the symbols printed on the tape. Each complete configuration also includes a D followed by one or more A's indicating the next m-configuration preceding the scanned symbol, for example:

DAAADCC

This sequence of letters appearing in a complete configuration indicates that the next m-configuration is q_3 and the next scanned symbol is a 1. Somewhere in the Standard Description of $\mathcal{M}$ is a sequence of letters matching these letters exactly. (If not, then something has gone wrong, and $\mathcal{M}$ is not circle-free.) All that $\mathcal{U}$ needs to do to determine the next configuration is to find a match. When $\mathcal{U}$ finds the matching configuration, it has immediate access to the configuration's operation — the symbol to be printed, a code indicating how to move the head, and the next m-configuration. $\mathcal{U}$ must then create a new complete configuration based on the last complete configuration and incorporating the printed character and the next m-configuration.

The Universal Machine might be easier to conceive if you consider that the first complete configuration of a machine's operation is trivial, and each step from one complete configuration to the next involves only a small change. It's really just a matter of comparing and copying symbols, and Turing has already defined an arsenal of m-functions that perform these very chores.

For now he's still talking about $\mathcal{M}'$ rather than $\mathcal{U}$, and $\mathcal{M}'$ only prints the complete configurations of $\mathcal{M}$.

One thing is lacking : at present the machine $\mathcal{M}'$ prints no figures.

That's true. In all this excitement we've forgot that $\mathcal{M}'$ (or $\mathcal{U}$) is only printing successive complete configurations of $\mathcal{M}$ on F-squares using letters A, C, and D and the colon separators, and it's probably using E-squares as a scratch pad. The real object of this game is to print 0s and 1s.

> We
> may correct this by printing between each successive pair of complete
> configurations the figures which appear in the new configuration but not
> in the old. Then (C$_1$) becomes
>
> $$DDA : 0 : 0 : DCCCDCCCDAADCDDC : DCCC.... \quad (C_2)$$
>
> It is not altogether obvious that the E-squares leave enough room for
> the necessary "rough work", but this is, in fact, the case.

The extra D at the beginning of line (C$_2$) is a typographical error. The only
difference between (C$_2$) and the beginning of (C$_1$) should be the two 0s and the
colons. These are the result of the first operation, so they are printed after the first
complete configuration.

Turing wants M' (and U) to print the same 0s and 1s that M prints, because
then it's possible to say that M' computes the same sequence as M. The only
difference is that these digits will now be buried in the output between successive
complete configurations of the machine.

This is why Turing requires his machines to print the computed numbers
consecutively, and to not change a number once it's been printed. Without this
requirement, the numbers printed by M' (and U) would be a total jumble.

Turing says that M' should print all figures (0s or 1s) "which appear in the new
configuration but not in the old." When you reduce a machine to the standard
form (that is, only one printed symbol and one head movement per operation),
there are frequently occasions when the machine scans a 0 or 1 symbol on its
way somewhere else. The machine must reprint the 0 or 1 in these cases. M'
should ignore the times that M prints a 0 or 1 over itself. M' (and, by implication,
the Universal Machine) should print a 0 or 1 only *when the scanned symbol is a
blank*.

Turing concludes this section by suggesting that the complete configurations
could be expressed in numerical form, but this is something he never uses:

> The sequences of letters between the colons in expressions such as
> (C$_1$) may be used as standard descriptions of the complete configurations.
> When the letters are replaced by figures, as in §5, we shall have a numerical
>
> [243]
>
> description of the complete configuration, which may be called its descrip-
> tion number.

Now let's forget all about $\mathcal{M}'$ and start looking at $\mathcal{U}$.

It is well known that Turing's description of the Universal Machine contains a few bugs. (It's quite surprising how few bugs it contains considering that Turing wasn't able to simulate it on a real computer.) In analyzing the Universal Machine, I am indebted to Emil Post's corrections[1] and an analysis by Donald Davies.[2]

Because the Universal Machine is so essential to Turing's arguments in the rest of his paper, he proves the existence of such a machine by actually constructing it in full, excruciating detail. Once you understand the basic mechanism, however, you might find these details to be rather tedious. No one will punish you if you don't assimilate every symbol and function in Turing's description.

> ### 7. *Detailed description of the universal machine.*
>
> A table is given below of the behaviour of this universal machine. The m-configurations of which the machine is capable are all those occurring in the first and last columns of the table, together with all those which occur when we write out the unabbreviated tables of those which appear in the table in the form of m-functions. *E.g.*, $\mathfrak{e}$ (anf) appears in the table and is an m-function.

The m-configuration anf is part of Turing's Universal Machine. Towards the end of the machine, a particular configuration has $\mathfrak{e}$(anf) in its *final m-config* column. The skeleton table for $\mathfrak{e}$ appears on page 239 of Turing's paper (and page 125 of this book):

$\mathfrak{e}(\mathfrak{C})$	ə	R	$\mathfrak{e}_1(\mathfrak{C})$
	Not ə	L	$\mathfrak{e}(\mathfrak{C})$
$\mathfrak{e}_1(\mathfrak{C})$	Any	R, E, R	$\mathfrak{e}_1(\mathfrak{C})$
	None		$\mathfrak{C}$

---

[1] In an appendix to the paper Emil Post, "Recursive Unsolvability of a Problem of Thue," *The Journal of Symbolic Logic*, Vol. 12, No. 1 (Mar. 1947), 1–11. The entire paper is reprinted in Martin Davis, ed., *The Undecidable* (Raven Press, 1965), 293–303. The appendix is reprinted in B. Jack Copeland, ed., *The Essential Turing* (Oxford University Press, 2004), 97–101.

[2] Donald W. Davies, "Corrections to Turing's Universal Computing Machine" in C. Jack Copeland, ed., *The Essential Turing*, 103-124. Anyone interested in programming a simulation of the Universal Machine will want to study Davies' paper.

Turing now shows the unabbreviated table when $\mathfrak{anf}$ is substituted for $\mathfrak{C}$:

Its unabbreviated table is (see p. 239)

$\mathfrak{e}(\mathfrak{anf})$	$\begin{cases} \text{ə} \\ \text{not ə} \end{cases}$	$\begin{matrix} R \\ L \end{matrix}$	$\begin{matrix} \mathfrak{e}_1(\mathfrak{anf}) \\ \mathfrak{e}(\mathfrak{anf}) \end{matrix}$
$\mathfrak{e}_1(\mathfrak{anf})$	$\begin{cases} \text{Any} \\ \text{None} \end{cases}$	$\begin{matrix} R,E,R \\ \, \end{matrix}$	$\begin{matrix} \mathfrak{e}_1(\mathfrak{anf}) \\ \mathfrak{anf} \end{matrix}$

Consequently $\mathfrak{e}_1(\mathfrak{anf})$ is an m-configuration of $\mathcal{U}$.

Turing begins by describing a tape encoded with the Standard Description of some machine. This is the tape the Universal Machine will read and interpret.

When $\mathcal{U}$ is ready to start work the tape running through it bears on it the symbol ə on an F-square and again ə on the next E-square; after this, on F-squares only, comes the S.D of the machine followed by a double colon "::" (a single symbol, on an F-square). The S.D consists of a number of instructions, separated by semi-colons.

That, by the way, is Turing's first use of the word *instructions* in this paper. The word is appropriate here because the configurations of the machines are now playing a different role; they have become instructions to the Universal Machine.

Earlier (in Section 5 on page 140 of this book) Turing showed each configuration followed by a semicolon, however, the Universal Machine requires that each instruction *begin* with a semicolon. This is just one of several little "bugs" in the description of the Universal Machine.

To illustrate the workings of $\mathcal{U}$, let's supply it with a simple $\mathcal{M}$. This machine is a simplified form of the machine that prints alternating 0s and 1s:

m-config.	symbol	operations	final m-config.
q_1	S_0	PS_1, R	q_2
q_2	S_0	PS_2, R	q_1

This simplified machine has just two configurations rather than four and doesn't skip any squares. Here's a tape prepared in accordance with Turing's directions, but with the semicolons preceding each instruction. Because the tape is so long, I've shown it on two lines:

| ə | ə | ; | | D | | A | | D | | D | | C | | R | | D | | A | | A | |

| | ; | | D | | A | | A | | D | | D | | C | | C | | R | | D | | A | | :: | | ... |

The double colon separates the instructions of M from the successive complete configurations of M that U will print. Turing reminds us how these instructions are coded:

> **Each instruction consists of five consecutive parts**
>
> (i) "D" followed by a sequence of letters "A". This describes the relevant m-configuration.

At least one A must follow a D to signify an m-configuration; that is, the configurations begin at q_1 and there is no q_0.

> (ii) "D" followed by a sequence of letters "C". This describes the scanned symbol.

For symbols, a D by itself means a blank; a D with one C means 0, and with two C's means 1.

> (iii) "D" followed by another sequence of letters "C". This describes the symbol into which the scanned symbol is to be changed.
>
> (iv) "L", "R", or "N", describing whether the machine is to move to left, right, or not at all.
>
> (v) "D" followed by a sequence of letters "A". This describes the final m-configuration.

The Universal Machine needs to print complete configurations, which require the letters A, C, and D, and it also needs to print the computable sequence, which is composed of 0s and 1s. The Universal Machine uses lower-case letters as markers in the E-squares. In summary:

> The machine U is to be capable of printing "A", "C", "D", "0", "1", "u", "v", "w", "x", "y", "z".

Turing forgot to include the colon (which separates the successive complete configurations) in this list.

> The S.D is formed from ";",
> "*A*", "*C*", "*D*", "*L*", "*R*", "*N*".

Turing next presents one last function that the Universal Machine requires.

[244]

Subsidiary skeleton table.

con $(\mathfrak{C}, \alpha)$	Not A	R, R	con($\mathfrak{C}, \alpha$)
	A	L, Pα, R	con$_1$($\mathfrak{C}, \alpha$)
con$_1$($\mathfrak{C}, \alpha$)	A	R, Pα, R	con$_1$($\mathfrak{C}, \alpha$)
	D	R, Pα, R	con$_2$($\mathfrak{C}, \alpha$)
con$_2$($\mathfrak{C}, \alpha$)	C	R, Pα, R	con$_2$($\mathfrak{C}, \alpha$)
	Not C	R, R	$\mathfrak{C}$

con $(\mathfrak{C}, \ \alpha)$. Starting from an *F*-square, *S* say, the sequence *C* of symbols describing a configuration closest on the right of *S* is marked out with letters α. → $\mathfrak{C}$.

con $(\mathfrak{C}, \ )$. In the final configuration the machine is scanning the square which is four squares to the right of the last square of *C*. *C* is left unmarked.

The *m*-function con stands for "configuration," and it's missing a line[3]:

con$_1$($\mathfrak{C}, \alpha$)   None   PD, R, Pα, R, R, R $\mathfrak{C}$

We'll see how this missing line comes into play shortly.

The job of the con function is to mark a configuration with the symbol given as the second argument. Suppose the head is on the semicolon preceding an instruction:

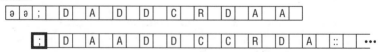

The con function moves right two squares at a time until it encounters an *A*. It prints an α to the left of the *A*. The con$_1$ function continues printing markers to the right of each *A* until it encounters a *D*. It prints a marker to the right of that

---

[3]As suggested by Post, "Recursive Unsolvability of a Problem of Thue," 7.

D as well and then goes to con$_2$. The con$_2$ function prints markers to the right of each C (if any). For this example, there are no C's in the configuration because the scanned square is a blank, so the result is:

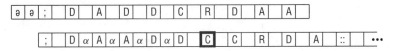

The explanatory paragraphs in the skeleton table for con are a bit confusing because Turing uses the letter C to stand for a whole sequence of symbols defining a configuration, and the same letter is part of the Standard Description. The first sentence of the second paragraph (beginning "In the final configuration") indicates that the head is left four squares to the right of the last square of the configuration (that is, the last square of the scanned character). The sentence "C is left unmarked" meaning "The configuration is left unmarked" applies only when the second argument to con is blank.

The description of the Universal Machine occupies just two pages in Turing's paper. Turing has previously defined his m-functions with such skill that in many cases, the m-configurations of $\mathcal{U}$ simply refer to a particular function. As usual, the machine begins with m-configuration b:

The table for $\mathcal{U}$.		
b	$\mathfrak{f}(b_1, b_1, ::)$	b. The machine prints
b$_1$ $R, R, P:, R, R, PD, R, R, PA$ anf		$: DA$ on the F-squares after $:: \rightarrow$ anf.

The m-function $\mathfrak{f}$ finds the double colon that separates the instructions from the complete configurations. As you'll recall, each complete configuration shows all the symbols on the tape, with the m-configuration preceding the scanned square. When a machine begins, the first m-configuration is q_1, which has a Standard Description of DA. That's what b$_1$ prints, starting with a colon that will delimit each complete configuration:

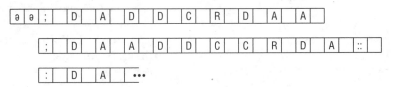

The next m-configuration of $\mathcal{U}$ is anf, which Donald Davies suggests stands for *anfang*, the German word for *beginning*. The $\mathfrak{g}$ function in the first line was mistakenly indicated as q in the tables of functions. It searches for the last occurrence of its second argument:

$\mathfrak{anf}$		$\mathfrak{g}(\mathfrak{anf}_1, :)$	$\mathfrak{anf}$. The machine marks the configuration in the last complete configuration with y. $\rightarrow$ $\mathfrak{tom}$.
$\mathfrak{anf}_1$		$\mathfrak{con}(\mathfrak{tom}, y)$	

After $\mathfrak{g}$ finds the colon (which precedes the current complete configuration), $\mathfrak{con}$ marks the m-configuration with the letter y. The additional line I've added to $\mathfrak{con}_1$ also comes into play: It prints a D (representing a blank square) and marks that square as well:

| ə | ə | ; | | D | | A | | D | | D | | C | | R | | D | | A | | A | |

| ; | | D | | A | | A | | D | | D | | C | | C | | R | | D | | A | | :: | |

| : | | D | y | A | y | D | y | ••• |

Whenever $\mathfrak{con}$ is marking an m-configuration in a complete configuration and comes to a blank square when it is expecting to find a D that represents the scanned symbol, $\mathfrak{con}_1$ prints a D. This is how the tape gets progressively longer as more squares are required.

Now the machine must locate the instruction whose configuration matches the symbols in the complete configuration marked with y. There are multiple instructions, of course, but they are easy to locate because each one is preceded by a semicolon. These instructions are tested starting with the last instruction and working towards the beginning. The m-configuration $\mathfrak{tom}$ looks like *fom* but is actually *kom*, possibly one of several abbreviations meant to suggest the word *compare*.

	;	R, Pz, L	$\mathfrak{con}(\mathfrak{tmp}, x)$	$\mathfrak{tom}$. The machine finds the last semi-colon not marked with z. It marks this semi-colon with z and the configuration following it with x.
$\mathfrak{tom}$	z	L, L	$\mathfrak{tom}$	
	not z nor ;	L	$\mathfrak{tom}$	

The first time through, tom finds the last (rightmost) instruction, prints a z following the semicolon, and then marks the configuration that follows using con.

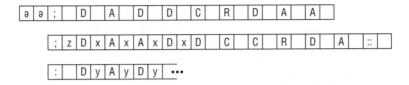

The z marker indicates that this instruction has been checked. On subsequent attempts to find a match, tom skips past all semicolons previously marked with z.

The m-configuration fmp (another abbreviation for *compare?*) uses cpe to compare the configuration marked x (which is the m-configuration and scanned symbol of an instruction) and the configuration marked y (which is current m-configuration and scanned symbol indicated in the complete configuration):

fmp	$cpe\big(e(fom, x, y), sim, x, y\big)$	fmp. The machine compares the sequences marked x and y. It erases all letters x and y. $\rightarrow$ sim if they are alike. Otherwise $\rightarrow$ fom.

The cpe function erases the markers as it compares the letters marked with those markers. If there's a match, then all the x and y markers have been erased, and we head to sim (meaning *similar*).

If the configurations marked x and y do not match (as they won't in our example), then the first argument of cpe takes over, which is an e (erase) function that erases all the remaining x and y markers and eventually retreats to fom to try the next instruction.

A little problem with the fmp function is that Turing never defined a version of e that has one m-configuration argument and two symbol arguments. Moreover, he can't go back to fom because some or all of the y markers have been erased by cpe. He really needs to go back to anf to mark the configuration again. Donald Davies suggests that the instruction should really read:

$$fmp \qquad cpe\big(e(e(anf, x), y), sim, x, y\big)$$

In our example, $\mathfrak{anf}_1$ will re-mark the m-configuration and scanned symbol in the complete configuration, and $\mathfrak{fom}$ will mark the next instruction (working backwards through the instructions):

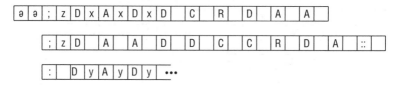

This time, the $\mathfrak{cpe}$ function invoked by $\mathfrak{fmp}$ will detect a match and head to $\mathfrak{sim}$. All the x and y markers will be gone, but the z markers remain. The leftmost z marker precedes the instruction that $\mathcal{U}$ must carry out. Turing summarizes the progress so far:

> $\mathfrak{anf}$. Taking the long view, the last instruction relevant to the last configuration is found. It can be recognised afterwards as the instruction following the last semi-colon marked z. $\rightarrow$ $\mathfrak{sim}$.

Actually, it's the *first* (leftmost) semicolon marked z, but the last instruction tested. The m-configuration $\mathfrak{sim}$ begins by using $\mathfrak{f}'$ to find that marker and position itself at the semicolon preceding the instruction. As you'll recall, the instruction has five parts: The m-configuration, the scanned symbol, the symbol to print, an L, N, or R, and the final m-configuration.

[245]

$\mathfrak{sim}$	$\mathfrak{f}'(\mathfrak{sim}_1, \mathfrak{sim}_1, z)$	
$\mathfrak{sim}_1$	$\mathfrak{con}(\mathfrak{sim}_2,)$	
$\mathfrak{sim}_2$ $\begin{cases} A \\ \text{not } A \end{cases}$	$\begin{matrix} & \mathfrak{sim}_3 \\ R, Pu, R, R, R & \mathfrak{sim}_2 \end{matrix}$	
$\mathfrak{sim}_3$ $\begin{cases} \text{not } A \\ A \end{cases}$	$\begin{matrix} L, Py & \mathfrak{e}(\mathfrak{mf}, z) \\ L, Py, R, R, R & \mathfrak{sim}_3 \end{matrix}$	

$\mathfrak{sim}$. The machine marks out the instructions. That part of the instructions which refers to operations to be carried out is marked with u, and the final m-configuration with y. The letters z are erased.

The m-configuration $\mathfrak{sim}_1$ refers to the $\mathfrak{con}$ function with a blank second argument. This essentially skips past the m-configuration and the scanned symbol, putting the head at the second character of the print operation.

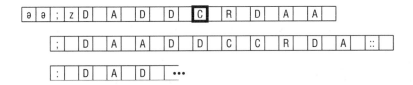

The second line for m-configuration $\mathfrak{sim}_2$ is incorrect: Emil Post suggests it should move the head *left* before printing a u. The two m-configurations $\mathfrak{sim}_2$ and $\mathfrak{sim}_3$ mark the operation (the symbol to be printed and the head-movement letter) and the next m-configuration. The $\mathfrak{e}$ function erases the z marker before heading to $\mathfrak{mf}$.

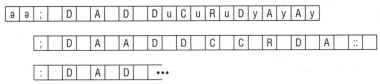

The m-configuration $\mathfrak{mf}$ (which looks like mf but is actually mk and perhaps stands for *mark*) now marks the last complete configuration. The first argument to the $\mathfrak{g}$ function (which is mistakenly q in the tables of functions) should be $\mathfrak{mf}_1$ rather than $\mathfrak{mf}$.

$\mathfrak{mf}$			$\mathfrak{g}(\mathfrak{mf}, :)$	
$\mathfrak{mf}_1$	not A	R, R	$\mathfrak{mf}_1$	
	A	L, L, L, L	$\mathfrak{mf}_2$	
$\mathfrak{mf}_2$	C	R, Px, L, L, L	$\mathfrak{mf}_2$	
	$:$		$\mathfrak{mf}_4$	
	D	R, Px, L, L, L	$\mathfrak{mf}_3$	
$\mathfrak{mf}_3$	not $:$	R, Pv, L, L, L	$\mathfrak{mf}_3$	
	$:$		$\mathfrak{mf}_4$	
$\mathfrak{mf}_4$			$\mathfrak{con}\big(\mathfrak{l}(\mathfrak{l}(\mathfrak{mf}_5)), \big)$	
$\mathfrak{mf}_5$	Any	R, Pw, R	$\mathfrak{mf}_5$	
	None	$P:$	$\mathfrak{sh}$	

$\mathfrak{mf}$. The last complete configuration is marked out into four sections. The configuration is left unmarked. The symbol directly preceding it is marked with x. The remainder of the complete configuration is divided into two parts, of which the first is marked with v and the last with w. A colon is printed after the whole. $\rightarrow \mathfrak{sh}$.

The m-configuration $\mathfrak{mf}$ uses $\mathfrak{g}$ to find the rightmost colon. That colon precedes the last complete configuration. The complete configuration is on F-squares and, in general, consists mostly of *D*'s followed by zero or more *C*'s, each of which represents a symbol on the tape. Buried somewhere within these symbols is an *m*-configuration, which is a *D* followed by one or more *A*'s.

The *m*-configuration $\mathfrak{mf}_1$ looks for the *m*-configuration buried within the complete configuration. When it finds an *A*, it moves the head left to the last symbol of the square that precedes the *m*-configuration. That square is marked with *x*. Then, $\mathfrak{mf}_3$ has the job of marking all the preceding characters with *v*.

When $\mathfrak{mf}_3$ gets to the colon, $\mathfrak{mf}_4$ takes over. It uses con to skip over the *m*-configuration and the scanned character. It stops when it finds something other than a *C*. Except for the scanned character, the other symbols are marked with *w*. Finally, $\mathfrak{mf}_5$ prints a colon.

Here's a complete configuration that's a bit more complex than the simple example we've been looking at:

| : | | D | | C | | D | | D | | A | | D | | C | | D | | D | | C | | | | ••• |

This complete configuration represents a tape starting with a 0 (*DC*) and a blank (*D*). The next square is the scanned square, indicated by the configuration q_1 (*DA*). The scanned square is a 0 (*DC*), which is followed by a blank (*D*) and a 0 (*DC*). When $\mathfrak{mf}$ is through with this, it looks like this:

| : | | D | v | C | v | D | x | D | | A | | D | | C | | D | w | D | w | C | w | : | | ••• |

The only thing unmarked is the configuration (which consists of the *m*-configuration *DA* and the scanned symbol *DC*).

In our much simpler example, there are no symbols to the left of the *m*-configuration and no symbols to the right of the scanned square, so the *v*, *x*, and *w* markers don't play a role:

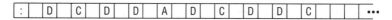

| ə | ə | ; | | D | | A | | D | | D | u | C | u | R | u | D | y | A | y | A | y |

| ; | | D | | A | | A | | D | | D | | C | | C | | R | | D | | A | | :: |

| : | | D | | A | | D | | : | | ••• |

Everything is now marked. The operation and final *m*-configuration of the instruction is marked with *u* and *y*, and portions of the complete configuration are marked with *v*, *x*, and *w*.

The Universal Machine needs to print a 0 or 1 if the instruction is printing a 0 or 1 except in those cases when a machine reprints a 0 and 1 because it's just scanned a 0 or 1. The Universal Machine should print a 0 or 1 only if the scanned square is blank. That's the job of $\mathfrak{sh}$ (which may stand for *show*).

$\mathfrak{sh}$			$\mathfrak{f}(\mathfrak{sh}_1, \text{inst}, u)$
$\mathfrak{sh}_1$		L, L, L	$\mathfrak{sh}_2$
$\mathfrak{sh}_2$	D	R, R, R, R	$\mathfrak{sh}_2$
	not D		inst
$\mathfrak{sh}_3$	C	R, R	$\mathfrak{sh}_4$
	not C		inst
$\mathfrak{sh}_4$	C	R, R	$\mathfrak{sh}_5$
	not C		$\mathfrak{pe}_2(\text{inst}, 0, :)$
$\mathfrak{sh}_5$	C		inst
	not C		$\mathfrak{pe}_2(\text{inst}, 1, :)$

$\mathfrak{sh}$. The instructions (marked u) are examined. If it is found that they involve "Print 0" or "Print 1", then 0: or 1: is printed at the end.

First, $\mathfrak{sh}$ locates the leftmost u marker, and $\mathfrak{sh}_1$ moves the head left three places to be positioned over the last symbol representing the scanned square. That symbol will be a D if the scanned square is a blank. If it's not D, then the rest of these m-configurations are skipped by heading to inst.

If the scanned character is a blank, then $\mathfrak{sh}_2$ goes to $\mathfrak{sh}_3$ (not $\mathfrak{sh}_2$ as the table indicates) and then $\mathfrak{sh}_3$, $\mathfrak{sh}_4$, and $\mathfrak{sh}_5$ check if the printed instruction is DC (to print 0) or DCC (print 1). If so, then $\mathfrak{pe}_2$ prints that figure and a colon at the end of the tape. The example tape now looks like this:

The $\mathfrak{sh}$ section of the table is obviously simplified by the use of binary numbers rather than decimal. Decimal numbers would require eight more m-configurations ($\mathfrak{sh}_6$ through $\mathfrak{sh}_{13}$) to print digits 2 through 9.

Whether a 0 or 1, or neither, is printed, the Universal Machine goes to inst (which may stand for *instruction* but perhaps *instigate* is more descriptive). The last remaining job is to render the next complete configuration of $\mathcal{M}$. The next complete configuration includes all the symbols in the current configuration marked x, v, and w because those symbols will remain unchanged. The m-configuration and the scanned square, however, will be replaced. They will be replaced with the m-configuration marked y and the symbol marked with u.

The inst table has another reference to the g function that was defined originally as q. Also, the ec_5 function on the fifth line should be ce_5 like the third and fourth lines.

[246]

inst			$g(l(inst_1), u)$	inst. The next complete
$inst_1$	α	R, E	$inst_1(\alpha)$	configuration is written down,
$inst_1(L)$			$ce_5 (ov, v, y, x, u, w)$	carrying out the marked instruc-
$inst_1(R)$			$ce_5 (ov, v, x, u, y, w)$	tions. The letters u, v, w, x, y
$inst_1(N)$			$ec_5 (ov, v, x, y, u, w)$	are erased. $\rightarrow$ anf.
ov			$e(anf)$	

The function ce_5 wasn't actually defined, nor was ce_4. Basing them on ce_3 we can easily create them:

$$ce_4 (\mathfrak{B}, \alpha, \beta, \gamma, \delta) \qquad ce(ce_3 (\mathfrak{B}, \beta, \gamma, \delta), \alpha)$$
$$ce_5 (\mathfrak{B}, \alpha, \beta, \gamma, \delta, \varepsilon) \qquad ce(ce_4 (\mathfrak{B}, \beta, \gamma, \delta, \varepsilon), \alpha)$$

The ce_5 function sequentially copies symbols marked α to the end of the tape, then symbols marked β, and so forth, erasing the markers in the process.

The m-configuration inst refers to g, which goes to the rightmost symbol marked u; that symbol is L, R, or N. The m-configuration $inst_1$ scans that symbol, erases it, and then goes to $inst_1(L)$, $inst_1(R)$, or $inst_1(N)$ depending on the symbol. It's clear what Turing wants to do here, but I really must protest the introduction of a new syntax at this point in the machine, particularly when it's not necessary. Let's replace the entire $inst_1$ configuration with the following:

$$inst_1 \begin{cases} L & R, E & ce_5 (ov, v, y, x, u, w) \\ R & R, E & ce_5 (ov, v, x, u, y, w) \\ N & R, E & ce_5 (ov, v, x, y, u, w) \end{cases}$$

In all three cases, the squares marked v are copied to the end of the tape first, and those marked w are copied last. The symbols marked v are all those on the left part of the complete configuration up to (and not including) the square to the left of the scanned square. That square is marked x. The symbols marked w are all those to the right of the scanned square.

The three copies in the middle of ce_5 depend on whether the head is moving left, right, or not at all. The order is:

Left: Next m-configuration / Symbol left of head / Printed symbol.
Right: Symbol left of head / Printed symbol / Next m-configuration.
None: Symbol left of head / Next m-configuration / Printed symbol.

For example, if the head is moving left, then the next m-configuration is inserted before the square to the left of the previous head position. If the head is moving right, the next m-configuration is to the right of the printed symbol.

Each of the ce_5 functions goes to $\mathfrak{ov}$ (which probably stands for *over*). The $\mathfrak{e}$ function erases all E-squares, and goes to $\mathfrak{anf}$ for the next move. Our tape now looks like this:

| ə | ə | ; | | D | | A | | D | | D | | C | | R | | D | | A | | A | | |

| | ; | | D | | A | | A | | D | | D | | C | | C | | R | | D | | A | | :: | |

| | : | | D | | A | | D | | : | | 0 | | : | | D | | C | | D | | A | | A | | ... |

The second complete configuration contains the symbols DC (meaning 0) followed by DAA, which indicates the new m-configuration q_2.

The Universal Machine as Turing has defined it has a few limitations. It cannot emulate just any general Turing Machine. It won't work right with any machine that moves its head anywhere left of its initial position because it has no way of inserting blanks to the left of the complete configurations. (Indeed, the process of inserting blanks to the *right* is something that Turing omitted in the $\mathfrak{con}$ function.) The Universal Machine also works correctly only with machines that replace blanks with 0s or 1s and do so in a uniform left-to-right manner. The Universal Machine can handle machines that perform otherwise, but it won't print the correct sequence of 0s and 1s.

Despite these limitations, and the little misprints and bugs, Turing has done something quite extraordinary. He has demonstrated the generality of computation by showing that a single universal machine can be suitably programmed to carry out the operation of any computing machine. Says one acclaimed book on computability: "Turing's theorem on the existence of a universal Turing machine [is] one of the intellectual landmarks of the last century."[4]

All of which prompts the question:

Did Alan Turing invent the computer?

---

[4]John P. Burgess, preface, in George S. Boolos, John P. Burgess, and Richard C. Jeffrey, *Computability and Logic*, fourth edition (Cambridge University Press, 2002), xi.

10 Computers and Computability

By imagining a computing machine that does almost nothing, Turing was actually conceiving a very versatile "general purpose" computer. This was a revolutionary concept. The common assumption at the time was that computers would be designed specifically for particular types of jobs. The early analog computer known as the Differential Analyzer (designed and built by M.I.T. professor Vannevar Bush and his students in the 1920s) exemplified this approach. The Differential Analyzer did something very important — solve ordinary differential equations — but that was all it did.

Even people deeply involved in building digital computers often didn't grasp the generality of digital logic. Howard Aiken, for example, was one of the computer's true pioneers and had been working with digital computers since 1937. Yet, in 1956 Aiken said:

> [I]f it should turn out that the basic logics of a machine designed for the numerical solution of differential equations coincide with the logics of a machine intended to make bills for a department store, I would regard this as the most amazing coincidence I have ever encountered.[1]

Turing, who visualized the computer as a logic machine, knew better. While most early computer builders thought in terms of hardware, Turing had been writing software since 1936. To Turing, even basic arithmetical operations like addition could be achieved in software. Compare Aiken's 1956 statement with what Turing wrote in 1950:

> This special property of digital computers, that they can mimic any discrete state machine, is described by saying that they are

[1]Paul Ceruzzi, *Reckoners: The Prehistory of the Digital Computer, from Relays to the Stored Program Concept, 1935–1945* (Greenwood Press, 1983), 43. Ceruzzi's source is Howard Aiken, "The Future of Automatic Computing Machinery," *Elektronische Rechenanlage und Informationsverarbeitung* (Darmstadt, 1956), 33.

> *universal* machines. The existence of machines with this property has the important consequence that, considerations of speed apart, it is unnecessary to design various new machines to do various computing processes. They can all be done with one digital computer, suitably programmed for each case. It will be seen that as a consequence of this all digital computers are in a sense equivalent.[2]

Turing includes the important qualification "considerations of speed apart." Some would argue that where computers are involved, speed isn't everything; it's the *only* thing. Whenever people want specialized computers — for example, to do computer-generated imagery (CGI) for a multimillion dollar Hollywood blockbuster — speed is usually a primary consideration, and beefed-up memory capacity doesn't hurt either. In actual number-crunching capabilities, however, all digital computers are universal.

Alan Turing's status in the general history of computing has never been quite clear. In one standard history[3] he barely merits mention, but when an eminent mathematician writes a history that treats the computer as a physical embodiment of mathematical concepts,[4] Turing becomes a principal player. How Turing fares in the computing history books really depends on whether the computer is approached from an engineering and commercial perspective, or from a mathematical and academic one.

One intriguing role that Turing played involves his relationship with John von Neumann. The two men first met in April 1935 when von Neumann came from Princeton to Cambridge to deliver a lecture course on almost-periodic functions. Soon after that, Turing decided he wanted to go to Princeton University himself.[5] They had contact again when Turing got to Princeton in the fall of 1936.[6] Von Neumann once claimed to have stopped reading papers in mathematical logic following the Gödel Incompleteness Theorem,[7] so it's not clear when von Neumann actually read "On Computable Numbers." The two mathematicians had other common mathematical interests (almost-periodic functions and group theory), and those are the subjects mentioned in von Neumann's letter of June 1, 1937, recommending Turing for a Procter Fellowship for his second year at Princeton.

[2]Alan Turing, "Computing Machinery and Intelligence," *Mind*, Vol. LIX, No. 236 (October 1950), 441–2.

[3]Martin Campbell-Kelly and William Aspray, *Computer: A History of the Information Machine* (Basic Books, 1996).

[4]Martin Davis, *The Universal Computer: The Road from Leibniz to Turing* (Norton, 2000).

[5]Andrew Hodges, *Alan Turing: The Enigma* (Simon & Schuster, 1983), p. 95.

[6]Hodges, *Alan Turing*, 118.

[7]Hodges, *Alan Turing*, 124.

Before Turing left Princeton in July 1938, von Neumann offered him a job at the Institute for Advanced Study as his assistant for $1,500 a year, but Turing turned down the offer. By that time, von Neumann had almost certainly read Turing's paper. For his biography of Turing, Andrew Hodges queried physicist Stanislaw Ulam (who was also at the IAS) on von Neumann's estimation of Turing. (Von Neumann himself died in 1957 at the age of 53.) Ulam recalled traveling with von Neumann in the summer of 1938, when von Neumann suggested a game of

> writing down on a piece of paper as big a number as we could, defining it by a method which indeed has something to do with some schemata of Turing's.... von Neumann had great admiration for him and mentioned his name and "brilliant ideas" to me already, I believe, in early 1939.... At any rate von Neumann mentioned to me Turing's name several times in 1939 in conversations, concerning mechanical ways to develop formal mathematical systems.[8]

These early points of contact between Turing and von Neumann become suddenly important in September 1944 when von Neumann arrived at the Moore School of Electrical Engineering of the University of Pennsylvania. Already under construction was a computer called the ENIAC (Electronic Numerical Integrator and Computer), a 30-ton behemoth designed under the supervision of John Presper Eckert (1919–1995) and John William Mauchly (1907–1980). Even as it was being constructed, the limitations of the ENIAC had become apparent and a successor was planned, to be called the EDVAC (Electronic Discrete Variable Automatic Computer).

> From the beginning, von Neumann's perspective was not simply that of a potential user, but of a scientific and technical contributor as well. In the remaining months of 1944 and throughout 1945, when he was not at Los Alamos, he took time to attend technical conferences on the EDVAC and to make technical contributions and suggestions on logic design.[9]

Yet, when a document appeared dated June 30, 1945, entitled "First Draft of a Report on the EDVAC"[10] with John von Neumann as the sole author, a controversy was ignited, and the smoke has yet to clear. The report emphasizes important

---

[8] Hodges, *Alan Turing*, 145.

[9] Nancy Stern, "John von Neumann's Influence on Electronic Digital Computing, 1944–1946," *Annals of the History of Computing*, Vol. 2 No. 4 (October 1980), 353.

[10] Reprinted in Brian Randell, ed., *The Origins of Digital Computers* (Springer, 1973).

concepts — that the computer should be electronic, that it should work with binary numbers, and that programs should be stored in memory — but it's never been fully determined whether von Neumann originated these concepts or if he simply articulated ideas that that had been floating around the Moore School since the ENIAC days. For decades, people have referred to "von Neumann architecture" when describing digital computers, but this term is slipping out of use, partially out of respect for those many others who contributed to concepts of computer architecture.

The "First Draft of a Report on the EDVAC" makes reference to just one other publication: a paper entitled "A Logical Calculus of the Ideas Immanent in Nervous Activity" published in the *Bulletin of Mathematical Biophysics*.[11] This reference reveals von Neumann's interest in the relationship between the computer and the human brain, but it's also interesting that the authors of this paper had based their concepts of the physiology of the brain on the functions of Turing Machines. The McCulloch and Pitts paper is also cited by Norbert Wiener (1894–1964) in his classic book *Cybernetics, or Control and Communication in the Animal and the Machine* (1948). I'll have more to say about McCulloch, Pitts, Wiener, and von Neumann in Chapter 17.

The physicist Stanley Frankel, who worked with von Neumann at Los Alamos, remembers von Neumann's enthusiasm about Turing's paper in 1943 or 1944:

> Von Neumann introduced me to that paper and at his urging I studied it with care. Many people have acclaimed von Neumann as the 'father of the computer' (in a modern sense of the term) but I am sure that he would never have made that mistake himself. He might well be called the midwife, perhaps, but he firmly emphasized to me, and to others I am sure, that the fundamental conception is owing to Turing — insofar as not anticipated by Babbage, Lovelace, and others. In my view von Neumann's essential role was in making the world aware of these fundamental concepts introduced by Turing and of the development work carried out in the Moore school and elsewhere.[12]

Throughout the latter 1940s, von Neumann seems to have mentioned the importance of Turing to several people. For example, in 1946, he wrote to Norbert

---

[11]W.S. MacCulloch and W. Pitts, "A Logical Calculus of the Ideas Immanent in Nervous Activity," *Bulletin of Mathematical Biophysics*, Vol. 5 (1943), 115–133.

[12]Letter quoted in B. Jack Copeland, ed., *The Essential Turing: The Ideas that Gave Birth to the Computer Age* (Oxford University Press, 2004), 22. This letter is part of a 6-page section on "Turing, von Neumann, and the Computer" in Copeland's guide to the "Computable Numbers" paper.

Wiener of "the great positive contribution of Turing ... one, definite mechanism can be 'universal.' "[13]

Although Alan Turing is remembered mostly for his writings, his name is also linked to three major computer projects.

The first was the Colossus, a code-breaking computer developed and built at Bletchley Park in 1943. It was designed by Thomas H. Flowers (1905–1998), who had become familiar with switching circuits and electronics from his work during the 1930s in the research laboratories of the Telephone Branch of the Post Office. Although some writers have assumed that Turing was involved in the Colossus project,[14] it appears he was not. He knew about it, of course, but he "declined the invitation to take a direct part."[15] Nevertheless, the influence of Turing's paper on the logical design of the Colossus was clearly acknowledged.[16]

Turing was much more involved in a computer project at the National Physical Laboratory (NPL) at Teddington in southwest London. In 1944 the director of NPL was Sir Charles Darwin (1887–1962), whose grandfather had published some influential books on biology. Darwin created a Mathematics Division which was given the job of developing automated computing machines.

J. R. Womersley, the head of the Mathematics Division, summoned Turing to NPL for an interview in June 1945.[17] Womersley had read "On Computable Numbers" and wanted Turing to design a computer called the Automatic Computing Engine, or ACE, and if the word "engine" evoked memories of Charles Babbage, that was deliberate.

Turing, having read von Neumann's EDVAC Report and having a few ideas about computers of his own, finished the "Proposal for Development in the Mathematics Division of an Automatic Computing Engine (or ACE)" before the end of 1945. Turing's report says that it "gives a fairly complete account of the proposed calculator" but recommends that it "be read in conjunction with J. von Neumann's 'Report on the EDVAC'."[18]

Turing's proposed machine was electronic, used binary numbers, and had a 1 megahertz clock rate, although bits were transferred serially. It used mercury delay line storage, which stored bits as acoustic pulses in tubes of mercury.

---

[13] B. Jack Copeland and Diane Proudfoot, "Turing and the Computer" in B. Jack Copeland, ed., *Alan Turing's Automatic Computing Engine: The Master Codebreaker's Struggle to Build the Modern Computer* (Oxford University Press, 2005), 116.

[14] Myself included in Charles Petzold, *Code: The Hidden Language of Computer Hardware and Software* (Microsoft Press, 1999), 244.

[15] Hodges, *Alan Turing*, 268.

[16] Hodges, *Alan Turing*, 554 (note 5.7).

[17] Introduction to B.E. Carpenter and R. W. Doran, *A.M. Turing's ACE Report of 1946 and Other Papers* (MIT Press, 1986), 5–6.

[18] *ACE Report*, 21.

A five-foot tube of mercury could store 1,024 bits. Each bit required about a millisecond to travel from one end of the tube to the other, whereupon it could be accessed and recycled to the beginning of the tube. Turing expected an addition of two 32-bit numbers to require 32 microseconds (that's one bit per clock cycle) and a 32-bit multiplication to require "rather over two milliseconds."[19]

Turing's design has a fairly small number of primitive instructions, mostly transfers between memory and registers. In this sense it resembles modern Reduced Instruction Set Computers (RISC), which incorporate fast hardware and do more complex jobs in software. Turing seems to have invented the *stack* — eventually a common form of computer storage analogous to the stack of plates in a cafeteria held aloft in a well by a spring. The last plate "pushed" on the stack becomes the next plate "popped" from the stack. Turing's routines for these two operations are called BURY and UNBURY.[20]

Turing presented a more personal vision of computing in a lecture to the London Mathematical Society on February 20, 1947. "[C]omputing machines such as the ACE... are in fact practical versions of the universal machine." The complexity of the job the machine must do "is concentrated on the tape" — that is, in software — "and does not appear in the universal machine proper in any way."[21] Turing recognized the importance of speed in the computer, of course, but he tended to emphasize the advantages of large storage:

> I believe that the provision of proper storage is the key to the problem of the digital computer, and certainly if they are to be persuaded to show any sort of genuine intelligence much larger capacities than are yet available must be provided. In my opinion this problem of making a large memory available at reasonably short notice is much more important than that of doing operations such as multiplication at high speed.[22]

As might be expected, Turing clearly recognized the advantages of binary numbers over decimal:

> Binary working is the most natural thing to do with any large scale computer. It is much easier to work in the scale of two than any other, because it is so easy to produce mechanisms which have two positions of stability.[23]

[19] *ACE Report*, 116.

[20] *ACE Report*, 76.

[21] *ACE Report*, 112–113.

[22] *ACE Report*, 112.

[23] *ACE Report*, 113–114

Towards the end of the talk, Turing speculated about machines that can modify their own instruction tables:

> It would be like a pupil who had learnt much from his master, but had added much more by his own work. When this happens I feel that one is obliged to regard the machine as showing intelligence.[24]

By September 1947, Turing was feeling frustrated about the lack of progress being made on the ACE. He requested a year's sabbatical at half pay and departed to Cambridge. The expectation at NPL was that he would return for at least another two years, but that never happened. (The Pilot ACE wasn't ready until 1950, and it deviated quite a bit from Turing's original proposal.)

Instead, Turing went to join Max Newman, who had been at the University of Manchester since 1945. Newman had obtained a grant for a new Computing Machine Laboratory and was building a computer called the Mark I. In June 1948, the Mark I became "the first EDVAC-type electronic stored-program computer to be completed."[25]

Turing joined the Manchester mathematics faculty and Newman's project in September. Two months later, an arrangement was reached with Ferranti Limited, a Manchester manufacturer of electronics, to develop a machine that Ferranti would market commercially.

Turing was mostly responsible for the programming aspects of the Mark I. Around 1951, Turing was given the job of writing the first "Programmers' Handbook" for the production machine, in which Turing defined programming as "an activity by which a digital computer is made to do a man's will, by expressing this will suitably on punched tapes."[26]

Rather than mercury delay lines, the Mark I used cathode ray tubes for storage. This type of storage — often called the Williams Tube — was pioneered by F. C. Williams, who had come to Manchester in December 1946. The data to be stored is sent to the CRT as electrical pulses, where it is displayed on the screen as an array of dots, each representing one bit. A different intensity or size of the dots distinguishes between 0 and 1. A metal plate in front of the tube picks up the charges from these dots and allows the tube to be refreshed or read. A second CRT would allow people to view the dots and examine the data. By 1947, each CRT was capable of storing 2,048 bits.

---

[24] *ACE Report*, 123.

[25] Martin Campbell-Kelly, "Programming the Mark I: Early Programming Activity at the University of Manchester," *Annals of the History of Computing*, Vol. 2, No. 2 (April 1980), 134.

[26] Campbell-Kelly, "Programming the Mark I", 147. The handbook is available at www.alanturing.net/turing_archive/archive/index/manchesterindex.html

The Mark I stored data in 40-bit words, which could also store two 20-bit instructions. These words were displayed on the CRTs in 5-bit groups, and so a base-32 notation developed where each 5-bit code was represented by the teleprinter character corresponding to that code. To read a number, it was necessary to know the code corresponding to each character. These character codes were not in alphabetical order, so following Turing's gallant lead, everybody who programmed for the Mark I was forced to memorize the 32-character sequence:

/E@A:SIU$\frac{1}{2}$DRJNFCKTZLWHYPQOBG"MXV£

Turing's involvement in these actual computer projects may cause us to lose sight of the simple fact that Turing's intent in his "Computable Numbers" paper was *not* to design a universal computing machine. The whole purpose of the paper was to use this hypothetical computer to help resolve the Entscheidungsproblem. There are still a few more steps. A crucial one is to demonstrate that Turing's machines are intrinsically limited in what they can do.

Turing stated in the introduction to his paper, "Although the class of computable numbers is so great, and in many ways similar to the class of real numbers, it is nevertheless enumerable" (his page 230; my page 66). In Section 5, he demonstrated how "To each computable sequence there corresponds at least one description number, while to no description number does there correspond more than one computable sequence. The computable sequences and numbers are therefore enumerable" (his page 241; my page 138).

Some doubts may still linger. It's obvious that the class of computable numbers contains at least some transcendentals. Turing Machines that calculate π or e or Liouville's constant are certainly possible. Surely transcendentals whose digits have some kind of order are computable by a Turing Machine. That's the game Ulam and von Neumann played while traveling together.

Nevertheless, the vast majority — no, no, no, let's be realistic about this and say *virtually all* — virtually all transcendentals are ostensibly streams of random digits. In the realm of real numbers, orderly or calculable sequences of digits are rare. Complete and total randomness is the rule.

How exactly do you make a machine that computes a number with no pattern? Do you just generate digits randomly?

Randomness is not something computers do very well, and yet computers are often called upon to behave randomly. Some statistics applications require random numbers, and computer games routinely need random numbers to vary the action. Without random numbers each hand of Solitaire would be exactly the same.

Programming languages often provide some standard way for programs to generate random numbers. For example, a computer program written in the C programming language can use a function named *rand* to obtain a random number between 0 and 32,767. The *rand* function begins with a number known as a *seed*, which by default is initially set to 1. Different *rand* functions may implement the actual algorithm in different ways; as an example, here's the implementation of *rand* found in Microsoft's version of C[27]:

```
int seed = 1;

int rand()
{
    return ((seed = seed * 214013 + 2531011) >> 16) & 32767;
}
```

The *rand* function multiplies *seed* by 214,013 and adds 2,531,011, and then stores that result back in *seed* for the next time *rand* is called; however, since *seed* is defined as a 32-bit signed integer, overflow or underflow may result. The result of the calculation is truncated to 32 bits, and if the highest bit is 1, the value is actually negative.[28] The calculation continues by shifting the result 16 bits, effectively dividing it by 65,536 and truncating any fractions. Finally, a Boolean AND operation is performed between the bits of that result and the bits of 32,767. That eliminates all bits except the bottom 15 and ensures that the result is between 0 and 32,767.

Even if you didn't follow this convoluted calculation, it should be obvious that in no way is this *rand* function generating random numbers! The function is entirely deterministic. Starting with a *seed* value of 1, repeated calls to the function always result in the calculation of the same series of numbers:

41
18,467
6,334
26,500
19,169
. . .

The first time a program calls *rand*, the function returns 41, and the 30,546[th] time a program calls *rand*, the function also returns 41, and then the cycle repeats.

Because this sequence is entirely determined by the seed and the algorithm, it is not truly random. It is instead called a *pseudo-random sequence*. If you performed certain statistical tests on the numbers generated by *rand*, they would appear to exhibit characteristics of randomness. In some applications a pseudo-random sequence is preferred to truly random numbers because it's possible to reproduce results and test that the program is working correctly.

---

[27] rand.c © 1985–1997, Microsoft Corporation. Some details in the *rand* function have been altered for purposes of clarity.

[28] A discussion of overflow and underflow may be found in my book *Code*, 153–154.

In games, however, generating the same sequence of random numbers is *not* desirable. For that reason, every time you deal a new hand of Solitaire, the program probably begins by obtaining the current time of the day down to seconds and milliseconds, and then uses that to set a new seed. Assuming you don't deal at the exact — down to the millisecond — same time of the day, you're getting what appears to be a random hand.

John von Neumann once said that "Any one who considers arithmetical methods of producing random digits is, of course, in a state of sin."[29] (This was right before he described arithmetical methods for producing random numbers.) Because computers generate random numbers incompetently, applications that *really* need random numbers go outside the computer and use dedicated hardware for this task. A hardware random number generator (RNG) might use ambient noise or quantum processes to generate random numbers.

Curiously enough, Alan Turing seems to have originated the idea of generating random numbers in hardware. Turing requested that the production model of the Mark I at the University of Manchester have a special instruction that generated a random number from a noise source. It turned out to be not quite as random as it should have been, but random enough to prevent it from being properly debugged.[30]

Let's assume we have a hardware RNG that works. We put it to use to generate a sequence of 0s and 1s just like a Turing Machine. Put a binary point in front and you can watch a real number — doubtlessly a transcendental number — being created right before your eyes. (If you tried this with a software pseudo-random sequence, eventually the seed would be recalculated and the sequence would begin again. The resultant number would have a repeating sequence of digits and that means it would be rational.)

Now define a Turing Machine that generates the very same real number as the hardware RNG. You can't do it. The only approach that duplicates the RNG is a Turing Machine that explicitly prints exactly the digits you need, but that's not a Turing Machine with a finite number of configurations.

Maybe the randomness of most real numbers is merely an illusion. After all, the digits of π appear to be random, but π is definitely computable. Maybe real numbers that appear to be random actually have some kind of underlying structure that we just don't know about. Maybe if we approach this question from a different direction, we might instead prove that the computable numbers are *not* enumerable. We might then be able to get a good night's sleep because we'd be comforted with the knowledge that every real number is computable.

---

[29]John von Neumann, *Collected Works, Volume V, Design of Computer, Theory of Automata, and Numerical Analysis* (Macmillan, 1963), 768. The statement was originally made at a symposium on Monte Carlo methods in 1949.

[30]Martin Campbell-Kelly, "Programming the Mark I", 136.

Turing needs to confront these possibilities head on.

8. *Application of the diagonal process.*

It may be thought that arguments which prove that the real numbers are not enumerable would also prove that the computable numbers and sequences cannot be enumerable*. It might, for instance, be thought that the limit of a sequence of computable numbers must be computable.

---

* *Cf.* Hobson, *Theory of functions of a real variable* (2nd ed., 1921), 87, 88.

Turing is alluding to Georg Cantor's first (1874) proof of the nonenumerability of the real numbers that I described beginning on page 24. It's likely that Turing didn't have access to Cantor's original publication so he refers instead to a text book by E. W. Hobson and published by Cambridge University Press.[31] Hobson follows Cantor very closely, even using much of the same notation.

Turing suggests that Cantor's exercise be repeated using an enumeration of computable numbers rather than real numbers. In both cases, the numbers approach a limit. In Cantor's proof, that limit has to be a real number (What else could it be?), but Cantor was able to demonstrate that the limit wasn't in the enumeration of real numbers, thus proving that the real numbers are not enumerable.

When the same process is attempted with computable numbers, the computable numbers also approach a limit. Could that limit also be a computable number? Turing's answer:

This is clearly only true if the sequence of computable numbers is defined by some rule.

By "sequence" Turing means the sequence of alphas and betas that approach the limit. That limit is a computable number only if we can compute it — that is, we

---

[31] The full title of this influential book by Cambridge mathematics professor Ernest William Hobson (1856–1933) is *The Theory of Functions of a Real Variable and the Theory of Fourier's Series*, and the first edition was published by Cambridge University Press in 1907. The second edition that Turing refers to dates from 1921, but so much new material had been added that a second *volume* had to be published in 1926. This Volume II was also referred to as a second edition. Volume I was revised as a third edition in 1927. The third edition of Volume I and the second edition of Volume II were republished by Harren Press in 1950 and Dover Books in 1957, and these might be the easiest editions to track down. The discussion that Turing refers to is on pages 84 and 85 of this third edition of Volume I. It is followed on pages 85 and 86 by Cantor's diagonal proof.

can devise some algorithm that tells us the numeric limit approached by these alphas and betas. That does not seem likely. If we don't have a way to compute this limit, it is not a computable number. It is yet another uncomputable real number, and hence we haven't disproved that computable numbers are enumerable.

> Or we might apply the diagonal process.

Turing puts the rest of the paragraph in quotation marks as if an intruder has burst into his paper trying to convince us that the computable numbers are not enumerable. Turing's adversary pursues a more notation-laden arithmetic variation of the diagonal process than the one I offered on page 28.

> "If the computable sequences are enumerable, let α_n be the n-th computable sequence, and let $\phi_n(m)$ be the m-th figure in α_n.

It's just notation. Each computable sequence is a series of 0s and 1s, and each of these binary digits is represented by ϕ, the Greek letter phi. The computable sequences can be listed with a superfluity of subscripts and indices like so:

$$\alpha_1 = \phi_1(1)\ \phi_1(2)\ \phi_1(3)\ \phi_1(4)\ \cdots$$
$$\alpha_2 = \phi_2(1)\ \phi_2(2)\ \phi_2(3)\ \phi_2(4)\ \cdots$$
$$\alpha_3 = \phi_3(1)\ \phi_3(2)\ \phi_3(3)\ \phi_3(4)\ \cdots$$
$$\cdots$$

> Let β be the sequence with $1 - \phi_n(n)$ as its n-th figure.

In other words, β is the diagonal with the 0s and 1s flipped:

$$\beta = (1 - \phi_1(1))\ (1 - \phi_2(2))\ (1 - \phi_3(3))\ (1 - \phi_4(4)) \cdots$$

> Since β is computable, there exists a number K such that $1 - \phi_n(n) = \phi_K(n)$ all n.

That is, for some K, there's an α_K in the enumerated list of computable numbers:

$$\beta = \alpha_K = \phi_K(1) \; \phi_K(2) \; \phi_K(3) \; \phi_K(4)\ldots$$

In general, for digit n,

$$1 - \phi_n(n) = \phi_K(n)$$

or

$$1 = \phi_K(n) + \phi_n(n)$$

Turing's adversary now uses this arithmetic argument to demonstrate that β can't exist:

> Putting $n = K$,

that is,

$$1 = \phi_K(K) + \phi_K(K)$$

> we have $1 = 2\phi_K(K)$, *i.e.* 1 is even. This is impossible. The computable sequences are therefore not enumerable".

Well, that's interesting. This mysterious intruder has just described how to compute a number called β based on the computable sequences in the enumerated list, but this computed number is not in the list. Therefore, the intruder says, the computable sequences are not enumerable.

But Turing remains calm, and says:

> The fallacy in this argument lies in the assumption that β is computable.

Fallacy? What fallacy? How can β not be computable? β is computed from the enumeration of computable sequences, so it has to be computable, right?

Well, not exactly.

Let's step back a moment. Turing originally defined computable numbers as those that are calculable by finite means. He constructed imaginary machines to compute these numbers, and he showed that each machine can be uniquely identified by a positive integer called a Description Number. Because integers are enumerable, Turing Machines are also enumerable, and therefore computable sequences are enumerable.

In one sense, enumerating the Turing Machines is as easy as enumerating the positive integers:

1
2
3
4
5
. . .

All the Turing Machines will appear in this list in the form of Description Numbers, and from the Description Number we can get the Standard Description, and then we can feed that to the Universal Machine to get the computable sequence.

Of course, we're missing something: We're missing a way to determine exactly which positive integers in that list are Description Numbers of circle-free machines.

As you may recall from the definitions in Section 2, a circle-free machine is one that goes on printing 0s and 1s forever. Although a machine that never stops may appear to be "out of control" or "gone crazy," circle-free machines are necessary to compute irrational numbers and those rational numbers with repeating digits. Even when printing rational numbers like .1 (the binary equivalent of $\frac{1}{2}$), it is preferable for the machine to be circle-free by printing 1 and then a continuous sequence of 0s:

.10000000 . . .

A *circular* machine, on the other hand, is one that gets stuck in an undesirable loop. A circular machine could keep printing 0s without advancing the head, for example, or it could forever print symbols other than 0 and 1.

The terms *circle-free* and *circular* are not optimally descriptive: A circle-free machine might spend the rest of eternity in a little loop that prints 0s or 1s, and that might be fine. A circular machine could get jammed because it's directed to an *m*-configuration that doesn't exist, and that's just one of many problems that could befall it.

We need to identify the Description Numbers of circle-free machines because those are the only ones qualified to be interpreted by the Universal Machine. We may have successfully enumerated all the Turing Machines (somewhere within that list of positive integers), but we haven't identified those that are circle-free, so we can't use them to generate computable sequences.

It's very clear that many integers are not Description Numbers of any machine whatsoever. We can easily determine (by human inspection or a Turing Machine) whether a particular integer is a *well-formed* Description Number, which means that it's divided into well-formed instructions, each of which begins with an m-configuration, and so forth. We might even determine whether the machine refers to m-configurations that aren't present. We could check whether certain m-configurations aren't used. We could also easily check to see whether any m-configurations include instructions that actually print 0s or 1s. Such a process would determine that the lowest well-formed Description Number is 31,334,317, and this is a circular machine. (It only prints blanks.) It's not until 313,324,317 that the first circle-free machine is encountered, and not until 313,325,317 that we find the first circle-free machine that prints from left to right.

Here's the very beginning of an enumeration of the positive integers where the first two circle-free print-to-the-right Turing Machines are identified:

1
2
3
4
5
...
313,325,317 ← This one prints 0's to the right
...
3,133,225,317 ← This one prints 1s to the right
...

These, of course, are the simplest of simple machines, and the method to identify them is simple as well. Much more difficult — actually, as Turing will show, impossible — is a machine that implements a *general process* to determine whether a particular integer is the Description Number of a circle-free machine.

That general process is precisely what we need to perform the diagonalization. Each digit of β is based on a different computable number, so computing β requires that all the circle-free Turing Machines be identified. Turing will show that these circle-free machines cannot be identified by finite means, which means that we can't explicitly enumerate the computable sequences. It is therefore simply not true that β is a computable sequence.

> It would be true if we could enumerate the computable sequences by finite means, but the problem of enumerating computable sequences is equivalent to the problem of finding out whether a given number is the D.N of a circle-free machine, and we have no general process for doing this in a finite number of steps.

Turing now makes a subtle shift in focus. He started by attempting to apply Cantor's diagonalization proof to computable sequences, but now he wants simply to explore what happens when we try to identify all the Description Numbers of circle-free machines.

> In fact, by applying the diagonal process argument correctly, we can show that there cannot be any such general process.

If, as Turing asserts, there's no general process for determining whether a particular integer is a Description Number of a circle-free machine, then β is not computable. That would invalidate the interloper's "proof" that the computable sequences are not enumerable. Nothing would then detract from our confidence that computable sequences are indeed enumerable and hence can't include all the real numbers.

Unfortunately, Turing begins the next paragraph rather vaguely:

> The simplest and most direct proof of this is by showing that, if this general process exists, then there is a machine which computes β.

I think he's saying that there cannot be a general process to determine whether a particular machine is circle-free because, if there were, we'd be able to compute β, and we know we can't compute β, because then the diagonal argument would be valid, and computable sequences would not be enumerable.

> This proof, although perfectly sound, has the disadvantage that it may leave the reader with a feeling that "there must be something wrong".

The paradox still nags at our consciences. For that reason, Turing will now prove more directly that there is no machine that will determine whether a particular integer is a Description Number of a circle-free machine.

> The proof which I shall give has not this disadvantage, and gives a certain insight into the significance of the idea "circle-free".

He might also have added that the implications go far beyond this little exercise in number theory.

All Turing wants now is a machine that extracts one digit from each computable sequence. He doesn't have to bother with subtracting the digits from one. He's actually going to try to compute something a little bit simpler than β:

> It depends not on constructing β, but on constructing β', whose n-th figure is $\phi_n(n)$.

On the very first page of Turing's paper (page 66 of this book) he said, "The computable numbers do not, however, include all definable numbers, and an example is given of a definable number which is not computable." Both β and β' are such definable numbers. β' is definable because instructions can be given for how to compute it: Enumerate the whole numbers starting at 1. For each number, determine whether it's a well-formed Description Number of a Turing Machine. If so, determine whether that machine is circle-free. If so, compute that number up to the n-th digit (where n is one more than the number of circle-free machines encountered so far). That digit is the n-th digit of β'.

You can see that β' is completely defined, but can it be computed?

Although Turing defined no instruction that would ever halt the machine, the problem that Turing is now attacking is studied more in the variation known as the *Halting Problem*. (The term originated in Martin Davis's 1958 book *Computability and Unsolvability*.[32]) Can we define a Turing Machine that will determine whether another Turing Machine will either halt or go on forever? If we substitute the idea of circularity for halting, it's a similar problem. Can one Turing Machine analyze another Turing Machine and determine its ultimate fate?

Turing begins by assuming there exists a machine that determines whether any arbitrary machine is circle-free. In the following discussion, he refers to the machine's Standard Description rather than the Description Number, but it doesn't really matter because it's trivial to convert between them.

> [247]
>
> Let us suppose that there is such a process; that is to say, that we can invent a machine $\mathcal{D}$ which, when supplied with the S.D of any computing machine $\mathcal{M}$ will test this S.D and if $\mathcal{M}$ is circular will mark the S.D with the symbol "u" and if it is circle-free will mark it with "s".

---

[32]Martin Davis, *Computability and Unsolvability* (McGraw-Hill, 1958), 70. Davis believes he first used the term in lectures in 1952. (See Copeland, *The Essential Turing*, 40, footnote 61.) The concept also shows up in Chapter 13 of Stephen Cole Kleene, *Introduction to Metamathematics* (Van Nostrand, 1952).

The machine $\mathcal{D}$ is the Decision machine. The "u" stands for *unsatisfactory* (meaning a circular machine) and the "s" for *satisfactory* (circle-free). Turing defined these terms at the end of Section 5 (his page 241, my page 142).

> By combining the machines $\mathcal{D}$ and $\mathcal{U}$ we could construct a machine $\mathcal{H}$ to compute the sequence β'.

Actually the $\mathcal{H}$ machine also needs to generate positive integers and then convert them to Standard Descriptions, but that's fairly trivial. For every positive integer that $\mathcal{H}$ generates, $\mathcal{H}$ uses $\mathcal{D}$ to determine whether the number defines a satisfactory machine. If so, then $\mathcal{H}$ passes that Standard Description to the Universal Machine $\mathcal{U}$ to compute the sequence. For the n-th computable sequence, $\mathcal{U}$ needs only to run the machine up to the nth digit. That digit then becomes the nth digit of β'. Because $\mathcal{U}$ is under the control of $\mathcal{H}$, $\mathcal{H}$ can stop $\mathcal{U}$ when it has the particular digit it needs.

It's necessary for $\mathcal{H}$ to check the Standard Description with $\mathcal{D}$ first because we don't want $\mathcal{U}$ to get stuck running an unsatisfactory machine. If $\mathcal{H}$ gives $\mathcal{U}$ the Standard Description of an unsatisfactory machine, and that unsatisfactory machine never prints a digit, then the process gets stuck and can't move forward.

Turing does not actually show us what this magic Decision machine $\mathcal{D}$ looks like, so that should be a big hint that such a machine is impossible. Just off hand, it seems like it would at least be very difficult. How can $\mathcal{D}$ determine that a particular machine is circle-free except by mimicking the machine and tracing through its every step?

At any rate, $\mathcal{D}$ is similar to $\mathcal{U}$ in that it works with a Standard Description (or, equivalently, a Description Number) encoded on a tape.

> The machine $\mathcal{D}$ may require a tape. We may suppose that it uses the E-squares beyond all symbols on F-squares, and that when it has reached its verdict all the rough work done by $\mathcal{D}$ is erased.

It leaves behind only an s or u for its final verdict.

> The machine $\mathcal{H}$ has its motion divided into sections. In the first $N - 1$ sections, among other things, the integers $1, 2, \ldots, N - 1$ have been written down and tested by the machine $\mathcal{D}$.

The term "divided into sections" does not mean that there exist different parts of $\mathcal{H}$ that handle the different numbers. Separate sets of configurations for each number would require that $\mathcal{H}$ be infinite. Turing is really referring to sequential operations over a period of time. The actual process must be a general one that applies to all integers: The $\mathcal{H}$ machine generates positive integers one after another, passes each in turn to $\mathcal{D}$ to determine whether it's satisfactory, and, if so, uses $\mathcal{U}$ to calculate a certain number of digits in the computable sequence.

> A certain number, say $R(N-1)$, of them have been found to be the D.N's of circle-free machines.

R just accumulates a count of circle-free machines that have already been encountered. The machine needs R to determine how many digits to calculate for each circle-free machine that turns up.

> In the N-th section the machine $\mathcal{D}$ tests the number N. If N is satisfactory, *i.e.*, if it is the D.N of a circle-free machine, then $R(N) = 1 + R(N-1)$ and the first $R(N)$ figures of the sequence of which a D.N is N are calculated.

If N is 3,133,225,317, for example, then $R(N-1)$ is 1. (See the list above of positive integers with the first two satisfactory machines identified.) Only one satisfactory machine has been discovered so far. The machine $\mathcal{D}$ will determine that N is indeed the Description Number of a circle-free machine. So, $R(N)$ is set to 2, and $\mathcal{U}$ calculates the first two digits of the machine defined by 3,133,225,317. Those two digits will both be 1. $\mathcal{H}$ uses the second of those digits as the second digit of β'. It's on its way!

> The $R(N)$-th figure of this sequence is written down as one of the figures of the sequence β' computed by $\mathcal{H}$.

The usual case, of course, is that the Description Number is either no machine at all or a circular machine.

> If N is not satisfactory, then $R(N) = R(N-1)$ and the machine goes on to the $(N+1)$-th section of its motion.

The point is that $\mathcal{H}$ must look at the potential Description Numbers one after another, and for each satisfactory Description Number, $\mathcal{H}$ must run the machine until the $R(N)$-th digit.

Turing now takes great pains to demonstrate that $\mathcal{H}$ is circle-free. $\mathcal{H}$ simply runs $\mathcal{D}$ for each potential Description Number and $\mathcal{D}$ is circle-free by the original assumptions.

> From the construction of $\mathcal{H}$ we can see that $\mathcal{H}$ is circle-free. Each section of the motion of $\mathcal{H}$ comes to an end after a finite number of steps. For, by our assumption about $\mathcal{D}$, the decision as to whether N is satisfactory is reached in a finite number of steps. If N is not satisfactory, then the N-th section is finished. If N is satisfactory, this means that the machine $\mathcal{M}(N)$ whose D.N is N is circle-free, and therefore its $R(N)$-th figure can be calculated in a finite number of steps. When this figure has been calculated and written down as the $R(N)$-th figure of β', the N-th section is finished. Hence $\mathcal{H}$ is circle-free.

$\mathcal{H}$ is a Turing Machine, so $\mathcal{H}$ has a Description Number (which Turing calls K). At some point, $\mathcal{H}$ will have to deal with its own Description Number. $\mathcal{H}$ will have to determine whether $\mathcal{H}$ is circle-free.

> Now let K be the D.N of $\mathcal{H}$. What does $\mathcal{H}$ do in the K-th section of its motion? It must test whether K is satisfactory, giving a verdict "s" or "u". Since K is the D.N of $\mathcal{H}$ and since $\mathcal{H}$ is circle-free, the verdict cannot be "u".

Then Turing also adds:

> On the other hand the verdict cannot be "s".

The fundamental problem is that $\mathcal{H}$ gets into an infinite recursion. Before $\mathcal{H}$ encounters the number K (the Description Number of itself) $\mathcal{H}$ has analyzed all positive integers 1 through $K - 1$. The number of circle-free machines so far is $R(K - 1)$ and the first $R(K - 1)$ digits of β' have been found.

What is the $R(K)$-th digit of β'? To get that digit, $\mathcal{H}$ has to trace through its own operation, which means it has to duplicate everything up to the point where it encountered K, and then the process begins again. That is why $\mathcal{H}$ cannot be circle-free.

> For if it were, then in the K-th section of its motion $\mathcal{H}$ would be bound to compute the first $R(K - 1) + 1 = R(K)$ figures of the sequence computed by the machine with K as its D.N and to write down the $R(K)$-th as a figure of the

> sequence computed by $\mathcal{H}$. The computation of the first $R(K) - 1$ figures
> would be carried out all right, but the instructions for calculating the
> $R(K)$-th would amount to "calculate the first $R(K)$ figures computed by
> H and write down the $R(K)$-th". This $R(K)$-th figure would never be
> found.

(In the penultimate line, H should be $\mathcal{H}$.)

$\mathcal{H}$ is generating a sequence of digits based on the sequences generated by other machines. That's pretty straightforward when we think of machines as generating sequences like the binary equivalent of 1/3, π, and the square root of 2, but where does $\mathcal{H}$ get digit K of this sequence that it's generating? It has to get that digit from itself, but that makes no sense because $\mathcal{H}$ gets digits only from other machines.

OK, so $\mathcal{H}$ has a little problem when encountering its own Description Number. Can't it just skip that one? Well, yes, it can, but as we've seen, every computable sequence can be calculated by a variety of different machines. Machines could calculate the same sequence in different ways, or they could have superfluous instructions. $\mathcal{H}$ would need to skip those similar machines as well. What about the machines that don't calculate β', but calculate something close to β', such as β' with its 27th and 54th digits swapped? There are an infinite number of such machines and avoiding them all puts quite a burden on $\mathcal{H}$ — an *impossible* burden.

> *I.e.*, $\mathcal{H}$ is circular, contrary both to what we have found in the last paragraph and to the verdict "*s*". Thus both verdicts are impossible and we conclude that there can be no machine $\mathcal{D}$.

There can be no general process to determine whether a machine is circle-free. By implication, there can be no computer program that will determine the ultimate fate of other computer programs.

Turing has also resolved the paradox of the diagonal process: He first established that computable numbers are enumerable, yet the diagonal process seemed to indicate that you could create a computable number not in the list. Turing has shown that the diagonal could *not* be calculated by finite means, and hence is not computable. Computable numbers may be enumerable, but they cannot actually be enumerated in a finite number of steps.

Turing is not quite finished with this section. He now hypothesizes a machine $\mathcal{E}$, which might stand for "ever print."

[248]

> We can show further that *there can be no machine $\mathcal{E}$ which, when supplied with the S.D of an arbitrary machine $\mathcal{M}$, will determine whether $\mathcal{M}$ ever prints a given symbol (0 say).*

Turing needs this $\mathcal{E}$ machine in the final section of the paper when he uses it to prove that the Entscheidungsproblem has no solution. Here he will prove that $\mathcal{E}$ cannot exist by first showing that the existence of $\mathcal{E}$ implies the existence of a process for determining whether a machine prints 0 infinitely often, but that implies the existence of a similar process to determine whether a machine prints 1 infinitely often. If you had the ability to determine whether a machine prints 0 infinitely often or 1 infinitely often (or both), you'd have the ability to determine whether a machine is circle-free. It's already been proven that such a process is impossible, so machine $\mathcal{E}$ must also be impossible.

> We will first show that, if there is a machine $\mathcal{E}$, then there is a general process for determining whether a given machine $\mathcal{M}$ prints 0 infinitely often.

Turing will demonstrate this through a rather odd method of defining variations of the arbitrary machine $\mathcal{M}$.

> Let $\mathcal{M}_1$ be a machine which prints the same sequence as $\mathcal{M}$, except that in the position where the first 0 printed by $\mathcal{M}$ stands, $\mathcal{M}_1$ prints $\bar{0}$. $\mathcal{M}_2$ is to have the first two symbols 0 replaced by $\bar{0}$, and so on. Thus, if $\mathcal{M}$ were to print
>
> $$ABA01AAB0010AB\ldots,$$
>
> then $\mathcal{M}_1$ would print
>
> $$ABA\bar{0}1AAB0010AB\ldots$$
>
> and $\mathcal{M}_2$ would print
>
> $$ABA\bar{0}1AAB\bar{0}010AB\ldots.$$

If you had a machine $\mathcal{M}$, could you define a machine that reads the Standard Description of $\mathcal{M}$ and manufactures the Standard Descriptions of $\mathcal{M}_1$, $\mathcal{M}_2$, and so forth? Turing says yes, and he calls this machine $\mathcal{F}$:

> Now let $\mathcal{F}$ be a machine which, when supplied with the S.D of $\mathcal{M}$, will write down successively the S.D of $\mathcal{M}$, of $\mathcal{M}_1$, of $\mathcal{M}_2$, ... (there is such a machine).

To convince ourselves that $\mathcal{F}$ is plausible, let's consider that very simple machine that alternatively prints 0 and 1, that is, the binary form of 1/3 without skipping any spaces:

q_1	None	P0, R	q_2
q_2	None	P1, R	q_1

That's machine $\mathcal{M}$. Here's machine $\mathcal{M}_1$:

q_1	None	P$\overline{0}$, R	q_4
q_2	None	P1, R	q_1
q_3	None	P0, R	q_4
q_4	None	P1, R	q_3

All the original configurations (all two of them) have simply been duplicated and given different m-configurations. In the first set of configurations, every line that printed 0 now prints $\overline{0}$ and then jumps to the appropriate configuration in the second set. $\mathcal{M}_2$ has three sets:

q_1	None	P$\overline{0}$, R	q_4
q_2	None	P1, R	q_1
q_3	None	P$\overline{0}$, R	q_6
q_4	None	P1, R	q_3
q_5	None	P0, R	q_6
q_6	None	P1, R	q_5

You might notice that these modified machines never enter configurations q_2, but that's just a fluke of this particular machine.

It is therefore entirely plausible that $\mathcal{F}$ exists. Notice the relationship between these $\mathcal{M}$ machines: If $\mathcal{M}$ never prints 0, then neither does $\mathcal{M}_1$, $\mathcal{M}_2$, and so forth. If $\mathcal{M}$ prints 0 just once, then $\mathcal{M}_1$ never prints 0, and neither does $\mathcal{M}_2$, and so forth. If $\mathcal{M}$ prints 0 twice, then $\mathcal{M}_1$ prints 0 once, $\mathcal{M}_2$ never prints 0, and so forth. If $\mathcal{M}$ prints 0 infinitely often, then so does $\mathcal{M}_1$, $\mathcal{M}_2$, and so forth.

You'll recall that $\mathcal{E}$ is assumed to determine whether a machine ever prints 0.

We combine $\mathcal{F}$ with $\mathcal{E}$ and obtain a new machine, $\mathcal{G}$. In the motion of $\mathcal{G}$ first $\mathcal{F}$ is used to write down the S.D of $\mathcal{M}$, and then $\mathcal{E}$ tests it, : 0 : is written if it is found that $\mathcal{M}$ never prints 0; then $\mathcal{F}$ writes the S.D of $\mathcal{M}_1$, and this is tested, : 0 : being printed if and only if $\mathcal{M}_1$ never prints 0, and so on.

$\mathcal{G}$ uses $\mathcal{F}$ to generate the Description Numbers of $\mathcal{M}$, $\mathcal{M}_1$, $\mathcal{M}_2$, and so forth, and $\mathcal{E}$ to determine whether the resultant machine ever prints 0. If the resultant machine never prints 0, $\mathcal{G}$ prints 0.

The result is this: If $\mathcal{M}$ never prints 0, or prints 0 only a finite number of times, then $\mathcal{G}$ prints 0 infinitely often. If $\mathcal{M}$ prints 0 infinitely often, then $\mathcal{G}$ never prints 0.

Now let us test $\mathcal{G}$ with $\mathcal{E}$. If it is found that $\mathcal{G}$ never prints 0, then $\mathcal{M}$ prints 0 infinitely often; if $\mathcal{G}$ prints 0 sometimes, then $\mathcal{M}$ does not print 0 infinitely often.

That means $\mathcal{G}$ can tell us that $\mathcal{M}$ prints 0 infinitely often. It tells us this by never printing 0.

Similarly there is a general process for determining whether $\mathcal{M}$ prints 1 infinitely often. By a combination of these processes we have a process for determining whether $\mathcal{M}$ prints an infinity of figures, *i.e.* we have a process for determining whether $\mathcal{M}$ is circle-free. There can therefore be no machine $\mathcal{E}$.

By another proof by contradiction, Turing has shown that $\mathcal{E}$ cannot exist because it would ultimately imply the existence of $\mathcal{D}$ — the machine that determines whether any machine is circle-free — and that machine cannot exist.

Turing finishes this section with a reminder that we really need to examine this assumed equivalence between human computers and Turing Machines because we've been relying on it quite a lot.

The expression "there is a general process for determining ..." has been used throughout this section as equivalent to "there is a machine which will determine ...". This usage can be justified if and only if we can justify our definition of "computable".

That examination will come in the next section.

Turing then hints at another aspect of this demonstration that won't be explored until Part III of this book. Turing began by interpreting the output of Turing Machines as "computable numbers," but machines can be more flexible than that. For example, consider a machine that prints a sequence like this:

0011010100010100010100010000010 . . .

That might look like a number, but it's actually the output of a "prime number" machine that we might denote by *IsPrime(n)*. For the *n*th figure in this sequence (beginning with *n* equal to zero), *IsPrime(n)* is 1 if *n* is prime, and 0 if *n* is not prime. The sequence printed by the machine indicates that 2, 3, 5, 7, 11, 13, 17, 19, 23, and 29 are all primes. Such a machine is entirely plausible, but it's not really computing a number. Instead it's telling us something about the natural numbers.

> For each of these "general process" problems can be expressed as a problem concerning a general process for determining whether a given integer n has a property $G(n)$ [e.g. $G(n)$ might mean "n is satisfactory" or "n is the Gödel representation of a provable formula"], and this is equivalent to computing a number whose n-th figure is 1 if $G(n)$ is true and 0 if it is false.

Turing has now, in a very small way that will become more apparent in Part III of this book, established a link between his computing machines and mathematical logic. The symbols 1 and 0 not only serve as binary digits, but — as George Boole realized many years ago — they can also symbolize *true* and *false*.

Consider a bunch of functions that have arguments of natural numbers and which return values of *true* and *false* (or 1 and 0):

IsPrime(n)
IsEven(n)
IsOdd(n)
IsLessThanTen(n)
IsMultipleOfTwentyTwo(n)

and so forth. These are sometimes known as Boolean functions, and they can be implemented by Turing Machines that print sequences of 0s and 1s for *n* equal to 0, 1, 2, 3, and so forth. The *IsOdd* function prints the same alternating sequence as Turing's first example machine.

Turing has established that these computable sequences are enumerable. So, too, are the actual function names! They can be alphabetized, for example. In Cantor's notation of transfinite numbers, the cardinality of the set of all computable and alphabetizable Boolean functions of natural numbers is $\aleph_0$, the cardinality of enumerable sets.

Each Boolean function returns *true* or 1 for a subset of the natural numbers. For example, *IsPrime* returns 1 for the following set of natural numbers:

$$\{2, 3, 5, 7, 11, 13, \ldots\}$$

Each of these Boolean functions is associated with a different subset of the natural numbers. As you might recall from Chapter 2, the set of all subsets is called a *power set*, and if the original set has a cardinality of $\aleph_0$, then the power set has a cardinality of $2^{\aleph_0}$.

The set of all *conceivable* Boolean functions has a cardinality of $2^{\aleph_0}$, while the set of all *computable* Boolean functions (and indeed, the set of all Boolean functions that can be described with a name in the English language) has a cardinality of $\aleph_0$. That's another big gap between the conceivable and the computable.

11 Of Machines and Men

A lan Turing wrote at the beginning of the first section of his paper (page 68 of this book) of his definition of computable numbers that "No real attempt will be made to justify the definitions given until we reach §9." We have now reached Section 9, and the pages that follow have been called by Turing's biographer Andrew Hodges "among the most unusual ever offered in a mathematical paper."[1]

Turing will attempt to demonstrate that the capabilities of a Turing Machine are equivalent to a human computer carrying out a well-defined mathematical process. Therefore, if an algorithmic process is insolvable by a Turing Machine, it is also unsolvable by a human. This idea — generally expressed more formally — has come to be known as the Turing thesis or (in a related form) the Church-Turing thesis. It's called a "thesis" because it's much too amorphous a concept to be subjected to a rigorous mathematical proof. The thesis nonetheless extends to other digital computers: Their computational capabilities are no greater than the Turing Machine.

Only the first part of Section 9 appears in this chapter; the remainder requires some background in mathematical logic and will conclude in Part III of this book. For the most part, I will not interrupt Turing's analysis. Here's a summary by Martin Davis:

> Turing's "analysis" is a remarkable piece of applied philosophy in which, beginning with a human being carrying out a computation, he proceeds by a process of elimination of irrelevant details, through a sequence of simplifications, to an end result which is the familiar model consisting of a finite state device operating on a one-way infinite linear tape.[2]

[1] Andrew Hodges, *Alan Turing: The Enigma* (Simon & Schuster, 1983), 104.
[2] Martin Davis, "Why Gödel Didn't Have Church's Thesis," *Information and Control*, Vol. 54, Nos. 1/2, (July/Aug. 1982), 14.

[249]

9. *The extent of the computable numbers.*

No attempt has yet been made to show that the "computable" numbers include all numbers which would naturally be regarded as computable. All arguments which can be given are bound to be, fundamentally, appeals to intuition, and for this reason rather unsatisfactory mathematically. The real question at issue is "What are the possible processes which can be carried out in computing a number?"

The arguments which I shall use are of three kinds.

(*a*) A direct appeal to intuition.

(*b*) A proof of the equivalence of two definitions (in case the new definition has a greater intuitive appeal).

(*c*) Giving examples of large classes of numbers which are computable.

The (*b*) argument is in Part III of this book; the (*c*) argument continues in Section 10 of Turing's paper.

Once it is granted that computable numbers are all "computable", several other propositions of the same character follow. In particular, it follows that, if there is a general process for determining whether a formula of the Hilbert function calculus is provable, then the determination can be carried out by a machine.

The "Hilbert function calculus" is the system of mathematical logic today commonly called "first-order predicate logic." It is within this logic that Hilbert defined the Entscheidungsproblem. It is unlikely that Turing knew that a process "carried out by a machine" is precisely what Heinrich Behmann called for in the earliest references to the Entscheidungsproblem (page 48). Behmann's address remained unpublished until recently.

I. [Type (*a*)]. This argument is only an elaboration of the ideas of § 1.

Computing is normally done by writing certain symbols on paper. We may suppose this paper is divided into squares like a child's arithmetic book. In elementary arithmetic the two-dimensional character of the paper is sometimes used. But such a use is always avoidable, and I think that it will be agreed that the two-dimensional character of paper is no essential of computation. I assume then that the computation is carried out on one-dimensional paper, *i.e.* on a tape divided into squares. I shall also suppose that the number of symbols which may be printed is finite. If we were to allow an infinity of symbols, then there would be symbols differing to an arbitrarily small extent†. The effect of this restriction of the number of symbols is not very serious. It is always possible to use sequences of symbols in the place of single symbols. Thus an Arabic numeral such as

[250]

17 or 999999999999999 is normally treated as a single symbol. Similarly in any European language words are treated as single symbols (Chinese, however, attempts to have an enumerable infinity of symbols). The differences from our point of view between the single and compound symbols is that the compound symbols, if they are too lengthy, cannot be observed at one glance. This is in accordance with experience. We cannot tell at a glance whether 9999999999999999 and 999999999999999 are the same.

---

† If we regard a symbol as literally printed on a square we may suppose that the square is $0 \leqslant x \leqslant 1, 0 \leqslant y \leqslant 1$. The symbol is defined as a set of points in this square, viz. the set occupied by printer's ink. If these sets are restricted to be measurable, we can define the "distance" between two symbols as the cost of transforming one symbol into the other if the cost of moving unit area of printer's ink unit distance is unity, and there is an infinite supply of ink at $x = 2, y = 0$. With this topology the symbols form a conditionally compact space.

In the next sentence, Turing refers to a "computer." He is, of course, talking about a *human* computer.

The behaviour of the computer at any moment is determined by the symbols which he is observing, and his "state of mind" at that moment. We may suppose that there is a bound B to the number of symbols or squares which the computer can observe at one moment. If he wishes to observe more, he must use successive observations. We will also suppose that the number of states of mind which need be taken into account is finite. The reasons for this are of the same character as those which restrict the number of symbols. If we admitted an infinity of states of mind, some of them will be "arbitrarily close" and will be confused. Again, the restriction is not one which seriously affects computation, since the use of more complicated states of mind can be avoided by writing more symbols on the tape.

In 1972, Kurt Gödel wrote a brief note regarding Turing's analysis in this section that he labeled "A philosophical error in Turing's work."[3] Gödel argued that "*mind, in its use, is not static, but constantly developing*" and that mental states of mind might even converge on the infinite. These disagreements represent a fundamental clash between those who believe the mind to be ultimately a mechanical process of the brain, and those who do not.

Let us imagine the operations performed by the computer to be split up into "simple operations" which are so elementary that it is not easy to imagine them further divided. Every such operation consists of some change of the physical system consisting of the computer and his tape. We know the state of the system if we know the sequence of symbols on the tape, which of these are observed by the computer (possibly with a special order), and the state of mind of the computer. We may suppose that in a simple operation not more than one symbol is altered. Any other changes can be split up into simple changes of this kind. The situation in regard to the squares whose symbols may be altered in this way is the same as in regard to the observed squares. We may, therefore, without loss of generality, assume that the squares whose symbols are changed are always "observed" squares.

Besides these changes of symbols, the simple operations must include changes of distribution of observed squares. The new observed squares must be immediately recognisable by the computer. I think it is reasonable to suppose that they can only be squares whose distance from the closest of the immediately previously observed squares does not exceed a certain fixed amount. Let us say that each of the new observed squares is within L squares of an immediately previously observed square.

In connection with "immediate recognisability", it may be thought that there are other kinds of square which are immediately recognisable. In particular, squares marked by special symbols might be taken as imme-

[251]

diately recognisable. Now if these squares are marked only by single symbols there can be only a finite number of them, and we should not upset our theory by adjoining these marked squares to the observed squares. If, on the other hand, they are marked by a sequence of symbols, we

---

[3] Kurt Gödel, *Collected Works, Volume II: Publications 1938–1974* (Oxford University Press, 1990), 306. Judson C. Webb's introduction beginning on page 292 — and particularly the identification on page 297 of Gödel's belief that the human mind has an existence separate from the physical matter of the brain — is helpful in understanding Gödel's remarks. Another analysis is Oron Shagrir, "Gödel on Turing on Computability," http://edelstein.huji.ac.il/staff/shagrir/papers/Goedel_on_Turing_on_Computability.pdf.

cannot regard the process of recognition as a simple process. This is a fundamental point and should be illustrated. In most mathematical papers the equations and theorems are numbered. Normally the numbers do not go beyond (say) 1000. It is, therefore, possible to recognise a theorem at a glance by its number. But if the paper was very long, we might reach Theorem 157767733443477; then, further on in the paper, we might find "... hence (applying Theorem 157767733443477) we have ...". In order to make sure which was the relevant theorem we should have to compare the two numbers figure by figure, possibly ticking the figures off in pencil to make sure of their not being counted twice. If in spite of this it is still thought that there are other "immediately recognisable" squares, it does not upset my contention so long as these squares can be found by some process of which my type of machine is capable. This idea is developed in III below.

When Turing describes "ticking the figures off in pencil," he is probably alluding to the similar machine operation of "marking" squares with non-numeric figures.

The simple operations must therefore include:

(*a*) Changes of the symbol on one of the observed squares.

(*b*) Changes of one of the squares observed to another square within *L* squares of one of the previously observed squares.

It may be that some of these changes necessarily involve a change of state of mind. The most general single operation must therefore be taken to be one of the following:

(*A*) A possible change (*a*) of symbol together with a possible change of state of mind.

(*B*) A possible change (*b*) of observed squares, together with a possible change of state of mind.

The operation actually performed is determined, as has been suggested on p. 250, by the state of mind of the computer and the observed symbols. In particular, they determine the state of mind of the computer after the operation is carried out.

That's just the previous page of his paper to which he's referring.

> We may now construct a machine to do the work of this computer. To each state of mind of the computer corresponds an "m-configuration" of the machine. The machine scans B squares corresponding to the B squares observed by the computer. In any move the machine can change a symbol on a scanned square or can change any one of the scanned squares to another square distant not more than L squares from one of the other scanned
>
> [252]
>
> squares. The move which is done, and the succeeding configuration, are determined by the scanned symbol and the m-configuration. The machines just described do not differ very essentially from computing machines as defined in § 2, and corresponding to any machine of this type a computing machine can be constructed to compute the same sequence, that is to say the sequence computed by the computer.

That is, the *human* computer.

At this point, we stop for now. Turing's second argument in this section begins with a reference to the "restricted Hilbert functional calculus," followed by a statement in that calculus, and for that some background is required that begins Part III of this book.

Turing's fascination with the connection between human brains and machines continued long beyond his 1936 paper on computable numbers. Turing's other famous paper, "Computing Machinery and Intelligence," was published in the October 1950 issue of the philosophy journal *Mind*.

"Can machines think?" Turing asks. He then devises a test with a human being sitting at a teletypewriter. (The modern equivalent might be instant messaging, or anything else that doesn't allow people to see or hear who they're communicating with.) Let the person ask questions and receive answers. If there's actually a computer on the other end, and the person can't tell that it's a computer, then we should say that the computer is intelligent.

This has come to be known as the Turing Test, and it remains as controversial as ever. Anybody who has a pat objection to the Turing Test should read Turing's paper, which already has answers to many reasonable objections.

Turing prefers to deal with this question in terms of "intelligence" rather than "thinking" because "thinking" implies a certain activity going on *inside* the computer.

> The original question, 'Can machines think?' I believe to be too meaningless to deserve discussion. Nevertheless I believe that at the end of the century the use of words and general educated opinion will have altered so much that one will be able to speak of machines thinking without expecting to be contradicted.[4]

[4]Alan Turing, "Computing Machinery and Intelligence," *Mind*, Vol. LIX, No. 236 (October 1950), 442.

The end of the century has passed and, if anything, more people than ever know that whatever computers do, it is not "thinking." We have not come to expect our computers to be intelligent, and generally we work best with our computer applications when we believe they will act in a completely deterministic way. A computer program that attempts to do something "intelligent" often seems to resemble a two-year old staring up from a newly crayoned wall and pleading, "But I thought you'd *like* it."

In the alternative universe of science fiction, Turing's prediction was right on target, as demonstrated by the most famous fictional computer of all time:

> Whether Hal could actually think was a question which had been settled by the British mathematician Alan Turing back in the 1940s. Turing had pointed out that, if one could carry out a prolonged conversation with a machine — whether by typewriter or microphone was immaterial — without being able to distinguish between its replies and those that a man might give, then the machine was thinking, by any sensible definition of the word. Hal could pass the Turing test with ease.[5]

Alan Turing would have turned 56 years old in 1968, the year that both the book and movie of *2001* came out. He might have been amused by the concept of a computer so intelligent that it would experience a nervous breakdown.

In the summer of 1950, Turing moved to a house in Wilmslow, about ten miles south of Manchester. He had become interested in morphogenesis, which is the study of how cells in an organism develop and differentiate themselves to exhibit various patterns and forms. The research involved running simulations on the Manchester computer.

On March 15, 1951, Alan Turing was elected a Fellow of the Royal Society in recognition of his work on Computable Numbers. His sponsors were Max Newman and Bertrand Russell. That evening, the BBC broadcast a talk Turing had recorded entitled "Can Digital Computers Think?" (No recording of this broadcast or any recording of Turing speaking is known to exist.)

In December 1951, a chain of events was set in motion that would have serious consequences. Turing met a young man on the streets of Manchester. Arnold Murray had a working-class background, he was on probation for theft, and he was unemployed. Turing and Murray had lunch, met again, and went back to Turing's home together. They met several times over the next month.

Late in January 1952, Turing discovered that his house had been burgled. He reported it to the police, who came and dusted for fingerprints. When Turing confronted Arnold Murray, Murray pleaded innocent but said he knew who did it — an acquaintance named Harry. The police also identified Harry from

[5] Arthur C. Clark, *2001: A Space Odyssey* (New American Library, 1968), ch. 16.

the fingerprints taken from Turing's house. Harry was already in custody for something else. When questioned about the Turing robbery, Harry gave the police an earful about what was going on between Turing and his friend.

On February 7, 1952, the day after George VI died and his eldest daughter Elizabeth ascended to the throne, the police called on Alan Turing. After some questioning, Turing admitted to them the nature of his relationship with Murray. This confession made Turing subject to arrest under Section 11 of the Criminal Law Amendment Act of 1885:

> Any male person who, in public or private, commits, or is a party to the commission of, or procures or attempts to procure the commission by any male person of, any act of gross indecency with another male person, shall be guilty of a misdemeanor, and being convicted thereof shall be liable at the discretion of the court to be imprisoned for any term not exceeding two years, with or without hard labour.[6]

The term "gross indecency" was not defined in the law, but was generally taken to mean acts such as mutual masturbation and oral sex. Other statutes covered the more serious offense of anal sex (or "buggery" as it was known within the British legal system).

Section 11 was a notorious law that was controversial from its very beginning. The Criminal Law Amendment Act of 1885 describes itself as "An Act to make further provision for the protection of women and girls, the suppression of brothels, and other purposes." The law raised the age of consent from 13 to 16, and contained several provisions intended to prevent women from exploitation, such as being drugged in brothels or abducted into prostitution.

The law had originally floundered in the House of Commons for a couple years but then became more urgent following a series of articles by liberal journalist William Thomas Stead (1849–1912) concerning child prostitution. Stead's courageous exposé culminated with his actual purchase of a 13-year old girl from her parents.

Following the public uproar over Stead's articles, the Bill was revived. Section 11 was introduced by Member of Parliament Henry Labouchère on August 6, 1885, and was added to the Act the next day, just a week before the Act eventually passed. There was some question at the time whether it was proper to add this section to a bill whose focus was the protection of young girls and women.[7]

---

[6]Wording obtained from http://www.swarb.co.uk/acts/1885Criminal_Law_AmendmentAct.shtml (accessed April 2008).

[7]H. Montgomery Hyde, *The Love That Dared Not Speak Its Name: A Candid History of Homosexuality in Britain* (Little, Brown and Company, 1970), 134. This book was originally published in England under the title *The Other Love*.

Section 11 specifically targeted men, and the acts covered under the term of "gross indecency" had never been illegal in Britain before, at least not when performed by consenting adults in private. Even at the time the "in private" clause seemed to allow the law to be used for blackmail.[8]

The most famous victim of Section 11 was Oscar Wilde (1854–1900), who was prosecuted under the law in 1895. Wilde served his time doing hard labor, which probably hastened his death.

By the 1950s, however, different methods of punishment were available. Turing pleaded guilty with the understanding that he was to be placed on a year's probation, during which he was to have hormone treatments.

Experiments with treating homosexuality using sex hormones had begun in the 1940s. At first it was believed that homosexuality resulted from insufficient male hormones, but the administration of testosterone actually had the opposite of the anticipated result. Female hormones were then tried on homosexual men, and those seemed to have more of a desired effect.[9] By the time of Turing's conviction, this treatment was known as organotherepy, but was also called "chemical castration" and seemed intended more to humiliate than anything else. The estrogen rendered Turing impotent and made his breasts grow.

The early 1950s were not a good time to be identified as a homosexual. In the United States, the "red scare" of the early 1950s soon metamorphosed into another type of witch hunt. There actually weren't very many communists working in the State Department, but there were plenty of closeted gay people working in government jobs in Washington D.C. "Over the course of the 1950s and 1960s, approximately 1,000 people were dismissed from the Department of State for alleged homosexuality."[10]

In theory, the term "security risk" could be applied to anyone who might have a tendency to divulge government secrets. In practice the term was basically a euphemism for "homosexual."[11] The assumption was that homosexuals could be blackmailed into revealing state secrets. However, the best example anyone could come up with of this actually happening involved the head of Austrian intelligence before World War I, and it was never quite clear what the real story was.[12]

What was happening to gays in the United States government also had implications for Great Britain. In 1951, the U.S. State Department began advising the British Foreign Office about "the homosexual problem" in the government, and later pressured the British government to be more diligent about supposed security problems regarding homosexuals.[13]

---

[8] Ibid, 136.

[9] Hodges, *Alan Turing*, 467–471.

[10] David K. Johnson, *The Lavender Scare: The Cold War Persecution of Gays and Lesbians in the Federal Government* (University of Chicago Press, 2004), 76.

[11] Johnson, *Lavender Scare*, 7–8.

[12] Johnson, *Lavender Scare*, 108–109.

[13] Johnson, *Lavender Scare*, 133.

Alan Turing's employment options were certainly becoming more restricted. A top-secret government job such as Turing had during the war would now be inconceivable, nor would Turing be able to travel to America again. A 1952 law prohibited admission to "aliens afflicted with psychopathic personality," which was interpreted to mean homosexuality.[14]

Was this enough to make Turing suicidal? We don't know.

On the streets of England as well as in the government, life was getting more difficult for gay men. When Sir John Nott-Bower was appointed Commissioner of the London Metropolitan Police in 1953, he swore he would "rip the cover off all London's filth spots." The same year the Home Office issued directives for a new drive against "male vice." At least one London magistrate was tired of coddling and wanted convicted men to be "sent to prison as they were in the old days." From the end of 1953 through early 1954, newspaper headlines heralded the prosecutions of several men.[15]

Had Turing a new relationship with a man who was now threatening to blackmail him?

Or was Turing's suicide merely a careless accident, as his mother believed?

It is indicative of our ignorance that one of the most persuasive explorations of Turing's state of mind during this period comes not from a history or biography but from a novel. Novelist Janna Levin (who is also a professor of astronomy and physics at Barnard College) portrays a man humiliated beyond his ability to express it:

> He doesn't know how to voice his humiliation or even how to experience it. It rattles around in him like a broken part, dislodged and loose in his metal frame. The humiliation won't settle on one place, sink in where it would no doubt fester but at least could be quarantined and possibly even treated. If not steadily eroded by the imperceptible buffing waves of time, then maybe more aggressively targeted, excised by his Jungian analyst. But the shame just won't burrow and bind.[16]

We just don't know what was different about the evening of June 7, 1954. We don't know what prompted Turing to dip his regular evening apple in cyanide before he went to bed.

He was found dead the next morning. Alan Turing was 41 years old.

---

[14]Hodges, *Alan Turing*, 474.

[15]Hyde, *The Love That Dared Not Speak Its Name*, 214-6.

[16]Janna Levin, *A Madman Dreams of Turing Machines* (Alfred A. Knopf, 2006), 214.

Das Entscheidungs problem

12 Logic and Computability

I n the summer of 1958, Chinese-born logician Hao Wang took a break from his teaching duties at Oxford to log some time with a state-of-the-art IBM 704 computer at the IBM Research Laboratory in Poughkeepsie, New York. On IBM punched cards Wang encoded theorems straight out of the pages of Alfred North Whitehead and Bertrand Russell's *Principia Mathematica*, published almost 50 years earlier. For example, theorem *11.26 is stated in the notation of *Principia Mathematica* as:

$$*11 \cdot 26. \ \vdash: .(\exists x) : (y).\phi(x,y) :\supset: (y) : (\exists x).\phi(x,y)$$

In Wang's punched card notation this became:

```
11*26/EXAYGXY-AYEXGXY
```

Wang wrote three programs to read these cards and prove the encoded theorems by applying various identities and inference rules that transformed the statements back into axioms. The bulk of time spent by these programs consisted of the mechanical processes of reading the cards and printing the steps of the proof. Wang estimated that the actual processing time in proving 220 theorems from chapters *1 through *5 of *Principia Mathematica* was less than three minutes, and an improved version of his third program was later able to prove 158 theorems from chapters *9 through *13 in about four minutes.[1]

Wang's program was not the first attempt to solve theorems by computer.[2] In 1954, Martin Davis used a computer built by the Institute for Advanced

[1] Hao Wang, "Toward Mechanical Mathematics", *IBM Journal of Research and Development*, Vol. 4, No. 1 (Jan. 1960), 2–22. Available at http://www.research.ibm.com/journal/rd/041/ibmrd0401B.pdf.

[2] Donald MacKenzie, "The Automation of Proof: A Historical and Sociological Exploration," *Annals of the History of Computing*, Vol. 17, No. 3 (Fall 1995), 7–29.

Study in Princeton to program Presburger's procedure for a simple, addition-only arithmetic. In the first known mathematical proof by computer, Davis's program demonstrated that a sum of two even numbers is also an even number.[3]

In 1957, Allen Newell, J.C. "Cliff" Shaw, and Herbert Simon published their results of a "Logic Theory Machine" programmed for the RAND Corporation's JOHNNIAC, a computer named for John von Neumann.[4] Newell, Shaw, and Simon also used *Principia Mathematica* as the source of the theorems. Being more interested in artificial intelligence than in mathematical logic, they wrote their program to imitate the way a human would prove the theorems (a "heuristic" approach, they called it). Hao Wang later pursued a more algorithmic method for better efficiency and a higher success rate.

Upon being informed by letter about the results of the Logic Theory Machine, Bertrand Russell reputedly wrote back, "I am delighted to know that 'Principia Mathematica' can now be done by machinery. I wish Whitehead and I had known of this possibility before we wasted 10 years doing it by hand."[5]

Principia Mathematica, in its three volumes and nearly 2,000 pages, was a monumental achievement in mathematics and logic. When Modern Library listed the 100 best nonfiction works of the twentieth century, *Principia Mathematica* came in at number 23.[6] There are, however, very few people qualified to make such a determination. Stephen Kleene, a student of Alonzo Church who later wrote the influential *Introduction to Metamathematics* (1952) and *Mathematical Logic* (1967), freely admitted that he never read the *Principia Mathematica*[7] and among the people who have made their marks in mathematical logic in the years since 1913, he is probably in the large majority.

The Introduction of *Principia Mathematica* states a goal of nothing less than "the complete enumeration of all the ideas and steps in reasoning employed in mathematics." This is the program (and philosophy of mathematics) known

---

[3]Martin Davis, "A Computer Program for Presburger's Algorithm," in Jörg Seikmann and Graham Wrightson, eds., *Automation of Reasoning 1: Classical Papers on Computational Logic, 1957-1966* (Springer-Verlag, 1983), 41–48.

[4]Allen Newell, J.C. Shaw, and H.A. Simon, "Empirical Explorations with the Logic Theory Machine: A Case Study in Heuristics", *Proceedings of the Western Joint Computer Conference*, Vol. 15 (1957), 218–239. Reprinted in Edward A. Feigenbaum and Julian Feldman, eds., *Computers and Thought* (MIT Press, 1995), 109–133.

[5]Quoted in Michael J. Beeson, "The Mechanization of Mathematics," in Christof Teuscher, ed., *Alan Turing: Life and Legacy of a Great Thinker* (Springer, 2004), 93.

[6]http://www.randomhouse.com/modernlibrary/100bestnonfiction.html.

[7]William Aspray, The Princeton Mathematics Community in the 1930s: An Oral-History Project. An interview with J. Barkley Rosser and Stephen C. Kleene in Madison, Wisconsin, on 26 April 1984, http://www.princeton.edu/~mudd/finding_aids/mathoral/pmc23.htm.

as *logicism* — the use of logic as a foundation for the rest of mathematics. To accomplish this feat, Whitehead and Russell employed a full arsenal of set-theoretic and logical tools. The idea of deliberately restricting their mathematical techniques would have seemed absurd.

Not so for David Hilbert, the man most closely associated with the philosophy of mathematics called *formalism*. Formalism focuses on axiomatic theories, and particularly in Hilbert's program, emphasized concepts such as consistency, soundness, completeness, and decidability.

Partially for pedagogical purposes and partially for analytical purposes, David Hilbert broke down the logic of *Principia Mathematica* into expanding subsets, each of which could be studied on its own. This approach was the basis of a course he taught at Göttingen in the winter of 1917–1918. In 1928 it became the 120-page book *Grundzüge der Theoretischen Logik* (*Principles of Mathematical Logic*) by David Hilbert and Wilhelm Ackermann, the book commonly known as Hilbert & Ackermann. This book is the source of the Entscheidungsproblem that is the primary focus of Turing's paper.

Turing refers explicitly to *Grundzüge der Theoretischen Logik* in his paper, as well as a later book by David Hilbert and Paul Bernays, *Grundlagen der Mathematik* (*Foundations of Mathematics*), the first volume of which was published in Berlin in 1934, and which is known as Hilbert & Bernays. (The second volume appeared in 1939 after the publication of Turing's paper.)

The next part of Turing's paper requires some familiarity with mathematical logic as developed in Hilbert & Ackermann. In the following overview of that logic I will use Turing's notation, which is *very* similar to the notation used in Hilbert & Ackermann. I will also mimic the approach of describing this logic as an expanding subset of features; this has become standard and is found in textbooks on mathematical logic by Alonzo Church, Stephen Kleene, Elliott Mendelson, Herbert B. Enderton, and many others.

I will begin with what Hilbert & Ackermann called *Aussagenkalkül*, later translated as the *sentential calculus*, but known better today as the *propositional calculus* or *propositional logic*.

I will then expand the logic to what Hilbert & Ackermann originally called the *engere Funktionenkalkül* or the *restricted functional calculus*. In the second edition of the book (1938) this was renamed as the *engere Prädikatenkalkül*, or restricted predicate calculus, but is better known today as *first-order* logic, or first-order predicate logic, or the first-order predicate calculus. Once a few concepts are introduced, I'll be able to distinguish between first-order logic and second-order logic, termed by Hilbert & Ackermann as the *erweiterte Funktionenkalkül* and later the *erweiterte Prädikatenkalkül*, or *extended predicate calculus*.

Propositional (or sentential) logic deals with entire declarative propositions (or sentences) that have a *truth value* — that is, they can be judged to be either true or false. Examples might be:

Today is Wednesday.
Seven is a prime number.
It's raining.
My mother's name is Barbara.
Ten is a perfect square.

Some of these sentences are true, some are false, and some may be true for me but false for you. (No fighting!) In propositional logic, sentences have single consistent truth values with no ambiguity, and the less we pretend that we're successfully analyzing anything except mathematical propositions, the less confused we'll be.

In propositional logic, sentences are often represented by capital italic letters. Letters from the early part of the alphabet (A, B, and C) often stand for particular sentences with fixed truth values, while the latter part of the alphabet (X, Y, and Z) are used as variable propositions.

We can combine individual propositions with certain connectives to make more complex sentences.

The first of these connectives is a lower-case v, from the Latin word *vel* meaning *or*, and specifically, an *inclusive or*, as opposed to *aut*, the Latin *exclusive or*. The sentence

$$X \vee Y$$

is true if either X or Y is true, or if both are true. A little truth table is helpful for displaying the possible combinations of X and Y:

X	Y	X v Y
false	false	false
false	true	true
true	false	true
true	true	true

It is permissible to omit the v symbol when there's no confusion. The formula

$$XY$$

is equivalent to:

$$X \vee Y$$

Notice that I did not represent this equivalence by writing the two formulas on the same line separated by an equal sign. The equal sign is not part of the language of the propositional calculus — or at least the propositional calculus as Hilbert & Ackermann formulated it.

When we say that one sentence is *equivalent* to another, we mean they have the same truth value if all the constituent sentences have the same corresponding truth values. We are expressing this equivalence in a human language, also known as a *metalanguage*. Carefully distinguishing the language of logic from the metalanguage tends to avoid confusion.

Hilbert & Ackermann allowed a metalanguage abbreviation of aq. (for "äquivalent" in German) or eq. (for "equivalent" in the English translation):

$$X \vee Y \quad eq. \quad XY$$

Remember that this abbreviation is *not* part of the language of propositional logic and is strictly for convenience.

The concept of "and" is represented by the ampersand, &. The formula

$$X \& Y$$

is true only if both X and Y are true, as shown in this truth table:

X	Y	X & Y
false	false	false
false	true	false
true	false	false
true	true	true

The "and" operation is often called *conjunction* from the use of the word in grammar; consequently, the "or" operation is often called *disjunction*, a much less familiar word.

It is obvious from the truth tables that:

$$X \vee X \quad eq. \quad X$$
$$X \& X \quad eq. \quad X$$

You can use both connectives in a compound sentence, in which case v is evaluated before &, and if that's not what you want, you can override it with parentheses, or you can use parentheses strictly for clarification.

$$X \& Y \vee Z \quad eq. \quad X \& (Y \vee Z)$$

Those sentences are not equivalent to:

$$(X \& Y) \vee Z$$

For example, if X is false, Y is true, and Z is true, then the first pair of sentences is false but the last sentence is true.

I won't belabor the various rules that exist to ensure that parentheses are always properly paired, and that connectives appear in sensible positions. These rules contribute to the concept of well-formed formulas or wffs (pronounced "woofs"). The words "true" and "false" are not part of the vocabulary of propositional logic, and neither are the letters "T" and "F", but for convenience you can use them to substitute for propositional letters. You can think of T as a sentence that is always true, and F as a sentence that is always false. From now on I'll use T and F in truth tables as well.

The following equivalences are obvious from the truth tables:

$$X \vee T \quad \text{eq.} \quad T$$
$$X \vee F \quad \text{eq.} \quad X$$
$$X \mathbin{\&} T \quad \text{eq.} \quad X$$
$$X \mathbin{\&} F \quad \text{eq.} \quad F$$

It is also obvious from the truth tables that both operations are commutative:

$$X \vee Y \quad \text{eq.} \quad Y \vee X$$
$$X \mathbin{\&} Y \quad \text{eq.} \quad Y \mathbin{\&} X$$

Both operations are also associative:

$$X \vee (Y \vee Z) \quad \text{eq.} \quad (X \vee Y) \vee Z$$
$$X \mathbin{\&} (Y \mathbin{\&} Z) \quad \text{eq.} \quad (X \mathbin{\&} Y) \mathbin{\&} Z$$

Both operations are distributive over each other:

$$X \vee (Y \mathbin{\&} Z) \quad \text{eq.} \quad (X \vee Y) \mathbin{\&} (X \vee Z)$$
$$X \mathbin{\&} (Y \vee Z) \quad \text{eq.} \quad (X \mathbin{\&} Y) \vee (X \mathbin{\&} Z)$$

If you replace F in the truth tables with 0, and T with 1, you'll see that conjunction is exactly equivalent to the multiplication of two one-digit binary numbers, and disjunction is somewhat similar to addition. For this reason, conjunction is sometimes called the "logical product" and disjunction is the "logical sum." However, there is some inconsistency in the use of these terms, so they're not encouraged.

Conjunction and disjunction are binary operations; the only unary operation is called the "not" or "negation" and is symbolized by a dash much like a minus sign:

X	$-$X
F	T
T	F

Turing's notation differs from that of Hilbert & Ackermann, who use a bar over the letter or larger expression. Negation is always evaluated first: The negation sign applies only to the symbol immediately following it. A double negative cancels out:

$$-\!-X \quad \text{eq.} \quad X$$

These two relationships are very basic:

$$X \text{ v} -X \quad \text{eq.} \quad T$$
$$X \,\&\, -X \quad \text{eq.} \quad F$$

Two of the most fundamental — but also the most interesting — logical relationships combine disjunction, conjunction, and negation. These are called De Morgan's Laws after the nineteenth century mathematician Augustus De Morgan (1806–1871), although the basic concept was known to Aristotle:

$$-(X \text{ v } Y) \quad \text{eq.} \quad -X \,\&\, -Y$$
$$-(X \,\&\, Y) \quad \text{eq.} \quad -X \text{ v } -Y$$

These equivalences are evident in common speech. For example, "It's not raining or snowing" or — $(X \text{ v } Y)$ is the same as "It's not raining, *and* it's not snowing" or $-X \,\&\, -Y$. When I'm informed, "You're certainly *not* rich and handsome, alas" or $-(X \,\&\, Y)$, I can only conclude, "I suppose I'm either poor or I'm ugly ... or both," or $-X \text{ v} -Y$.

Notice that De Morgan's Laws can be written with all the negation signs clumped together:

$$X \text{ v } Y \quad \text{eq.} \quad -(-X \,\&\, -Y)$$
$$X \,\&\, Y \quad \text{eq.} \quad -(-X \text{ v } -Y)$$

In the truth tables for the v and & operations, you can change all the falses to trues and all the trues to falses, and you end up with the truth table for the opposite operation. This is known as the "principle of duality" and it applies to complex sentences as well. Here's one:

$$X \,\&\, -Y \text{ v } Z$$

Negate everything and swap v and & (but remember to keep any implied parentheses intact) and the new sentence is the negation of the original sentence:

$$-X \text{ v } (Y \,\&\, -Z)$$

If you wanted to verify that these two sentences are, in fact, negations of each other, you might construct a little truth table to test all the values:

X	Y	Z	X & —Y v Z	—X v (Y & —Z)
F	F	F	F	T
F	F	T	F	T
F	T	F	F	T
F	T	T	F	T
T	F	F	T	F
T	F	T	T	F
T	T	F	F	T
T	T	T	T	F

The final two columns have opposite truth values, so:

$$X \& -Y \vee Z \quad \text{eq.} \quad -(-X \vee (Y \& -Z))$$

There is no operator for the *exclusive* or, but the following formula does it:

$$(X \vee Y) \& -(X \& Y)$$

Here's a truth table that shows how the sentence works:

X	Y	X v Y	X & Y	(X v Y)& —(X & Y)
F	F	F	F	F
F	T	T	F	T
T	F	T	F	T
T	T	T	T	F

The exclusive-or is just like the regular disjunction except when both X and Y are true.

If you apply De Morgan's Laws to the second half of the sentence for exclusive-or, you get:

$$(X \vee Y) \& (-X \vee -Y)$$

You might like the symmetry of this version more.

Computer circuitry uses an exclusive-or to calculate the sum of two binary digits, and a conjunction for the carry bit.[8]

The third binary operation is the tricky one. It's called "implication." You can read $X \to Y$ as "X implies Y" or "if X, then Y." Be forewarned that many people have a "something wrong here" reaction when first confronting the truth table for implication:

X	Y	X → Y
F	F	T
F	T	T
T	F	F
T	T	T

The top two entries might seem strange. If X is false, why should $X \to Y$ be true regardless of the value of Y? One way to look at it is to begin by assuming $X \to Y$ is true. If $X \to Y$ is true and X is true, then Y must be true. However, if X isn't true then what does that say about Y? Nothing. Y can be anything. That's why $X \to Y$ can be true if X is false regardless of Y.

---

[8]Charles Petzold, *Code: The Hidden Language of Computer Hardware and Software* (Microsoft Press, 1999), ch. 12.

Consider the sentence, "If it's raining then it's precipitating." That sentence is true if it's raining but it's also true if it's not raining. The only time that sentence is false is when it's raining but not precipitating.

Implication is used a lot in mathematical logic. Very often to the left of the implication sign is a formula that we know to be true. If we can then show that the sentence itself is true, we can conclude that the formula on the right is true.

Implication is not commutative and not associative. However,

$$X \rightarrow Y \quad \text{eq.} \quad -Y \rightarrow -X$$

The second sentence is called the *contrapositive*. If it's raining then I'm taking an umbrella. I don't have my umbrella so it must not be raining. Implication has a very simple relationship with disjunction:

$$X \rightarrow Y \quad \text{eq.} \quad -X \vee Y$$

In other words, $X \rightarrow Y$ is true if either X is false or Y is true. It's also possible to express implication in terms of conjunction:

$$X \rightarrow Y \quad \text{eq.} \quad -(X \& -Y)$$

If a conjunction of any number of terms is on the left of the implication sign, then any one of those terms can be on the right:

$$X \& Y \rightarrow X$$
$$X \& Y \rightarrow Y$$

Hilbert & Ackermann describe a biconditional (or "if and only if") operation symbolized with a tilde:

X	**Y**	**X ~ Y**
F	F	T
F	T	F
T	F	F
T	T	T

$X \sim Y$ is true only if X and Y have the same truth values. Turing does not use the biconditional at all in his paper. Still, it's instructive to observe that it is equivalent to the conjunction of implications going both ways:

$$X \sim Y \quad \text{eq.} \quad (X \rightarrow Y) \& (Y \rightarrow X)$$

If you accept that this equivalence makes sense, then the only way it works is if $T \rightarrow T$ is true (which we all accept) and $F \rightarrow F$ is also true (which is one of the iffy ones). Also, $T \rightarrow F$ and $F \rightarrow T$ must have opposite truth values. Everybody agrees that $T \rightarrow F$ must be false, which means that $F \rightarrow T$ must be true. This confirms the correctness of the truth table for implication.

Suppose I give you the following sentence:

$$X \vee Y \vee (-X \, \& -Y)$$

What can you tell me about it? Is it true or false? You might object and say that you can't tell whether it's true or false unless you know the values of X and Y. I'll then suggest that you set up a truth table to test all the combinations of X and Y. Here it is:

X	Y	$X \vee Y \vee (-X \, \& -Y)$
F	F	T
F	T	T
T	F	T
T	T	T

Regardless of the individual values of X and Y, this sentence is always true. We say that such a sentence is a *tautology*, or that it is *universally valid*. Universally valid sentences are much loved in mathematical logic because they are true regardless of the truth values of the individual propositions.

Let's try another:

X	Y	$X \, \& \, Y \, \& -X$
F	F	F
F	T	F
T	F	F
T	T	F

That sentence is never true. It is a *contradiction*. The negation of a tautology is a contradiction, and the negation of a contradiction is a tautology.

Here's a third:

X	Y	$X \vee (Y \, \& -Y)$
F	F	F
F	T	F
T	F	T
T	T	T

This sentence is sometimes true and sometimes false depending on the values of X and Y. This sentence is said to be *satisfiable* — the sentence has the ability to be true with a certain combination of propositional values.

A sentence that is universally valid (a tautology) is also considered to be satisfiable. A sentence is universally valid if and only if the negation of that sentence is not satisfiable.

For any sentence, we can use a truth table to determine whether that sentence is universally valid, a contradiction, or merely satisfiable. The process of evaluating a truth table is mechanical. It doesn't require any special inspiration, insights, or intuition. If you're a computer programmer, you can easily imagine writing a program that reads a sentence in propositional logic, evaluates it, and prints the words "valid" or "contradiction" or "satisfiable."

For this reason, we say that sentences in the propositional calculus are *decidable*. A *decision procedure* exists to determine the validity, or satisfiability, of any arbitrary sentence in propositional logic.

In other words, the Entscheidungsproblem for the propositional calculus has been solved. We can all go home early today.

This is not to say that a truth table is always practical. Suppose a sentence has 100 propositional variables. The number of lines in the truth table is 2^{100} or 1,267,650,600,228,229,401,496,703,205,376, or about 10^{30}, which is a very large number. Even with a futuristic computer that processes each line in 1 nanosecond — a billionth of a second, or the length of time required for light to travel approximately one foot — the processing time would be 38 trillion years, about 3,000 times the current age of the universe.

The good news is this: If you restrict yourself to 55 propositional variables, and you're still able to process each line in 1 nanosecond, you'd only have to wait about a year. Each new variable doubles the processing time. In computability and complexity theory, the computing time for processing truth tables is known as *exponential time* because it relates exponentially to the size of the problem.

For those reasons, solutions other than truth tables are valuable for evaluating sentences in propositional logic. These techniques often involve putting the sentence in a *normal form*, which is either a conjunction of multiple terms, each of which is a disjunction of variables, or a disjunction of multiple terms, each of which is a conjunction of variables.

This concludes my all-too-hasty overview of propositional logic. We must move on because propositional logic is insufficient for many purposes. The big problem with propositional logic is that we're dealing with entire declarative sentences, and we can't relate the internals of different sentences to each other. Propositional logic fails when attempting to analyze Aristotelian syllogisms ("All men are mortal; Socrates is a man; hence...") or the straightforward sorites devised by Lewis Carroll ("No kitten, that loves fish, is unteachable; No kitten without a tail can play with a gorilla; Kittens with whiskers always love fish; No teachable kitten has green eyes; No kittens have tails unless they have whiskers; hence...[9]").

We can make logic more powerful by introducing *propositional functions* or *predicates*. (The first term is the one that Turing prefers; the second is somewhat more modern. I'll use the two terms interchangeably.) The term *predicate* comes from grammar, in which sentences are divided into subjects and predicates. For

---

[9]Lewis Carroll, *Symbolic Logic: Part I. Elementary* (Macmillan, 1896), 118. The solution is "No kitten with green eyes will play with a gorilla." But you knew that!

example, in the sentence "The politician speaks great truths," the subject is "The politician" and the predicate is "speaks great truths."

The introduction of predicates is the first step to turning propositional logic into first-order predicate logic. Whenever we use predicates, we're restricting ourselves to a specific *domain* or population. In real life, this domain is very often the natural numbers. Individuals from this population are *arguments* to the predicates.

In Hilbert & Ackermann (and in Turing), predicates look like functions, but they only have values of true and false. I like to use whole words or multiple words for my predicates, such as *IsPrime*. The domain of the *IsPrime* predicate consists of natural numbers, so that *IsPrime*(7) is true but *IsPrime*(9) is false. Individuals from the domain can be symbolized by lower-case letters that serve as variables, for example *IsPrime*(x).

Whenever a predicate has an explicit argument, then the predicate with its argument becomes a proposition. For example, *IsPrime*(10) is the same as the proposition "Ten is a prime." This is one way in which predicate logic relates to propositional logic.

Predicates can have multiple arguments. Suppose you're dealing with a domain consisting of your friends, all of whom have unique names. The predicate *Loves*(x, y) is true if person x loves person y. For example, *Loves*(Pat, Terry) is the same as the proposition "Pat loves Terry." Some predicates have commutative arguments, but not this one, so *Loves*(Pat, Terry) is *not* the same as *Loves*(Terry, Pat).

We can combine predicates with the same connectives used with propositional logic. The sentence

$$Loves(Pat, \ Terry) \ \& \ Loves(Terry, \ Pat)$$

is true if they both love each other, and

$$Loves(Pat, \ Terry) \ \sim \ Loves(Terry, \ Pat)$$

is true if their feelings (whatever they may be) are reciprocated.

What does this mean?

$$Loves(x, \ Pat)$$

It's not quite entirely clear. If it has any meaning at all, we might guess that it means that *everybody* loves Pat. Or maybe at least *somebody* loves Pat.

To avoid ambiguities like these, we must also introduce two *quantifiers*, which Turing calls *quantors*. The first is the *universal quantifier*, which consists of the variable enclosed in parentheses before the predicate:

$$(x)Loves(x, \ Pat)$$

The x in parentheses means "for all x." That formula is true if "for all x, x loves Pat." It's true if everybody loves Pat. This formula

$$(x)Loves(Pat, \ x)$$

is true if Pat loves everybody. The symbol ∀ is often used for the universal quantifier, but not by Hilbert & Ackermann or Turing.

The second type of quantifier is the *existential quantifier*, which translates as "there exists." Hilbert & Ackermann use a regular E for the existential quantifier but Turing prefers the more common ∃. For example,

$$(\exists x)Loves(x, \; Terry)$$

means that "there exists an x such that x loves Terry" or somebody loves Terry — at least one person, even if that person is Terry.

In first-order logic (what Hilbert & Ackermann called the *restricted* calculus), quantifiers are applied only to variables denoting individuals from the domain. In second-order logic (or the *extended* calculus), quantifiers can be applied to variables representing propositional functions. Turing's paper involves only first-order logic.

If we're dealing with a *finite* population, then the universal quantifier can be expressed as a conjunction, and the existential quantifier as a disjunction. For example, suppose our entire population consists of just Pat, Terry, and Kim. The formula:

$$(x)Loves(Kim, \; x)$$

is equivalent to the conjunction:

$$Loves(Kim, \; Pat) \; \& \; Loves(Kim, \; Terry) \; \& \; Loves(Kim, \; Kim)$$

All those individual predicates must be true for the sentence to be true. The formula

$$(\exists x)Loves(Kim, \; x)$$

is equivalent to:

$$Loves(Kim, \; Pat) \; v \; Loves(Kim, \; Terry) \; v \; Loves(Kim, \; Kim)$$

Only one of the predicates need be true for the sentence to be true.

If you recall the duality of De Morgan's Theorem and you apply that to these two formulas, you probably won't be inordinately surprised to discover that the universal and existential quantifiers can be represented in terms of each other when negation is introduced. These two equivalent formulas are true if not everyone loves Terry:

$$—(x)Loves(x, \; Terry) \quad eq. \quad (\exists x)—Loves(x, \; Terry)$$

The following two formulas are both true if nobody loves Terry:

$$(x)—Loves(x, \; Terry) \quad eq. \quad —(\exists x)Loves(x, \; Terry)$$

Similarly,

$$(x)Loves(x, \; Terry) \quad eq. \quad —(\exists x)—Loves(x, \; Terry)$$

The formula on the right can be translated as, "it is not the case that there exists someone who does not love Terry." Similarly,

$$(\exists x)Loves(x,\ Terry)\quad eq.\quad -(x)-Loves(x,\ Terry)$$

It is not the case that nobody loves Terry.

When American mathematician Charles Sanders Peirce (1839–1914) developed his logical quantifiers, he used the symbol $\sum$, commonly associated with summation, for the existential quantifier and $\prod$, the symbol for a compound product, for the universal quantifier, further emphasizing the relationship between logic and binary arithmetic.

The x that I've been using in these formulas is known as a *bound variable* because it is attached to the quantifier. It serves the same role as a variable function argument. Any variable that is not part of a universal or existential quantifier is known as a *free variable*. In the following formula, x is bound but y is free:

$$(\exists x)Loves(x,\ y)$$

Free or bound variables can be changed, but only if they don't clash with other variables. For example, we can change the x in the preceding formula to z:

$$(\exists z)Loves(z,\ y)$$

The formula has exactly the same meaning, but we can't change the bound variable to a y because it would then clash with the free variable and become something completely different.

A single formula cannot contain a bound variable and a free variable that are the same. A formula in first-order logic containing no free variables can be referred to as a *sentence* or a *proposition*. It is not proper to use these words to describe formulas that contain free variables.

Bound variables have a scope often indicated by parentheses. In the following sentence, x is bound throughout the parenthetical expression:

$$(x)[Loves(x,\ Kim)\ \&\ Loves(x,\ Pat)]$$

Notice the use of brackets instead of parentheses just to make the statement more readable. The sentence means that everybody loves Kim and loves Pat; it has the same meaning as:

$$(x)Loves(x,\ Kim)\ \&\ (x)Loves(x,\ Pat)$$

Now those two bound variables are independent of each other, and one or the other can be changed:

$$(y)Loves(y,\ Kim)\ \&\ (x)Loves(x,\ Pat)$$

The following statement is true if someone loves both Kim and Pat:

$$(\exists x)[Loves(x,\ Kim)\ \&\ Loves(x,\ Pat)]$$

However, the meaning changes when you separate the two predicates:

$$(\exists x)Loves(x,\ Kim)\ \&\ (\exists x)Loves(x,\ Pat)$$

Now there's someone who loves Kim and someone who loves Pat, but it's not necessarily the same person.

Now replace the conjunction I've been using in the last several formulas with a disjunction:

$$(x)[Loves(x,\ Kim)\ v\ Loves(x,\ Pat)]$$

That's true if every person either loves Kim or loves Pat (or both). It's true if Terry loves Kim but not Pat, and if Terry loves Pat but not Kim. The sentence meaning changes when you separate the two predicates:

$$(x)Loves(x,\ Kim)\ v\ (x)Loves(x,\ Pat)$$

This is true only if everybody loves Kim or everybody loves Pat or everybody loves both.

Here's an existential quantifier applied over a disjunction:

$$(\exists x)[Loves(x,\ Kim)\ v\ Loves(x,\ Pat)]$$

There exists a person who loves either Kim or Pat or both. Separating the two predicates retains the meaning:

$$(\exists x)Loves(x,\ Kim)\ v\ (\exists x)Loves(x,\ Pat)$$

Two basic relationships apply to all propositional functions. In both examples, A is a predicate and a is a member of the domain. The first relationship is:

$$(x)A(x)\ \rightarrow\ A(a)$$

If the predicate is true for everyone, then it's true for any individual. The second is this:

$$A(a)\ \rightarrow\ (\exists x)A(x)$$

Quantifiers can be stacked. For example,

$$(\exists x)(y)Loves(x,\ y)$$

This is interpreted as if the quantifiers were grouped like this:

$$(\exists x)[(y)Loves(x,\ y)]$$

It's true if there exists a person who loves everybody. The meaning is not quite the same when you switch the order of the quantifiers:

$$(y)(\exists x)Loves(x,\ y)$$

This is true if everyone is loved by somebody, but not necessarily by the same person. For example, if Kim loves Kim, and Terry loves Terry, but they don't love each other, then:

$$(y)(\exists x)Loves(x,\ y)$$

is true but,

$$(\exists x)(y)Loves(x,\ y)$$

is not. If the sentence beginning with the existential quantifier is true, however, then so is the other one. This relationship is encapsulated in Theorem *11.26 from *Principia Mathematica* that you saw at the beginning of this chapter:

$$*11\cdot 26.\ \vdash:\ .(\exists x):(y).\phi(x,\ y):\supset:(y):(\exists x).\phi(x,\ y)$$

where $\phi(x, y)$ is a predicate. In the notation that Turing uses, that's:

$$(\exists x)(y)\phi(x,\ y)\ \rightarrow\ (y)(\exists x)\phi(x,\ y)$$

When a string of consecutive universal quantifiers appears in a formula, they can be rearranged without changing anything. The same is true for a string of existential quantifiers. (Convert the sentence to a compound conjunction or disjunction to convince yourself this is so.) In general, however, a series of interspersed universal quantifiers and existential quantifiers cannot be rearranged without changing the meaning of the formula.

Just as with propositional logic, formulas can be evaluated without regard to the meanings of the domain and the predicates. The formula

$$(x)[F(x)\ v -F(x)]$$

is considered to be *universally valid* because it's true regardless of the domain and the definition of the propositional function F. The following formula, however, is never true:

$$(\exists x)(F(x)\ \&\ -F(x))$$

Such a formula is said to be *refutable*. Then there are the formulas that fall somewhere in between. This one is very simple:

$$(x)F(x)$$

It's easy to come up with a domain for x and a function F where this is true. Suppose the domain consists of natural numbers and F means "greater than or equal to zero." It's equally easy to identify a domain and function where it's false. Suppose F returns true if the argument is prime. This formula is said to be "satisfiable" because it's true under some interpretations.

Validity and satisfiability are flip sides of the same problem because the concepts are related: A sentence is either satisfiable or refutable. If sentence $\mathfrak{A}$ is valid, then it is also satisfiable (but not necessarily the other way around). If $\mathfrak{A}$ is satisfiable but not valid, then —$\mathfrak{A}$ is also satisfiable but not refutable. $\mathfrak{A}$ is valid if and only if —$\mathfrak{A}$ is not satisfiable.

The words *validity* and *satisfiability* are sometimes associated with a *semantic* approach to mathematical logic, so called because it's referring to the truth meaning of the sentences involved.

Another approach to mathematical logic is *syntactic* in nature. You begin with axioms and derive theorems. Such theorems are said to be *provable*, meaning that they are a consequence of the axioms. With the syntactic approach to logic, it's not necessary to get involved with messy — possibly metaphysical — concepts of truth.

For propositional logic, Hilbert & Ackermann stated four rather obvious axioms derived from *Principia Mathematica*:

(a) $X \vee X \rightarrow X$
(b) $X \rightarrow X \vee Y$
(c) $X \vee Y \rightarrow Y \vee X$
(d) $(X \rightarrow Y) \rightarrow (Z \vee X \rightarrow Z \vee Y)$

Although the axioms refer only to disjunction and implication, we can apply them to conjunction as well if we define X & Y as an abbreviation for —(—X v—Y).

For first-order logic, Hilbert & Ackermann added two more axioms. For any predicate F, the following statements are axioms:

(e) $(x)F(x) \rightarrow F(y)$
(f) $F(y) \rightarrow (\exists x)F(x)$

In addition to the axioms are rules for obtaining complex statements from primitive statements:

1. Substitution: A propositional variable can be consistently replaced with a formula while avoiding clashes among bound and free variables; free and bound variables can be changed if clashes are avoided; predicates can be replaced with formulas.
2. Implication: If formula $\mathfrak{A}$ is true, and if formula $\mathfrak{A} \rightarrow \mathfrak{B}$ is true, then $\mathfrak{B}$ is true.

This second rule is known as *modus ponens* (mode of affirmation). It seems to be obvious, but it really must be an axiom. You can't derive it, and if you think you can, you might want to take a look at Lewis Carroll's essay "What the Tortoise Said to Achilles."[10]

---

[10]Lewis Carroll, "What the Tortoise Said to Achilles," *Mind*, New Series, Vol. 4, No. 14 (Apr. 1895), 278–280, and frequently republished.

Anything that can be derived from these six axioms and two rules is known as a *theorem*. The derivation itself is known as a *proof*. Any formula that is the result of a proof is said to be *provable*. A theorem is a provable formula.

For example, if $\mathfrak{A}$ and $\mathfrak{B}$ are both theorems, then by axiom (c) and rule (1) we can say that

$$\mathfrak{A} \vee \mathfrak{B} \;\rightarrow\; \mathfrak{B} \vee \mathfrak{A}$$

is provable and hence also a theorem.

The rules go both ways: You can begin with axioms and use the rules to derive theorems, or you can begin with a formula and use the rules to convert it into an axiom, in which case you can classify the formula as a theorem. The automated proof programs I discussed at the beginning of this chapter began with theorems from *Principia Mathematica* and applied the axioms and substitution rules to reduce them to axioms.

As you can see, Hilbert's formalization of mathematics seemed to reduce it to a mechanical process of symbol manipulation. This was evident to Henri Poincaré (1854–1912), who wrote that "we might imagine a machine where we put in axioms at one end and take out theorems at the other, like that legendary machine in Chicago where pigs go in alive and come out transformed into hams and sausages."[11]

You can even mechanically *enumerate* all the theorems in a systematic manner. You begin with the axioms, which you extend to any number of propositional variables and any number of predicates, and then you apply the substitution and implication rules in every possible combination.

By definition, a theorem is a formula that is derivable from the axioms, so this enumeration of theorems yields every possible theorem. A question then raises itself: Are these theorems the same as the universally valid formulas? Or might there be some universally valid formulas that cannot be generated based on the axioms?

Using Hilbert and Ackermann's book as a springboard, Kurt Gödel established the equivalence between the semantic and syntactic approaches to first-order logic first in his 1929 doctoral thesis, "Über die Vollständigkeit des Logikkalküls" ("On the Completeness of the Calculus of Logic"), and then in the 1930 paper "Die Vollständigkeit der Axiome des logischen Funktionenkalküls" ("The Completeness of the Axioms of the Functional Calculus of Logic").

Prior to Gödel, it had already been known that every provable formula was also universally valid. This is known as *soundness*, and it's essential to a logical

---

[11] Henri Poincaré, *Science and Method*, translated by Francis Maitland (Thomas Nelson & Sons, 1914; Dover, 2003), 147.

system. What Gödel proved was that every universally valid formula was also provable. This is one possible definition of "completeness" of a logical system, and indeed, the titles of Gödel's papers refer to *Vollständigkeit* — completeness. Gödel's Completeness Theorem demonstrated that the axioms are complete — that the axiomatic system proposed by Hilbert & Ackermann for the pure predicate logic is sufficient for enumerating every universally valid statement in that logic.

It might be supposed that the enumeration of theorems and Gödel's Completeness Theorem provide the basis for a decision procedure for first-order logic. For example, suppose you want to determine the provability of formula $\mathfrak{A}$. You begin enumerating all the theorems and comparing them with $\mathfrak{A}$. If $\mathfrak{A}$ is not provable, however, you won't get a match, and you won't know when to stop.

Yes, I know that you're cleverer than that: Your approach is to enumerate all the theorems and compare each theorem *and its negation* to $\mathfrak{A}$ (or you compare each theorem to $\mathfrak{A}$ and its negation). You're *still* not guaranteed to get a match because $\mathfrak{A}$ might be merely satisfiable and not universally valid or refutable. For this reason, an enumeration-based decision procedure is said to be only *semi-decidable*. Only if you know beforehand that either $\mathfrak{A}$ or $—\mathfrak{A}$ is universally valid will the procedure successfully come to a conclusion. Even after Gödel's 1930 papers, the Entscheidungsproblem for first-order logic was still an open question.

Gödel's more famous paper was published in 1931, and involved an application of first-order logic to basic arithmetic — addition and multiplication. Using this arithmetic, Gödel was able to associate a number with every formula and every proof. Gödel created a predicate named Bew for *beweisbar*, meaning *provable*, and was able to apply this predicate to the Gödel number of its negation, creating a formula that asserts its own unprovability.

Thus, within a logical system supporting basic arithmetic, it is possible to develop propositions that can be neither proved nor disproved. Although this concept has come to be known as the Gödel Incompleteness Theorem, the title of the paper is actually "Über formal unentscheidbare Sätze der *Principia mathematica* under verwandter Systeme I" ("On Formally Undecidable Propositions of *Principia Mathematica* and Related Systems I").[12] The title refers not to completeness or incompleteness but to *unentscheidbare Sätze* — undecidable propositions.

Does Gödel's Incompleteness Theorem spell doom for a general decision procedure? Not necessarily, although a general decision procedure certainly seemed more unlikely in 1931 than in 1930. Gödel's Incompleteness Theorem is about undecidable propositions, while the Entscheidungsproblem concerns the

---

[12] All three Gödel papers I've cited are most conveniently available in Kurt Gödel, *Collected Works: Volume I, Publications 1929–1936* (Oxford University Press, 1986).

existence of a general process to determine the provability of any given formula. A decision procedure, if it existed, would classify an undecidable proposition as unprovable.

The early computer programs that proved theorems from the pages of *Principia Mathematica* definitely did *not* do so by starting with the axioms and systematically deriving all provable formulas. The Newell-Simon-Shaw paper refers to this as the "British Museum algorithm," so called because it's akin to searching through the British Museum and examining each object in hopes of discovering the precise one you want. This brute-force approach was rejected by these early researchers as soon as it was considered. As Martin Davis put it,

> [I]t was all too obvious that an attempt to generate a proof of something non-trivial by beginning with the axioms of some logical system and systematically applying the rules of inference in all possible directions was sure to lead to a gigantic combinatorial explosion.[13]

Only one programmer operated without fear of combinatorial explosions, and that was Alan Turing. Turing's imaginary computers have unlimited storage and all the time in the world, so Turing can journey where more machine-bound programmers fear to tread.

In the previous chapter I left off in the middle of Section 9, "The extent of the computable numbers." Turing had begun Section 9 with a need to convince us that the numbers computable by his machine include "all numbers which would naturally be regarded as computable" (pg. 249 of Turing's paper; page 190 in this book).

Turing then began with a section headed by Roman numeral I (meaning the first of several arguments) and "Type (*a*)" meaning "A direct appeal to intuition." The next section coming up begins with a heading of Roman numeral II because it's the second of Turing's arguments, and "Type (*b*)" which he indicated was "A proof of the equivalence of two definitions (in case the new definition has greater intuitive appeal)."

The single sentence that follows this heading has three footnotes. The first footnote only clarifies that he's talking about the restricted functional calculus, which is what we know as first-order predicate logic. I want you to ignore the second footnote for the moment. I'll discuss it soon enough.

---

[13]Martin Davis, "The Early History of Automated Deduction," in Alan Robinson and Andrei Voronkov, eds., *Handbook of Automated Reasoning* (MIT Press, 2001), Vol. I, 3–15.

II.   [Type (*b*)].

If the notation of the Hilbert functional calculus[†] is modified so as to be systematic, and so as to involve only a finite number of symbols, it becomes possible to construct an automatic[‡] machine, $\mathcal{K}$, which will find all the provable formulae of the calculus[§].

[†] The expression "the functional calculus" is used throughout to mean the *restricted* Hilbert functional calculus.

[‡] It is most natural to construct first a choice machine (§2) to do this. But it is then easy to construct the required automatic machine. We can suppose that the choices are always choices between two possibilities 0 and 1. Each proof will then be determined by a sequence of choices $i_1, i_2, \ldots, i_n$ ($i_1 = 0$ or 1, $i_2 = 0$ or 1, $\ldots, i_n = 0$ or 1), and hence the number $2^n + i_1 2^{n-1} + i_2 2^{n-2} + \cdots + i_n$ completely determines the proof. The automatic machine carries out successively proof 1, proof 2, proof 3, ...

[§] The author has found a description of such a machine.

I believe Turing calls the machine $\mathcal{K}$ to stand for the German word *Kalkül*. Although not entirely obvious in this sentence, you'll see eventually that Turing is describing a British Museum algorithm. The machine $\mathcal{K}$ begins with axioms either already encoded on the tape or, alternatively, the machine begins by writing the axioms on the tape. These are the basic axioms of first-order logic plus whatever other axioms are required for additional predicates. The machine implements the inference rules progressively to generate all the provable statements of the calculus.

Turing requires that the notation of first-order logic "be modified so as to be systematic." Surely we don't want to worry about the equivalence of statements that differ solely in the use of variable names or unnecessary parentheses. For example, these three statements must be regarded as identical:

$$(x)(\exists y)\phi(x, y)$$
$$(y)(\exists x)\phi(y, x)$$
$$(x)(\exists y)(\phi(x, y))$$

The notation can be made systematic by requiring that variables always be of the form x_i, and that they must appear in a particular formula in numeric order of the subscript. Moreover, parentheses must be used only where they're needed to govern the order of operations. Alternatively (and most likely in a practical machine), the formulas could be encoded in a prefix notation that makes parentheses unnecessary, such as the so-called Polish notation that Jan Łukasiewicz (1878–1956) invented specifically for propositional logic. Rather than

$$(A \text{ v } B) \text{ \& } (C \text{ v } D)$$

the statement would be encoded as:

&vABvCD

What's important here is that this machine generates all provable formulas. We know from the Gödel Completeness Theorem that this collection is the same as all universally valid formulas.

I believe that Turing is attempting here to appeal to those early readers of his paper who might be skeptical about the ability of his machines to compute real numbers of any arbitrary degree of complexity. In 1936 there was much more trust in the efficacy of first-order logic than computing machines. From an implementation viewpoint, this $\mathcal{K}$ machine seems quite feasible. It is certainly much simpler than machines that compute real numbers such as the seventh root of 10. Machine $\mathcal{K}$ works solely with strings of symbols and pastes them together in various ways through rules of substitution. Much of the string comparison and substitution logic has already been presented in the functions Turing used in the Universal Machine.

The second footnote of this sentence — the footnote that begins, "It is most natural to construct . . ." — actually seems to describe a somewhat different approach that would be more suitable for propositional logic than first-order logic. Given a fixed number n of propositional variables, you can develop a system to generate all well-formed formulas by interspersing these variables with the logical connectives. For each of these formulas, you then test whether the formula is a tautology using a truth-table approach.

If this well-formed formula has n propositional variables, then 2^n tests are required to determine whether the formula is valid. If you think of true and false as the binary digits 1 and 0, then each test corresponds to an n-digit binary number where each digit represents the truth value of one variable. In Turing's footnote, this n-digit binary number is slightly incorrect, and the 2^n term at the beginning must be deleted. The trials can be numbered beginning with 0 and ending with $(n-1)$ to correspond with the value of the n-digit binary number.

Although Turing needs to use this $\mathcal{K}$ machine to generate statements in first-order logic rather than propositional logic, you'll see that whenever he requires integers, he only requires a *finite* domain of non-negative integers. At no time does he require an infinite domain, so conceivably his first-order formulas could be converted to propositional formulas, and he could then use a truth-table solution.

The introduction of natural numbers into a system of first-order logic is always somewhat messy but pretty much essential if we're going to apply the logic to numeric concepts. Merging numbers into logic usually begins with a variation of the Peano Axioms. These are five axioms extracted from an original nine axioms presented by Giuseppe Peano in his small 1889 book *The Principles of Arithmetic, Presented by a New Method*,[14] but based on Richard Dedekind's 1888 pamphlet *Was sind und was sollen die Zahlen? (What are and What should be the Numbers?)*.[15]

The Peano Axioms are built around the concept of a "successor," which is intuitively the number that comes right after a number. For example, the successor to 12 is 13. The Peano Axioms ensure that every number has a successor, and that this successor is unique. Only one number is not the successor to any number. In Peano's formulation, that number is 1, but these days the natural numbers are generally defined to begin with zero.

Here's one version of the Peano Axioms in plain English:

1. Zero is a number.
2. Every number has a successor that is also a number.
3. Zero is not the successor to any number.
4. Two numbers that are the successors to the same number are equal.
5. If something is true for zero, and if the fact that it's true for some number implies that it's true for the successor of that number, then it's true for all numbers.

The fifth axiom is commonly known as the principle of mathematical induction, and it forms the basis of many mathematical proofs about the natural numbers. (Turing will use it twice in proofs in the next two chapters.) Nevertheless, expressing induction in the language of first-order logic is problematic. Induction is inherently a concept of second-order logic because it must apply to all predicates that have arguments of natural numbers. The concept of equality is a second-order concept as well, and that's why you'll see a reluctance among logicians — and Turing in this paper — to introduce a predicate that is true if two arguments are equal.

Even the task of encapsulating the first four Peano Axioms in the language of first-order logic is not trivial and (as you'll see) Turing's representation is inadequate. This problem has no real effect on his proof or conclusions, but it's certainly disturbing.

Another problem involves representing the natural numbers themselves. The quaint tradition of using 0, 1, 2, 3, and so forth simply will not do. Nothing except centuries of convention and the brutal indoctrination of grammar school tells us

---

[14]Excerpted in Jean van Heijenoort, ed., *From Frege to Gödel: A Source Book in Mathematical Logic, 1879–1931* (Harvard University Press, 1967), 83–97. Complete version available in *Selected Works of Giuseppe Peano*, translated and edited by Hubert C. Kennedy (George Allen & Unwin, 1973), 101–134.

[15]Reprinted in William Ewald, ed., *From Kant to Hilbert: A Source Book in the Foundations of Mathematics* (Oxford University Press, 1996), Vol. II, 787–833.

that the successor of 12 is 13. Particularly if we're conceiving mechanical forms of symbol manipulation, a much better approach is to have symbols that themselves convey the concept of successorship.

In the first volume of *Grundlagen der Mathematik* (1934) — a book that Turing later refers to in his paper — Paul Bernays uses prime marks to indicate that one number is the successor to another. For example, if a is a number, then a' is the successor to that number, and a'' is the next successor. Bernays also uses the symbol 0 to represent zero, in which case $0'$ is the successor to zero, and $0''$ is the next successor.[16] What number is it *really*? Just count the prime marks on the 0. The earliest example I've seen of this notation in the works of Hilbert and his followers is in David Hilbert's 1927 "Foundations of Mathematics."[17]

Turing doesn't take *quite* this approach. He is apparently reluctant to use even the 0 symbol. Instead he uses the symbol u as the first natural number. (He's somewhat vague whether u is 0 or 1 or even if it matters. In my examples I've assumed that u is 0.) The successors of u are then u', u'', u''' and so forth. This notation could get unwieldy for large numbers, and it doesn't let us represent an arbitrary number such as n or x. Taking a cue from Hilbert & Bernays, Turing uses the notation $u^{(r)}$ to indicate r prime marks on u. For example, u''''' can be represented as $u^{(5)}$, which we know as the number of fingers on one human hand.

Turing defines a propositional function $N(x)$ which is true if x is a non-negative integer. If we're restricting ourselves to a universe of non-negative integers anyway, this function doesn't really tell us anything, but Turing finds it useful to express the Peano Axioms.

Turing also defines a propositional function $F(x, y)$ which is true if y is the successor to x, or in common arithmetic, $y = x + 1$. Keep in mind that F does not *provide* the successor or *calculate* the successor. It is what programmers call a Boolean function. It is intended to be true only if y is actually the successor to x.

Once you have a good successor predicate (named *Succ*, for example, just to distinguish it from Turing's), and you've established an axiom for mathematical induction, it's possible to define a predicate named $Sum(x, y, z)$ that is true if z equals $x + y$. The *Sum* predicate is based on the following three axioms:

$(x)Sum(x, u, x)$

$(x)Sum(u, x, x)$

$(x)(y)(z)(r)(s)(Sum(x, y, z) \,\&\, Succ(y, r) \,\&\, Succ(z, s) \rightarrow Sum(x, r, s))$

The first two axioms define the addition of zero to any number. The third says that if $x + y = z$ and $r = y + 1$ and $s = z + 1$ then $x + r = s$.

---

[16]David Hilbert and Paul Bernays, *Grundlagen der Mathematik*, Volume I (Springer, 1934), 218.

[17]David Hilbert, "Foundations of Mathematics," *From Frege to Gödel*, 467.

It's possible to define a *Product(x, y, z)* predicate similarly:

(x)*Product(x, u, u)*

(x)*Product(u, x, u)*

(x)(y)(z)(r)(s)(*Product(x, y, z)* & *Succ(y, r)* & *Sum(z, x, s)*
  → *Product(x, r, s)*)

The first two axioms define multiplication by zero, and the third says that if $x \times y = z$ and $r = y + 1$ and $z + x = s$ then $x \times r = s$.

Let's go a little further. The predicate *IsEven(x)* can be defined as:

$$(\exists y)Product(y, u'', x)$$

IsEven(x) is true if there exists a *y* such that $x = y \times 2$. The predicate *IsOdd(x)* is the same as —*IsEven(x)*, and here I'll stop because I have enough for my examples.

Now let *α* be a sequence, and let us denote by $G_\alpha(x)$ the proposition "The *x*-th figure of *α* is 1", so that[‖] —$G_\alpha(x)$ means "The *x*-th figure of *α* is 0".

[‖] The negation sign is written before an expression and not over it.

That footnote is where Turing indicates he's using a negation symbol that differs from Hilbert's. This *α* is a sequence that we'd normally compute by designing a dedicated machine. Turing suggests here that we instead derive predicates that are true and false corresponding to digits 1 and 0. For example, the sequence corresponding to the square root of two, developed in Chapter 6, begins:

1011011010 . . .

If we number the digits beginning with 0, then $G_\alpha(0)$ is true, $G_\alpha(1)$ is false, $G_\alpha(2)$ is true, $G_\alpha(3)$ is true, $G_\alpha(4)$ is false, and so on. That's likely quite a complex predicate. A much easier sequence is Turing's Example I machine:

0101010101 . . .

This sequence, you'll recall, is the binary equivalent of 1/3. A propositional function that describes this sequence is easy if we define $G_\alpha(x)$ as *IsOdd(x)*.

Suppose further that we can find a set of properties which define the sequence *α* and which can be expressed in terms of $G_\alpha(x)$ and of the propositional functions *N(x)* meaning "*x* is a non-negative integer" and *F(x, y)* meaning "$y = x + 1$".

Here is Turing's introduction of two predicates he will use through much of the remainder of the paper. F is the successor function so crucial to defining the natural numbers. I am much less convinced of the need for the N function if the domain is explicitly restricted to the natural numbers.

I'm not sure what Turing means by a "set of properties." What we really want here are axioms that support the propositional functions from which $G_\alpha(x)$ is composed. In my simple example, these axioms would include the axioms for the *Sum* and *Product* predicates.

> When we join all these formulae together conjunctively, we shall have a formula, $\mathfrak{A}$ say, which defines α.

The conjunction of the axioms doesn't really define α so much as provide a foundation for defining α.

> The terms of $\mathfrak{A}$ must include the necessary parts of the Peano axioms, viz.,
>
> $$(\exists u)\, N(u) \mathrel{\&} (x)\,(N(x) \to (\exists y)\, F(x,y)) \mathrel{\&} (F(x,y) \to N(y)),$$
>
> which we will abbreviate to P.

The P is for Peano, of course. This is a conjunction of three terms. The first indicates that u exists; the second says that for every x there is a y that is its successor, that the third indicates that a successor to a number is also a natural number. This formula does *not* establish the uniqueness of zero, or the uniqueness of successors, and that's a problem. Hilbert & Bernays has the following three axioms for the successor function (which they call S).[18]

$$(x)(\exists y)S(x,y)$$
$$(\exists x)(y)\!-\!S(y,x)$$
$$(x)(y)(r)(s)(S(x,r)) \mathrel{\&} S(y,r) \mathrel{\&} S(s,x) \to S(s,y)$$

The first asserts that every number has a successor; the second says that there exists a number that does not have a predecessor; the third says that if r is the successor to x and y, and x is the successor to s, then y is also the successor to s, essentially establishing the uniqueness of successors.

> When we say "$\mathfrak{A}$ defines α", we mean that $-\mathfrak{A}$ is not a provable formula, and also that, for each n, one of the following formulae (A_n) or

---

[18]Hilbert and Bernays, *Grundlagen der Mathematik*, Volume I, 209. I've modified the notation a bit to agree with Turing's.

(B_n) is provable.

$$\mathfrak{A} \,\&\, F^{(n)} \rightarrow G_\alpha(u^{(n)}), \qquad\qquad (A_n)\P$$

$$\mathfrak{A} \,\&\, F^{(n)} \rightarrow (-G_\alpha(u^{(n)})), \qquad\qquad (B_n),$$

where $F^{(n)}$ stands for $F(u, u') \,\&\, F(u', u'') \,\&\, \ldots F(u^{(n-1)}, u^{(n)})$.

¶ A sequence of r primes is denoted by $^{(r)}$.

The footnote on the identifier for the (A_n) formula refers to the convention of using a superscript in parentheses to indicate a series of prime marks. Turing also uses a superscript on his successor function F to indicate a conjunction of successor functions, essentially saying that 1 is the successor to 0, 2 is the successor to 1, and so forth.

Turing's conjunction of successor functions is inadequate because it does not establish that these successors are unique. For example, what is the truth value of $F(u', u''')$? Nothing is telling us that this is false. One simple possible correction expands $F^{(n)}$ greatly (although still finitely) by including negations of all successor predicates that are not true, such as $—F(u, u'')$ and $—F(u', u)$, stopping at $u^{(n)}$.

The n here is the digit number, starting with digit 0 and progressively getting higher. The sequence is generated from digit 0, digit 1, digit 2, and so forth. The computation of each digit requires only a finite number of non-negative integers, so the $F^{(n)}$ formula is a finite conjunction of terms. In some cases, however, the formula might require a few more integers. For example, for digit 0, the formulas indicate that only u is required, but in my example u'' is also required for the definition of the $IsOdd$ function, so the superscript on F should really be the greater of n and 2.

With that little fix, the following formulas will be provable:

$$B_0 : \quad \mathfrak{A} \,\&\, F^{(2)} \rightarrow —IsOdd(u)$$

$$A_1 : \quad \mathfrak{A} \,\&\, F^{(2)} \rightarrow IsOdd(u')$$

$$B_2 : \quad \mathfrak{A} \,\&\, F^{(2)} \rightarrow —IsOdd(u'')$$

$$A_3 : \quad \mathfrak{A} \,\&\, F^{(3)} \rightarrow IsOdd(u''')$$

$$B_4 : \quad \mathfrak{A} \,\&\, F^{(4)} \rightarrow —IsOdd(u'''')$$

$$A_5 : \quad \mathfrak{A} \,\&\, F^{(5)} \rightarrow IsOdd(u''''')$$

and so forth. $\mathfrak{A}$, you'll recall, includes all the axioms required to support the $IsOdd$ function. These results correspond to the first six digits of the sequence: 0, 1, 0, 1,

0, 1. Notice that 1 digits correspond to A_n being provable, and 0 digits correspond to the provability of B_n.

> [253]
>
> I say that α is then a computable sequence: a machine $\mathcal{K}_\alpha$ to compute α can be obtained by a fairly simple modification of $\mathcal{K}$.

The $\mathcal{K}$ machine, you'll recall, generated all provable formulas from the axioms.

> We divide the motion of $\mathcal{K}_\alpha$ into sections. The n-th section is devoted to finding the n-th figure of α. After the $(n-1)$-th section is finished a double colon :: is printed after all the symbols, and the succeeding work is done wholly on the squares to the right of this double colon. The first step is to write the letter "A" followed by the formula (A_n) and then "B" followed by (B_n).

For this example and n equal to 5, the machine first writes "A" and "B" followed by the two possibilities:

$$\textbf{A}\ \mathfrak{A}\ \&\ F^{(5)} \rightarrow IsOdd(u''''') \quad \textbf{B}\ \mathfrak{A}\ \&\ F^{(5)} \rightarrow {-\!\!-} IsOdd(u''''')$$

Not exactly, however: The "A" and "B" won't be boldfaced, the $\mathfrak{A}$ term will be the explicit conjunction of all the axioms, $F^{(5)}$ will be an explicit conjunction of more axioms, *IsOdd* will probably be a negation of the *Product* function shown earlier, and all the functions will probably be given more cryptic names.

The point, however, is that one or the other of these two statements will be provable. The machine has the entire tape to the right of these two printed formulas to do its work. Perhaps it first writes the axioms on the tape and then begins the work to derive the provable formulas.

> The machine $\mathcal{K}_\alpha$ then starts to do the work of $\mathcal{K}$, but whenever a provable formula is found, this formula is compared with (A_n) and with (B_n). If it is the same formula as (A_n), then the figure "1" is printed, and the n-th section is finished. If it is (B_n), then "0" is printed and the section is finished. If it is different from both, then the work of $\mathcal{K}$ is continued from the point at which it had been abandoned. Sooner or later one of the formulae (A_n) or (B_n) is reached; this follows from our hypotheses about α and $\mathfrak{A}$, and the known nature of $\mathcal{K}$. Hence the n-th section will eventually be finished. $\mathcal{K}_\alpha$ is circle-free; α is computable.

It is conceivable that the $\mathcal{K}_\alpha$ machine could be generalized much like Turing's universal machine. It could begin with a tape on which the axioms have already been encoded. Simply encode different axioms and a different function on the tape, and the machine could calculate any sequence that is definable through first-order logic.

It can also be shown that the numbers α definable in this way by the use of axioms include all the computable numbers. This is done by describing computing machines in terms of the function calculus.

Turing will actually describe a computing machine in terms of first-order logic in the last section of his paper and the next chapter of this book. For now, he wants to remind the reader that not every number can be computed by a machine, particularly a sequence that tells us with 0s and 1s which Description Numbers are those of satisfactory machines.

It must be remembered that we have attached rather a special meaning to the phrase "$\mathfrak{A}$ defines α". The computable numbers do not include all (in the ordinary sense) definable numbers. Let δ be a sequence whose n-th figure is 1 or 0 according as n is or is not satisfactory. It is an immediate consequence of the theorem of § 8 that δ is not computable. It is (so far as we know at present) possible that any assigned number of figures of δ can be calculated, but not by a uniform process. When sufficiently many figures of δ have been calculated, an essentially new method is necessary in order to obtain more figures.

Turing has now finished with his second argument to justify that his machines can compute numbers commonly regarded as computable. The third argument follows. You might recall Turing's reliance on a human computer's "state of mind." Some readers might regard that human state of mind as too amorphous a concept to be encapsulated in a machine.

I'll let this chapter conclude without interrupting Turing's short description of how a state of mind can actually be built into the structure of a machine.

III. This may be regarded as a modification of I or as a corollary of II.

We suppose, as in I, that the computation is carried out on a tape; but we avoid introducing the "state of mind" by considering a more physical and definite counterpart of it. It is always possible for the computer to break off from his work, to go away and forget all about it, and later to come back and go on with it. If he does this he must leave a note of instructions (written in some standard form) explaining how the work is to be continued. This note is the counterpart of the "state of mind". We will suppose that the computer works in such a desultory manner that he never does more than one step at a sitting. The note of instructions must enable him to carry out one step and write the next note. Thus the state of progress of the computation at any stage is completely determined by the note of

[254]

instructions and the symbols on the tape. That is, the state of the system may be described by a single expression (sequence of symbols), consisting of the symbols on the tape followed by Δ (which we suppose not to appear elsewhere) and then by the note of instructions. This expression may be called the "state formula". We know that the state formula at any given stage is determined by the state formula before the last step was made, and we assume that the relation of these two formulae is expressible in the functional calculus. In other words, we assume that there is an axiom $\mathfrak{A}$ which expresses the rules governing the behaviour of the computer, in terms of the relation of the state formula at any stage to the state formula at the preceding stage. If this is so, we can construct a machine to write down the successive state formulae, and hence to compute the required number.

13 Computable Functions

When was the last time you put your personal computer to work calculating the infinite digits of an irrational number? Unless you're one of those people who recreationally run programs that calculate millions of digits of π, it's unlikely that any program you use calculates more digits than your favorite calculator utility.

While it is obvious that Alan Turing established many principles and concepts of computer programming in his paper, computing the infinite digits of real numbers is certainly not typical of the activities of computers past, present, or future.

Instead, computers perform complex tasks that programmers have divided into small chunks called functions or procedures or subroutines or methods (depending on the particular programming language). These functions generally perform some specific job in a finite period of time. They begin with some input, crunch that input to create output, and then end, releasing control to some other function.

The concept of functions originated in mathematics. In general terms, a function is a mathematical entity that transforms input into output. The input is known as the *argument* to the function, or the *independent* variable; the output is known as the function's *value*, or the *dependent* variable. Often functions are restricted to particular types of numbers or other objects. The allowable input is known as the function's *domain*. The possible resultant output values is known as the *range*.

Turing mentioned the concept of "computable functions" in the first paragraph of his paper as a topic for future exploration:

> Although the subject of this paper is ostensibly the computable *numbers*, it is almost equally easy to define and investigate computable functions of an integral variable or a real or computable variable, computable predicates, and so forth. . . . I hope shortly to give an account of the relations of the computable numbers, functions, and so forth to one another. This will include a development of the theory of functions of a real variable expressed in terms of computable numbers.

Turing didn't pursue these topics in precisely this way. As you'll discover in Chapter 17, the concept of a computable function later became quite important when Stephen Kleene (in his 1952 book *Introduction to Metamathematics*) and Martin Davis (in his 1958 book *Computability and Unsolvability*) reformulated the Turing Machine to calculate integer functions rather than to compute real numbers.

In a sense, we've already seen machines that implement functions. The Universal Machine is such an animal because it takes as input a Standard Description of a machine and creates output containing the complete configurations of that machine, as well as the sequence the machine would have computed.

What about more traditional functions? What would they look like? Consider the trigonometric sine function. The input is a number representing an angle, generally in units of degrees or radians. That angle is assumed to be part of a right triangle. The sine function calculates the ratio of the opposite side of that triangle to the hypotenuse. More generally (and to define the sine function for angles greater than 90 degrees) a line is drawn from the origin on a Cartesian coordinate system to any point. For the angle that line makes with the X axis (measured in a counter-clockwise direction), the sine function returns the ratio of the distance from the end of the line to the X axis to the length of the line.

The domain of the sine function comprises all real numbers, although the function cycles in value every 360 degrees or 2π radians. The range — the values of the function — consists of real numbers from -1 to 1, inclusive.

The actual calculation of the sine function involves an infinite series, where x is in radians:

$$\sin(x) = x - \frac{x^3}{3!} + \frac{x^5}{5!} - \frac{x^7}{7!} + \cdots$$

This is the formula that today's computers use to calculate the sine function, although generally the calculation occurs in the computer's processor chip rather than in software.

Computers cannot store arbitrary real numbers because real numbers have an infinite number of decimal places. Instead, computers approximate real numbers with rational numbers. In 1985, the Institute of Electrical and Electronics Engineers (IEEE) published the IEEE Standard for Binary Floating-Point Arithmetic that's used by many computer systems to store numbers in a form suitable for representation with scientific notation. The popular double-precision format, for example, stores a number using 64 bits: 1 bit for the sign (positive or negative), 11 for the exponent, and 52 for the mantissa, providing precision approximately equivalent to 16 decimal digits.[1] The real number 123.456 is essentially stored as two integers: 8,687,443,681,197,687 (the mantissa) and 46 (the exponent), because $8{,}687{,}443{,}681{,}197{,}687 \div 2^{46}$ approximately equals 123.456. That ratio is a rational number, not a real number.

---

[1] Charles Petzold, *Code: The Hidden Language of Computer Hardware and Software* (Microsoft Press, 1999), ch. 23.

When a computer calculates a sine, this approximation is essential because it allows the function to finish in a finite period of time. Although the sine function is calculated as an infinite series of terms, the absolute value of the terms gets smaller and smaller. The function can stop when the terms no longer make a difference in the desired precision of the result.

A Turing Machine, however, revels in infinite precision. When computing real numbers, it just keeps going and going and going. When calculating the sine function, that could be a real problem because each of the infinite number of terms has an infinite number of digits. For example, suppose the angle is a simple 1 radian. The second term is 1/6, which requires an infinite number of digits regardless of whether the number base is decimal or binary. If the machine needs to calculate infinite digits of the second term, how can it move on to the third term?

One workable strategy is to calculate the first digit from each term in succession until the term is so small that the first digit of the term is zero, and then calculate the second digit from each term until the term is so small that the first two digits of the term are zero, and so forth. This is obviously a complex process, particularly if you don't want the machine to erase any digits of the result after it has calculated them.

Implementing the sine function is only one problem. Where does the input come from?

Perhaps our immediate instinct is to let a human user of the machine somehow "type in" the angle when the machine needs it. This is a concept obviously inspired by today's world of interactive computers and onscreen calculators, but the Turing Machine would need to be redesigned somewhat to accept input of this sort. That's a bit more work than we're ready for at this moment.

A second option is to "hard code" the input to the function within the machine itself. For example, we could design a machine that specifically calculates the sine of 37.85 degrees. Although the machine would be limited to calculating the sine of this particular angle, we might hope that we've designed the machine so it's fairly easy to modify it for other angles.

A third approach is to encode the angle on the tape. The machine reads the input, calculates the sine, and prints the result back on the tape. (I can tell you like this approach! So do I.)

A fourth approach is to let the machine generate its own input. For example, the machine could first calculate the sine of zero degrees, then one degree, then two degrees, and so forth, printing each result on the tape to create a whole "table" of values. This approach would require the machine to limit itself to a finite number of digits per result.

A fifth approach involves two different machines. The first machine computes a real number, and the second machine computes the sine of that number. When I speak of two machines, I'm really speaking of one machine that implements the logic of the two machines. We've already seen machines combined in this way.

In Section 8 (page 181-182 of this book) Turing combined a decision machine $\mathcal{D}$ with the Universal Machine $\mathcal{U}$ to create a machine $\mathcal{H}$ that analyzes standard descriptions. The advantage to this approach is that we can "plug in" a different first machine when we need to calculate the sine of a different angle.

None of these approaches is entirely free from problems. The big problem is that the input to the sine function is a real number (at least in theory) and so is the output, and real numbers have an infinite number of digits. It is not possible to type in an infinite number of digits, or encode those digits on the tape.

In fact, even if you restrict yourself to nice, simple angles with a finite number of decimal places, the sine function requires radians. There are π radians in 180 degrees, so a seemingly simple angle of 10 degrees is actually $\pi/18$ radians — a transcendental number with an infinite number of decimal places.

Now, we've got ourselves into a situation where one machine needs to calculate $\pi/18$ while a second machine calculates the sine of that value, and both machines are actually implemented in the same "meta-machine." The second machine can't wait for the first machine to finish before beginning its own calculation! The two machines need to work in tandem, a programming technique sometimes known as *dovetailing*: As the machine calculating the angle completes a new digit, then the machine calculating the sine of that angle must take over and calculate a new digit of the result. This back-and-forth interplay between the two machines continues forever.

At this point, you probably won't be surprised to learn that the Turing Machines reformulated by Stephen Kleene and Martin Davis compute only *number-theoretic* functions, that is, functions whose domains and ranges are both restricted to non-negative integers. Both authors encode function input as strokes or tick marks. For example, the number 7 is represented by simple vertical lines in 8 consecutive squares. (The number 0 requires 1 stroke.)

Generally, when you're calculating a function, you don't want the calculation to go on forever. You want the function to finish so you can examine the result. For this reason, the reformulated Turing Machines described by Kleene and Davis *halt* when they're finished with a calculation. Obviously, a machine dedicated to adding or multiplying non-negative integers does not need to run forever. In the Kleene and Davis formulation, machines that don't halt are considered *bad* machines. Determining whether a Turing Machine will properly complete its calculation and halt was termed — by Davis — as the *halting problem*. The halting problem has subsequently become closely identified with Turing Machines, but the concept is foreign to Turing's original paper.

Now that we've done a little bit of thinking about the inherent problems in creating Turing Machines that work with functions of real numbers, we're ready to study the approaches that Turing suggests in Section 10 of his paper.

Section 10 is actually a continuation of Section 9. At the beginning of that earlier section, Turing had promised three kinds of arguments concerning the computing ability of his machines. The third was "Giving examples of large classes of numbers which are computable" and that is the subject of Section 10. At the same time, Turing veers somewhat from his primary focus of computable numbers and instead voyages into the realm of computable functions.

Section 10 is probably the least analyzed part of Turing's paper, and often the toughest to parse. He is terse and sometimes obscure, and I am not confident that I have always nailed his arguments with complete accuracy.

It's perhaps not surprising that Turing begins by discussing a "computable function of an integral variable," and that the "simplest" way of defining such a function requires that both the domain and range be non-negative integers.

10. *Examples of large classes of numbers which are computable.*

It will be useful to begin with definitions of a computable function of an integral variable and of a computable variable, etc. There are many equivalent ways of defining a computable function of an integral variable. The simplest is, possibly, as follows. If γ is a computable sequence in which 0 appears infinitely[†] often, and n is an integer, then let us define $\xi(\gamma, n)$ to be the number of figures 1 between the n-th and the $(n + 1)$-th figure 0 in γ. Then $\phi(n)$ is computable if, for all n and some γ, $\phi(n) = \xi(\gamma, n)$.

[†] If $\mathcal{M}$ computes γ, then the problem whether $\mathcal{M}$ prints 0 infinitely often is of the same character as the problem whether $\mathcal{M}$ is circle-free.

I need an example. Let our function ϕ (the Greek letter phi) be something simple like this

$$\phi(n) = 2n + 1$$

for non-negative integer n. So,

$\phi(0) = 1$
$\phi(1) = 3$
$\phi(2) = 5$
$\phi(3) = 7$

. . .

The sequence γ (the Greek letter gamma) that corresponds to this function is this:

01011101111101111110...

Notice between each successive pair of zeros are one 1, then three 1s, then five 1s, seven 1s, and so forth, corresponding to the values of the function $\phi(n)$ for each successive non-negative integer n.

Is γ a computable sequence? It certainly looks computable to me. That means that $\phi(n)$ is a computable function, and the machine that computes γ runs forever, computing all the values of the function.

Turing approaches this computable function from a direction opposite to my example: He presupposes a sequence γ that contains 0 infinitely often, mentions a function $\xi(\gamma, n)$ (the Greek letter xi) that indicates the number of 1s between each consecutive pair of zeros, and equates $\phi(n)$ to $\xi(\gamma, n)$.

In this sense, any machine that computes a sequence in which 0 appears infinitely often is also computing a function of positive integers, although in general we can't determine which machines actually fit this criterion.

Now Turing hypothesizes a predicate corresponding to the ϕ function, so that the calculation of the function becomes analogous to the logic-based calculation of numbers Turing demonstrated in Section 9 of his paper and the previous chapter of this book.

> An equivalent definition is this. Let $H(x, y)$ mean $\phi(x) = y$.

Let's use the same example. The function with a change in the independent variable is:

$$\phi(x) = 2x + 1$$

We can define $H(x, y)$ using the predicates I described in the previous chapter:

$$(\exists z)\,(Product(u'', x, z)\ \&\ Sum(z, u', y))$$

This formula is true if there exists a z such that it's true that 2 times x equals z, and also true that z plus 1 equals y.

> Then, if we can find a contradiction-free axiom $\mathfrak{A}_\phi$, such that $\mathfrak{A}_\phi \to P$,

$\mathfrak{A}_\phi$ must be a conjunction of the axioms for the predicates required to define H (in this case *Product* and *Sum*) and P, so the implication holds trivially.

> and if for each integer n there exists an integer N, such that
> $$\mathfrak{A}_\phi \ \& \ F^{(N)} \rightarrow H(u^{(n)}, u^{(\phi(n))}),$$

You'll recall that $F^{(N)}$ is an abbreviation for the conjunction of successor functions. N must be at least as large as the greater of n and $\phi(n)$, and possibly larger. In our example, for n equal to 10, $\phi(n)$ equals 21. Internal to the H function, the numbers 1 and 2 are required, and z is 20. Therefore, N must be at least 21 in order to define sufficient numbers, but it could be greater than both n and $\phi(n)$ in some cases.

> and such that, if $m \neq \phi(n)$, then, for some N',
> $$\mathfrak{A}_\phi \ \& \ F^{(N')} \rightarrow (-H(u^{(n)}, u^{(m)}),$$

A right parenthesis is missing towards the end. In summary, the predicate H is true when the first argument is n and the second is $\phi(n)$, but false otherwise. For this second formula, N' must also be at least as great as m, but you'll see shortly that values of m greater than n don't really get involved in the show.

> then ϕ may be said to be a computable function.

There Turing ends his discussion without really describing how it's supposed to work. It's another modification of the $\mathcal{K}$ machine that enumerates all provable formulas. The machine that Turing described in Section 9 enumerates these provable formulas for successive values of n, printing a 1 or a 0 for each value of n according to the truth value of the predicate G.

This new problem requires a $\mathcal{K}_\gamma$ machine that will calculate the γ sequence described earlier

0101110111110111111110 ...

where each run of 1s is the value of the $\phi(n)$ function for successive values of n. The big difference is that this machine enumerates all provable formulas not just for successive values of n but varying values of n and m.

For each new value of n and m, the machine begins by printing formulas A and B (using the terminology established with the earlier machine)

$$\text{A } \mathfrak{A}_\phi \ \& \ F^{(N)} \ \rightarrow \ H(u^{(n)}, u^{(m)}) \text{ B } \mathfrak{A}_\phi \ \& \ F^{(N')} \ \rightarrow \ (-H(u^{(n)}, u^{(m)}))$$

and then tries to match one or the other of these formulas by generating all provable formulas.

The machine begins with n equal to zero. This is the argument to the function $\phi(n)$ and the first argument to the predicate $H(n, m)$. For each new value of n, the machine prints a zero and sets m to zero. This m is possibly a result of the function $\phi(n)$ and the second argument to the predicate $H(n, m)$.

For each new value of m, the machine begins generating all provable formulas. If formula B is matched, then the machine prints a 1 because that value of m is not the result of the $\phi(n)$ function. The machine increments m, prints new versions of A and B, and begins generating provable formulas again. If formula A is matched, then that value of m is the result of $\phi(n)$, and the machine moves on to the next value of n. For the next value of n the machine begins by printing a zero and setting m back to zero.

In this way, the machine prints the γ sequence where each run of 1s indicates the value of the function for increasing integer arguments.

> We cannot define general computable functions of a real variable, since there is no general method of describing a real number,

This is the problem I discussed earlier with encoding a real number on a tape for a function to access.

> but we can define a computable function of a computable variable.

This requires the calculation of the computable number and the computable function to work in tandem. In perhaps the simplest case, after each new digit of the variable is calculated, the computable function takes over and prints a new digit of the result. Both the computable variable and the computable function maintain the same level of precision in terms of significant digits.

Turing's example of such a function is the trigonometric tangent. Turing wants to calculate the tangent for a variety of computable numbers — in fact, all computable numbers — but he doesn't indicate any criterion for a calculation to stop and the next one to begin.

> If n is satisfactory, let γ_n be the number computed by $\mathcal{M}(n)$, and let
> $$\alpha_n = \tan\left(\pi \left(\gamma_n - \tfrac{1}{2}\right)\right),$$
> [255]
> unless $\gamma_n = 0$ or $\gamma_n = 1$, in either of which cases $\alpha_n = 0$.

A footnote coming up indicates this is not the only possible function, but it is a simple one for Turing's purposes. Because Turing Machines compute real numbers between 0 and 1, the number γ_n will be between 0 and 1 regardless of the machine. The argument to the tangent function is between $-1/2\pi$ and $1/2\pi$, which are angles in units of radians, equivalent to angles from $-90°$ to $90°$.

> Then, as n runs through the satisfactory numbers, α_n runs through the computable numbers[†].
>
> ---
>
> [†] A function α_n may be defined in many other ways so as to run through the computable numbers.

The tangent of values between $-90°$ and $90°$ range from $-\infty$ to ∞, thus sweeping through the entire continuum of real numbers. (Strictly speaking, the tangents of $-90°$ and $90°$ are undefined, which is why Turing treats those cases separately.) With just a few exceptions, the results of the tangent function will be transcendental numbers.

It is only later that Turing suggests that we can actually define a Turing Machine that calculates the tangent of an angle. Like the sine function, the tangent is calculated by an infinite series

$$\tan(x) = x + \frac{x^3}{3} + \frac{x^5}{3 \cdot 5} + \frac{x^7}{3 \cdot 5 \cdot 7} + \cdots$$

where x ranges from $-\pi/2$ to $\pi/2$.

> Now let $\phi(n)$ be a computable function which can be shown to be such that for any satisfactory argument its value is satisfactory[‡]. Then the function f, defined by $f(\alpha_n) = \alpha_{\phi(n)}$, is a computable function and all computable functions of a computable variable are expressible in this form.
>
> ---
>
> [‡] Although it is not possible to find a general process for determining whether a given number is satisfactory, it is often possible to show that certain classes of numbers are satisfactory.

The $\phi(n)$ function has a domain and range of description numbers of satisfactory machines. Perhaps we're limiting ourselves to machines in a particular format simple enough to be established as satisfactory. The $\phi(n)$ function modifies the description number, essentially reprogramming the machine, so that it calculates something else. For example, $\phi(n)$ might reprogram a machine so that instead of calculating x, it doubles the value and adds 1, essentially implementing the function $2x + 1$.

> Similar definitions may be given of computable functions of several variables, computable-valued functions of an integral variable, etc.
> I shall enunciate a number of theorems about computability, but I shall prove only (ii) and a theorem similar to (iii).

The ten theorems that follow are identified with lowercase Roman numerals. The proofs of (ii) and (iii) occupy the last two pages of Section 10 of the paper.

> (i) A computable function of a computable function of an integral or computable variable is computable.

In other words, we can stack these things. We can start with a machine that computes a number, and then apply another machine that implements a function of that number, and then apply another machine that implements another function of the result of the first function. Like the earlier machine based on the trigonometric tangent, these machines can't wait until the previous stage has completed. The machines must work in tandem, passing information from one stage to another, perhaps as each digit is calculated.

> (ii) Any function of an integral variable defined recursively in terms of computable functions is computable. *I.e.* if $\phi(m, n)$ is computable, and r is some integer, then $\eta(n)$ is computable, where
>
> $$\eta(0) = r,$$
>
> $$\eta(n) = \phi\left(n, \eta(n-1)\right).$$

Watch out: The Greek eta (η) looks a bit like the italic n. The "function of an integral variable" is η. The "computable function" is $\phi(m, n)$. As an example, let's suppose that r equals 1 and the function $\phi(m, n)$ is defined simply as

$$\phi(m, n) = m \cdot n$$

which I'm sure is computable. Let's calculate a few values of η.

$\eta(0) = r = 1$
$\eta(1) = \phi(1, \eta(0)) = \phi(1, 1) = 1 \cdot 1 = 1$
$\eta(2) = \phi(2, \eta(1)) = \phi(2, 1) = 2 \cdot 1 = 2$
$\eta(3) = \phi(3, \eta(2)) = \phi(3, 2) = 3 \cdot 2 = 6$
$\eta(4) = \phi(4, \eta(3)) = \phi(4, 6) = 4 \cdot 6 = 24$
$\eta(5) = \phi(5, \eta(4)) = \phi(5, 24) = 5 \cdot 24 = 120$
. . .

This $\eta(n)$ function is a recursive definition of the factorial function. Towards the end of this section, Turing will prove that an integral function such as $\eta(n)$ defined in terms of the computable function $\phi(m, n)$ is itself computable.

> (iii) If $\phi (m, n)$ is a computable function of two integral variables, then $\phi(n, n)$ is a computable function of n.

This sounds trivial, but Turing takes the opportunity to do something interesting. The proof concludes this chapter.

> (iv) If $\phi(n)$ is a computable function whose value is always 0 or 1, then the sequence whose n-th figure is $\phi(n)$ is computable.

For example, suppose the function *IsPrime(n)* returns 1 if n is a prime number and 0 otherwise. Turing is asserting that the following sequence is computable:

0011010100010100010100010000010. . .

I've only shown the first 31 digits for n starting at zero. The digits set to 1 correspond to the prime numbers 2, 3, 5, 7, 11, 13, 17, 19, 23, and 29.

Turing next refers to Dedekind's theorem. Here's the statement of that theorem from the first chapter of G.H. Hardy's *A Course of Pure Mathematics*, which is possibly where Turing first encountered the theorem when he began reading the book in 1931 in preparation for attending Cambridge that fall.

> **Dedekind's theorem.** If the real numbers are divided into two classes L and R in such a way that
>
> (i)   every number belongs to one or other of the two classes,
> (ii) each class contains at least one number,
> (iii) any member of L is less than any member of R,

then there is a number α, which has the property that all the numbers less than it belong to L and all the number greater than it to R. The number α itself may belong to either class.[2]

This is apt to be a little mystifying on first encounter, but it describes a fundamental difference between the rational numbers and the real numbers, and specifically, how the real numbers form a continuum but the rational numbers do not.

Visualize a number line that runs from negative infinity on the left to positive infinity on the right. If you want, you can consider just a section of this number line. Cut it into two parts. (This is known as the Dedekind Cut.) Some of the numbers are on the left (L in the theorem) and some are on the right (R).

You can cut the line at 1.5, for example, so that everything in L is less than 1.5 and everything in R is greater than 1.5. What about 1.5 itself? It's your choice whether it's in L or R. You might put it in L, in which case it's the greatest number in L. In that case, R has no lowest number. In other words, there's no number in R that is lower than all the others. Or, 1.5 might be in R, in which case it's the least number in R, and L has no greatest number.

Now cut the line at the square root of 2. If the number line consists of just *rational* numbers, then everything in L is less than the square root of 2, and everything in R is greater than the square root of 2. Because the square root of 2 is not rational, it belongs to neither L nor R. Moreover, L has no greatest number and R has no least number. The line has a discontinuity at the square root of 2.

If the number line consists of *real* numbers, however, then the square root of 2 must belong to either L or R. You can't define a cut of the real numbers so that the cut point doesn't belong to either L or R. This is why the real numbers form a continuum but the rational numbers do not.

Dedekind's theorem does not hold in the ordinary form if we replace "real" throughout by "computable".

[2]G.H. Hardy, *A Course of Pure Mathematics*, 10th edition (Cambridge University Press, 1952), 30. The Dedekind Theorem is not covered in the first edition (1908) of Hardy's book but does appear in the sixth edition (1933). I have not been able to examine editions between those. Turing read Hardy's book before going to Cambridge in 1931 and might have obtained the fifth edition (1928) at that time. Hardy's book is not the only place Turing might have encountered Dedekind's Theorem. A discussion appears in Chapter 34 of Bertrand Russell, *The Principles of Mathematics* (Cambridge University Press, 1903), Chapter 7 of Bertrand Russell, *Introduction to Mathematical Philosophy* (George Allen & Unwin, 1919, 1920), and in the first chapter of E. W. Hobson's *The Theory of Functions of a Real Variable and the Theory of Fourier's Series*, a book that Turing referred to in §8 of his paper. Dedekind's pamphlet "*Stetigkeit und Irrationale Zahlen*" describing this concept was published in 1872; the first English translation appeared in Richard Dedekind, *Essays on the Theory of Numbers*, trans. Wooster W. Beman (Open Court Press, 1901; Dover, 1963) as "Continuity and Irrational Numbers." The translation was completely revised for William Ewald, ed., *From Kant to Hilbert: A Source Book in the Foundations of Mathematics* (Oxford University Press, 1996), Vol. II, 765–779.

The computable numbers do not form a continuum because you can make a Dedekind Cut at a non-computable number. Perhaps the number is too complex (that is, too random) to be defined algorithmically, or perhaps you can *define* the number — for example, the number contains one digit from every computable number — but you can't compute that number. This cut divides the computable numbers into two parts so that L has no greatest number and R has no least number.

> **But it holds in the following form :**

Note the Roman numeral that follows: This is Turing's theorem (v) coming up. The propositional function $G(\alpha)$ that Turing introduces here is true if the argument — a computable number — is less than (or perhaps less than or equal to) some fixed number ξ (the Greek letter xi).

The $G(\alpha)$ function divides the computable numbers into two classes L — the computable numbers for which $G(\alpha)$ returns true — and R — the numbers for which $G(\alpha)$ returns false. In Hardy's statement of Dedekind's Theorem, requirement (i) is satisfied because $G(\alpha)$ is either true or false for every computable number.

> **(v) If $G(\alpha)$ is a propositional function of the computable numbers and**
>
> **(a) $(\exists\alpha)\,(\exists\beta)\{G(\alpha)\,\&\,(-G(\beta))\}$,**

Turing's (a) formula is equivalent to Hardy's requirement (ii), that each class contain at least one member.

> **(b) $G(\alpha)\,\&\,(-G(\beta)) \rightarrow (\alpha < \beta)$,**

Turing's (b) formula is equivalent to Hardy's requirement (iii). If $G(\alpha)$ is true, then α is in L, and if $G(\beta)$ is false, then β is in R, and α is less than β.

> **and there is a general process for determining the truth value of $G(\alpha)$, then**
>
> **[256]**
>
> **there is a computable number ξ such that**
>
> $$G(\alpha) \rightarrow \alpha \leq \xi,$$
>
> $$-G(\alpha) \rightarrow \alpha \geq \xi.$$

The "general process for determining the truth value of $G(\alpha)$" is crucial. Because ξ is a computable number, in the general case it cannot be explicitly stored somewhere within the definition of $G(\alpha)$. Nevertheless, it would be possible for a machine to compute that number by narrowing in on the value. In fact, the machine to compute ξ would do so by testing ever more accurate values in $G(\alpha)$.

> In other words, the theorem holds for any section of the computables such that there is a general process for determining to which class a given number belongs.

In the next sentence, the term "sequence of computable numbers" might be a little confusing because almost from the beginning of his paper, Turing has used the term "computable sequence" to refer to the digits that a machine generates. The "sequence" he's speaking of here is an ordered collection of computable numbers.

> Owing to this restriction of Dedekind's theorem, we cannot say that a computable bounded increasing sequence of computable numbers has a computable limit. This may possibly be understood by considering a sequence such as
> $$-1, -\tfrac{1}{2}, -\tfrac{1}{4}, -\tfrac{1}{8}, -\tfrac{1}{16}, \tfrac{1}{2}, \ldots .$$

This little passage was the subject of a discussion on the `sci.logic` newsgroup a few years ago. The thread is archived beginning at http://sci.tech-archive.net/Archive/sci.logic/2004-08/2244.html. One supposition was that the 1/2 at the end was wrong, and it really should have been $-1/32$. That fix makes the sequence look prettier but it can't be what Turing had in mind because now the sequence is apparently approaching zero, which is certainly a computable limit.

The more plausible conjecture is that Turing is presenting a sequence that seems to be heading toward a computable limit, but really is not. The sequence might even be bounded by -1 and 1, perhaps, but that doesn't tell us whether the limit is truly computable.

> On the other hand, (v) enables us to prove
>
> (vi) If α and β are computable and $\alpha < \beta$ and $\phi(\alpha) < 0 < \phi(\beta)$, where $\phi(\alpha)$ is a computable increasing continuous function, then there is a unique computable number γ, satisfying $\alpha < \gamma < \beta$ and $\phi(\gamma) = 0$.

Turing is alluding to a computable function that is perhaps a polynomial:

$$\phi(x) = 5x^3 - 3x^2 - 7$$

It is well known that any real polynomial with an odd degree (the largest exponent) has at least one real root — that is, a value x for which the polynomial equals zero.

For polynomial $\phi(x)$ you can narrow in on that root by observing that $\phi(1)$ equals -5 and $\phi(2)$ equals 21. The root must be between 1 and 2.

The numbers 1 and 2 are α and β in Turing's statement; you can see that $\alpha < \beta$ and $\phi(\alpha) < 0 < \phi(\beta)$. Because the function is continuous (that is, it has no gaps), there is a value γ between α and β for which $\phi(\gamma)$ equals zero. The objective is to calculate it. We can choose a number midway between α and β, which would be 1.5 in this example, and find $\phi(1.5)$, which is 3.125. Because this value is greater than zero, let 1.5 be the new β. Now we know that the root is somewhere between 1 and 1.5. Now try 1.25; $\phi(1.25)$ equals -1.921875, which is less than zero so 1.25 is the new α. Now we know that the root is between 1.25 and 1.5. Each step restricts the root to a smaller interval and, in effect, computes it.

Roughly speaking, a sequence of numbers is said to *converge* if the absolute values of the differences between successive numbers in the sequence get smaller and smaller. (I say "roughly" because these differences might not get smaller at the beginning of the sequence.) Any real number can be represented as a convergent sequence of rational numbers. This is most simply demonstrated using a sequence of rational numbers like these:

$a_0 = 3$
$a_1 = 3.1$
$a_2 = 3.14$
$a_3 = 3.141$
$a_4 = 3.1415$
$a_5 = 3.14159$
$\ldots$

These are all rational numbers, yet they are getting closer and closer to the irrational number we know as π. The sequence is convergent because the difference between successive numbers is getting smaller. The difference between a_3 and a_4 is 0.0005 but the difference between a_4 and a_5 is 0.00009.

Mathematically, this difference is often represented by a lower-case epsilon, ϵ. You can choose any arbitrary value of ϵ as small as you want, for example 0.0001. A particular sequence converges if there's some number N that corresponds to this ϵ so that for all $n > N$ and $m > N$, the absolute value of the difference between the numbers is less than the arbitrary number we've chosen: $|a_n - a_m| < \epsilon$. In the above example, for ϵ equal to 0.0001, N is 3 because $|a_4 - a_5| < 0.0001$ and so are the differences between all a_n and a_m where n and m are greater than 3.

Turing defines computable convergence similarly.

> *Computable convergence.*
>
> We shall say that a sequence β_n of computable numbers *converges computably* if there is a computable integral valued function $N(\epsilon)$ of the computable variable ϵ, such that we can show that, if $\epsilon > 0$ and $n > N(\epsilon)$ and $m > N(\epsilon)$, then $|\beta_n - \beta_m| < \epsilon$.

The numbers in the sequence must be computable, and Turing also requires that ϵ be computable and $N(\epsilon)$ be a computable function.

> We can then show that
>
> (vii) A power series whose coefficients form a computable sequence of computable numbers is computably convergent at all computable points in the interior of its interval of convergence.

A power series is an infinite summation of the form:

$$a_0 + a_1 x + a_2 x^2 + a_3 x^3 + a_4 x^4 + \ldots$$

As I showed earlier, you can represent a trigonometric sine function as a power series:

$$\sin(x) = x - \frac{x^3}{3!} + \frac{x^5}{5!} - \frac{x^7}{7!} + \cdots$$

The coefficients (that is, the a_i values) are 1, 0, $-1/3!$, 0, $1/5!$, 0, $-1/7!$, and so forth. These coefficients are certainly a computable sequence. Some power series converge only when x equals zero. Other power series converge for a range of x values, called the *interval of convergence*. It is well known that the sine function converges for all x. Because the coefficients are computable, it's possible for a machine to determine whether they're convergent.

> (viii) The limit of a computably convergent sequence is computable.

It's also possible to have a sequence of functions that converge to a particular function. If this convergence occurs for a particular value to the function, then it is said to be *pointwise* convergence. A much stronger convergence of functions is *uniform* convergence, which is independent of the value to the function.

And with the obvious definition of "uniformly computably convergent":

(ix)   The limit of a uniformly computably convergent computable sequence of computable functions is a computable function. Hence

(x)   The sum of a power series whose coefficients form a computable sequence is a computable function in the interior of its interval of convergence.

From these theorems, Turing concludes that all algebraic numbers are computable as well as some popular transcendental numbers:

From (viii) and $\pi = 4(1 - \frac{1}{3} + \frac{1}{5} - \ldots)$ we deduce that π is computable.
From $e = 1 + 1 + \dfrac{1}{2!} + \dfrac{1}{3!} + \ldots$ we deduce that e is computable.

[257]

From (vi) we deduce that all real algebraic numbers are computable.

Algebraic numbers, recall, are the roots of polynomial equations.

From (vi) and (x) we deduce that the real zeros of the Bessel functions are computable.

The Bessel functions are solutions to a common form of differential equations, and the zeros are where the functions have a value of zero. The last conclusion also encompasses the trigonometric functions, logarithms, exponentials, and a host of lesser-known functions.

Turing promised a proof of theorem (ii), which asserted that any function of an integral variable defined recursively in terms of computable functions is computable.

Proof of (ii).

Toward the beginning of Section 10, Turing defined a predicate $H(x, y)$ that is true if $\phi(x) = y$, and then showed how a machine can prove formulas involving $H(u^{(n)}, u^{(\phi(n))})$ and $-H(u^{(n)}, u^{(m)})$ where $m \neq \phi(n)$. That proof established the computability of the function $\phi(x)$.

This current proof is based on the earlier one, but instead of the function $\phi(x)$ he has the function $\eta(x)$, where

$$\eta(0) = r$$

$$\eta(n) = \phi(n, \eta(n-1))$$

> Let $H(x, y)$ mean "$\eta(x) = y$", and let $K(x, y, z)$ mean "$\phi(x,y) = z$".

For the factorial example,

$$\phi(x, y) = x \cdot y$$

so $K(x, y, z)$ is simply $Product(x, y, z)$.

> $\mathfrak{A}_\phi$ is the axiom for $\phi(x,y)$.

This $\mathfrak{A}_\phi$ axiom requires support for the $K(x, y, z)$ predicate. For the factorial example, the axiom would include the axioms for the successor, Sum, and $Product$ predicates. The axiom for $\eta(x)$ is more elaborate:

> We take $\mathfrak{A}_\eta$ to be
>
> $\mathfrak{A}_\phi$ & P & $(F(x,y) \to G(x,y))$ & $(G(x,y)$ & $G(y,z) \to G(x,z))$
>
> & $(F^{(r)} \to H(u, u^{(r)}))$ & $(F(v,w)$ & $H(v,x)$ & $K(w,x,z) \to H(w,z))$
>
> & $[H(w,z)$ & $G(z,t)$ v $G(t,z) \to (-H(w,t))]$.

This is Turing's third use of a predicate named G, all of which are defined differently. This one, however, is fundamental: It's the "greater-than" function, and amazingly, Turing didn't actually get around to clarifying what this function does until the *Proceedings of the London Mathematical Society* published Turing's corrections to his paper.[3] (Those corrections appear in Chapter 16 of this book.) In that correction paper, Turing says that $G(x, y)$ is to have the interpretation "x precedes y," or $y > x$. As usual the F predicate is the successor function.

$\mathfrak{A}_\eta$ consists of a conjunction of seven terms, beginning with $\mathfrak{A}_\phi$ and P. The third term indicates that if y is the successor of x, then y is greater than x, and the last term on the first line states the transitivity of the G function (if y is greater than x and z is greater than y, then z is greater than x).

---

[3]Alan Turing, "On Computable Numbers, with an Application to the Entscheidungsproblem. A Correction," *Proceedings of the London Mathematical Society*, 2nd Series, Vol. 43 (1937), 544–546.

The first term on the second line asserts that $H(u, u^{(r)})$ is true, which means that $\eta(0) = r$. The second term is this:

$$(F(v, w) \;\&\; H(v, x) \;\&\; K(w, x, z) \rightarrow H(w, z))$$

Translating to the functions that aren't predicates, if $w = v + 1$, and $\eta(v) = x$, and $\phi(w, x) = z$, then $\eta(w) = z$, or:

$$\eta(v + 1) = \phi(v + 1, \eta(v))$$

which is another way to state the general formula for $\eta(n)$ for n greater than 0.

The final term of $\mathfrak{A}_\eta$ is this:

$$[H(w, z) \;\&\; G(z, t) \;v\; G(t, z) \rightarrow (-H(w, t))]$$

Notice the pair of G predicates with their arguments switched. This is the sole reason for incorporating the G function into this axiom; either one or the other of these G terms is true if z does not equal t. The whole term asserts that if $H(w, z)$ is true, then for all values t that do not equal z, $H(w, t)$ is not true, in other words, $\eta(w) \neq t$.

I would be more comfortable if the formula for $\mathfrak{A}_\eta$ included a bunch of universal quantifiers, but in their absence they are implied.

> I shall not give the proof of consistency of $\mathfrak{A}_\eta$. Such a proof may be constructed by the methods used in Hilbert and Bernays, *Grundlagen der Mathematik* (Berlin, 1934), p. 209 *et seq.* The consistency is also clear from the meaning.

This is the first volume of a book largely written by Swiss mathematician Paul Bernays and begun when he was at Göttingen. Being Jewish, Bernays lost his professorship at the university in 1933 and moved to Zürich in 1934. The second volume of *Grundlagen der Mathematik* (*Foundations of Mathematics*) was published in 1939. The book was highly regarded at the time, but was never translated into English. Bernays played another role in Turing's paper. In the published correction to his paper, Turing indicates that he "is indebted to P. Bernays for pointing out these errors." Alonzo Church's short paper showing that the Entscheidungsproblem has no solution[4] received similar scrutiny, and it too was followed with a correction[5] containing the footnote, "The author is indebted to Paul Bernays for pointing out this error..."

---

[4] Alonzo Church, "A Note on the Entscheidungsproblem," *The Journal of Symbolic Logic*, Vol. 1, No. 1 (Mar. 1936), 40–41.

[5] Alonzo Church, "Correction to *A Note on the Entscheidungsproblem*," *The Journal of Symbolic Logic*, Vol. 1, No. 3 (Sept. 1936), 101–102.

Although Bernays was at the Institute for Advanced Study from 1935 to 1936, he had gone back to Zurich before Turing arrived in Princeton, and apparently he and Turing never met.

The page to which Turing refers is the beginning of a section on number theory. It is on that very page that Bernays introduces an R predicate that is the same as Turing's G predicate. The axioms that Bernays lists for his greater-than predicate (which I've converted slightly to Turing's notation) demonstrate to what extent Turing is gliding over the details:

$$(x)—R(x, x)$$

$$(x)(y)(z)(R(x, y) \mathrel{\&} R(y, z) \rightarrow R(x, z))$$

$$(x)(\exists y)R(x, y)$$

The third axiom reminds us that there exists a number that is not greater than any other number. That number is usually 0 or 1, depending on one's definition of natural numbers. That same page in *Grundlagen der Mathematik* lists the axioms for Bernay's successor function called S:

$$(x)(\exists y)S(x, y)$$

$$(\exists x)(y)—S(x, y)$$

$$(x)(y)(r)(s)(S(x, r) \mathrel{\&} S(y, r) \mathrel{\&} S(s, x) \rightarrow S(s, y))$$

It's quite surprising that Turing refers to a page of a book that defines predicates that he uses in his paper, but with axioms that he ignores.

Turing's approach here is an induction proof, a type of proof particularly suited for number theory and other applications where only natural numbers are involved. In an induction proof, a formula (or something) is proved first for zero. This is usually easy. Then, an assumption is made that the formula is true for n, and the formula is proved for $n + 1$ based on that assumption. It's not necessary to prove the formula for all n, only that truth for n implies truth for $n + 1$. Since the formula was first proved for 0, it's true for $0 + 1$ or 1, and because it's true for 1, it's true for $1 + 1$ or 2, and so forth.

Turing's induction proof is a little different. He leaves the proof of the zero case for later and begins with the induction part, showing that if the formula is assumed to be true for $n - 1$, it's also true for n. The assumption comes first.

> **Suppose that, for some n, N, we have shown**
> $$\mathfrak{A}_\eta \mathrel{\&} F^{(N)} \rightarrow H(u^{(n-1)}, u^{(\eta(n-1))}),$$

The following formula is a direct consequence of the $\mathfrak{A}_\phi$ axiom that supports the K propositional function.

then, for some M,

$$\mathfrak{A}_\phi \ \& \ F^{(M)} \to K(u^{(n)}, u^{(\eta(n-1))}, u^{(\eta(n))}),$$

Also, since $\mathfrak{A}_\eta \to \mathfrak{A}_\phi$ trivially,

$$\mathfrak{A}_\eta \ \& \ F^{(M)} \to K(u^{(n)}, u^{(\eta(n-1))}, u^{(\eta(n))})$$

This also remains true if we form a conjunction with a couple terms on the right side that we know to be true. One is a trivial successor function that is implied by $F^{(M)}$ and the other is the original H predicate assumption:

$$\mathfrak{A}_\eta \ \& \ F^{(M)} \to F(u^{(n-1)}, u^{(n)}) \ \& \ H(u^{(n-1)}, u^{(\eta(n-1))})$$
$$\& \ K(u^{(n)}, u^{(\eta(n-1))}, u^{(\eta(n))}),$$

This is beginning to take the form of something in the $\mathfrak{A}_\eta$ axiom, and Turing pulls it out:

and

$$\mathfrak{A}_\eta \ \& \ F^{(M)} \to [F(u^{(n-1)}, u^{(n)}) \ \& \ H(u^{(n-1)}, u^{(\eta(n-1))})$$
$$\& \ K(u^{(n)}, u^{(\eta(n-1))}, u^{(\eta(n))}) \to H(u^{(n)}, u^{(\eta(n))})].$$

To the right of the first implication sign is the penultimate term of the $\mathfrak{A}_\eta$ axiom, with values of $u^{(n)}$, $u^{(n-1)}$, $u^{(\eta(n))}$, and $u^{(\eta(n-1))}$ substituted for w, v, z, and x, respectively. Combining those two formulas,

Hence

$$\mathfrak{A}_\eta \ \& \ F^{(M)} \to H(u^{(n)}, u^{(\eta(n))}).$$

This completes the induction part of the proof. Turing has not yet shown that the formula is true for zero. This he does now.

Also

$$\mathfrak{A}_\eta \ \& \ F^{(r)} \to H(u, u^{(\eta(0))}).$$

This is just a term of the axiom with $\eta(0)$ substituted for r. Now we know that the formula is true for all n.

Hence for each n some formula of the form

$$\mathfrak{A}_\eta \ \& \ F^{(M)} \to H(u^{(n)}, u^{(\eta(n))})$$

is provable.

It's now necessary to show that for $m \neq \eta(n)$ — not $\eta(u)$ as Turing has it in the next sentence — the axioms imply the negation of H.

> Also, if $M' \geq M$ and $M' \geq m$ and $m \neq \eta(u)$, then
>
> $$\mathfrak{A}_\eta \,\&\, F^{(M')} \rightarrow G(u^{\eta((n))}, u^{(m)}) \text{ v } G(u^{(m)}, u^{(\eta(n))})$$

That is, if $m \neq \eta(n)$ then m is either greater than or less than $\eta(n)$.

> [258]
>
> and
>
> $$\mathfrak{A}_\eta \,\&\, F^{(M')} \rightarrow \big[\{G(u^{(\eta(n))}, u^{(m)}) \text{ v } G(u^{(m)}, u^{(\eta(n))})$$
> $$\&\, H(u^{(n)}, u^{(\eta(n))})\} \rightarrow (-H(u^{(n)}, u^{(m)}))\big].$$

To the right of the first implication sign is a restatement of the last term of the $\mathfrak{A}_\eta$ axiom, rearranged somewhat and with values of $u^{(n)}$, $u^{(m)}$, and $u^{(\eta(n))}$ substituted for w, t, and z, respectively. Combining these two formulas,

> Hence $\qquad\qquad \mathfrak{A}_\eta \,\&\, F^{(M')} \rightarrow (-H(u^{(n)}, u^{(m)})).$
>
> The conditions of our second definition of a computable function are therefore satisfied.

By "second definition" Turing means the demonstration beginning with the sentence "An equivalent definition is this," beginning on page 236 of this book. He has established that he can create two statements of the following form:

$$\mathfrak{A}_\eta \,\&\, F^{(M)} \rightarrow H(u^{(n)}, u^{(\eta(n))})$$

$$\mathfrak{A}_\eta \,\&\, F^{(M')} \rightarrow (-H(u^{(n)}, u^{(m)}))$$

For every value of n and m, one or the other is provable.

> Consequently η is a computable function.

The next proof contains the final appearance of tables of a Turing Machine in this paper (and this book). This machine is intended to prove Turing's theorem (iii), which states that if $\phi(m, n)$ is a computable function of two integral variables, then $\phi(n, n)$ is a computable function of n.

This proof illustrates a technique of computing a function whose domain is the natural numbers but whose range is real numbers. The function is computed for multiple successive arguments (n equals 0, 1, 2, and so forth), but the computation of the function is stopped when n digits have been calculated.

> *Proof of a modified form of* (iii).
>
> Suppose that we are given a machine $\mathcal{N}$, which, starting with a tape bearing on it əə followed by a sequence of any number of letters "F" on F-squares and in the m-configuration $\mathfrak{b}$, will compute a sequence γ_n depending on the number n of letters "F".

The tape looks something like this:

ə	ə	F		F		F		F		F													...

What's interesting about this machine is that it's the closest that Turing comes in this paper to describing something that works much like the reformulated Turing Machines described by Kleene and Davis. This machine reads a non-negative integer encoded on the tape as a series of letters "F" and then computes a function of that integer. The Kleene and Davis machines implement number-theoretic functions, but in the spirit of Turing's eternally running machines, he's implicitly assumed that the sequence γ_n is something more complex — perhaps the cube root of n. If the machine begins by reading five "F" characters (like the tape shown above), it will calculate the cube root of 5.

> If $\phi_n(m)$ is the m-th figure of γ_n, then the sequence β whose n-th figure is $\phi_n(n)$ is computable.

For example, the function $\phi_5(12)$ returns the twelfth binary digit of the cube root of 5. Turing presents a new computable sequence β that contains one digit from the ϕ_n function for each n. In my example, the first digit of the sequence β is the first digit of the cube root of 1, the second digit is the second digit of the cube root of 2, and so forth.

Turing has begun by assuming that this machine (be it a cube-root machine or something different) already exists. He is going to modify this machine, in part by changing some of the existing instructions and in part by adding some new instructions to create a somewhat different machine.

The new machine must work with a variable number of "F" characters: First no characters, then one "F", then two "F" characters and so forth. After calculating n digits (where n is the number of "F" characters plus 1) it must essentially stop that calculation and then start over with an additional "F" character governing what it does. This new machine will *not* print its 0 and 1 digits in consecutive F-squares. They will be printed in order from left to right, but they will be buried in other output from the machine.

Turing wants his original machine in a standard form so he can modify it easily.

> We suppose that the table for $\mathcal{N}$ has been written out in such a way that in each line only one operation appears in the operations column.

For these modifications, Turing needs to introduce some new characters, including the Greek upper-case letters xi and theta. He also needs to replace three characters anywhere they occur in the table for this machine.

> We also suppose that $\Xi, \Theta, \bar{0},$ and $\bar{1}$ do not occur in the table, and we replace ə throughout by Θ, 0 by $\bar{0}$, and 1 by $\bar{1}$.

When Turing says "replace ə throughout by Θ," he doesn't mean on the tape. The tape still needs to begin with two schwa sentinels. He means that any line in the table that reads a schwa should be modified to read a theta.

Turing doesn't say it here, but the machine modifications also require that the symbols h and k are not used by this machine, and that configurations $\mathfrak{c}, \mathfrak{u}, \mathfrak{u}_1, \mathfrak{u}_2,$ $\mathfrak{u}_3, \mathfrak{v}, \mathfrak{v}_1, \mathfrak{v}_2, \mathfrak{v}_3$ are available for new definitions.

> Further substitutions are then made. Any line of form
>
> | $\mathfrak{A}$ | α | $P\bar{0}$ | $\mathfrak{B}$ |
> |---|---|---|---|
>
> we replace by
>
> | $\mathfrak{A}$ | α | $P\bar{0}$ | $\mathrm{re}(\mathfrak{B}, \mathfrak{u}, h, k)$ |
> |---|---|---|---|

The line being replaced originally printed a 0 rather than a $\bar{0}$. The $\mathfrak{A}$ and $\mathfrak{B}$ configurations, and the scanned character α, are just placeholders here. You may recall re as a "replace" function; here re replaces the first h on the tape with a k, and then goes to configuration $\mathfrak{B}$. If it doesn't find an h, it goes to configuration $\mathfrak{u}$.

As defined in Section 4, the $\mathfrak{re}$ function uses the $\mathfrak{f}$ function, which relies upon a schwa sentinel. That function should *not* be altered to search for a theta sentinel instead.

This is how the new machine essentially intercepts the operation of the original machine whenever it prints a digit. When the machine begins working with a new number of "F" characters, the number of h characters on the tape will be one more than the number of "F" characters. Thus, the machine prints $\overline{0}$ rather than 0 h times before going to configuration $\mathfrak{u}$.

	and any line of the form			
	$\mathfrak{A}$	α	$P\overline{1}$	$\mathfrak{B}$
by	$\mathfrak{A}$	α	$P\overline{1}$	$\mathfrak{re}(\mathfrak{B}, v, h, k)$

The $\mathfrak{u}$ and $\mathfrak{v}$ configurations need to print actual 0 and 1 characters without overlines, and then prepare the tape for the next number of "F" characters and essentially restart the machine. Turing will show only the $\mathfrak{u}$ configuration but $\mathfrak{v}$ is very similar.

and we add to the table the following lines:		
$\mathfrak{u}$		$\mathfrak{pe}(\mathfrak{u}_1, 0)$
$\mathfrak{u}_1$	$R, Pk, R, P\Theta, R, P\Theta$	$\mathfrak{u}_2$
$\mathfrak{u}_2$		$\mathfrak{re}(\mathfrak{u}_3, \mathfrak{u}_3, k, h)$
$\mathfrak{u}_3$		$\mathfrak{pe}(\mathfrak{u}_2, F)$

After the $\mathfrak{u}$ configuration prints an actual 0, $\mathfrak{u}_1$ prints a k and two thetas, which to the machine represents a new sentinel. The $\mathfrak{u}_2$ and $\mathfrak{u}_3$ configurations replace each k with an h. (Recall that the h characters were changed to k in the previous alternation.) For each k changed to an h, an F is also printed at the end. In Turing's table, an infinite loop exists because $\mathfrak{u}_2$ always hops to $\mathfrak{u}_3$ and $\mathfrak{u}_3$ always hops to $\mathfrak{u}_2$. The replace function needs to be:

$$\mathfrak{re}\,(\mathfrak{u}_3, \mathfrak{b}, k, h)$$

If no more k characters are available to change to h, the machine needs to start over at configuration $\mathfrak{b}$, which is the starting configuration of the original machine. The $\mathfrak{v}$ configurations are similar except that $\mathfrak{v}$ prints 1 rather than 0.

and similar lines with v for $\mathfrak{u}$ and 1 for 0 together with the following line	
$\mathfrak{c}$	$R, P\Xi, R, Ph$	$\mathfrak{b}.$

Another bug, unfortunately. It actually shouldn't print an *h* here, but should print the new-style sentinel:

$$\mathfrak{c} \qquad R, P\Xi, R, P\Theta, R, P\Theta$$

> We then have the table for the machine $\mathcal{N}'$ which computes β. The initial *m*-configuration is $\mathfrak{c}$, and the initial scanned symbol is the second ə.

Let's see if this really works. We have a machine $\mathcal{N}$ that is a modified version of $\mathcal{N}$ that calculates the cube root of however many "F" characters it reads from the tape. Machine $\mathcal{N}$ begins with a tape with just two schwas in configuration $\mathfrak{c}$:

ə	ə																											•••

Configuration $\mathfrak{c}$ prints a xi and two thetas:

ə	ə	Ξ	Θ	Θ																				•••

The xi isn't actually used anywhere. Now the machine branches to configuration $\mathfrak{b}$ and the machine proceeds normally but using the two thetas for a sentinel instead of the schwas. There are no "F" characters to be read, so it's calculating the cube root of zero. When it comes time to print the first $\bar{0}$ it also tries to replace the first *h* with a *k*. There are no *h* characters so the machine branches to configuration $\mathfrak{u}$. This configuration prints a real 0 on the tape, followed by a *k* and two thetas:

ə	ə	Ξ	Θ	Θ	...			0	k	Θ	Θ										•••

The $\mathfrak{u}_2$ and $\mathfrak{u}_3$ configurations comprise a little loop to replace each *k* with an *h* and print an *F*:

ə	ə	Ξ	Θ	Θ	...			0	h	Θ	Θ	F									•••

There are no more *k*'s to change to *h*, so now the machine goes to *m*-configuration $\mathfrak{b}$, and the machine essentially starts over to calculate the cube root of 1. The first digit is 1, so the machine prints a $\bar{1}$ and changes the *h* to a *k*. It continues. The next digit is a zero, so it prints a $\bar{0}$. There are no more *h*'s, so the machine branches to $\mathfrak{u}$ again to print the real zero, followed by a *k* and two thetas:

ə	ə	Ξ	Θ	Θ	...		0	k	Θ	Θ	F	...		0	k	Θ	Θ			•••

Now for every *k*, the *k* is changed to an *h* and an F is printed:

| ə | ə | Ξ | ⊖ | ⊖ | ... | | | 0 | h | ⊖ | ⊖ | F | ... | | | 0 | h | ⊖ | ⊖ | F | F | | | ••• |

There's another bug here, but this one I didn't fix. The "F" characters need to be on *F*-squares so they need a space between them. Regardless, there are no more *k* characters to change to *h* so the machine branches to *m*-configuration b to begin calculating the cube root of 2.

With the conclusion of Section 10, Turing is satisfied that he has defined a model for computation that formally encompasses anything that an algorithm might require. He is now ready to demonstrate that the Entscheidungsproblem can have no solution.

14 The Major Proof

Some mathematical proofs are straightforward; others need to come through the back door. This second category surely includes *reductio ad absurdum* proofs, which begin by assuming the opposite of what needs to be proven, and then demonstrate that the initial assumption leads to a contradiction.

Then there are the proofs that don't bother coming through the front door *or* the back door. These proofs instead seem to avoid the subject entirely by building an elaborate structure that at times appears both mysterious and indulgent. Just when the whole point of the exercise has become entirely obscured and you've long since abandoned hopes of ever seeing a solution, the clever mathematician drops through the chimney and exclaims with a hearty "Ta-dah!" that the proof has been completed. (Just don't get any soot on the carpet.)

In a sense, the final section of Turing's paper is the most important part because it is here that he shows that "the Entscheidungsproblem cannot be solved." This was an important conclusion at the time, but the structure Turing built to support this result — the imaginary device now known as the Turing Machine — ultimately would become more interesting and fruitful than the actual proof that must now command our attention.

Turing laid the foundation for this proof in Section 8. It didn't seem to be very important at the time, but he was careful to establish that you cannot design a Turing Machine that implements a general finite process to determine whether another Turing Machine ever prints the digit 0. The two intermediary sections (9 and 10) served to establish that Turing's concept of machine computability was equivalent to our conventional notions of human computability.

In Section 11, Turing shows how the functionality of a computing machine can be expressed in the language of first-order predicate logic. He then constructs a formula in this logic that is provable if and only if the machine ever prints the digit 0. If that formula is decidable — that is, if we can determine whether it's provable — then we'd have a general process for determining whether a machine ever prints 0, and we already know we can't have one.

11. *Application to the Entscheidungsproblem.*

The results of §8 have some important applications. In particular, they can be used to show that the Hilbert Entscheidungsproblem can have no solution. For the present I shall confine myself to proving this particular theorem. For the formulation of this problem I must refer the reader to Hilbert and Ackermann's *Grundzüge der Theoretischen Logik* (Berlin, 1931), chapter 3.

The book was actually published in 1928. Chapter 3 is about a third of the 120-page four-chapter book, and is entitled "Der engere Funktionenkalkül" or "The Restricted Functional Calculus," what we know today as first-order predicate logic. The authors state:

> *Das Entscheidungsproblem ist gelöst, wenn man ein Verfahren kennt, das bei einem vorgelegten logischen Ausdruck durch endlich viele Operationen die Entscheidung über die Allgemeingültigkeit bzw. Erfüllbarkeit erlaubt. . . . [Das] Entscheidungsproblem muß als das Hauptproblem der mathematischen Logik bezeichnet werden.*[1]

> The decision problem is solved when we know a procedure with a finite number of operations that determines the validity or satisfiability of any given expression. . . . The decision problem must be considered the main problem of mathematical logic.

The use of the words *validity* and *satisfiability* by Hilbert and Ackermann indicate a so-called semantic formulation of the decision problem. Twenty-five years later, Wilhelm Ackermann continued examining the Entscheidungsproblem from a semantic perspective in his short book *Solvable Cases of the Decision Problem* (North-Holland Publishing Company, 1954).

Referring to Hilbert's restricted functional calculus with the letter **K** (perhaps for *Kalkül*), Turing employs a somewhat different vocabulary to describe the decision problem.

I propose, therefore, to show that there can be no general process for determining whether a given formula 𝔄 of the functional calculus **K** is provable, *i.e.* that there can be no machine which, supplied with any one 𝔄 of these formulae, will eventually say whether 𝔄 is provable.

---

[1]David Hilbert and Wilhelm Ackermann, *Grundzüge der Theoretischen Logik* (Springer, 1928), 73, 77.

By using the word *provable* rather than *validity* or *satisfiability*, Turing reveals that he is approaching the decision problem from a syntactic perspective. The syntactic approach to logic is relative to a system of axioms and inference rules. A formula is considered to be provable (that is, the formula is a theorem) if the formula is an axiom, or if it is derivable from the axioms using the inference rules. The semantic and syntactic approaches to first-order logic were established to be equivalent by Gödel's Completeness Theorem of 1930.

Following the discussions in Sections 9 and 10, Turing has earned the right to assert that if a machine can't be designed to implement a general decision procedure, then there is no general decision procedure that a human could carry out either.

Back in 1936, readers of Turing's paper not steeped in the nuances of completeness, incompleteness, and decidability might have been confused about the relationship between Gödel's incompleteness proof — described in a paper whose title actually mentioned "unentscheidbare Sätze" or "undecidable propositions" — and Turing's proof. Indeed, on the first page of his paper, Turing said that "conclusions are reached which are superficially similar to those of Gödel" (page 67 of this book). He needs to elaborate on that subject a bit more.

> It should perhaps be remarked that what I shall prove is quite different from the well-known results of Gödel[†]. Gödel has shown that (in the formalism of Principia Mathematica) there are propositions 𝔄 such that neither 𝔄 nor — 𝔄 is provable. As a consequence of this, it is shown that no proof of consistency of Principia Mathematica (or of **K**) can be given within that formalism. On the other hand, I shall show that there is no general method which tells whether a given formula 𝔄 is provable in **K**, or, what comes to the same, whether the system consisting of **K** with — 𝔄 adjoined as an extra axiom is consistent.
>
> ───────────────
>
> † *Loc. cit.*

Gödel's theorem and Turing's theorem approach decidability from opposite directions. Gödel's theorem shows the existence of propositions that can be neither proved nor disproved; these propositions are said to be undecidable.

The "general method" that Turing refers to is a decision procedure — an algorithm that analyzes any arbitrary formula and determines whether it is provable or not provable. Turing will prove that no general decision procedure can exist.

Even with the existence of undecidable propositions, a decision procedure could still conceivably exist. When analyzing Gödel's undecidable proposition, it would identify both the proposition and its negation as unprovable.

> If the negation of what Gödel has shown had been proved, *i.e.* if, for each
> $\mathfrak{A}$, either $\mathfrak{A}$ or $-\mathfrak{A}$ is provable, then we should have an immediate solution
> of the Entscheidungsproblem. For we can invent a machine $\mathcal{K}$ which will
> prove consecutively all provable formulae. Sooner or later $\mathcal{K}$ will reach
> either $\mathfrak{A}$ or $-\mathfrak{A}$. If it reaches $\mathfrak{A}$, then we know that $\mathfrak{A}$ is provable. If it
> reaches $-\mathfrak{A}$, then, since **K** is consistent (Hilbert and Ackermann, p. 65), we
> know that $\mathfrak{A}$ is not provable.

Well, okay, but obviously Turing's handy-dandy $\mathcal{K}$ machine (now making its
final appearance in this paper) is certainly *not* what Hilbert had in mind when
he formulated the Entscheidungsproblem. Regardless of how "mechanical" or
"machine-like" any hypothetical decision procedure was supposed to be, it was
still envisioned as something that a human being could manage rather than a
computer requiring millennia of processing time and all the world's memory
resources.

Gödel's result has not provided the basis of a general decision procedure.
Turing's proof is still required.

> Owing to the absence of integers in **K** the proofs appear somewhat
> lengthy. The underlying ideas are quite straightforward.
> Corresponding to each computing machine $\mathcal{M}$ we construct a formula
> Un $(\mathcal{M})$ and we show that, if there is a general method for determining
> whether Un $(\mathcal{M})$ is provable, then there is a general method for deter-
> mining whether $\mathcal{M}$ ever prints 0.

Is Turing giving away the punch line by naming the formula Un for Undecidable?
This Un($\mathcal{M}$) formula functions as a counter-example — a formula that no general
decision procedure can successfully analyze.

As you'll recall, a machine consists of a series of configurations associated with
operations. Beginning with the pages of his paper where Turing presented the
Universal Machine, he's been using the word *instructions* to refer to these elements
of the machine.

Turing needs to represent this computing machine in the language of first-order
logic. Each instruction will be converted to a formula that indicates how the
instruction affects the complete configurations of the machine. The complete
configurations, you'll recall, are snapshots of the tape after each move of the
machine. The complete configuration also includes the next m-configuration of
the machine and the next scanned character.

Turing first presents several propositional functions (known as predicates in
more modern terminology). Like all propositional functions, they have values
of true or false. In all cases, the arguments to these functions are non-negative

integers signifying the squares of the tape and the complete configurations. The squares of the tape are assumed to be numbered beginning at zero, which implies that the tape has a beginning and is infinite in only one direction.

Complete configurations are also assumed to be consecutively numbered. A number pair (x, y) identifies a particular square y in complete configuration x. Although I'll be using actual numbers in my examples, no numbers or examples appear in Turing's discussion.

Let's recall Turing's Example I machine that printed alternating 0s and 1s on every other square. Here are the first 10 complete configurations. I've identified these complete configurations with numbers in the leftmost column. (The heading means "Complete Configuration x.") I've identified the squares of the tape with numbers across the top. I've also replaced Turing's original configuration letters with subscripted q's.

CC x	0	1	2	3	4	5	6	7	...
				--SQUARE Y--					
0	q_1								
1	0	q_2							
2	0		q_3						
3	0		1	q_4					
4	0		1		q_1				
5	0		1		0	q_2			
6	0		1		0		q_3		
7	0		1		0		1	q_4	
8	0		1		0		1		
9	0		1		0		1		
...	0		1		0		1		

This particular machine prints only in every other square, so only the even-numbered squares contain numbers. An m-configuration appearing in a square indicates that's the square being scanned in this complete configuration.

Many of Turing's propositional functions include subscripts that are part of the name of the function. These propositional functions are defined in isolation, but you'll soon see how Turing uses them to describe an entire machine.

The interpretations of the propositional functions involved are as follows :

$R_{S_t}(x, y)$ is to be interpreted as "in the complete configuration x (of $\mathcal{M}$) the symbol on the square y is S".

The final S before the end quotation mark is missing a subscripted l. As you'll recall, the character S_0 is a blank, S_1 is 0, and S_2 is 1. For the Machine I example, $R_{S_2}(5, 2)$ is true because digit 1 appears in complete configuration 5 on square 2, but $R_{S_2}(5, 6)$ is false because digit 1 does not appear in complete configuration 5 in square 6.

[260]

$I(x, y)$ is to be interpreted as "in the complete configuration x the square y is scanned".

For the Example I machine, the function $I(6, 6)$ is true because in complete configuration 6 the next scanned square is 6, but $I(6, y)$ is false for any other square y.

$K_{q_m}(x)$ is to be interpreted as "in the complete configuration x the m-configuration is q_m.

An end quotation mark is missing in that sentence. For the Example I machine, the function $K_{q_2}(5)$ is true but $K_{q_3}(5)$ and $K_{q_2}(7)$ are false.

$F(x, y)$ is to be interpreted as "y is the immediate successor of x".

Or, in the quaint notation of arithmetic, $y = x + 1$. Using the notation for natural numbers that Turing introduced earlier, the predicate $F(u''', u'''')$ is true, but with proper axiomatization, $F(u''', u'''')$ should be false.

So far, Turing has just developed propositional functions that describe the complete configurations of a machine in operation. He hasn't equated these to the table that describes the actual machine. The standard form of a machine contains only one print instruction and one move instruction per line. Each line of the table consists of an m-configuration q_i, a scanned symbol S_j, a printed symbol S_k (which could be the same as S_j), head movement left, right, or not at all, and a new m-configuration q_l.

Turing next gives a definition for something he calls Inst (for "instruction"). This is not a propositional function, but an abbreviation for an expression built from the propositional functions just presented. Each Inst expression is associated with a line of the machine table. The expression describes how these particular combinations of m-configurations, symbols, and head movement affect the complete configuration:

Inst $\{q_i\, S_j\, S_k\, L\, q_l\}$ is to be an abbreviation for

$$(x,y,x',y') \left\{ (R_{S_j}(x,y) \& I(x,y) \& K_{q_i}(x) \& F(x,x') \& F(y',y)) \right.$$

$$\rightarrow \left(I(x',y') \& R_{S_k}(x',y) \& K_{q_l}(x') \right.$$

$$\left. \left. \& (z) \Big[F(y',z)\, \mathrm{v}\, (R_{S_j}(x,z) \rightarrow R_{S_k}(x',z)) \Big] \right) \right\}.$$

This is one of three possible Inst expressions and applies to the case where the head moves left. That's what the L among the arguments of Inst means.

The initial $(x,\ y,\ x',\ y')$ is an abbreviation for four universal quantifiers $(x)(y)(x')(y')$. The bound variables x and x' are two consecutive complete configurations; toward the end of the first line you'll see an F predicate (the first of two) indicating that x' is the successor of x. The bound variables y and y' are two adjacent squares. For an instruction in which the head moves left, y' equals y minus 1, or y is the successor of y', as the second F predicate in the first line indicates.

The other three predicates in the first line indicate the conditions for this particular instruction. The complete configuration is x, the scanned square is y, the scanned symbol is S_j, and the configuration is q_i.

The second line begins with an implication sign and applies to the entire remainder of the expression. These are predicates that describe the complete configuration that results from this instruction. In the next complete configuration x', the square y' is scanned; square y now has the symbol S_k and the new m-configuration is q_l.

Inst concludes with an expression on the third line that *should* indicate that all other squares except square y remain the same. These other squares are indicated with the bound variable z. Either z is the successor of y' (in which case it's equal to y and was the target of a print operation) or ... but here the rest of Turing's formula is wrong. What it says is that in all other squares, S_j becomes S_k, which makes no sense.

A better version of the Inst expression is among the corrections that Turing listed in a follow-up paper published in the *Proceedings of the London Mathematical Society* about a year after the original. That correction (page 310 of this book) is not quite right either, but here's what the last line should be:

$$\& (z) \Big[F(y',z)\, \mathrm{v}\, \Big(\big[R_{S_0}(x,z) \rightarrow R_{S_0}(x',z)\big] \& \big[R_{S_1}(x,z) \rightarrow R_{S_1}(x',z)\big] $$

$$\& \ldots \& \big[R_{S_M}(x,z) \rightarrow R_{S_M}(x',z)\big] \Big) \Big] \Big) \Big\}$$

The $S_0, S_1, \ldots S_M$ subscripts in the R function are all the symbols that $\mathcal{M}$ can print. In other words, for all squares z, either z is the successor of y' (which means z is y — the square that was altered) or the symbol on that square remains the same from complete configuration x to complete configuration x'.

The Inst expression that Turing just presented is for the head moving left.

> Inst $\{q_i \, S_j \, S_k \, R \, q_l\}$ and   Inst $\{q_i \, S_j \, S_k \, N \, q_l\}$
>
> **are to be abbreviations for other similarly constructed expressions.**

Just for a little variety (and as a convenient reference in the pages ahead), the following box shows the complete correct expression for an instruction where the head moves right:

Inst $\{q_i S_j S_k R q_l\}$ is an abbreviation for:

$$(x, y, x', y') \left\{ (R_{S_j}(x, y) \& I(x, y) \& K_{q_i}(x) \& F(x, x') \& F(y, y')) \right.$$
$$\rightarrow (I(x', y') \& R_{S_k}(x', y) \& K_{q_l}(x')$$
$$\& (z)[F(z, y') \vee ([R_{S_0}(x, z) \rightarrow R_{S_0}(x', z)] \&$$
$$[R_{S_1}(x, z) \rightarrow R_{S_1}(x', z)] \&$$
$$\ldots \&$$
$$\left. [R_{S_m}(x, z) \rightarrow R_{S_m}(x', z)])])) \right\}$$

This expression is mostly the same as the instruction for the head moving left except that the $F(y', y)$ term becomes $F(y, y')$ to indicate that the new scanned square is to the right of the last scanned square, and $F(y', z)$ becomes $F(z, y')$ in the latter part of the expression to indicate that z equals y.

For the Example I machine, the m subscript in the R_{S_m} function has a maximum value of 2 because the machine only prints symbols S_0 (blank), S_1 (zero), and S_2 (one).

> Let us put the description of $\mathcal{M}$ into the first standard form of §6. This description consists of a number of expressions such as "$q_i \, S_j \, S_k \, L \, q_l$" (or with R or N substituted for L).

Actually it's Section 5 where Turing develops this standard form. The Example I machine appears on page 241 of his paper (page 139 of this book) like this:

$$q_1 S_0 S_1 R q_2; \ q_2 S_0 S_1 R q_3; \ q_3 S_0 S_2 R q_4; \ q_4 S_0 S_0 R q_1;$$

Each of these four quintuples becomes an Inst expression.

> Let us form all the corresponding expressions such as Inst $\{q_i S_j S_k L q_l\}$ and take their logical sum. This we call Des $(\mathcal{M})$.

That is, the *Description* of machine $\mathcal{M}$. The term "logical sum" can be a bit ambiguous so in the corrections paper (page 311 of this book) Turing substitutes the word "conjunction." In other words, all the Inst terms can be joined with ampersands to represent a complete machine in the language of first-order logic.

Des($\mathcal{M}$) for the Example I machine is an abbreviation for:

$$\text{Inst}\{q_1 S_0 S_1 R q_2\} \ \& \ \text{Inst}\{q_2 S_0 S_1 R q_3\} \ \&$$
$$\text{Inst}\{q_3 S_0 S_2 R q_4\} \ \& \ \text{Inst}\{q_4 S_0 S_0 R q_1\}$$

Now Turing will incorporate that Des($\mathcal{M}$) formula into a larger formula he calls Un($\mathcal{M}$) for *Undecidable*. This Un formula is an implication of the form:

> Some machine $\rightarrow$ Prints zero

The formula uses the successor function F as well as the propositional function N that is true if the argument is a natural number.

The formula Un $(\mathcal{M})$ is to be

$$(\exists u)\Big[N(u) \ \& \ (x)(N(x) \rightarrow (\exists x')F(x,x'))$$
$$\& \ (y,z)\big(F(y,z) \rightarrow N(y) \ \& \ N(z)\big) \ \& \ (y)R_{S_0}(u,y)$$
$$\& \ I(u,u) \ \& \ K_{q_1}(u) \ \& \ \text{Des}(\mathcal{M})\Big]$$
$$\rightarrow (\exists s)(\exists t)\big[N(s) \ \& \ N(t) \ \& \ R_{S_1}(s,t)\big].$$

The implication sign at the beginning of the fourth line divides the formula into the two parts. Each part has an expression in brackets preceded by one or two existential quantifiers.

The last line is the easiest part: It simply says that there exist two numbers s and t such that the character S_1 (a zero) appears in complete configuration s on square t of the tape. In Section 8, Turing proved that there is no algorithm that will tell us whether an arbitrary machine ever prints zero, so I trust you're beginning to see Turing on his way down the mathematical chimney.

The Un($\mathcal{M}$) formula begins by asserting the existence of a number u (the number zero) that serves as both the number of the first complete configuration and the first scanned square. The remainder of the first line just indicates that for each number x there's another number x' that is the successor of x.

The second line is a little wordy but simply asserts that for complete configuration u (zero) and every square y on the tape, the symbol on square y is S_0, or
blank. This is the initial condition of the tape. The third line contains an I function
to establish that in complete configuration zero, the scanned square is zero, and a
K function to set the initial m-configuration to q_1. This is followed by the Des(M)
expression that describes the machine itself.

From the previous formula Turing extracts just the part in square brackets and
provides another abbreviation:

$[N(u) \& \dots \& \text{Des}(M)]$ may be abbreviated to $A(M)$.

The proposition $A(M)$ encompasses the starting conditions of the machine and the
machine's description, but has a free variable of u.

In the published correction to the paper, Turing took note of a problem that
ripples through this proof and which I discussed in Chapter 12. He has not
established that successors are unique. For this reason he defines a propositional
function $G(x, y)$ that is true if y is greater than x, and an expression Q that is
intended to replace the P representation of the Peano Axioms:

Q is an abbreviation for:

$$(x)(\exists w)(y,z)\left\{F(x,w) \& \left(F(x,y) \to G(x,y)\right)\right.$$
$$\& \left(F(x,z) \& G(z,y) \to G(x,y)\right)$$
$$\& \left[G(z,x) \text{ v } \left(G(x,y) \& F(y,z)\right) \text{ v }\right.$$
$$\left.\left.\left(F(x,y) \& F(z,y)\right) \to \left(-F(x,z)\right)\right]\right\}$$

With this definition taking care of the natural numbers, the $A(M)$ abbreviation
becomes much simpler. It's a conjunction of Q, the starting conditions for the
machine, and the machine description:

$A(M)$ is an abbreviation for:

$$Q \& (y)R_{S_0}(u,y) \& I(u,u) \& K_{q_1}(u) \& \text{Des}(M)$$

In $A(M)$, u is a free variable. That variable becomes bound in the Un(M) formula:

Un(M) is the formula:

$$(\exists u)A(M) \to (\exists s)(\exists t)R_{S_1}(s,t)$$

I've removed the $N(x)$ predicates because the domain of all these propositional functions is implicitly assumed to be the natural numbers. Referring to the definitions of the R, I, K, and F predicates, and the Inst and Des formulas, Turing says:

> When we substitute the meanings suggested on p. 259–60 we find that Un $(\mathcal{M})$ has the interpretation "in some complete configuration of $\mathcal{M}$, S_1 (*i.e.* 0) appears on the tape".

Because the expression on the left of the implication sign in Un($\mathcal{M}$) includes the description of the machine and its starting conditions, it is our assumption that it is true. These are the axioms. To the right of the implication sign is an expression that is true if the machine prints a zero sometime during its run time. Therefore, the formula Un($\mathcal{M}$) is itself true if the right side is true — that is, if the machine ever prints zero — and false if the machine never prints zero. Does there exist an algorithm that will determine whether Un($\mathcal{M}$) is provable? If so, then there also exists an algorithm that will tell us if an arbitrary machine ever prints zero.

Notice that Turing refers to the "suggested" meaning of the propositional functions. Much of the remainder of the proof will be based on a purely syntactic interpretation of the formulas without requiring that we take into account the precise meaning of these functions.

Turing now wants to show that Un($\mathcal{M}$) is provable if and only if S_1 appears on the tape. He tackles each half of this proof in two lemmas (subsidiary proofs) that he soon refers to as Lemma 1 and Lemma 2, but which he first refers to as (*a*) and (*b*):

> Corresponding to this I prove that
>
> (*a*) If S_1 appears on the tape in some complete configuration of $\mathcal{M}$, then Un($\mathcal{M}$) is provable.
>
> (*b*) If Un($\mathcal{M}$) is provable, then S_1 appears on the tape in some complete configuration of $\mathcal{M}$.
>
> When this has been done, the remainder of the theorem is trivial.

The harder part is Lemma 1, which Turing now repeats verbatim.

> [261]
>
> LEMMA 1. *If S_1 appears on the tape in some complete configuration of $\mathcal{M}$, then Un($\mathcal{M}$) is provable.*
>
> We have to show how to prove Un($\mathcal{M}$).

As before, u is what we commonly know as zero, u' is 1, u'' is 2, and $u^{(n)}$ means a u with n prime marks and represents the number n.

In addition, Turing slips in some new notation in the next sentence of his paper that involves three new functions named $r(n, m)$, $i(n)$, and $k(n)$. These are not propositional functions because they return integers. The n argument is a complete configuration and m is a square of the tape.

The $r(n, m)$ function returns an *index* of the character that appears in complete configuration n on square m. This index is 0 for a blank, 1 for zero, 2 for a 1, and so forth, so that $S_{r(n,m)}$ is the character that appears in complete configuration n on square m. Turing will combine this r function as a subscript for S with the R propositional function:

$$R_{S_{r(n,m)}}(n, m)$$

That predicate is always true, although Turing will instead use superscripted u terms for the arguments to R:

$$R_{S_{r(n,m)}}\left(u^{(n)}, u^{(m)}\right)$$

Turing allows himself to use n and m in the r function but requires $u^{(n)}$ and $u^{(m)}$ in the R predicate.

The second new function that Turing introduces is $i(n)$, which returns the number of the scanned square in complete configuration n, so that the predicate

$$I\left(u^{(n)}, u^{(i(n))}\right)$$

is always true because it refers to the complete configuration n and the scanned square $i(n)$. The third new function $k(n)$ returns the *index* of the m-configuration in complete configuration n, so that $q_{k(n)}$ is the m-configuration in complete configuration n. The predicate

$$K_{q_{k(n)}}\left(u^{(n)}\right)$$

is always true because it indicates that in complete configuration n, the m-configuration is $q_{k(n)}$.

Let us suppose that in the n-th complete configuration the sequence of symbols on the tape is $S_{r(n, 0)}, S_{r(n, 1)}, \ldots, S_{r(n, n)}$, followed by nothing but blanks, and that the scanned symbol is the $i(n)$-th, and that the m-configuration is $q_{k(n)}$.

In complete configuration 0, the tape is entirely blank. In complete configuration 1, possibly one non-blank symbol appears on the tape. In general, in complete configuration n, a maximum of n symbols appear on the tape (and quite likely fewer). Turing represents this sequence of symbols beginning at square 0 as $S_{r(n,0)}$, $S_{r(n,1)}, \ldots, S_{r(n,n)}$. If he's actually listed $n + 1$ symbols here rather than n, that's no problem because some of these r functions undoubtedly return 0 and hence refer to blank squares.

Then

we may form the proposition

$$R_{S_{r(n,0)}}(u^{(n)}, u) \,\&\, R_{S_{r(n,1)}}(u^{(n)}, u') \,\&\, \ldots \,\&\, R_{S_{r(n,n)}}(u^{(n)}, u^{(n)})$$

$$\&\, I\left(u^{(n)}, u^{(i(n))}\right) \,\&\, K_{q_{k(n)}}(u^{(n)})$$

$$\&\, (y)F\left((y, u') \vee F(u, y) \vee F(u', y) \vee \ldots \vee F(u^{(n-1)}, y) \vee R_{S_0}(u^{(n)}, y)\right),$$

which we may abbreviate to CC_n.

That is, "complete configuration n." The first line includes a conjunction of functions corresponding to the symbols on the first $n + 1$ squares. The second line includes functions referring to the scanned square $i(n)$ and the m-configuration $q_{k(n)}$.

Toward the beginning of the third line, the F that appears right after the universal quantifier should be inside the large parentheses. Just as the first line indicates the symbols that appear on squares numbered 0 through n, this last line indicates that squares numbered greater than n contain blanks. That's the R predicate that appears at the very end. The universal quantifier of y ranges over all squares. Either u' is the successor to square y (i.e., y is 0) or square y is the successor to u (i.e., y is 1), or square y is the successor to u' (i.e., y is 2) and so forth up through the case where the square y is the successor to $n - 1$ (i.e., y is n). If y is none of those cases, then square y contains a blank symbol.

Here's the corrected version:

CC_n is an abbreviation for:

$$R_{S_{r(n,0)}}(u^{(n)}, u) \,\&\, R_{S_{r(n,1)}}(u^{(n)}, u') \,\&\, \ldots \,\&\, R_{S_{r(n,n)}}(u^{(n)}, u^{(n)})$$

$$\&\, I(u^{(n)}, u^{(i(n))}) \,\&\, K_{q_{k(n)}}(u^{(n)})$$

$$\&\, (y)\left(F(y, u') \vee F(u, y) \vee F(u', y) \vee \ldots \vee F(u^{(n-1)}, y) \vee R_{S_0}(u^{(n)}, y)\right),$$

When n equals zero, the first line drops out, and much of the third line as well. CC_0 is an abbreviation for:

$$I(u, y) \,\&\, K_{q_1}(u) \,\&\, (y)R_{S_0}(u, y)$$

As before, $F(u,u')$ & $F(u',u'')$ & ... & $F(u^{(r-1)}, u^{(r)})$ is abbreviated to $F^{(r)}$.

I shall show that all formulae of the form $A(\mathcal{M})$ & $F^{(n)} \to CC_n$ (abbreviated to CF_n) are provable.

The $A(\mathcal{M})$ formula, you'll recall, combined the starting condition of the machine (a blank tape, an m-configuration of q_1, scanned square number zero) with the Des($\mathcal{M}$) expression, which was a description of the machine. The Des($\mathcal{M}$) expression combined multiple Inst expressions. Each Inst expression indicated how the instruction changed a symbol on the scanned square, changed the m-configuration, and changed the square to be scanned.

Turing is essentially defining a CF_n formula for each complete configuration n.

CF_n is an abbreviation for:

$$A(\mathcal{M}) \,\&\, F^{(n)} \to CC_n$$

Here are the first few of these CF_n formulas:

CF_0: $A(\mathcal{M}) \to CC_0$
CF_1: $A(\mathcal{M})$ & $F(u, u') \to CC_1$
CF_2: $A(\mathcal{M})$ & $F(u, u')$ & $F(u', u'') \to CC_2$
CF_3: $A(\mathcal{M})$ & $F(u, u')$ & $F(u', u'')$ & $F(u'', u''') \to CC_3$
...

The meaning of CF_n is "The n-th complete configuration of $\mathcal{M}$ is so and so", where "so and so" stands for the actual n-th complete configuration of $\mathcal{M}$. That CF_n should be provable is therefore to be expected.

Turing shows that the CF_n formulae are provable with an induction proof. He proves first that CF_0 is provable, and then shows that if CF_n is provable, so is CF_{n+1}.

CF_0 is certainly provable, for in the complete configuration the symbols are all blanks, the m-configuration is q_1, and the scanned square is u, i.e. CC_0 is

$$(y) R_{S_0}(u,y) \,\&\, I(u,u) \,\&\, K_{q_1}(u).$$

This is simply a rearranged version of the CC_0 formula I showed earlier. The expression for $A(\mathcal{M})$ is this:

$$Q \,\&\, (y)R_{S_0}(u,y) \,\&\, I(u,u) \,\&\, K_{q_1}(u) \,\&\, \text{Des}(\mathcal{M})$$

$A(\mathcal{M})$ contains precisely the same R, I, and K predicates as CC_0.

$A(\mathcal{M}) \to CC_0$ is then trivial.
We next show that $CF_n \to CF_{n+1}$ is provable for each n.

If you look at the expression for CF_n, you'll see that

$$CF_n \to CF_{n+1}$$

is just an abbreviation for the formula:

$$\left[A(\mathcal{M}) \& F^{(n)} \to CC_n\right] \to \left[A(\mathcal{M}) \& F^{(n+1)} \to CC_{n+1}\right]$$

This is the much harder part of the induction proof, but proving this implication will let us say that $CF_0 \to CF_1$ is provable, $CF_1 \to CF_2$ is provable, and so forth, so that all CF_n expressions are provable.

There are three cases to consider, according as in the move from the n-th to the $(n+1)$-th configuration the machine moves to left or to right or remains stationary. We suppose that the first case applies, *i.e.* the machine moves to the left. A similar argument applies in the other cases.

In the first part of the next sentence Turing defines integers a, b, c, and d based on the r, i, and k functions introduced earlier, but these definitions are a little mixed up:

If $r(n, i(n)) = a$, $r(n+1, i(n+1)) = c$, $k(i(n)) = b$, and $k(i(n+1)) = d$,

In Turing's published correction to this paper, he untangles the definitions. They all refer to complete configuration n and should be:

$a = k(n)$, the index of the m-configuration
$b = r(n, i(n))$, the index of the symbol in scanned square $i(n)$
$c = k(n+1)$, the index of the next m-configuration
$d = r(n+1, i(n))$, the index of the new symbol in square $i(n)$

The a and c abbreviations are subscripts on q; the b and d abbreviations are subscripts on S. These abbreviations exist solely to simplify the remainder of the sentence and a few items that follow:

then Des $(\mathcal{M})$ must include Inst $\{q_a\, S_b\, S_d\, L\, q_c\}$ as one of its terms, *i.e.*

$$\text{Des}(\mathcal{M}) \to \text{Inst}\{q_a\, S_b\, S_d\, L\, q_c\}.$$

Because Des consists of the conjunction of all of the Inst terms, if Des is true then any individual Inst term is also true, and the implication is true. $A(\mathcal{M})$ is a conjunction of Des and other expressions, hence:

$$A(\mathcal{M}) \rightarrow \text{Des}(\mathcal{M})$$

Combining these two implications, we have:

$$A(\mathcal{M}) \rightarrow \text{Inst}\ \{q_a S_b S_d L q_c\}$$

The expression $F^{(n+1)}$ is an abbreviation for a conjunction of F predicates that are also assumed to be axioms. Because $F^{(n+1)}$ is true, we can add it to both sides of that formula as a conjunction:

Hence $\qquad A(\mathcal{M})\ \&\ F^{(n+1)} \rightarrow \text{Inst}\,\{q_a\, S_b\, S_d\, L\, q_c\}\ \&\ F^{(n+1)}$.

But $\qquad \text{Inst}\{q_a\, S_b\, S_d\, L\, q_c\}\ \&\ F^{(n+1)} \rightarrow (CC_n \rightarrow CC_{n+1})$

is provable,

Another fix is required: The conjunction on the left must also include Q to affirm the uniqueness of the successors:

$$\text{Inst}\ \{q_a S_b S_d L q_c\}\ \&\ Q\ \&\ F^{(n+1)} \rightarrow (CC_n \rightarrow CC_{n+1})$$

If you replace the a, b, c, and d subscripts in the Inst expression, you'll see that it refers to the particular Inst instruction that causes complete configuration n to advance to complete configuration $(n + 1)$:

$$\text{Inst}\ \{q_{k(n)} S_{r(n,i(n))} S_{r(n+1,i(n))} L q_{k(n+1)}\}\ \&\ Q\ \&\ F^{(n+1)} \rightarrow (CC_n \rightarrow CC_{n+1})$$

This formula is equivalent to

$$(CC_n\ \&\ \text{Inst}\ \{q_{k(n)} S_{r(n,i(n))} S_{r(n+1,i(n))} L q_{k(n+1)}\}\ \&\ Q\ \&\ F^{(n+1)}) \rightarrow CC_{n+1}$$

and intuitively it seems very obvious: CC_{n+1} is implied by CC_n in conjunction with the particular Inst instruction that causes CC_n to advance to CC_{n+1}. However, showing that this is provable by manipulating the propositional functions involved is rather messy due to the complexity of the Inst and CC_n abbreviations.

The two statements that Turing has just presented are provable,

and so therefore is

$$A(\mathcal{M})\ \&\ F^{(n+1)} \rightarrow (CC_n \rightarrow CC_{n+1})$$

That's a statement of the form $X \rightarrow (Y \rightarrow Z)$ and it's fairly easy to show that it's equivalent to $(X \rightarrow Y) \rightarrow (X \rightarrow Z)$, so:

$$\left(A(\mathcal{M}) \mathbin{\&} F^{(n+1)} \to CC_n\right) \to \left(A(\mathcal{M}) \mathbin{\&} F^{(n+1)} \to CC_{n+1}\right)$$

Recall that F with a superscript is an abbreviation for a conjunction of F predicates, so that $F^{(n+1)} \to F^{(n)}$ and $(A(\mathcal{M}) \mathbin{\&} F^{(n+1)}) \to (A(\mathcal{M}) \mathbin{\&} F^{(n)})$

[262]

and $\qquad \left(A(\mathcal{M}) \mathbin{\&} F^{(n)} \to CC_n\right) \to \left(A(\mathcal{M}) \mathbin{\&} F^{(n+1)} \to CC_{n+1}\right),$

Both those parenthetical expressions are of the form of the abbreviation CF_n,

i.e. $\qquad\qquad\qquad\qquad CF_n \to CF_{n+1}.$
CF_n is provable for each n.

The induction proof showing that CF_n is provable is concluded, but we're not finished with the lemma yet because we really need to prove $\mathrm{Un}(\mathcal{M})$.

Now it is the assumption of this lemma that S_1 appears somewhere, in some complete configuration, in the sequence of symbols printed by $\mathcal{M}$; that is, for some integers N, K,

where N is the number of a complete configuration and K is a square,

CC_N has $R_{S_1}(u^{(N)}, u^{(K)})$ as one of its terms, and therefore $CC_N \to R_{S_1}(u^{(N)}, u^{(K)})$ is provable.

This is so because any term in a conjunction implies that term.

We have then
$$CC_N \to R_{S_1}(u^{(N)}, u^{(K)})$$
and $\qquad\qquad\quad A(\mathcal{M}) \mathbin{\&} F^{(N)} \to CC^N.$

That superscript on CC should actually be a subscript, but it's the definition CF_N which Turing has just shown is provable for all N (although previously he used a lower-case n rather than upper-case N).

So far, Turing has been dealing with formulas that have contained a free variable named u.

We also have

$$(\exists u)A(\mathcal{M}) \to (\exists u)(\exists u')\ldots(\exists u^{(N')})(A(\mathcal{M}) \& F^{(N)}),$$

where $N' = \max(N, K)$.

Actually, K (which is the square on which the zero appears) can never be greater than N (the complete configuration), so N' is always equal to N. The expression $A(\mathcal{M}) \& F^{(N)}$ on the right was just shown to imply CC_N, which was just shown to imply $R_{S_1}(u^{(N)}, u^{(K)})$

And so

$$(\exists u)A(\mathcal{M}) \to (\exists u)(\exists u')\ldots(\exists u^{(N')})R_{S_1}(u^{(N)}, u^{(K)}),$$

The R function doesn't require the existence of all integers from u through $u^{(N')}$. It just requires $u^{(N)}$ and $u^{(K)}$, so most of those existential quantifiers can be removed, and we're left with:

$$(\exists u)A(\mathcal{M}) \to (\exists u^{(N)})(\exists u^{(K)})R_{S_1}(u^{(N)}, u^{(K)}),$$

If we replace $u^{(N)}$ with s and $u^{(K)}$ with t, we get:

$$(\exists u)A(\mathcal{M}) \to (\exists s)(\exists t)R_{S_1}(s, t),$$

This is precisely the definition of $\mathrm{Un}(\mathcal{M})$ that you'll see in a little box on page 268. It is peculiarly not, however, the definition of $\mathrm{Un}(\mathcal{M})$ implied by Turing in his original text. He had $N(s)$ and $N(t)$ in the expression on the right of the implication sign, but those predicates simply indicate that s and t are natural numbers, and that fact has been implied.

Beginning with the premise "If S_1 appears on the tape in some complete configuration of $\mathcal{M}$," we've just proved a formula that was defined as $\mathrm{Un}(\mathcal{M})$,

i.e. $\mathrm{Un}(\mathcal{M})$ is provable.

This completes the proof of Lemma 1.

The second lemma is much shorter, and requires only interpreting the formula using the propositional functions defined earlier.

LEMMA 2. *If* $\mathrm{Un}(\mathcal{M})$ *is provable, then* S_1 *appears on the tape in some complete configuration of* $\mathcal{M}$.

If we substitute any propositional functions for function variables in a provable formula, we obtain a true proposition. In particular, if we substitute the meanings tabulated on pp. 259–260 in Un($\mathcal{M}$), we obtain a true proposition with the meaning "S_1 appears somewhere on the tape in some complete configuration of $\mathcal{M}$".

Now Turing has established that Un($\mathcal{M}$) is provable if and only if S_1 appears on the tape in some complete configuration of $\mathcal{M}$.

We are now in a position to show that the Entscheidungsproblem cannot be solved. Let us suppose the contrary. Then there is a general (mechanical) process for determining whether Un($\mathcal{M}$) is provable. By Lemmas 1 and 2, this implies that there is a process for determining whether $\mathcal{M}$ ever prints 0, and this is impossible, by § 8. Hence the Entscheidungsproblem cannot be solved.

In retrospect, it was a piece of cake, wouldn't you agree?

It shouldn't be surprising at all that Un($\mathcal{M}$) is a rather complex formula. If it were much simpler, it might be of a form that could be analyzed by a decision procedure. Instead, Un($\mathcal{M}$) includes A($\mathcal{M}$) as one of its terms, and A($\mathcal{M}$) includes Q and Des($\mathcal{M}$) among its terms, and Des($\mathcal{M}$) is a conjunction of all the Inst terms that make up the machine. Each Inst term has five universal quantifiers, Q has three universal quantifiers and one existential quantifier, A($\mathcal{M}$) has another universal quantifier, and Un($\mathcal{M}$) has three existential quantifiers.

This complex nesting of quantifiers wouldn't make a difference in the solvability of the proposition if it happened to contain only monadic predicates, that is, predicates with only one argument. In 1915, Leopold Löwenheim (1878–1957) proved that propositions containing only monadic predicates were decidable.[2]

By the time Turing wrote his paper, much additional progress had been made in finding decision procedures for special cases of formulas. Generally, when applying decision procedures, a formula is first converted to *prenex normal form*, which means that the formula is manipulated so that all quantifiers (in non-negated form) are moved to the beginning of the formula and precede an expression called the "matrix" that contains no quantifiers.

Over the years, various mathematicians discovered decision procedures for classes of formulas in prenex normal form that begin with a particular pattern of

[2]Leopold Löwenheim, "Über Möglichkeiten im Relativekalkül," *Mathematische Annalen*, Vol. 76 (1915), 447–470. Translated as "On Possibilities in the Calculus of Relatives," in Jean van Heijenoort, ed., *From Frege to Gödel: A Source Book in Mathematical Logic, 1879–1931* (Harvard University Press, 1967), 228–251.

quantifiers. In the literature on decision problems,[3] this pattern of quantifiers is shown using the ∀ and ∃ symbols for the universal and existential quantifiers. A numeric superscript indicates a particular number of quantifiers; an asterisk means any number.

In 1928, Paul Bernays and Moses Schönfinkel (1889–1942) published a decision procedure for sentences beginning with ∃*∀* (any number of existential quantifiers followed by any number of universal quantifiers). In 1928, Wilhelm Ackermann gave a decision procedure for ∃*∀∃* (any number of existential quantifiers followed by one universal quantifier, followed by any number of existential quantifiers). In 1932 Gödel showed a decision procedure for two universal quantifiers between any number of existential quantifiers: ∃*∀²∃*.

Also explored in connection with the decision problem were *reduction classes*. A reduction class consists of all sentences that begin with a particular pattern of quantifiers. Sentences in various reduction classes were proven to have a decision procedure only if *all* sentences have a decision procedure. In 1920, Skolem proved that ∀*∃* defines a reduction class and in 1933 Gödel narrowed that to ∀³∃*.

Before the proofs of Church and Turing, it was not known whether these reduction classes had decision procedures — only that if there existed a decision procedure for the reduction class, there would also exist a *general* decision procedure. A consequence of the Church and Turing papers was that these reduction classes were undecidable. In 1932, Gödel had shown a decision procedure for sentences with the prefix ∃*∀²∃* and by extension ∀²∃*. After Turing's proof, it was known that sentences with the prefix ∀³∃* were undecidable. With the addition of one little universal quantifier, a decidable sentence of form ∀²∃* tips to an undecidable sentence of form ∀³∃*.

In the following paragraph, Turing uses the word *quantor* to refer to quantifiers.

> In view of the large number of particular cases of solutions of the Entscheidungsproblem for formulae with restricted systems of quantors, it
>
> [263]
>
> is interesting to express Un($\mathcal{M}$) in a form in which all quantors are at the beginning. Un($\mathcal{M}$) is, in fact, expressible in the form
>
> $$(u)(\exists x)(w)(\exists u_1)\ldots(\exists u_n)\mathfrak{B}, \qquad (\mathrm{I})$$
>
> where $\mathfrak{B}$ contains no quantors, and $n = 6$.

Turing has proved that sentences with the prefix ∀∃∀∃⁶ (using the customary notation) form a reduction class. There can be no decision process for sentences with this prefix.

---

[3] Most notably, Egon Börger, Erich Grädel, and Yuri Gurevich, *The Classical Decision Problem* (Springer, 1997). This book and its bibliography should be consulted for papers concerning the Entscheidungsproblem and its partial solutions.

> By unimportant modifications we can obtain a formula, with all essential properties of Un($\mathcal{M}$), which is of form (I) with $n = 5$.

In the correction to this paper, Turing notes that this last number should be 4, so the reduction class is further narrowed to $\forall\exists\forall\exists^4$.

In 1962, Swiss logician Julius Richard Büchi (1924–1984) took another swing at the Entscheidungsproblem using Turing Machines, and managed to simplify the proof somewhat.[4] He showed that sentences of the form $\exists\&\forall\exists\forall$ form a reduction class. (Such a sentence is a conjunction of two terms, each preceded by its own quantifier or quantifiers.) Büchi's paper also laid the groundwork for proving that $\forall\exists\forall$ sentences form a reduction class, which means there can be no general decision procedure even for sentences with the seemingly simple prefix of $\forall\exists\forall$.

Mathematicians do the world big favors when they develop methods for solving problems, but they perform an equal service when they prove that something has no solution. There is no way to trisect an angle with ruler and compass, no way to square the circle, and no way to prove Euclid's fifth postulate from the first four. There are no integer solutions to $x^n + y^n = z^n$ for n greater than 2, there is no way to establish consistency of arithmetic within the system, and there is no general decision procedure for first-order logic.

We can stop wasting our time trying to find one. Knowing what's impossible is just as important as knowing what's possible.

---

[4] J. Richard Büchi, "Turing-Machines and the Entscheidungsproblem," *Mathematische Annalen*, Vol. 148, No. 3 (June 1962), 201–213.

15 The Lambda Calculus

In 1983 or 1984, when Alonzo Church was about 80 years old, he was invited to speak at the Center for the Study of Language and Information at Stanford University, and was taken on a little tour featuring CSLI's Xerox Dandelion computers. These computers were running LISP, a programming language developed by John McCarthy (b. 1927). Church was told how LISP was based on the lambda calculus that Church had invented some 50 years earlier.

Church confessed that he didn't know anything about computers, but that he once had a student who did.[1] By that time, of course, everyone knew who Alan Turing was.

The lambda calculus developed by Alonzo Church in the early 1930s provided a means for Church to prove that that there is no general decision procedure for first-order predicate logic. Alan Turing learned of this proof prior to the publication of his own paper on computable numbers and the Entscheidungsproblem. He was then obliged to add an appendix to his paper that described how his approach and Church's approach were basically equivalent. That appendix is the subject of this chapter.

If the concepts behind the lambda calculus seem familiar, it is because they have been quite influential in the development of programming languages. Fairly early it was noticed that a structural relationship existed between the lambda calculus and programming languages classified as *procedural* or *imperative*, such as the early programming language ALGOL,[2] from which languages such as Pascal and C derived, as well as the many derivatives of C such as C++, Java, and C#. Programs written in procedural languages are structured around the concept of passing data around to procedures (also called subroutines or methods) that process this data in various ways.

---

[1] María Manzano, "Alonzo Church: His Life, His Work and Some of His Miracles," *History and Philosophy of Logic*, Vol. 18 (1997), 212.

[2] P. J. Landin, "A Correspondence Between ALGOL 60 and Church's Lambda-Notation," *Communications of the ACM*, Vol. 8, No. 2 (Feb. 1965), 89–101; Vol. 8, No. 3 (Mar. 1965), 158–165.

The lambda calculus has had a more direct influence on *functional* programming languages, such as LISP, APL, Haskell, Scheme, and F#. In a functional language the functions are arranged more like a chain where each function gets the output from the previous one. Functional languages often allow the manipulation of functions in much the same way that procedural languages manipulate data. While functional languages have not achieved the mainstream popularity of procedural languages, they have recently been enjoying something of a renaissance.

Alonzo Church was born in 1903 in Washington, D.C., and spent most of his professional life at Princeton University. He attended Princeton as an undergraduate and then earned his Ph.D. in mathematics at the age of 24. He spent two years as a National Research Fellow, and then came back to Princeton, where he taught from 1929 until his retirement in 1967. Church then had a supplemental career at UCLA until 1990.

Church was a hard-working and meticulous man. He spoke in carefully constructed complete sentences and worked late into the night. Church's classes often began with an elaborate ritual of cleaning the blackboard, sometimes involving a pail of water. When working on a mathematical problem, he would use different colored inks, and when he needed more colors, he would mix his own using various proportions of the standard colors. When he finished with a page he wished to preserve, he would cover it with Duco, a lacquer that Church found particularly suited for the purpose because it did not warp the paper.[3]

Church supervised 31 doctoral dissertations, including those of Stephen Kleene (1931), John Barkley Rosser (1934), Leon Henkin (1947), Martin Davis (1950), Hartley Rogers (1952), and Raymond Smullyan (1959), as well as Alan Turing (1938).[4]

It is often assumed that Alonzo Church founded the Association for Symbolic Logic because he was the first editor of *The Journal of Symbolic Logic*. He did not actually found the organization, but he did guide the journal on a very illustrious course, highlighted by his valuable bibliographies on the literature of logic.

The story of the lambda calculus begins with work that Church did while he was a National Research Fellow from 1927 to 1929. At the time, mathematicians wanted to get a handle on the amorphous concept of *effective calculability*. To understand the limits and capability of numeric calculations, it was necessary to define functions in a formal and systematic manner, that is, as symbols and strings with definite rules. What was the best way to do this? Could it then be shown that these functions fully encapsulated effective calculability?

---

[3] Herbert B. Enderton, "Alonzo Church: Life and Work," introduction to *Collected Works of Alonzo Church* (MIT Press, forthcoming). Preprint available at http://www.math.ucla.edu/~hbe/church.pdf.

[4] Herbert B. Enderton, "In Memoriam: Alonzo Church, 1903–1995," *The Bulletin of Symbolic Logic*, Vol. 1, No. 4 (1995), 486–488.

Church's first paper on the subject was received by *The Annals of Mathematics* on October 5, 1931, and published the following April.[5] It is here that Church introduced a lower-case lambda (λ) to represent functions.

Part of the impetus for a new notation was a certain ambiguity in the traditional representation of functions. Consider the following expression:

$$x^2 + 5x + 7$$

By itself, that expression is syntactically correct, yet we're not sure what we're supposed to do with it. This is much clearer:

$$f(x) = x^2 + 5x + 7$$

That's a traditional function notation where x is a bound (or independent) variable. We can change that bound variable to whatever we want, as long as there won't be a collision with anything else in the function:

$$f(y) = y^2 + 5y + 7$$

We can now represent a value of the function with an expression such as $f(4)$. We know to substitute the 4 for the independent variable and calculate a value of the function:

$$f(4) = (4)^2 + 5 \cdot (4) + 7 = 43$$

You may be amazed when you realize this, but there's no standard way to represent the function expression (that is, the expression $y^2 + 5y + 7$) together with a specific value for y. Once we stick the 4 in for y, we lose the independent variable. If you were put in charge of fixing this deficiency and developing a notation for representing a function with a value, perhaps you might come up with something like this:

$$[y^2 + 5y + 7](4)$$

That's not too bad, but what if the expression had multiple independent variables? This is rather ambiguous:

$$[y^2 + 5y + 18x - 2xy + 7](4)$$

Even if you allowed this

$$[y^2 + 5y + 18x - 2xy + 7](4,\ 5)$$

you're assuming that the values for x and y are specified in a particular order.

In *Principia Mathematica*, Alfred North Whitehead and Bertrand Russell adopted the notation of a circumflex for classes that satisfied certain functions: $\hat{y}$. Church

---

[5] Alonzo Church, "A Set of Postulates for the Foundation of Logic," *The Annals of Mathematics*, 2nd Series, Vol. 33, No. 2 (Apr. 1932), 346–366.

wanted to move the circumflex in front of the variable, like $\hat{\ }y$, but for typographical reasons the symbol was soon changed to a lambda[6]: λy.

Church's notation evolved somewhat over the years. In the following discussion, I will attempt to be consistent with the notation eventually used by Turing in the appendix to his paper. A function of one variable is represented with this general syntax

$$\lambda x[M]$$

where M is an expression containing the bound variable x. For the earlier example, you can denote the function as:

$$\lambda x[x^2 + 5x + 7]$$

A function with a value for the bound variable is written with the general syntax:

$$\{F\}(A)$$

F is a function, and if F has an independent variable, then the formula represents the function where A can replace that independent variable. If the function has an independent variable x, for example, the general notation is:

$$\{\lambda x[M]\}(A)$$

For the example function, this becomes:

$$\{\lambda x[x^2 + 5x + 7]\}(A)$$

If the value of x is to be 4, then you can write it like so:

$$\{\lambda x[x^2 + 5x + 7]\}(4)$$

There we have it: We've successfully notated a function together with a value for the independent variable.

A function with two independent variables has the general form

$$\{\{F\}(A)\}(B)$$

but for convenience and readability it can be shortened to:

$$\{F\}(A, B)$$

If you put an actual function in for F, it looks like this:

$$\{\lambda x \lambda y[y^2 + 5y + 18x - 2xy + 7]\}(A, B)$$

We now know that A is to be substituted for x and B is to be substituted for y because that's the order of the lambdas at the beginning.

---

[6]J. Barkley Rosser, "Highlights of the History of Lambda-Calculus," *Annals of the History of Computing*, Vol. 6, No. 4 (Oct. 1984), 337–349.

Additional notational shortcuts are allowed. The curly braces can be eliminated if there's no confusion, so that

$$\{F\}(A, B)$$

becomes

$$F(A, B)$$

which looks like regular function notation, except that the F expression actually contains some lambdas:

$$\lambda x \lambda y[M](A, B)$$

Church also allowed the brackets to be replaced by a single dot following the string of lambdas:

$$\lambda x \lambda y.M(A, B)$$

This is the form in which you'll see most of the lambda expressions in the pages that follow.

After Church established the basic lambda notation, he introduced expressions for the common logical operators and rules of substitution to convert formulas into equivalent formulas. Church defined these rules of conversion very formally, but they can be boiled down to the following:

I. You can change a particular bound variable (for example, x to y) if the new variable doesn't collide with anything else in the formula.

II. In a formula $\{\lambda x.M\}(N)$, if N doesn't contain anything named x, you can substitute N for all occurrences of x in M, at which point the formula becomes just M with N substituted for the original x.

III. The reverse of II is allowed.

A year and a half after that first paper on lambda functions, Church published a second.[7] Church revised his list of postulates and emphasized "the entirely formal character of the system which makes it possible to abstract from the meaning of the symbols and to regard the proving of theorems (of formal logic) as a game played with marks on paper according to a certain arbitrary set of rules."[8] That concept is very much in the formalist tradition.

Church also introduced the abbreviation *conv* meaning "by conversion" to indicate one formula converted into an equivalent formula by rule I, II, or III. For example,

$$\lambda x[x^2 + 5x + 7](A) \text{ conv } A^2 + 5A + 7$$

Church concluded this second paper with a short section on positive integers. He used lambda notation to define the symbol 1, the successor, addition, and

---

[7] Alonzo Church, "A Set of Postulates for the Foundation of Logic (Second Paper)," *The Annals of Mathematics*, 2nd Series, Vol. 34, No. 4 (Oct. 1933), 839–864.

[8] Ibid, 842.

multiplication operations, and the five Peano Axioms, and declared, "Our program is to develop the theory of positive integers on the basis which we have just been describing, and then, by known methods or appropriate modifications of them, to proceed to a theory of rational numbers and a theory of real numbers."[9]

The next steps in this process consisted of papers by Church's student Stephen Cole Kleene — whose last name is pronounced "klay-nee" — with the assistance of John Barkley Rosser (1907–1989). In 1934 Kleene laid some foundational work in "Proof by Cases in Formal Logic,"[10] and simplified the notation for multiple lambdas. Instead of

$$\lambda x \lambda y M$$

you can use

$$\lambda xy M$$

Kleene's doctoral thesis was adapted and published in 1935 as the two-part "A Theory of Positive Integers in Formal Logic."[11] The prerequisites for this paper are Church's two papers and Kleene's earlier paper, but the second part also alludes to a forthcoming paper by Church and Rosser.[12]

Although the lambda calculus as developed by Church, Kleene, and Rosser is quite extensive and involves logic as well as arithmetic, I want to focus on some elementary arithmetic just so you get a taste of how addition and multiplication can be implemented through pure symbol manipulation.

When defining the natural numbers, it's always necessary to begin with either 0 or 1; Church and Kleene begin with 1, and here's the symbol for it:[13]

$$1 \rightarrow \lambda fx.f(x)$$

The arrow means "stands for" or "is an abbreviation for." The formula itself may seem a little strange. Actually, it probably seems *extremely* strange, but it's merely a definition, so it needn't make sense right away. With the more verbose notation, it is:

$$1 \rightarrow \{ \lambda fx[f(x)] \}$$

Thus, 1 is actually a function with the two bound variables f and x. Just offhand, those two variables seem like two more variables than are needed to define a simple number.

---

[9] Ibid, 864.

[10] S. C. Kleene, "Proof by Cases in Formal Logic," *The Annals of Mathematics*, 2nd Series, Vol. 35, No. 3 (July 1934), 529–544.

[11] S. C. Kleene, "A Theory of Positive Integers in Formal Logic, Part I," *American Journal of Mathematics*, Vol. 57, No. 1 (Jan. 1935), 153–173; Vol. 57, No. 2 (Apr. 1935), 219–244.

[12] Alonzo Church and J. B. Rosser, "Some Properties of Conversion," *Transactions of the American Mathematical Society*, Vol. 39, No. 3 (May 1936), 472–482.

[13] I'll be showing the definitions as they appear in the first 10 pages of Kleene's "A Theory of Positive Integers in Formal Logic, Part I."

This is the successor function:

$$S \rightarrow \lambda\rho fx.f(\rho(f, x))$$

Again, I agree, very strange. Although we expect the successor function to have a bound variable, we hardly expect it to have *three* bound variables.

The symbol 2 is fortunately defined as you might expect:

$$2 \rightarrow S(1)$$

If we actually want to apply the successor function to 1, we must make sure that the bound variables are all unique, so let's use the following equivalent expression for 1:

$$1 \rightarrow \lambda ab.a(b)$$

When working with lambda expressions, functions and variables often shift roles. In the progressive derivation of converted formulas below, I use curly braces selectively to identify the function with a bound variable being replaced in that step.

The function $S(1)$ can also be written as $\{S\}(1)$ or like this:

$$\{ \lambda\rho fx.f(\rho(f, x)) \}(\lambda ab.a(b))$$

The first bound variable in the successor function is ρ, so the expression for 1 replaces ρ in that function, and the ρ after the λ disappears:

$$\lambda fx.f(\lambda ab.a(b)(f, x))$$

This formula now contains another function with two arguments:

$$\lambda fx.f(\{ \lambda ab.a(b) \}(f, x))$$

Substitute the f for a and x for b:

$$\lambda fx.f(f(x))$$

and we're done.

Whereas the number 1 was originally defined as

$$1 \rightarrow \lambda fx.f(x)$$

the number 2 is:

$$2 \rightarrow S(1) \text{ conv } \lambda fx.f(f(x))$$

Compare the converted expression for 2 with the expression for 1 and you'll see an additional f and pair of parentheses to the right of the dot. Now express 2 with different variables as $\lambda ab.a(a(b))$ and try determining the next successor $\{S\}(2)$:

$$\{ \lambda\rho fx.f(\rho(f, x)) \}(\lambda ab.a(a(b)))$$

Again, substitute 2 for ρ:

$$\lambda fx.f(\{ \lambda ab.a(a(b)) \}(f, x))$$

Substitute f for a and x for b:

$$\lambda fx.f(f(f(x)))$$

That's the lambda expression for 3. I suspect you're beginning to see the pattern. What we want most from an abstract representation of the positive integers is the sense of some kind of succession. This notation shows that succession: Each successive integer has an additional nested appearance of the first bound variable.

Kleene defined the addition operator like this:

$$+ \rightarrow \lambda \rho \sigma fx.\rho(f,\ \sigma(f,x))$$

Skeptical? Let's add 2 and 3. First we need to make all the bound variables different. I'll use $\lambda ab.a(a(b))$ for 2 and $\lambda cd.c(c(c(d)))$ for 3 so that $\{+\}(2, 3)$ is:

$$\{\ \lambda \rho \sigma fx.\rho(f,\ \sigma(f,x))\ \}(\lambda ab.a(a(b)),\ \lambda cd.c(c(c(d))))$$

In the + function, substitute the formula for 2 for ρ and substitute the formula for 3 for σ:

$$\lambda fx.\lambda ab.a(a(b))(f, \{\ \lambda cd.c(c(c(d)))\ \}(f,x))$$

The substituted 3 is now a function where f is substituted for c and x for d:

$$\lambda fx.\{\ \lambda ab.a(a(b))\ \}(f, f(f(f(x))))$$

Now that substituted 2 is a function where f is substituted for a and $f(f(f(x)))$ for b:

$$\lambda fx.f(f(f(f(f(x)))))$$

And we're done. The answer is the same as $S(S(S(S(1))))$ or what we commonly refer to as 5.

Interestingly, the multiplication function is simpler than the addition function:

$$\times \rightarrow \lambda \rho \sigma x.\rho(\sigma(x))$$

Let's try it with 2 and 3. We can write $\{\times\}(2, 3)$ as:

$$\{\ \lambda \rho \sigma x.\rho(\sigma(x))\ \}(\lambda ab.a(a(b)), \lambda cd.c(c(c(d))))$$

Substitute the formula for 2 for ρ and the formula for 3 for σ:

$$\lambda x.\lambda ab.a(a(b)) (\{\ \lambda cd.c(c(c(d)))\ \}(x))$$

Now 3 has become a function where x is substituted for c:

$$\lambda x.\{\ \lambda ab.a(a(b))\ \}(\lambda d.x(x(x(d))))$$

Now 2 has become a function. Substitute the expression on the right for a:

$$\lambda x.\lambda b.\lambda d.x(x(x(d))) (\{\ \lambda d.x(x(x(d)))\ \}(b))$$

In the function on the right, substitute b for d

$$\lambda x.\lambda b.\{\ \lambda d.x(x(x(d)))\ \} (x(x(x(b))))$$

and finish with the final substitution for d:

$$\lambda xb.x(x(x(x(x(x(b))))))$$

That's 6, which is certainly the product of 2 and 3.

The functional definition of numbers allows you to do some odd things, for example

$$\{2\}(3)$$

or:

$$\{\lambda ab.a(a(b))\}(\lambda cd.c(c(c(d))))$$

If you carry out the laborious substitutions, you'll eventually end up with

$$\lambda bd.b(b(b(b(b(b(b(b(b(d)))))))))$$

or 9, which not coincidentally is 3 to the second power. That's why exponentiation of m to the n power is defined simply as:

$$\lambda mn.nm$$

Here is a system where multiplication is seemingly simpler than addition and exponentiation is the simplest of them all. As Church, Kleene, and Rosser experimented with the lambda calculus, they found that they could express anything they could think of in lambda notation — a characteristic later called λ-definability. "Church had been speculating, and finally definitely proposed, that the λ-definable functions are all the effectively calculable functions."[14]

Kurt Gödel had come to the Institute for Advanced Study in 1933, and in the spring of 1934 he delivered some lectures at Princeton on his Incompleteness Theorem, and also on recursive functions, which are functions built up from basic primitive functions.[15] The impetus for Gödel's interest in recursive functions was a letter he received in 1931 from Jacques Herbrand (1908–1931), the brilliant young French mathematician who died while mountain climbing in the Alps.

At the time, however, Gödel believed that neither lambda functions nor recursive functions were sufficient to encompass all of what we think of informally as effective calculability.

In 1936, Church published "An Unsolvable Problem of Elementary Number Theory"[16] that actually contains the first appearance of the term "λ-definable."

---

[14] Stephen C. Kleene, "Origins of Recursive Function Theory," *Annals of the History of Computing*, Vol. 3, No. 1 (Jan. 1981), 59.

[15] Based on notes taken by Kleene and Rosser, Gödel's lectures were circulated but not formally published until 1965 when they were included in Martin Davis, ed., *The Undecidable* (Raven Press, 1965), 41–71. They were subsequently published in Kurt Gödel, *Selected Works: Volume I, Publications 1929–1936* (Oxford University Press, 1986), 346–371.

[16] Alonzo Church, "An Unsolvable Problem of Elementary Number Theory," *American Journal of Mathematics*, Vol. 58, No. 2 (Apr. 1936), 345–363.

(Previously Kleene had just used the terms "definable" or "formally definable" for expressing logical and arithmetic operations in terms of the lambda notation.) Church refers to his earlier papers and Kleene's two papers, as well as to two forthcoming papers by Kleene that explore the relationship between recursive functions and λ-definable functions.[17] Using Gödel numbering, Church was able to construct an unsolvable problem just as Gödel constructed an undecidable proposition.

With this foundation, Church published the two-page "A Note on the Entscheidungsproblem" in the very first issue of *The Journal of Symbolic Logic* (which he also edited), with the conclusion, "*The general case of the Entscheidungsproblem of the engere Functionenkalkül is unsolvable.*"[18] The paper was received by the *Journal* on April 15, 1936, six weeks before Turing's submission to the *London Mathematical Society* on May 28, 1936.

Turing probably spent a good part of the summer of 1936 reading the various papers by Alonzo Church and Stephen Kleene that I've cited here, learning the lambda calculus and examining how it related to his computing machines. Turing's three-page appendix is indicated as being received by the London Mathematical Society on August 28; at the end Turing added "The Graduate College, Princeton University, New Jersey, USA" in anticipation of his future home. He did not leave England for the United States until September 23, arriving in New York on the 29th.[19]

Added 28 August, 1936.

APPENDIX.

Computability and effective calculability

The theorem that all effectively calculable (λ-definable) sequences are computable and its converse are proved below in outline.

The "in outline" qualification means that there will be some gaps in the proof.

It is assumed that the terms "well-formed formula" (W.F.F.) and "conversion" as used

---

[17]S. C. Kleene, "General Recursive Functions of Natural Numbers," *Mathematische Annalen*, Vol. 112, No. 1 (Dec. 1936), 727–742; reprinted in Martin Davis, ed., *The Undecidable* (Raven Press, 1965), 237–252. S. C. Kleene, "λ-Definability and Recursiveness," *Duke Mathematical Journal*, Volume 2, Number 2 (1936), 340–353.

[18]Alonzo Church, "A Note on the Entscheidungsproblem," *The Journal of Symbolic Logic*, Vol. 1, No. 1 (Mar. 1936), 40–41. See also Alonzo Church, "Correction to a Note on the Entscheidungsproblem," *The Journal of Symbolic Logic*, Vol. 1, No. 3 (Sep. 1936), 101–102.

[19]Andrew Hodges, *Alan Turing: The Enigma* (Simon & Schuster, 1983), 116.

by Church and Kleene are understood. In the second of these proofs the existence of several formulae is assumed without proof; these formulae may be constructed straightforwardly with the help of, *e.g.*, the results of Kleene in "A theory of positive integers in formal logic", *American Journal of Math.*, 57 (1935), 153–173, 219–244.

By "second of these proofs," Turing means the converse: that every computable sequence is also λ-definable.

The W.F.F. representing an integer n will be denoted by N_n.

Using Kleene's definitions of 1 and subsequent numbers — but with bound variables consistent with what Turing soon shows — N_1 is $\lambda xy.x(y)$, N_2 is $\lambda xy.x(x(y))$, and N_n is $\lambda xy.x(x(x(x \dots (y) \dots)))$.

We shall say that a sequence γ whose n-th figure is $\phi_\gamma(n)$ is λ-definable or effectively calculable if $1 + \phi_\gamma(u)$ is a λ-definable function of n,

The argument of the second occurrence of ϕ_γ should (like the first occurrence) be n rather than u, so the expression is $1+\phi_\gamma(n)$. The nth digit of a computable sequence γ is either 0 or 1, but the lambda calculus as defined by Church and Kleene involves only *positive* integers, not including zero. The function $\phi_\gamma(n)$ can't be λ-definable because zero is not λ-definable. For this reason, 1 is added so the numbers are 1 and 2.

i.e. if there is a W.F.F. M_γ such that, for all integers n,

$$\{M_\gamma\}\, (N_n) \text{ conv } N_{\phi_\gamma(n)+1},$$

i.e. $\{M_\gamma\}(N_n)$ is convertible into $\lambda xy.x(x(y))$ or into $\lambda xy.x(y)$ according as the n-th figure of λ is 1 or 0.

The λ in the last line is wrong; it should be the "nth figure of γ." The function M_γ for the value N_n (indicating the digit of the sequence) is convertible into either $\lambda xy.x(x(y))$, which is 2, or $\lambda xy.x(y)$, which is 1, corresponding to the digits 1 and 0.

For example, if the fifth digit of γ is 1, then $\phi_{\gamma(5)}$ is 1, and

$$\{M_\gamma\}(N_5) \text{ conv } N_{\phi_\gamma(5)+1}$$

which means

$$\{M_\gamma\}(N_5) \text{ conv } N_2$$

> To show that every λ-definable sequence γ is computable, we have to show how to construct a machine to compute γ. For use with machines it is convenient to make a trivial modification in the calculus of conversion. This alteration consists in using x, x', x'', ... as variables instead of $a, b, c, \ldots$.

Turing hasn't used any variables named a, b, or c here, but he has used x and y. He wants all variables in a standard form because some comparing and matching will be going on. This is similar to the requirement in Section 8 (page 221 of this book) that first-order predicate logic be "modified so as to be systematic" before it can be processed by a machine.

> We now construct a machine L which, when supplied with the formula M_γ, writes down the sequence γ. The construction of L is somewhat similar to that of the machine $\mathcal{K}$ which proves all provable formulae of the functional calculus. We first construct a choice machine L_1, which, if supplied with a W.F.F., M say, and suitably manipulated, obtains any formula into which M is convertible. L_1 can then be modified so as to yield an automatic machine L_2 which obtains successively all the formulae
>
> [264]
>
> into which M is convertible (cf. foot-note p. 252).

Of the five footnotes on page 252 of his paper, Turing is referring to the second (page 221 of this book) where he discusses the machine that proves all provable formulae of first-order logic. This machine is similar and probably quite a bit simpler considering the very systematic way in which lambda expressions are converted.

> The machine L includes L_2 as a part. The motion of the machine L when supplied with the formula M_γ is divided into sections of which the n-th is devoted to finding the n-th figure of γ. The first stage in this n-th section is the formation of $\{M_\gamma\}(N_n)$. This formula is then supplied to the machine L_2, which converts it successively into various other formulae. Each formula into which it is convertible eventually appears, and each, as it is found, is compared with
>
> $$\lambda x\Big[\lambda x'\big[\{x\}(\{x\}(x'))\big]\Big], \quad i.e.\ N_2,$$
>
> and with $\quad\quad \lambda x\big[\lambda x'[\{x\}(x')]\big], \quad i.e.\ N_1.$

These are just verbose expressions for the numbers 2 and 1. In implementing a machine to convert λ expressions, you want absolute consistency in the notation, and that's easiest with no syntactical shortcuts.

If it is identical with the first of these, then the machine prints the figure 1 and the n-th section is finished. If it is identical with the second, then 0 is printed and the section is finished. If it is different from both, then the work of L_2 is resumed. By hypothesis, $\{M_\gamma\}(N_n)$ is convertible into one of the formulae N_2 or N_1; consequently the n-th section will eventually be finished, *i.e.* the n-th figure of γ will eventually be written down.

Turing skips a line before commencing the more difficult converse of the proof: How to develop a lambda expression that encapsulates the workings of a particular machine.

To prove that every computable sequence γ is λ-definable, we must show how to find a formula M_γ such that, for all integers n,

$$\{M_\gamma\}(N_n) \text{ conv } N_{1+\phi_\gamma(n)}.$$

That's just the same formula as before but with a rearranged subscript on the final N. Now the job involves not describing a machine to manipulate lambda functions, but defining a lambda function that imitates a machine.

Let $\mathcal{M}$ be a machine which computes γ and let us take some description of the complete configurations of $\mathcal{M}$ by means of numbers, *e.g.* we may take the D.N of the complete configuration as described in § 6.

In the discussion that follows, I'm going to be referring to "configuration numbers," which are simply consecutive integers 0, 1, 2, 3, and so forth that increase as the machine operates. For any particular machine and for each configuration number there is an associated Description Number of the complete configuration. These are generally very large numbers that include codes to describe the symbols already printed on the tape, as well as the next m-configuration.

Let $\xi(n)$ be the D.N of the n-th complete configuration of $\mathcal{M}$.

Turing's n is what I'm calling the configuration number, while $\xi(n)$ is a Description Number.

The table for the machine $\mathcal{M}$ gives us a relation between $\xi(n+1)$ and $\xi(n)$ of the form

$$\xi(n+1) = \rho_\gamma\big(\xi(n)\big),$$

where ρ_γ is a function of very restricted, although not usually very simple, form : it is determined by the table for $\mathcal{M}$.

This ρ_γ function converts from one Description Number to the next. The input is generally a long number, and the output is another long number. This function must basically find within this long sequence a pattern of numbers corresponding to an m-configuration and scanned symbol, and construct the next complete configuration based on the machine table, possibly including a new printed symbol and changing the m-configuration and next scanned symbol.

Turing's description of this function as "not usually very simple" is right on target. The function essentially needs to break apart the Description Number into individual digits to examine them. Because the Description Number is a decimal number, the function can extract a piece of any length by first dividing the big number by a power of 10 and ignoring the fractional part, and then dividing by another power of 10 and keeping the remainder. Although the ρ_γ function is unquestionably complex, it's certainly conceivable.

ρ_γ is λ-definable (I omit the proof of this), *i.e.* there is a W.F.F. A_γ such that, for all integers n,

$$\{A_\gamma\}(N_{\xi(n)}) \text{ conv } N_{\xi(n+1)}.$$

A_γ is essentially the same function as ρ_γ except expressed in the language of the lambda calculus. It converts Description Numbers to Description Numbers.

Let U stand for

$$\lambda u\Big[\{\{u\}(A_\gamma)\} (N_r) \Big],$$

where $r = \xi(0)$;

The uppercase U at the beginning of the sentence should have a subscripted γ because it is based on a particular computable sequence. N_r is the Description Number of the complete configuration when the machine begins — the number 313. The number corresponds to the Standard Description DAD, which means m-configuration q_1 (DA) and scanning a blank square (D). The variable u is the configuration number, that is, 0, 1, 2, and so forth as the machine progresses. The enclosure of u in curly brackets to indicate a function may not seem to make sense, but you'll see shortly that it works just fine.

then, for all integers n,

$$\{U_\gamma\}(N_n) \text{ conv } N_{\xi(n)}.$$

The argument to the U_γ function is the configuration number (0, 1, 2, and so forth). Turing asserts that this function is convertible into the Description Number of that configuration. Let's try it out for configuration 4, which involves converting the expression $\{U_\gamma\}(N_4)$ or:

$$\{\, \lambda u[\{\{u\}(A_\gamma)\}(N_{\xi(0)})]\,\}(\lambda xy.x(x(x(x(y)))))$$

I've used $N_{\xi(0)}$ rather than N_r in the U_γ function just so we don't forget that the subscript refers to a Description Number. Replace u in the function with the expression for 4:

$$\{\{\, \lambda xy.x(x(x(x(y))))\}(A_\gamma)\}(N_{\xi(0)})$$

Now replace x with A_γ:

$$\{\, \lambda y.A_\gamma(A_\gamma(A_\gamma(A_\gamma(y))))\,\}(N_{\xi(0)})$$

Finally, replace y with $N_{\xi(0)}$:

$$A_\gamma(A_\gamma(A_\gamma(A_\gamma(N_{\xi(0)}))))$$

The first application of A_γ on $N_{\xi(0)}$ results in $N_{\xi(1)}$ and the next application results in $N_{\xi(2)}$ and so forth, so the final result is $N_{\xi(4)}$, as Turing claimed. Now you see why it made sense for u to be a function in the U_γ definition: It essentially compounds u nested occurrences of the A_γ function.

[265]

It may be proved that there is a formula V such that

$$\{\{V\}(N_{\xi(n+1)})\}(N_{\xi(n)}) \begin{cases} \text{conv } N_1 & \text{if, in going from the } n\text{-th to the } (n+1)\text{-th} \\ & \text{complete configuration, the figure 0 is} \\ & \text{printed.} \\ \text{conv } N_2 & \text{if the figure 1 is printed.} \\ \text{conv } N_3 & \text{otherwise.} \end{cases}$$

The function V basically analyzes the Description Numbers of two consecutive complete configurations and determines whether a 0 or 1 was printed, or neither. It's another complex but conceivable function.

Let W_γ stand for

$$\lambda u[\{\{V\}(\{A_\gamma\}(\{U_\gamma\}(u)))\}(\{U_\gamma\}(u))],$$

so that, for each integer n,

$$\{\{V\}(N_{\xi(n+1)})\}(N_{\xi(n)}) \text{ conv } \{W_\gamma\}(N_n),$$

The formula on the left side of this statement is the one that is convertible to either N_1, N_2, or N_3. It's easiest to demonstrate this conversion by starting with the converted result or:

$$\{W_\gamma\}(N_n)$$

Replace W_γ with the expression that Turing just showed us:

$$\left\{\lambda u\left[\left\{\{V\}\left(\{A_\gamma\}\left(\{U_\gamma\}(u)\right)\right)\right\}\left(\{U_\gamma\}(u)\right)\right]\right\}(N_n)$$

Replace u with N_n:

$$\left\{\{V\}\left(\{A_\gamma\}\left(\{U_\gamma\}(N_n)\right)\right)\right\}\left(\{U_\gamma\}(N_n)\right)$$

The expression $\{U_\gamma\}(N_n)$ is convertible to $N_{\xi(n)}$, so:

$$\left\{\{V\}\left(\{A_\gamma\}\left(N_{\xi(n)}\right)\right)\right\}(N_{\xi(n)})$$

The expression $\{A_\gamma\}(N_{\xi(n)})$ is convertible to $N_{\xi(n+1)}$, and this is what we were after:

$$\{\{V\}(N_{\xi(n+1)})\}(N_{\xi(n)})$$

With this little proof, we now know that $\{W_\gamma\}(N_n)$ is convertible to N_1, N_2, or N_3, depending on whether the progress from the n-th to the $(n+1)$-th complete configuration results in a 0 or 1 being printed, or otherwise.

and let Q be a formula such that

$$\{\{Q\}(W_\gamma)\}\,(N_s)\text{ conv }N_{r(z)},$$

where $r(s)$ is the s-th integer q for which $\{W_\gamma\}(N_q)$ is convertible into either N_1 or N_2.

In the formula, the subscript on the final N is obviously $r(s)$ and not $r(z)$. Only some of the complete configurations involve a 0 or 1 being printed. The $r(s)$ function reveals which these are. For example, if a 0 or 1 was printed in complete configurations 1, 4, 6, 7, and so forth, then $r(1)$ returns 1, $r(2)$ returns 4, $r(3)$ returns 6, $r(4)$ returns 7, and so forth.

Then, if M_γ stands for

$$\lambda w\left[\{W_\gamma\}\left(\{\{Q\}(W_\gamma)\}\,(w)\right)\right],$$

it will have the required property†.

---

† In a complete proof of the λ-definability of computable sequences it would be best to modify this method by replacing the numerical description of the complete configurations

by a description which can be handled more easily with our apparatus. Let us choose certain integers to represent the symbols and the m-configurations of the machine. Suppose that in a certain complete configuration the numbers representing the successive symbols on the tape are $s_1 s_2 \ldots s_n$, that the m-th symbol is scanned, and that the m-configuration has the number t; then we may represent this complete configuration by the formula

$$[[N_{s_1}, N_{s_2}, \ldots, N_{s_{m-1}}], [N_t, N_{sm}], [N_{s_{m+1}}, \ldots, N_{s_n}]],$$

where

$$[a, b] \text{ stands for } \lambda u[\{\{u\}(a)\}(b)],$$

$$[a, b, c] \text{ stands for } \lambda u\Big[\Big\{\{\{u\}(a)\}(b)\Big\}(c)\Big],$$

etc.

In the second half of Turing's demonstration he set out for himself the job of finding a formula M_γ such that for all n,

$$\{M_\gamma\}(N_n) \text{ conv } N_{1+\phi_\gamma(n)}$$

The formula tells us whether the n-th digit of the sequence is a 0 or 1. Let's begin with:

$$\{M_\gamma\}(N_n)$$

Substitute the formula that Turing just derived for M_γ:

$$\{\lambda w[\{W_\gamma\}(\{\{Q\}(W_\gamma)\})(w))]\}(N_n)$$

Replace w with N_n:

$$\{W_\gamma\}(\{\{Q\}(W_\gamma)\})(N_n))$$

The expression within the parentheses was shown to be convertible into $N_{r(n)}$, so:

$$\{W_\gamma\}(N_{r(n)})$$

That formula was shown to be convertible into N_1, N_2, or N_3 depending on whether 0 or 1 is printed in complete configuration $r(n)$ or something else. Nevertheless, $r(n)$ is defined as returning only those complete configurations that result in a 0 or 1 being printed.

The footnote shows a complete configuration separated into the parts of the tape before the next scanned symbol and after the next scanned symbol. The lambda expressions that Turing suggests represent these parts of the tape can be quite long, and grow in size with each complete configuration.

Here the paper ends.

The Graduate College,
Princeton University,
New Jersey, U.S.A.

Turing's more rigorous proof did not pursue the approach he outlined here for the converse. The paper "Computability and λ-Definability" was received by *The Journal of Symbolic Logic* on September 11, 1937, less than a year after he had arrived in Princeton.[20] The paper begins:

> Several definitions have been given to express an exact meaning corresponding to the intuitive idea of 'effective calculability' as applied for instance to functions of positive integers. The purpose of the present paper is to show that the computable functions introduced by the author are identical with the λ-definable functions of Church and the general recursive functions due to Herbrand and Gödel and developed by Kleene. It is shown [in this paper] that every λ-definable function is computable and that every computable function is general recursive.

Turing first shows that λ-definable functions are computable by showing a Turing Machine — probably more complex than Turing's universal machine — that can parse and convert λ functions.

The second half of the proof shows that computable functions are recursive. Turing didn't need to show that computable functions were λ-definable because Stephen Kleene had already shown (in "λ-Definability and Recursiveness") that recursive functions are λ-definable. All three definitions of effective calculability were then linked in equivalence.

In later years, Turing would often allude to those amazing imaginary machines he conceived while lying in Grantchester meadows in the summer of 1935, but he would never again show actual tables of a machine in any published article. When he wrote his doctoral thesis[21] under Church, it was all recursive functions and λ functions.

---

[20] Alan Turing, "Computability and λ-Definability," *The Journal of Symbolic Logic*, Vol. 2, No. 4 (Dec. 1937), pp. 153–163.

[21] Alan Turing, "Systems of Logic Based on Ordinals," *Proceedings of the London Mathematical Society*, 2nd Series, Vol. 45, No. 1 (1939), 161–228.

16 Conceiving the Continuum

Real life is often much messier and more complex than the histories that attempt to capture it in a series of consecutive sentences and paragraphs. Historians must smooth out the rough edges, omit peripheral personages, and avoid distracting digressions. This simplification sometimes distorts as much as it attempts to illuminate. The resultant series of events might seem unnaturally inevitable, as if nothing could have happened to make it go differently, and even imply that these events led to the best of all possible outcomes. Sometimes the result is what British historian Herbert Butterfield (1900–1979) called "a Whig interpretation of history" after those nineteenth-century writers who portrayed the history of the British Empire as leading progressively and inexorably toward modern parliamentary democracy.

Histories of science, mathematics, and technology are particularly susceptible to Whig interpretations. We are the beneficiaries of the "correct" scientific theories and the "proper" technologies, so we can identify a chain back through history, associating effects to causes that have led to this inevitable outcome. Floundering missteps are de-emphasized, and if historical disagreements or feuds are discussed, they always result in the proper vanquishing of anyone trying to impede the progress that led to the glorious moment we're all here to celebrate.

In relating the history of the Turing Machine, for example, it is tempting to mold the past into a coherent series of progressive intellectual achievements — from Cantor and Frege, through Russell and Hilbert, to Gödel and Church and Turing — culminating in a single mathematical paper published in 1936. To keep this book reasonably short and focused, this is precisely what I've done.

In the process, I've ignored some dissenting views. As in any field of intellectual endeavor, controversies and disagreements have often peppered the history of mathematics.[1] In the late nineteenth century and throughout the twentieth century, these controversies frequently involved the philosophy of mathematics, and very often, the nature of infinity.

---

[1] See Hal Hellman, *Great Feuds in Mathematics: Ten of the Liveliest Disputes Ever* (Wiley, 2006), for entertaining blow-by-blow recaps.

The philosophy of mathematics is a broad and complex field, but perhaps the most fundamental question is both simple and unnerving:

To what extent do mathematical entities exist independently of the human beings who study them?

Do mathematicians simply discover mathematical patterns that already exist within the intrinsic fabric of the universe in much the same way that astronomers discover stars and other celestial bodies? Or do mathematicians *invent* mathematics like an engineer designs a new vacuum cleaner or a composer writes an opera? As that great popularizer of mathematics history Morris Kline (1908–1992) much more poetically put it,

> Is then mathematics a collection of diamonds hidden in the depths of the universe and gradually unearthed, or is it a collection of synthetic stones manufactured by man, yet so brilliant nevertheless that they bedazzle those mathematicians who are already partially blinded by pride in their own creations?[2]

On one side of this debate are the *realists* or *Platonists*, who believe, in Roger Penrose's words, in "the objectivity of mathematical truth. Platonic existence, as I see it, refers to the existence of an objective external standard that is not dependent upon our individual opinions nor upon our particular culture."[3]

At the other extreme are the *constructivists*, who see mathematics as a strictly human invention. To the constructivists, the seeming permanence and transcendence of mathematics is merely an illusion enhanced by the human skill of pattern recognition — a skill engineered in our brains through millions of years of evolution.

Between these two extremes lie plenty of gradations, each with its own descriptive name and advocates, some of whom probably already resent my crude categorization of a gradated range between two extremes.

Most working mathematicians would probably categorize themselves as residing in the Platonic region of this landscape. The Platonic concept of mathematics dominates our culture and appeals to our instincts. When we shout, "Eureka!" we are saying "I have found it" and not "I have made it." Over 100 years after David Hilbert addressed the Second International Congress of Mathematicians, we still thrill at his words:

> However unapproachable these problems may seem to us and however helpless we stand before them, we have, nevertheless, the firm conviction that their solution must follow by a finite

---

[2] Morris Kline, *Mathematics: The Loss of Certainty* (Oxford University Press, 1980), 323.
[3] Roger Penrose, *The Road to Reality: A Complete Guide to the Laws of the Universe* (Alfred A. Knopf, 2005), 13.

number of purely logical processes ... This conviction of the solvability of every mathematical problem is a powerful incentive to the worker. We hear within us the perpetual call: There is the problem. Seek its solution. You can find it by pure reason, for in mathematics there is no *ignorabimus*.[4]

Now that's a Platonist speaking: The solutions are out there. We need only to find them. Even after Hilbert's hopes of proofs of completeness, consistency, and decision procedures were dashed, the Platonist instinct still survived. Prominent among the Platonists, in fact, was Kurt Gödel.

Differences in mathematical philosophy are not just a matter of ideology, but also focus on propriety. Certain basic assumptions underlie all mathematical proofs. Yet, some of these assumptions were developed in the world of finite objects and become problematic when applied to infinite collections.

"Thinking about infinity is not straightforward," Aristotle (384–322 BCE) observed, and we can imagine his students nodding in solemn agreement. "There are a lot of intractable consequences whether you assume that there is or is not such a thing as infinity."[5]

To navigate this treacherous terrain in Book III of his *Physics*, Aristotle helpfully differentiated between an *actual* or *completed* infinity, and a *potential* infinity. A potential infinity is the infinity of the natural numbers: After each one comes another. Subdividing something into smaller and smaller pieces is also a potential infinity. These are processes that occur over time and which never end. "Generally speaking, the infinite exists by one thing being taken after another. What is taken is always finite on its own, but always succeeded by another part which is different from it."[6]

Actual infinity, however, does *not* exist in Aristotle's cosmology, and he makes several arguments why it can't exist. He very wisely notes, "Infinity turns out to be the opposite of what people say it is. It is not 'that which has nothing beyond itself' that is infinite, but 'that which always has something beyond itself'."[7]

Aristotle does not even allow infinity to exist as a mental concept:

> [I]t is absurd to rely on what can be thought by the human mind, since then it is only in the mind, not in the real world, that any excess and defect exist. It is possible to think of any one of us as

[4]As quoted in Ben H. Yandell, *The Honors Class: Hilbert's Problems and Their Solvers* (A. K. Peters, 2002), 395.

[5]Aristotle, *Physics*, translated by Robin Waterfield (Oxford World's Classics, 1996), Book III, Chapter 4, page 65.

[6]*Ibid*, Book III, Chapter 6, page 72.

[7]*Ibid*, Book III, Chapter 6, page 73.

being many times bigger than he is and to make him infinitely large, but a person does not become superhumanly large just because someone thinks he is; he has to be so in fact, and then it is merely coincidental that someone is thinking it.[8]

Aristotle was no Platonist.

Not everyone accepted Aristotle's rejection of infinity. Philosopher Stephan Körner (1913–2000) observed that Aristotle's conceptions

were never unanimously accepted. Philosophers of the Platonic tradition, including Augustinian theologians, always regarded the notion of infinite given totalities, whether they are continua or not, as legitimate. They were not troubled by the inapplicability of such a notion to sense experience, since for them mathematics was not an abstraction from — much less a description of — sense experience, but a description of reality; and reality was not apprehended by the senses, but by reason.[9]

Mathematicians have often been troubled by completed infinities and try to work with infinite processes in a safe way. It is precisely the recognition of the difference between completed infinity and potential infinity that persuades us to write the mathematical formula

$$\lim_{n \to \infty} \left(1 + \frac{1}{n}\right)^n$$

rather than:

$$\left(1 + \frac{1}{\infty}\right)^{\infty}$$

The first formula expresses a limit. Where does that expression go when n gets very, very, very large? It heads toward the number we know as the Euler constant or e, approximately equal to 2.71828...

The second formula uses the symbol ∞ as a completed infinity, and as a result, is pure gibberish.

The rigorous definition of a mathematical limit was developed by German mathematician Karl Weierstrass (1815–1897), although earlier mathematicians had come close. The concept was essential for putting the differential and integral calculus on a sound mathematical basis. Prior to the concept of the limit, calculus was based on the "infinitesimal," a number not quite zero (because it could still

---

[8]Ibid, Book III, Chapter 8, page 76–7.

[9]Stephan Körner, "Continuity," in Paul Edwards, ed., *The Encyclopedia of Philosophy* (Macmillan, 1967), Vol. 2, 205.

be manipulated like a finite quantity) but close enough to zero that it could eventually be ignored. Calculus still has remnants of these infinitesimals in the notation dx.

Another nineteenth-century German mathematician, Leopold Kronecker (1823–1891), had very strong views about the use of completed infinities in mathematics. Kronecker is best known for the aphorism "God created the integers; everything else is the work of man."[10] The mention of a supreme being — or more precisely, the identification of mathematical entities that exist independently of human beings — might *seem* to make Kronecker a Platonist, but it's the "everything else" that reveals him to be a strict constructivist. Kronecker wanted to base all of mathematics on finite constructions involving finite integers. He had issues even with the concept of limits and definitions of irrational numbers.

One of Kronecker's former students began pursuing mathematical research that was completely outrageous — not only defining collections of infinite objects, but promiscuously *counting* these infinite objects, and then performing arithmetical operations on these values. Kronecker objected to these techniques and at times even inhibited their publication, with the result that today Kronecker is best known for the evil and maniacal persecution of this former student, Georg Cantor.

A Kronecker-centric view of these events reveals this persecution to reside more in Cantor's paranoid worldview than in Kronecker's actual intentions.[11] Still, history is written by the victors. Cantor's set theory and his distinction between enumerable and non-enumerable collections proved to be extremely useful, so Kronecker has largely ended up with the discarded theorems of mathematics history.

Cantor's concept of transfinite numbers is extremely Platonic — even a bit, well, trippy. Here's Cantor writing in 1883:

> We can speak of the actuality or existence of the integers, finite as well as infinite, in *two* senses ... First, we may regard the integers as actual in so far as, on the basis of definitions, they occupy an entirely determinate place in our understanding ... But then, reality can also be ascribed to numbers to the extent that they must be taken as an expression or copy of the events and relationships in the external world which confronts the intellect ... Because of the thoroughly realistic but, at the same time, no

---

[10] This quotation is not found in Kronecker's works. It first appeared in print in 1893 as "Die ganzen Zahlen hat der liebe Gott gemacht, alles andere ist Menschenwerk." See William Ewald, ed., *From Kant to Hilbert: A Source Book in the Foundations of Mathematics* (Oxford University Press, 1996), Vol. II, 942. In his 1922 address "The New Grounding of Mathematics. First Report," Hilbert quoted it with integer in the singular: "Die ganze Zahl schuf der liebe Gott, alles andere ist Menschenwerk." See *From Kant to Hilbert*, Vol. II, 1120.

[11] Harold Edwards, "Kronecker's Place in History," in William Aspray and Philip Kitcher, eds., *History and Philosophy of Modern Mathematics* (University of Minnesota Press, 1988), 139–144.

less idealistic foundation of my point of view, I have no doubt
that these two sorts of reality always occur together in the sense
that a concept designated in the first respect as existent always
also possesses in certain, even infinitely many, ways a transient
reality. . . . This linking of both realities has its true foundation in
the *unity* of the *all to which we ourselves belong*.[12]

In previous chapters, I've discussed the logicism of Bertrand Russell (derived
from Frege and Peano) and the formalism of David Hilbert. In the early twentieth
century, another movement and philosophy stood in opposition to these endeavors.
This was called *intuitionism*, and it came from the mind of Dutch mathematician
Luitzen Egbertus Jan Brouwer (1881–1966).

Gloomy and pessimistic with a mystical bent, Brouwer looms over the early
twentieth century like a stern schoolmaster appalled by the chaos he sees around
him. Brouwer scholar Walter P. van Stigt describes Brouwer's outlook on life as "a
blend of romantic pessimism and radical individualism." In an early treatise entitled
Life, Art and Mysticism (1905), Brouwer "rails against industrial pollution and man's
domination of nature through his intellect and established social structures, and
promotes a return to 'Nature' and to mystic and solitary contemplation."[13]

Brouwer attended and then taught at the University of Amsterdam. Although his
dissertation was on the foundations of mathematics (presaging his later interests),
much of his early work was in the field of topology.

Brouwer coined the term "intuitionism" to describe his idea of how mathematical
entities are formulated by the mind. They are objects of thought, and their symbolic
representation on paper is a necessary evil to convey these thoughts from one
person to another. In contrast, formalism focuses more on a manipulation of
symbols that takes place entirely on paper — little more than a game with
meaningless rules.

As the programs of Russell and Hilbert began taking shape, it became clear that
Cantor's work had become widely accepted. In Brouwer's view (as well as that of
Henri Poincaré), the extensive use of Cantor's set theory and transfinite numbers
could only lead to mathematical catastrophes.

Brouwer wasn't entirely opposed to conceptions of infinity. He accepted the idea
of infinite sets, but only if these sets were constructable and enumerable — that is,
could be placed in a one-to-one correspondence with the integers. As early as 1913,
Brouwer was emphasizing that "the intuitionist recognizes only the existence of
denumerable sets . . . aleph-null is the only infinite power of which the intuitionists

[12]Georg Cantor, "Foundations of a General Theory of Manifolds: A Mathematico-Philosophical
Investigation into the Theory of the Infinite," in *From Kant to Hilbert*, Vol. II, pgs. 895–6.
[13]Walter P. van Stigt, "Brower's Intuitionist Program," in Paolo Mancosu, ed., *From Brouwer to Hilbert: The
Debate on the Foundations of Mathematics in the 1920s* (Oxford University Press, 1998), 5.

recognize the existence."[14] A set of real numbers must be prohibited precisely because the members are not enumerable. The only way you can define a set of the real numbers is to assert that the set contains all real numbers. You can't show the first few with an ellipsis, or define some kind of rule for inclusion. There is no rule; there is no sequence; you can't construct the set; hence there can be no such set. Much of Cantor's theory of transfinite numbers is therefore simply "without meaning to the intuitionist."[15]

Between 1918 and 1928, Brouwer published papers on intuitionist critiques of the formalist program, as well as papers attempting to provide a new foundation for mathematics free of problems and paradoxes. In particular, Brouwer found fault with the law of the excluded middle, which is the principle that either something has a certain property or it does not. While such a law certainly applies to finite collections, Brouwer felt it had been foolishly applied to infinite collections.

In one famous example,[16] Brouwer took on the common belief that the limit of a convergent sequence is always less than zero, equal to zero, or greater than zero. (This is related to the law of the excluded middle in the sense that either the limit is less than zero or it's not less than zero.)

Here's a definition of a sequence:

$$c_n = \left(-\tfrac{1}{2}\right)^n \qquad \text{for } n < k$$

$$c_n = \left(-\tfrac{1}{2}\right)^k \qquad \text{for } n \geq k$$

The first few values in the sequence are $-\tfrac{1}{2}, \tfrac{1}{4}, -\tfrac{1}{8}, \tfrac{1}{16}, -\tfrac{1}{32}$, so this sequence is clearly converging to zero when n is less than k. Moreover, when n is greater than k, then all the remaining c_n values are just $\left(-\tfrac{1}{2}\right)^k$, so that's the value to which the sequence converges.

Here's the catch: The value k is the position within the digits of π where the consecutive digits 0123456789 first appear.

Does c_n converge to a value less than zero, or to a value greater than zero, or to zero itself? It depends on whether k is odd, even, or nothing at all. The Platonist would claim that the limit of the c_n sequence is an actual number, even if we don't know what it is. The constructivist would counter by asserting that because this limit can't be constructed, it does not exist. It is undefined. It falls through the cracks of the law of the excluded middle.

---

[14]L. E. J. Brouwer, "Intuitionism and Formalism," *Bulletin of the American Mathematical Society*, Vol. 20 (1913), 81–96.

[15]Ibid.

[16]L. E. J. Brouwer, "On the Significance of the Principle of Excluded Middle in Mathematics, Especially in Function Theory" (1923), in Jean van Heijenoort, ed., *From Frege to Gödel: A Source Book in Mathematical Logic, 1879–1931* (Harvard University Press, 1967), 337.

Brouwer was once lecturing about this indeterminate sequence and someone pointed out that although *we* may not know how c_n converges, God certainly knows. "I do not have a pipeline to God," Brouwer responded.[17]

We know now that Brouwer's sequence actually *does* converge, although this fact became known only some three decades after Brouwer's death.[18] Consecutive digits of 0123456789 begin at the $17{,}387{,}594{,}880^{\text{th}}$ digit of π, so c_n converges to $2^{-17{,}387{,}594{,}880}$. Now that Brouwer's original sequence is ruined, it's easy to come up with another criterion for k. Let's redefine k as the position within the digits of π where a million consecutive 7s appear. Because the digits of π appear to be equally distributed in a random manner, these million consecutive 7s are likely to be out there somewhere. (Or maybe not. Although many mathematicians might believe that any possible sequence of digits occurs in π, this has never been proved. Some possible sequences in π simply can not be found without resources greater than the universe.)

As a consequence of rejecting the law of the excluded middle for infinite sets, Brouwer also denied the legitimacy of certain *reductio ad absurdum* proofs, and even Hilbert's contention that every mathematical problem is solvable!

Logic is affected as well. The law of the excluded middle is expressed in propositional logic as:

$$-X \vee X$$

In the classical logic of Whitehead and Russell and Hilbert, that formula is equivalent to

$$X \rightarrow X$$

and they're both equivalent to:

$$-(X \ \& \ -X)$$

The implication $X \rightarrow X$ is a symbolic representation of the ancient philosophical principle of identity ("something is what it is"), while the last of the three formulas symbolizes the principle of contradiction: Something can't both have a particular property and not have that property. In Aristotelian logic, these are all separate and distinct concepts, but with the "blunt instrument" of propositional logic they collapse into synonymous formulas.[19]

To David Hilbert, the restrictions that Brouwer wished to impose on mathematical thought were just too constricting. Hilbert was extremely reluctant to give up his tools, even if he acknowledged that some care need be taken. "We shall carefully investigate those ways of forming notions and those modes of inference that are fruitful; we shall nurse them, support them, and make them usable,

[17]Constance Reid, *Hilbert* (Springer, 1970, 1996), 184.

[18]Jonathan Borwein, The Brouwer-Heyting Sequence, http://www.cecm.sfu.ca/~jborwein/brouwer.html.

[19]Floy E. Andrews, "The Principle of Excluded Middle Then and Now: Aristotle and *Principia Mathematica*," *Animus*, Vol. 1 (1996), http://www2.swgc.mun.ca/animus/1996vol1/andrews.pdf.

whenever there is the slightest promise of success. No one shall be able to drive us from the paradise that Cantor created for us."[20] Still, Hilbert tried to adopt some stricter criteria for proofs that would not require the use of infinity.

The sniping back and forth between Hilbert and Brouwer escalated to the breaking point. In 1928 Hilbert dismissed Brouwer from the editorial board of the journal *Mathematische Annalen*. Albert Einstein, who was one of the three principal editors, resigned in protest. The event left Brouwer bitter and disillusioned, and he barely published anything for a decade. He died at the age of 85 after being struck by a car outside his home.

It is not known whether Turing had any contact with intuitionist concepts prior to writing his paper on computable numbers. Max Newman — the Cambridge professor whose lectures on the foundations of mathematics inspired Turing and who guided Turing's paper to publication — almost certainly knew of Brouwer from their mutual work in topology. Max Newman co-authored the official obituary of Brouwer for the Royal Society.[21] (This is no ordinary obituary: It's 30 pages long and includes a 5-page bibliography of Brouwer's works.) Nevertheless, Newman wrote only that section of the obituary about Brouwer's work in topology, and even this was some three decades after Turing's paper.

Turing's paper occupies a strange secluded islet between formalism and constructivism. His machines certainly reduce algorithms to a series of predefined manipulations of printed symbols, yet Turing's distinction between real numbers and computable numbers — and his identification of the computable numbers as that subset of the real numbers that can actually be calculated — has a decidedly constructivist flavor. Turing's definition of the computable numbers later led to a mathematical theory of "computable analysis" that parallels the classical "real analysis."[22]

Very much in tune with Brouwer's thinking is the idea that a computation of a number is a process that occurs over *time*. The digits don't exist until the machine computes them, and Turing Machines cannot be successfully analyzed by a finite general process to determine what they might do sometime in the future. There is no algorithm that lets you determine from the Description Number of a machine whether the machine will ever print a 0 or a 1, or whether it will print only a finite number of 0s and 1s, or whether it will ever print the consecutive digits 0123456789. If there were such an algorithm, we could apply it to the machine that computes the infinite digits of π. We could determine whether the machine will ever print the consecutive digits 0123456789 (or a million 7s in a row), and we would know at least whether Brouwer's sequence converges to zero.

---

[20] David Hilbert, "On the Infinite" (1925) in *From Frege to Gödel*, 375–6.

[21] G. Kreisel and M. H. A. Newman, "Luitzen Egbertus Jan Brouwer. 1881–1966," *Biographical Memoirs of Fellows of the Royal Society*, Vol. 15 (Nov. 1969), 39–68.

[22] See, for example, Oliver Aberth, *Computable Analysis* (McGraw-Hill, 1980).

The existence of such an algorithm would actually suggest the autonomous Platonic existence of the infinite digits of π and every other irrational number. These infinite digits would exist without actually being calculated. Such an algorithm does not exist, however; we are forced to grind out the digits to know what they are.

As you've seen, sometimes Turing likes to define a number whose digits require analyzing other machines; these numbers turn out not to be computable. Brouwer does something analogous in his 1921 paper "Does Every Real Number Have a Decimal Expansion?"[23] in which he defines a real number whose digits are based (once again) on the occurrences of certain patterns in the infinite digits of π.

Despite these interesting connections, I see no evidence of any familiarity with Brouwer's intuitionism in the paper that Turing submitted to the London Mathematical Society in 1936. Turing's work and his conclusions are so unusual that I suspect he wasn't working within *anyone's* prescribed philosophical view of mathematics.

In the fall of 1936, however, Turing went to Princeton to study with Alonzo Church, and was subsequently likely exposed to a somewhat wider vista of mathematical possibility and thought, possibly including Brouwerian intuitionism.

Church certainly had contact with intuitionism. When he received his Ph.D. from Princeton in 1927, he had two years on a National Research Fellowship.

> I spent a year at Harvard and a year in Europe, half the year at Göttingen, because Hilbert was there at the time, and half the year in Amsterdam, because I was interested in Brouwer's work, as were some of those advising me. . . . I think he wasn't teaching. He was quite old. I used to take the train out to his residence, way out in the country.[24]

The "quite old" characterization is a bit off: At the time Church gave this interview, he was 80 years old, but in 1929, Brouwer was only 48. Perhaps Brouwer's battles of the previous years had truly taken a toll.

Subsequently, Church seemed to have a certain sensitivity (though not an allegiance) to intuitionist concerns. Church's first paper on the lambda calculus begins with the sentence "In this paper we present a set of postulates for the foundation of formal logic, in which we avoid use of the free, or real, variable, and in which we introduce a certain restriction on the law of the excluded middle

---

[23]Reprinted in *From Brouwer to Hilbert*, 28–35.

[24]William Aspray, The Princeton Mathematics Community in the 1930s: An Oral-History Project. An interview with Alonzo Church at the University of California on 17 May 1984, http://www.princeton .edu/~mudd/finding_aids/mathoral/pmc05.htm.

as a means of avoiding the paradoxes connected with the mathematics of the transfinite."[25]

An interest in intuitionism also shows up in the work of Church's student Stephen Kleene. Kleene included a section on intuitionism in his book *Introduction to Metamathematics* (1952) and later co-authored the book *The Foundations of Intuitionistic Mathematics* (1965). A 1953 photograph of Brouwer — taken in Madison, Wisconsin, where Kleene taught at the time — appears in Kleene's article on the history of recursive function theory.[26]

Turing might also have been influenced by Hermann Weyl, who was at the Institute for Advanced Study during this time. Weyl received his doctorate at Göttingen under Hilbert, taught at the University of Zürich, and returned to Göttingen in 1930 to succeed Hilbert, only to be forced to leave Germany in 1933 because his wife was Jewish. Between about 1919 and 1928, Weyl pursued mathematics from an intuitionist perspective, and never lost interest in it.

Turing's brief foray into intuitionist thinking occurs in a short follow-up paper he wrote while at Princeton containing some corrections to his paper on computable numbers. As I described on page 63, the original paper appeared in the *Proceedings of the London Mathematical Society*, Volume 42, Parts 3 (issued November 20, 1936) and 4 (issued December 23, 1936). The parts published from October 1936 through April 1937 were collectively published as Second Series, Volume 42.

The follow-up paper appeared in the *Proceedings of the London Mathematical Society*, Volume 43, Part 7 (issued December 30, 1937). It was later included in the Second Series, Volume 43, which included parts issued from May through December, 1937.

[544]

ON COMPUTABLE NUMBERS, WITH AN APPLICATION TO THE ENTSCHEIDUNGSPROBLEM. A CORRECTION

By A. M. TURING.

In a paper entitled "On computable numbers, with an application to the Entscheidungsproblem"* the author gave a proof of the insolubility of the Entscheidungsproblem of the "engere Funktionenkalkül". This proof contained some formal errors† which will be corrected here: there

---

[25] Alonzo Church, "A Set of Postulates for the Foundation of Logic," *The Annals of Mathematics*, second Series, Vol. 33, No. 2 (Apr. 1932), 346.
[26] Stephen C. Kleene, "Origins of Recursive Function Theory," *Annals of the History of Computing*, Vol. 3. No. 1 (Jan. 1981), 62.

are also some other statements in the same paper which should be modified, although they are not actually false as they stand.

Proc. London Math. Soc. (2), 42 (1936–7), 230–265.
†The author is indebted to P. Bernays for pointing out these errors.

This three-page paper is sharply divided into two parts. The first part involves corrections to formulas and statements that appear in the proof of the insolubility of the Entscheidungsproblem in Section 11 of the paper. I have already incorporated those corrections into my commentary in Chapter 14. For the sake of completeness, here is that part of the paper. I will interrupt it only twice.

The expression for $\text{Inst}\{q_i\, S_j\, S_k\, L\, q_l\}$ on p. 260 of the paper quoted should read

$$(x,y,x',y')\left\{\left(R_{S_j}(x,y)\ \&\ I(x,y)\ \&\ K_{q_i}(x)\ \&\ F(x,x')\ \&\ F(y',y)\right)\right.$$

$$\rightarrow\left(I(x',y')\ \&\ R_{S_k}(x',y)\ \&\ K_{q_l}(x')\ \&\ F(y',z)\ \text{v}\ \left[\left(R_{S_0}(x,z)\rightarrow R_{S_0}(x',z)\right)\right.\right.$$

$$\left.\left.\&\ \left(R_{S_1}(x,z)\rightarrow R_{S_1}(x',z)\right)\ \&\ \ldots\ \&\ \left(R_{S_M}(x,z)\rightarrow R_{S_M}(x',z)\right)\right]\right)\Bigg\},$$

$S_0, S_1, \ldots, S_M$ being the symbols which $\mathcal{M}$ can print.

This correction is not quite right either. It's missing a universal quantifier for z that should appear right before the $F(y', z)$ term in the second line and apply to the remainder of the formula. The version shown on page 265 of this book is correct.

The statement on p. 261, line 33, viz.

$$\text{``Inst}\{q_a\, S_b\, S_d\, L\, q_c\}\ \&\ F^{(n+1)}\rightarrow(CC_n\rightarrow CC_{n+1})$$

is provable" is false (even with the new expression for $\text{Inst}\{q_a\, S_b\, S_d\, Lq_c\}$): we are unable for example to deduce $F^{(n+1)}\rightarrow(-F(u,u''))$ and therefore can never use the term

$$F(y',z)\,\text{v}\,\left[\left(R_{S_0}(x,z)\rightarrow R_{S_0}(x',z)\right)\ \&\ \ldots\ \&\ \left(R_{S_M}(x,z)\rightarrow R_{S_M}(x',z)\right)\right]$$

[545]

in $\text{Inst}\{q_a\, S_b\, S_d\, Lq_c\}$.

This is where Turing acknowledges that his formulation of the natural numbers was flawed.

To correct this we introduce a new functional variable G [$G(x, y)$ to have the interpretation "x precedes y"]. Then, if Q is an abbreviation for

$$(x)(\exists w)(y,z)\left\{ F(x,w) \,\&\, \left(F(x,y) \rightarrow G(x,y)\right) \,\&\, \left(F(x,z) \,\&\, G(z,y) \rightarrow G(x,y)\right)\right.$$

$$\left.\&\, \left[G(z,x) \vee \left(G(x,y) \,\&\, F(y,z)\right) \vee \left(F(x,y) \,\&\, F(z,y)\right) \rightarrow \left(-F(x,z)\right)\right]\right\}$$

the corrected formula Un($\mathcal{M}$) is to be

$$(\exists u)A(\mathcal{M}) \rightarrow (\exists s)(\exists t)\, R_{S_1}(s,t),$$

where $A(\mathcal{M})$ is an abbreviation for

$$Q \,\&\, (y)R_{S_0}(u,y) \,\&\, I(u,u) \,\&\, K_{q_1}(u) \,\&\, \mathrm{Des}(\mathcal{M}).$$

The statement on page 261 (line 33) must then read

$$\mathrm{Inst}\{q_a \, S_b \, S_d \, Lq_c\} \,\&\, Q \,\&\, F^{(n+1)} \rightarrow (CC_n \rightarrow CC_{n+1}),$$

and line 29 should read

$$r\left(n,\, i(n)\right) = b, \quad r\left(n+1,\, i(n)\right) = d, \quad k(n) = a, \quad k(n+1) = c.$$

For the words "logical sum" on p. 260, line 15, read "conjunction". With these modifications the proof is correct. Un($\mathcal{M}$) may be put in the form (I) (p. 263) with $n = 4$.

A blank line follows that paragraph to conclude the first of the two parts of the correction. The second part concerns a different matter altogether, and refers to a paragraph occurring much earlier in the paper.

Some difficulty arises from the particular manner in which "computable number" was defined (p. 233).

The relevant paragraph is on page 76 of this book and reads: "A sequence is said to be computable if it can be computed by a circle-free machine. A number is computable if it differs by an integer from the number computed by a circle-free machine."

Turing's use of the word "intuitive" in the next sentence must be interpreted in its common sense; if Turing had been referring to anything related to Brouwer he would have used the word "intuitionist." Moreover, it is clear from a statement that follows that this hypothesis does *not* satisfy intuitionist requirements, even if it satisfies intuitive ones.

> If the computable numbers are to satisfy intuitive requirements we should have:
>
> *If we can give a rule which associates with each positive integer n two rationals a_n, b_n satisfying $a_n \leqslant a_{n+1} < b_{n+1} \leqslant b_n, b_n - a_n < 2^{-n}$, then there is a computable number α for which $a_n \leqslant \alpha \leqslant b_n$ each n.*   (A)

In intuitionist circles, a "rule" is a construction. For n starting at zero, 2^{-n} equals the binary numbers $1, 0.1, 0.01, 0.001$, and so forth, so this rule associates successive pairs of rational numbers that get closer and closer to each other — one binary digit closer in value for each new value of n. Normally we would claim this process to be a convergent series.

> A proof of this may be given, valid by ordinary mathematical standards, but involving an application of the principle of excluded middle.

The problem is that the rule might involve something that cannot be established one way or the other, such as the appearance of a particular unknown series of consecutive digits in the infinite expansion of π. Turing will come up with a more Turingesque example shortly.

> On the other hand the following is false:
>
> *There is a rule whereby, given the rule of formation of the sequences a_n, b_n in (A) we can obtain a D.N. for a machine to compute α.*   (B)

Take careful note that he's identifying this statement as false.

> That (B) is false, at least if we adopt the convention that the decimals of numbers of the form $m/2^n$ shall always terminate with zeros, can be seen in this way.

Numbers of the form $m/2^n$ are a subset of rational numbers. They are of particular interest in connection with Turing Machines because the binary representation of such a number has only a finite number of 1s. For example, the rational number $12345/65536$ in binary is:

$0.0011\ 0000\ 0011\ 1001\ 0000 \ldots$

Because 65,536 is 2^{16}, only the first 16 binary digits after the decimal point are potentially non-zero (depending on the numerator), and the rest are zero. Any number of the form $m/2^n$ where m is less than 2^n begins with a maximum of n non-zero binary digits and then continues forever with zeros.

Turing is going to give a rule for the formation of a_n and b_n, but this rule is based on the sequence printed by another machine named $\mathcal{N}$.

> Let $\mathcal{N}$ be some machine, and define c_n as follows: $c_n = \frac{1}{2}$ if $\mathcal{N}$ has not printed a figure 0 by the time the n-th complete configuration is reached $c_n = \frac{1}{2} - 2^{-m-3}$ if 0 had first been printed at the m-th
>
> [546]
>
> complete configuration $(m \leq n)$. Put $a_n = c_n - 2^{-n-2}$, $b_n = c_n + 2^{-n-2}$.

Let's look at an example. Suppose $\mathcal{N}$ is a machine that prints the sequence 1111101.... Here's a calculation of c_n, a_n, and b_n:

n	SEQUENCE	c_n	a_n	b_n
0	1	$\frac{1}{2}$	$\frac{1}{2} - \frac{1}{4} = \frac{64}{256}$	$\frac{1}{2} + \frac{1}{4} = \frac{192}{256}$
1	1	$\frac{1}{2}$	$\frac{1}{2} - \frac{1}{8} = \frac{96}{256}$	$\frac{1}{2} + \frac{1}{8} = \frac{160}{256}$
2	1	$\frac{1}{2}$	$\frac{1}{2} - \frac{1}{16} = \frac{112}{256}$	$\frac{1}{2} + \frac{1}{16} = \frac{144}{256}$
3	1	$\frac{1}{2}$	$\frac{1}{2} - \frac{1}{32} = \frac{120}{256}$	$\frac{1}{2} + \frac{1}{32} = \frac{136}{256}$
4	1	$\frac{1}{2}$	$\frac{1}{2} - \frac{1}{64} = \frac{124}{256}$	$\frac{1}{2} + \frac{1}{64} = \frac{132}{256}$
5	0	$\frac{127}{256}$	$\frac{127}{256} - \frac{1}{128} = \frac{125}{256}$	$\frac{127}{256} + \frac{1}{128} = \frac{129}{256}$
6 ...	1	$\frac{127}{256}$	$\frac{127}{256} - \frac{1}{256} = \frac{126}{256}$	$\frac{127}{256} + \frac{1}{256} = \frac{128}{256}$

The value c_n is always $\frac{1}{2}$ until the first zero in the sequence. If the first zero in the sequence is at position m (5 in the example), then c_n becomes $(2^{(m+2)} - 1) / 2^{(m+3)}$ for n greater than or equal to m.

> Then the inequalities of (A) are satisfied,

The a_n values always increase; the b_n values always decrease. The absolute values of the differences between a_n and b_n are always less than 2^{-n}. (Actually, the differences are always 2^{-n-1}.)

> and the first figure of α is 0 if $\mathcal{N}$ ever prints 0 and is 1 otherwise.

In the example, the limit is clearly 127/256, so the α sequence calculated by this machine is 011111110000... representing that rational number. If the first 0 in the sequence appears at n equal to 4, the limit is 63/128, so the α sequence is 011111100000.... Only if 0 never appears in the sequence will the limit be $\frac{1}{2}$, equivalent to the sequence 100000000000....

We clearly have a rule for the formulation of a_n and b_n, but this rule is based on a sequence printed by some other machine $\mathcal{N}$; such a rule requires a procedure to determine whether a machine such as $\mathcal{N}$ ever prints the digit zero.

The first figure of α is 1 if $\mathcal{N}$ never prints zero, and 0 otherwise, so,

> If (B) were true we should have a means of finding the first figure of α given the D.N. of $\mathcal{N}$: *i.e.* we should be able to determine whether $\mathcal{N}$ ever prints 0, contrary to the results of § 8 of the paper quoted.

The "paper quoted" is Turing's original paper. The next statement is something of a shocker, and it may initially seem wrong to you (as it did to me at first):

> Thus although (A) shows that there must be machines which compute the Euler constant (for example) we cannot at present describe any such machine, for we do not yet know whether the Euler constant is of the form $m/2^n$.

The Euler constant that Turing mentions here is *not* the famous e that serves as the base of natural logarithms, but the somewhat less famous Euler constant γ (gamma) that is calculated like so,

$$\gamma = \lim_{n \to \infty} \left(1 + \frac{1}{2} + \frac{1}{3} + \cdots \frac{1}{n} - \ln(n) \right)$$

or, perhaps more revelatory, as the difference between the summation and the integral of the function $1/x$,

$$\gamma = \lim_{n \to \infty} \left(\sum_{i=1}^{n} \frac{1}{i} - \int_{1}^{n} \frac{1}{x} dx \right)$$

and which approximately equals 0.57721566490153286....

This Euler constant is also known as the Euler-Mascheroni constant. Euler came up with the formula for the constant in 1734, and he calculated it to 16 digits in 1781. Lorenzo Mascheroni (1750–1800) got his name attached to the constant by calculating 32 digits in 1790 (although only the first 19 digits were correct) and by first using the letter γ to represent the number.[27]

Turing did not pick this constant randomly. One famous aspect of this constant is that no one knows whether it's rational or irrational, and if it is irrational, whether it's algebraic or transcendental. It was not known in 1937 and it is still not known in 2008.

The quotation from David Hilbert earlier in this chapter referring to "unapproachable" problems is actually preceded by the sentence: "Take any definite unsolved problem, such as the question as to the irrationality of the Euler-Mascheroni constant C, or the existence of an infinite number of prime numbers of the form $2^n + 1$. However unapproachable these problems may seem to us . . ." The status of the Euler-Mascheroni constant was considered *so* unapproachable that Hilbert did not include it in his list of 23 challenges for the new century.

If the Euler constant is rational, it might be the case that its denominator is a power of two. If that is so, the binary representation concludes with an infinite string of zeros.

If you had a Turing Machine to calculate γ, certainly there is no general process to determine whether γ is of the form $m/2^n$ because that would be equivalent to determining whether the machine prints only a finite number of 1s, and that is not possible. That much is very clear.

Turing is asserting something much more severe: that knowledge of the rationality or irrationality of the Euler constant is necessary to define a Turing Machine that computes the number — that the machine itself needs to "know" whether γ concludes with an infinite string of 0s or not. This might come as a surprise to anyone who has actually coded computer algorithms to calculate thousands and millions of digits of γ.

Yet, Turing has a valid point, and it relates to the inability of his machines to erase digits once they're printed: When a number is of the form $m/2^n$ where m is less than 2^n, we expect the machine to print all 0s after the first n digits. A machine that calculates the Euler constant will *not* behave in this manner because the algorithm approximates the Euler constant with ever smaller (but finite) terms. If the Euler constant is truly of the form $m/2^n$, the machine would indeed need to "know" this fact to calculate the exact value. Otherwise, the machine would always be approximating a number that it properly should nail precisely. Any non-zero digit after the first n digits is simply wrong — and very problematic because it can't be erased under Turing's conventions — but these non-zero digits are also unavoidable.

However much you may appreciate Turing's interesting analysis of the problems with the Euler constant, you're likely to find his solution to be worse than the problem.

---

[27] Julian Havil, *Gamma: Exploring Euler's Constant* (Princeton University Press, 2003), 89.

This disagreeable situation can be avoided by modifying the manner in which computable numbers are associated with computable sequences, the totality of computable numbers being left unaltered. It may be done in many ways* of which this is an example.

---

* This use of overlapping intervals for the definition of real numbers is due originally to Brouwer.

If the intuitionist aura that hangs over this section of the paper wasn't quite evident before, the proof is in the footnote, which alludes to Brouwer's definition of real numbers.

The real-number continuum has always been a problematic concept because of the way it combines discrete and continuous properties. Each real number appears to be a precise point on the continuum, yet we don't feel entirely comfortable saying that the continuum is the composite of all these discrete points — particularly after Cantor has informed us that these discrete points can't even be enumerated.

Brouwer attempted to define real numbers in a manner that preserved both the continuous and discrete qualities of the continuum while avoiding completed infinities.

The tool that Brouwer invented for this process is known as a "choice sequence." Choice sequences come in several varieties, but for use in constructing a real number, they are potentially infinite sequences of pairs of rational numbers. Each successive pair defines an interval nested within the preceding interval. For example, here's a possible choice sequence of pairs of nested rational numbers:

$$[3, 4]$$
$$[3.1, 3.2]$$
$$[3.14, 3.15]$$
$$[3.141, 3.142]$$
$$\cdots$$

In the classical sense, this choice sequence is converging, and we enthusiastically note that it seems to be converging to the number π. However, when speaking of Brouwerian choice sequences, it is essential to avoid the concept of "convergence" because that implies a completed infinity. Each of the items in the sequence defines a continuous range between the two endpoints. This is how the choice sequence preserves the idea of continuity. The sequence does not have a *limit* of π. Instead, it maintains a type of *halo*[28] around the number π. This halo indeed

---

[28]The term comes from Edmund Husserl (1859–1938). See Mark van Atten, Dirk van Dalen, and Richard Tieszen, "Brouwer and Weyl: The Phenomenology and Mathematics of the Intuitive Continuum," *Philosophia Mathematica*, Vol. 10, No. 2 (2002), 207.

gets smaller and smaller in time as the sequence grows longer and the intervals get tighter, but the halo never shrinks to the precise dimensionless irrational number.

One Brouwer scholar clarifies the difference between Brouwer's choice sequences and traditional limits this way:

> It is worth stressing that intuitionistically, the choice sequence, growing in time, itself is the real number.... On Brouwer's construal, one knows very well what the real number is, for it is the proceeding sequence itself. It is not the case that a choice sequence is a method to approximate a real number that lies in transcendent reality waiting to be reached by the subject.[29]

In the intuitionist continuum, real numbers are always incomplete — unfinished and never to be finished — and exhibiting a non-zero dimension.

The choice sequence I showed above is probably generated from some kind of algorithm. Consequently, it is called a "lawlike" choice sequence. There are also "non-lawlike" or "lawless" choice sequences, in which each term is chosen by some kind of agent (such as the mathematician) determining how the sequence develops. The mathematician can even flip a coin to determine the items in the choice sequence.

> We can think of a non-lawlike choice sequence as a kind of intuition even though it is quite different in some respects from a lawlike intuition. It is still a sequence carried out in time by a subject (or transcendent ego), only part of which is actually completed. We would actually complete only a finite initial segment of it, it will be associated with filling out the horizon of an intention directed toward a real number, and we should think of it as a 'medium of free becoming.' It should be noted that we are speaking here of a choice sequence as a process, as a sequence of acts developing in time.[30]

Choice sequences can also be combinations of lawlike and lawless sequences, for example, by performing predetermined arithmetical operations on multiple lawless sequences.

[29]Mark van Atten, *On Brouwer* (Wadsworth, 2004), 31.

[30]van Atten, van Dalen, and Tieszen, "Brouwer and Weyl: The Phenomenology and Mathematics of the Intuitive Continuum," 212.

Two choice sequences might be considered equal if they start out the same and continue to be the same for awhile, such as these two sequences:

[3, 4]	[3, 4]
[3.1, 3.2]	[3.1, 3.2]
[3.14, 3.15]	[3.14, 3.15]
[3.141, 3.142]	[3.141, 3.142]

Then an interval might come up that causes the sequences to be not equal but overlapping:

[3.141, 3.14175]   [3.14125, 3.142]

Perhaps the sequences become equal again:

[3.14125, 3.14175]   [3.14125, 3.14175]

What happens in the future is anyone's guess.

It may seem as if a lawlike sequence is completely defined by the algorithm that produces it, and hence represents an actual discrete point on the continuum.

> Even so, it is clear that for a correct understanding of a choice
> sequence as representing a point on the intuitive continuum,
> the sequence should be considered as a sequence in progress,
> whether it is lawlike or not. In the case of non-lawlike sequences
> this may be easiest to grasp, but the same holds for lawlike
> sequences. For if, on the contrary, a lawlike sequence is con-
> ceived of as a finished object, we may be seduced into thinking
> of the point in the classical atomistic way again. But then the
> continuum would be disrupted. In other words, the condition
> that the point never 'is' but always 'becomes' preserves the con-
> tinuum.[31]

These concepts should actually be somewhat familiar to readers of Turing's paper because we have experience with Turing Machines. We think of a Turing Machine (or its Description Number) as representing a real number, but the machine always generates digits over a period of time. It is never finished, and we can never determine from the Description Number of the machine exactly what that number is actually going to become.

In binary, the digits of $\pi/4$ are:

.11001001000011111101101010101010001000...

[31] Ibid, 212–213.

(I'm using $\pi/4$ rather than π so the number is between 0 and 1.) A Turing Machine that calculates the digits of $\pi/4$ can actually be interpreted as calculating choice sequences. When the machine calculates the first digit of 1, that digit doesn't indicate the number 0.1; the digit actually represents a range from 0.10000000... to 0.11111111... because that's the range of possible real numbers that begin with 0.1. Keeping in mind that the sequence 0.11111111... is equal to 1, the nested choice sequences generated by such a machine are:

$$[0.1, 1.0]$$
$$[0.11, 1.00]$$
$$[0.110, 0.111]$$
$$[0.1100, 0.1101]$$
$$[0.11001, 0.11010]$$
$$[0.110010, 0.110011]$$
$$[0.1100100, 0.1100110]$$
$$\cdots$$

In this sense, a normal Turing Machine that follows Turing's conventions (that is, never erasing a printed digit) generates a Brouwerian choice sequence representing a computable real number. The process occurs over time and never completes.

If Turing sees this elegant connection in the same way I do, he doesn't acknowledge it. Obviously he didn't have the same opportunity I did to read twenty-first century scholars decode Brouwer's difficult papers. If Turing read any Brouwer — or received some Brouwerian concepts second-hand — it might have been something like Brouwer's article "*Die Struktur des Kontinuums*"[32] from 1928, which describes using choice sequences as a type of tree structure that fans out and covers a section of the continuum with overlapping intervals. This could have given Turing an idea how to translate computable sequences into computable numbers. Besides the need to fix the problem associated with the Euler constant, Turing might also have been concerned that his machines always compute numbers between 0 and 1, and he felt he needed to go beyond that range.

In Turing's original conception, a computable sequence becomes a real number simply by prefixing a binary point. The revised concept is much more complex:

> Suppose that the first figure of a computable sequence γ is i and that this is followed by 1 repeated n

---

[32] Translated as L. E. J. Brouwer, "The Structure of the Continuum" in *From Kant to Hilbert*, Vol. II, 1186–1197.

times, then by 0 and finally by the sequence whose r-th figure is c_r; then the sequence γ is to correspond to the real number

$$(2i - 1)n + \sum_{r=1}^{\infty}(2c_r - 1)(\tfrac{2}{3})^r.$$

The i figure represents the sign of the number: 0 for negative and 1 for positive. The series of 1 figures repeated n times is the integer part of the number. A zero is required to terminate the run; it functions something like a binary point. The figures that follow make up the fractional part of the number, which is always of the form

$$\pm\frac{2}{3} \pm \frac{4}{9} \pm \frac{8}{27} \pm \frac{16}{81} \pm \frac{32}{243} \pm \ldots$$

where the c_r figures determine whether each of the terms gets a plus sign (for 1) or a minus sign (for 0).

For example, suppose a machine prints the following sequence:

1 111110 11011 ...

I've inserted some spaces just to make it easier to translate into a number. The first digit is 1 meaning a positive number. The next five digits are 1s terminated with a zero so the integer part is 5. The fractional part is:

$$\frac{2}{3} + \frac{4}{9} - \frac{8}{27} + \frac{16}{81} + \frac{32}{243}$$

At this stage of the process the complete number is $5\frac{278}{243}$ or $6\frac{35}{243}$. Notice that the computed number actually has an integer part of 6 rather than 5. If the figures representing the fractional part of the number are all 1s, the fractional part is

$$\frac{2}{3} + \frac{4}{9} + \frac{8}{27} + \frac{16}{81} + \frac{32}{243} + \ldots$$

which converges to 2. Similarly, if the figures representing the fractional part are all 0s, the fractional part converges to -2. A sequence that has an encoded integer part of N can actually resolve to $N-2$ through $N + 2$, creating overlapping intervals.

If the machine which computes γ is regarded as computing also this real number then (B) holds.

That is, if there is a rule for formulating the sequences a_n and b_n that close in on a number, we can obtain a Description Number of the machine. Internally, the machine calculates a_n and b_n and then chooses to print a 0 or 1 based on the need to subtract or add $(2/3)^n$ to bring the computed number within this new range.

In the process, we're now stuck with this single method of computing numbers based on converging bounds. It is no longer possible to write simple machines that compute rational numbers such as $\frac{1}{2}$, or $\frac{1}{4}$. These numbers must now be approximated like all others. For example, the sequence for $\frac{1}{2}$ is now:

0 0 1010 1101 0100 1101...

The first two digits represent the sign (positive) and the binary point. The digits that follow indicate terms of 2/3, −4/9, 8/27, −16/81, and so forth. The portion of the sequence shown here computes $\frac{1}{2}$ to an accuracy somewhat greater than 3 decimal digits or 10 binary digits.

The advantage is that the machine doesn't have to "know" that it's really computing a rational number of the form $m/2^n$. It doesn't need to "know" when to abandon the calculation and settle into an infinite string of 0s. Even a sequence that terminates in an infinite run of 0s or 1s is associated with a number built from an infinite string of decreasing but finite terms.

There are other ways to compute $\frac{1}{2}$. Here's one alternative:

0 10 0101 0010 1011 0010...

The first digit is the sign (positive) but the next two digits represent the number 1. The digits that follow indicate terms of −2/3, 4/9, −8/27, 16/81, and so forth, the opposite of the digits in the first sequence.

> The uniqueness of representation of real numbers by sequences of figures is now lost, but this is of little theoretical importance, since the D.N.'s are not unique in any case.
>
> The Graduate College,
> Princeton, N.J., U.S.A.

Here Turing's short paper of corrections ends, seemingly without pity that this sudden paradigm shift has left us just a bit disoriented. We might feel some satisfaction that we now have a definition of computable numbers that is less mathematically troublesome, but it hardly compensates for the queasiness of being set adrift on the philosophically uncertain waves of the continuum.

IV And Beyond

17 Is Everything a Turing Machine?

No matter how well you understand the concept and workings of the Turing Machine, it won't help you actually build a computer. Digital computers are built from transistors or other switching mechanisms, such as relays or vacuum tubes. These transistors are assembled into logic gates that implement simple logical functions, which then form higher-level components such as registers and adders.[1]

The Turing Machine is built from — well, Turing never tells us. Turing didn't intend for his machines to function as blueprints for actual computers. The machines serve instead as a simplified abstract model of computation, whether performed by human or machine. Turing's initial purpose for creating the Turing Machine was the very specific goal of proving that there is no general decision procedure for first-order logic. Only later did the imaginary devices begin contributing to our understanding of the theory of computing. This transition took about 20 years, after which the Turing Machine became a subject of study within the discipline we now know as computer science.

Adapting the Turing Machine for purposes other than Turing's proof required that the machine be reformulated somewhat. Most of Turing's machines spend the rest of infinity computing the digits of some real number between 0 and 1. A much more common task in mathematics — as well as computer programming — is the computation of a function. A function requires one or more numbers as input, also called the arguments to the function. Based on that input the function calculates output, also known as the value of the function.

One important class of functions is the number-theoretic functions, so called because the input and output are both limited to natural numbers. Turing devised a technique to compute number-theoretic functions in Section 10 of his paper (page 235 of this book) by printing runs of consecutive 1 figures separated by single 0 figures. The number of consecutive 1s in the first run is the value of the

---

[1] This hierarchy is described in Charles Petzold, *Code: The Hidden Language of Computer Hardware and Software* (Microsoft Press, 1999).

function for an argument of 0; the number of consecutive 1s occurring next is the value of the function for 1; and so forth.

One mathematician to take a good long critical look at Turing's number-theoretic function machines was Stephen Cole Kleene. Kleene was a student of Alonzo Church at Princeton and received his Ph.D. in 1934, after which he began teaching at the University of Wisconsin in Madison.

Kleene later wrote, "While fully honoring Turing's conception of what his machines could do, I was skeptical that his was the easiest way to apply them to the computation of number-theoretic functions. In any case, only a total function $\phi(x)$ could be computed in this way."[2] Turing's technique doesn't work for partial functions, which are functions valid for only a proper subset of the natural numbers.

Beginning in the spring of 1941, Kleene began pursuing a different approach in a seminar on the foundations of mathematics that he taught at the University of Wisconsin. Kleene's reformulated Turing Machines were later featured in Chapter XIII of his now-classic 1952 book *Introduction to Metamathematics*.

Kleene's version of the Turing Machine still reads symbols, writes symbols, and moves left and right along a tape. However, it is limited to only one symbol, which is a simple vertical line, called a *tick* or *tally* mark. The machine differentiates between this symbol and a blank square. A natural number is represented by a series of tick symbols in consecutive squares delimited by blank squares. Because Kleene begins his natural numbers with 0, one tick mark represents 0, two tick marks represents 1, and so forth. Kleene appears to be the first author to show a sample Turing Machine tape as a diagram in his text.[3]

Turing's machines generally begin with a blank tape. Kleene's reformulated machines begin with a tape on which the input to a function is already encoded as one or more runs of consecutive tick marks separated by blanks. Kleene's machines then compute the value of the function and encode that number back on the tape. The first example Kleene shows is a successor function that calculates the next number after the encoded number; it performs this amazing feat by simply printing another tick mark after the existing run of tick marks.

Kleene's function-calculating machines require only a finite period of time to calculate, so the machine can stop when it's finished. There is no specific "stop" or "halt" configuration, but there are what Kleene calls "passive situations" where there is no place for the machine to go. When a machine is instructed to switch to a configuration that does not exist, "the machine is said then to *stop*. The situation in which it stops we call the *terminal situation* or *output*."[4]

---

[2]Stephen C. Kleene, "Origins of Recursive Function Theory," *Annals of the History of Computing*, Vol. 3, No. 1 (Jan. 1981), 61.

[3]Stephen C. Kleene, *Introduction to Metamathematics* (D. Van Nostrand, 1952), 358–360.

[4]Kleene, *Introduction to Metamathematics*, 358.

In Turing's conception, a good machine — which Turing calls a circle-free machine or a satisfactory machine — never stops. In Kleene's reformulation, a good machine finishes the function and then halts. A Kleene machine that gets into an infinite loop and never stops is a bad machine. In this respect, Kleene's machines obviously are much closer in concept to conventional mathematical and computer functions that calculate output from input in a finite number of steps.

As I discussed in Chapter 15, by 1936 there existed three different formulations of the intuitive notion of effective calculability:

- Turing Machines;
- recursive functions as defined by Kurt Gödel in 1934 based on a suggestion of Jacques Herbrand and further explored by Kleene; and
- λ-definable functions developed by Church and his students, most prominently Kleene.

The equivalence of these three formulations was established partially by Turing in the appendix to his paper on computable numbers and more rigorously in his 1937 paper "Computability and λ-Definability," and by Stephen Kleene in his 1936 paper "λ-Definability and Recursiveness." These days the term "recursive function" is nearly synonymous with "computable function."

Stephen Kleene was the first person to come up with terms to describe how these formalizations capture the intuitive notion of calculability. It is in *Introduction to Metamathematics* that Kleene first states something he explicitly calls *Church's thesis*: "*Every effectively calculable function (effectively decidable predicate) is general recursive.*" Two chapters later Kleene says: "Turing's thesis that every function which would naturally be regarded as computable is computable under his definition, i.e. by one of his machines, is equivalent to Church's thesis. . ."[5]

In a 1967 book, Kleene combined the two theses into one:

> Turing's and Church's theses are equivalent. We shall usually refer to them both as *Church's thesis*, or in connection with that one of its three versions which deals with "Turing machines" as the *Church-Turing thesis*.[6]

Since then, "Church-Turing thesis" has become the preferred term.

Introduction to Metamathematics is obviously a book for mathematicians. Six years later, another now-classic book crossed the line from mathematics into computer science.

Martin Davis was born in 1928 in New York City. He took his Ph.D. at Princeton University in 1950 with a dissertation entitled *On the Theory of Recursive*

---

[5] Kleene, *Introduction to Metamathematics*, 300, 376.
[6] Stephen Cole Kleene, *Mathematical Logic* (John Wiley & Sons, 1967; Dover, 2002), 232.

Unsolvability. Davis's thesis advisor was Alonzo Church, who had also been Kleene's thesis advisor in 1934 and Turing's in 1938.

In a course that Davis taught at the University of Illinois, he began speaking of the problem of determining whether a Turing Machine finishes its calculation as the "halting problem," perhaps as early as 1952.[7] This phrase became more widely known following the publication of Davis's book *Computability and Unsolvability* in 1958. In the book's Preface, Davis slyly notes, "Although there is little in this volume that is actually new, the expert will perhaps find some novelty in the arrangement and treatment of certain topics," and then clarifies: "In particular, the notion of the Turing machine has been made central in the development."[8]

Whereas the Turing Machine doesn't make an appearance until page 321 of Kleene's *Introduction to Metamathematics*, and doesn't get deeply involved in the discussion until Chapter 13, in Davis's *Computability and Unsolvability* the Turing Machine is right up front: on the first page of the first chapter.

Like Kleene, Davis denotes the natural numbers with successive tick marks and uses the machines to compute functions. Examples of machines that perform addition, subtraction, and multiplication begin on page 12.

Although *Computability and Unsolvability* is ostensibly a mathematics textbook, Davis realized that the book "because of its relevance to certain philosophical questions and the theory of digital computers [is] of potential interest to nonmathematicians."[9]

To further accentuate the difference, *Computability and Unsolvability* was published in a new McGraw-Hill Series in Information Processing and Computers. Even within that series, the book was unique. Other books in the series focused on the "practical" topics of computer hardware and programming. Titles published in this series in 1958 and 1959 included *Analog Simulation: Solution of Field Problems*; *High-Speed Data Processing*; *Digital Computer Primer*; *Digital Computing Systems*; and *A Primer of Programming for Digital Computers*.

Martin Davis's *Computability and Unsolvability* can truly be said to have initiated the study of computability as a topic that later became part of the standard curriculum for computer science majors.

It is on page 70 of *Computability and Unsolvability* that Davis introduces a term used frequently in connection with Turing Machines:

> Now, let *Z* be a simple Turing machine. We may associate with *Z* the following decision problem:
>
> *To determine, of a given instantaneous description α, whether or not there exists a computation of Z that begins with α.*

---

[7]See B. Jack Copeland, *The Essential Turing* (Oxford University Press, 2004), 40, footnote 61.
[8]Martin Davis, *Computability and Unsolvability* (McGraw-Hill, 1958: Dover, 1982), vii–viii.
[9]Davis, *Computability and Unsolvability*, vii.

> That is, we wish to determine whether or not Z, if placed in a given initial state, will eventually halt. We call this problem the *halting problem* for Z.[10]

Later on that same page, Davis formulates a theorem: "*There exists a Turing machine whose halting problem is recursively unsolvable.*"

The widespread influence of Martin Davis's book is such that the halting problem is now forever associated with Turing Machines despite the fact that Turing's original machines never halt!

Aside from speed, memory capability, and ever fancier human-interface devices, all modern computers are basically the same. Every computer that can emulate a Turing Machine — and that's a very easy requirement — is a universal computer. Moreover, any universal computer can emulate any other universal computer.

Some very early computers were *not* as powerful as the Turing Machine. Apparently the first computer to be at least *potentially* universal was the machine that Konrad Zuse built called the Z3, constructed between 1938 and 1941.[11] If built, Charles Babbage's Analytical Engine of the 1830s would have qualified as a universal machine, even though it would have been constructed from gears rather than switching mechanisms. Virtually all computers built since 1944 have been universal machines.

One crucial element of a universal machine is *programmability*. There must be some way to introduce a stream of instructions into the computer and have the computer respond. In modern computers, these instructions are bytes in memory called machine code. In Zuse's machine, instructions were encoded as holes punched in 35mm movie film. Babbage's machine would have used punched cards similar to those that controlled Jacquard silk-weaving looms.

Some early computers could be programmed only with an inflexible sequence of instructions. A universal machine must be able to skip around in the instruction stream based on the values of previous calculations. This feature is known as *conditional branching*, and it is essential for implementing calculational loops.

Computer programming languages are often called "Turing complete" if the syntax of the language allows them to mimic a Turing Machine.

The basic HyperText Markup Language (HTML) used extensively on the Web is not intended for computation and is certainly not Turing complete. JavaScript often used within HTML is certainly Turing complete, as are virtually all programming languages in use today. Any Turing-complete programming language can emulate any other Turing-complete language.

[10]Davis, *Computability and Unsolvability*, 70.

[11]Raúl Rojas, "How to Make Zuse's Z3 a Universal Computer," *IEEE Annals of the History of Computing*, Vol. 20, No. 3 (1998), 51–54.

The Turing Machine not only established the basic requirements for effective calculability but also identified limits: No computer or programming language known today is more powerful than the Turing Machine; no computer or programming language can solve the halting problem; no computer or programming language can determine the ultimate destiny of another computer program. You can't get around these limitations with a "better" programming language or a different kind of machine. At best you can only do jobs faster. You can rig up thousands of processors to perform in parallel, and you can strive to create quantum computers that perform massively parallel computations, but you simply can't bring infinity any closer to this hopelessly finite world in which we live.

Regardless of the limitations of the Turing Machine, some mathematicians have journeyed into the realm of *hypercomputation* and described machines that transcend the Turing limit. Alan Turing himself partially instigated this research by briefly describing a magical "oracle" in his Ph.D. thesis, the difficult 1939 paper "Systems of Logic Based on Ordinals":

> Let us suppose we are supplied with some unspecified means
> of solving [undecidable] number-theoretic problems; a kind of
> oracle as it were. We shall not go any further into the nature
> of this oracle apart from saying that it cannot be a machine. With
> the help of the oracle we could form a new kind of machine (call
> them *o*-machines), having as one of its fundamental processes
> that of solving a given number-theoretic problem.[12]

Perhaps we'd all like a little oracle in our lives to help with the really tough questions. Researchers exploring hypercomputation have built on the oracle idea and introduced other features into Turing Machines so that they are not bound by normal real-life limitations. While interesting mathematical constructs, these hypercomputers are never quite practical because they violate basic laws of physics, such as accelerating time so that each step of the computation takes half as long as the previous step. Martin Davis has even gone so far as to refer to the "myth" of hypercomputation and compares the hypercomputationalists to trisectors of the angle and inventors of perpetual motion machines.[13]

To my mind, explorations into hypercomputation are valuable more for the questions they raise about computational universality. Alan Turing designed his imaginary machine to model the basic operations of a human computer in

---

[12] Alan Turing, "Systems of Logic Based on Ordinals," *Proceedings of the London Mathematical Society*, Series 2, Volume 45 (1939), 172–173.

[13] Martin Davis, "The Myth of Hypercomputation," in Christof Teuscher, ed., *Alan Turing: Life and Legacy of a Great Thinker* (Springer, 2004), 195–211.

mechanically carrying out a precise algorithm. He discovered that these machines have some inherent limitations. In the decades since, we have built computers that are computationally equivalent to Turing Machines and hence have those same constraints. We see no practical way to go beyond these limitations.

For that reason, the universality of computation — both in capability and limitations — seems very fundamental to any type of data-processing activity. These limitations seem as ingrained in the fabric of the natural world as the laws of thermodynamics.

If the Turing Machine has inherent limitations that seemingly can't be overcome without breaking the laws of physics, then what exactly are the implications for *natural* mechanisms that perform computational or logical operations? This question becomes most profound (and perhaps even a bit troubling) when we consider the two most important "natural mechanisms" in our lives that we might want to investigate in this way: the human mind, and the universe itself.

Strictly speaking, the Turing thesis involves only an equivalence between Turing Machines and mechanical algorithms. It does not necessarily imply that there can never be a computing machine that can outperform the Turing Machine, or that such machines violate some kind of known universal law.[14]

Perhaps we're missing something. Perhaps there's some kind of mysterious physical mechanism that can perform some powerful computational operation that simply can't be emulated on the Turing Machine. Does the model of the Turing Machine really help us to understand the human mind and the universe? Or are we foolishly bringing the most complex objects we know down to the level of a reductionist machine that can't even properly add?

The legacy of the Turing Machine outside the fields of mathematics and computing began several years after the 1936 publication of Turing's paper with the fortuitous meeting between Warren McCulloch (1898–1969) and Walter Pitts (1923–1969).

As a youngster in Detroit, the brilliant Walter Pitts taught himself Latin and Greek, philosophy and mathematics, and consequently was regarded by his family as a freak. He ran away to Chicago when he was 15. Homeless, Pitts spent much time in the park, where he made the acquaintance of an old man named Bert. He and Bert had similar interests in philosophy and mathematics, and Bert suggested that he read a book by University of Chicago professor Rudolf Carnap (1891–1970) — probably *The Logical Syntax of Language* published in 1937. Walter Pitts read the book and then headed to Carnap's office to discuss

---

[14]For a concise critique with a good bibliography see C. Jack Copeland, "The Church-Turing Thesis," Stanford Encyclopedia of Philosophy, http://plato.stanford.edu/entries/church-turing.

some problems that he had discovered. The old man named Bert turned out to be Bertrand Russell.[15]

If you don't believe that story, perhaps this one is more plausible: During the time that Bertrand Russell was teaching at the University of Chicago, he was taking a stroll through Jackson Park when he spotted a young man reading Carnap's book. They began talking, and Russell took Walter Pitts to Carnap's office.[16]

Then there is this one: When Pitts was 12 years old and still living in Detroit, he was chased by some bullies and took refuge in a library. When the library closed, he was trapped inside. He decided to read Whitehead and Russell's *Principia Mathematica*, and remained in the library for three days, finally sending a letter to Russell pointing out some errors. When Russell wrote back inviting him to Cambridge, Pitts decided to become a mathematician.[17]

What is known for sure is that Walter Pitts did attend a lecture by Bertrand Russell in Chicago in 1938, and that he also visited Rudolf Carnap's office the same year. Carnap was impressed with the young man and wanted to help him out by giving him a student job, but he didn't even know Pitts' name, and there was no way to find him.[18]

Pitts was "a shy, introverted lost soul, with glasses, bad teeth, a habit of twirling his hair, a slight nervous tremor, and a tendency to bump into things."[19] (Later on, during the Second World War, Pitts received a 4F classification from the draft board and was labeled "pre-psychotic," yet he was also recruited for the Manhattan Project and received top-secret clearance.[20]) After Carnap tracked down Pitts almost a year after the office visit, Pitts began studying logic with Carnap and attending classes at the University of Chicago, including seminars given by the red-bearded Ukrainian-born Nicolas Rashevsky (1899–1972).

Rashevsky had received his doctorate in theoretical physics from the University of Kiev, and immigrated to the United States in 1924. He became interested in applying mathematical models to biological processes, a discipline that relied on empirical research done by others, but which involved no laboratory work of

[15]The story is attributed to McCulloch's former student Manual Blum in Pamela McCorduck, *Machines Who Think: A Personal Inquiry into the History and Prospects of Artificial Intelligence*, 25th anniversary edition (A. K. Peters, 2004), 89. Blum also tells the story in Manual Blum, "Notes on McCulloch-Pitts' *A Logical Calculus of the Ideas Immanent in Nervous Activity*" in Rook McCulloch, ed., *Collected Works of Warren S. McCulloch* (Intersystems Publications, 1989), Vol. I, 31. A variation is recounted in an interview with Michael A. Arbib in James A. Anderson and Edward Rosenfeld, eds., *Talking Nets: An Oral History of Neural Networks* (MIT Press, 1998), 218.

[16]Interview with Jack D. Cowan in *Talking Nets*, 104.

[17]Interview with Jerome Y. Lettvin in *Talking Nets*, 2. In Jerome Y. Lettvin, "Warren and Walter," *Collected Works of Warren S. McCulloch*, Vol. II, 514–529, Pitts spent a week in the library reading *Principia Mathematica*, but only when the library was open.

[18]Neil R. Smalheiser, "Walter Pitts," *Perspectives in Biology and Medicine*, Vol. 43, No. 2 (Winter 2000), 218.

[19]Smalheiser, "Walter Pitts," 22.

[20]Ibid.

its own. By 1934, Rashevsky had even come up with a name to explain what he was doing: *mathematical biophysics*. In 1935, he became the first Assistant Professor of Mathematical Biophysics at the University of Chicago. A book entitled *Mathematical Biophysics* followed in 1938, and then a journal, the *Bulletin of Mathematical Biophysics* in 1939, devoted to publishing papers of Rashevsky and his followers. [21]

In 1942 and 1943, Pitts published three papers in the *Bulletin of Mathematical Biophysics*, and around this time was introduced to Warren McCulloch.

Warren McCulloch grew up in New Jersey and first attended Haverford, a Quaker college in Pennsylvania. Shortly after McCulloch entered the college in 1917, the teacher and philosopher Rufus Jones (1863–1948) — who about this time helped found the American Friends Service Committee — asked McCulloch "What is Thee going to be? . . . And what is Thee going to do?" McCulloch said he had no idea, "but there is one question I would like to answer. What is a number, that a man may know it, and a man, that he may know a number?" To which Rufus Jones could only respond, "Friend, Thee will be busy as long as Thee lives."[22]

McCulloch attended Yale to study philosophy and psychology, got his M.D. at the College of Physicians and Surgeons in New York in 1927, treated people with severe brain injuries at Bellevue Hospital Center in New York City, and worked with insane patients at Rockland State Hospital.[23] Back at Yale in 1934, McCulloch worked with Dusser de Barenne (1885–1940), who had pioneered the technique of mapping functional areas of the brain by applying strychnine to exposed portions of a cat's brain and observing what happens. In 1941, McCulloch moved to the Neuropsychiatric Institute of the University of Illinois.

McCulloch was a swashbuckling figure who "looked like Moses; he had this long beard and bushy eyebrows [and] a strange gleam in his eye. He really looked like he was crazy a lot of the time. He had gray eyes, and when they got really bright and glaring, he looked like a spectacle."[24] McCulloch was gregarious, "found a bottle [of Scotch] each night a fine lubricant for his side of the conversion,"[25] and was a big storyteller. (The stories about Walter Pitts meeting Bertrand Russell in Jackson Park all ultimately came from McCulloch.) McCulloch wrote poetry, discoursed on philosophy, and flaunted his polymathic learning whenever possible.

---

[21] Tara H. Abraham, "Nicholas Rashevsky's Mathematical Biophysics," *Journal of the History of Biology*, Vol. 37, No. 2 (Summer 2004), 333–385.

[22] Warren S. McCulloch, "What is a Number, That a Man May Know it, and a Man, That he May Know a Number?", *Collected Words of Warren S. McCulloch*, Vol. IV, 1226.

[23] Much of the biographical information on McCulloch comes from Michael A. Arbib, "Warren McCulloch's Search for the Logic of the Nervous System," *Perspectives in Biology and Medicine*, Vol. 43, No. 2 (Winter 2000), 193–216.

[24] Interview with Jack D. Cowan in *Talking Nets*, 102.

[25] Arbib, "Warren McCulloch's Search for the Logic of the Nervous System," 202.

It's not quite clear how Warren McCulloch and Walter Pitts were introduced, but they immediately hit it off, even to the extent of Pitts moving into the McCulloch household. McCulloch was attempting to formulate a theory of the workings of the brain, and Pitts' knowledge of mathematical logic was exactly what he needed. They hammered out a paper over the McCulloch kitchen table with McCulloch's daughter Taffy drawing the article's illustrations.[26] The historic paper that resulted from this first collaboration between McCulloch and Pitts was "A Logical Calculus of Ideas Immanent in Nervous Activity" published in Rashevsky's *Bulletin of Mathematical Biophysics* in 1943.

From research in the second half of the nineteenth century, scientists had known that the nervous system consisted of cells called neurons, and that these neurons seemed to be connected in a network. Additional research in the twentieth century had shown that these neurons worked much like switches that are triggered when a stimulus reaches a threshold.[27]

To McCulloch and Pitts, these neurons resembled logical functions, so they modeled the neurons with a form of propositional logic using Rudolf Carnap's notation. One crucial element not in traditional logic was a time delay between input and output; this time delay allowed neurons to be organized in circular patterns so that signals could be kept active just circling through the network. The McCulloch-Pitts paper defines axioms for this simplified model and then proceeds to prove some theorems.

"A Logical Calculus of Ideas Immanent in Nervous Activity" doesn't have many precursors. The bibliography consists solely of Carnap's *Logical Syntax of Language*, Hilbert and Ackermann's *Grundzüge der Theoretischen Logik* (spelled *"Grundüge"*), and Whitehead and Russell's *Principia Mathematica*. On page 15 of this 19-page paper, McCulloch and Pitts reveal a little broader reading when they conclude

> first, that every net, if furnished with a tape, scanners connected
> to afferents, and suitable efferents to perform the necessary
> motor-operations, can compute only such numbers as can a
> Turing machine; second, that each of the latter numbers can
> be computed by such a net ... This is of interest in affording a
> psychological justification of the Turing definition of
> computability and its equivalents, Church's λ-definability and
> Kleene's primitive recursiveness: If any number can be com-
> puted by an organism, it is computable by these definitions and
> conversely.[28]

[26] Arbib, "Warren McCulloch's Search for the Logic of the Nervous System," 199.

[27] Tara H. Abraham, "(Physio)logical Circuits: The Intellectual Origins of the McCulloch-Pitts Neural Networks," *Journal of the History of the Behavioral Sciences*, Vol. 38, No. 1 (Winter 2002), 19.

[28] W. S. McCulloch and W. Pitts, "A Logical Calculus in the Ideas Immanent in Nervous Activity," *Bulletin of Mathematical Biophysics*, Vol. 5 (1943), 129. Also in *Collected Works of Warren S. McCulloch*, Vol. I, 357.

Several years later, in 1948, McCulloch made the Turing connection more explicit. He explained that he was searching for a way to develop a theory in neurophysiology,

> and it was not until I saw Turing's paper that I began to get going the right way around, and with Pitts' help formulated the required logical calculus. What we thought we were doing (and I think we succeeded fairly well) was treating the brain as a Turing machine; that is, as a device which could perform the kind of functions which a brain must perform if it is only to go wrong and have a psychosis. . . . The delightful thing is that the very simplest set of appropriate assumptions is sufficient to show that a nervous system can compute any computable number. It is that kind of a device, if you like — a Turing machine.[29]

Still later (in 1955), McCulloch was blunter: "Pitts and I showed that brains were Turing machines, and that any Turing machine could be made out of neurons,"[30] although current knowledge was insufficient to put this equivalence to any practical use:

> To the theoretical question, Can you design a machine to do whatever a brain can do? the answer is this: If you will specify in a finite and unambiguous way what you think a brain does do with information, then we can design a machine to do it. Pitts and I have proved this construction. But can you say what you think brains do?[31]

The McCulloch and Pitts paper might have languished in mathematical biophysical obscurity had it not caught the attention of two major figures in twentieth-century computing: Norbert Wiener and John von Neumann.

Norbert Wiener was the product of the most notorious experiment in home-schooling since the regimen endured by John Stuart Mill. Both men later wrote memoirs about the experience of being molded into a prodigy by overbearing fathers; in Wiener's case, the scars remained raw and unhealed for most of his life. For years he battled a bipolar disorder without diagnosis, combining periods of brilliant research with inexplicable rages and suicidal despair.

---

[29]Warren McCulloch in Lloyd A. Jeffress, ed., *Cerebral Mechanisms in Behavior: The Hixon Symposium* (John Wiley & Sons, 1951), 32–33.
[30]Warren S. McCulloch, "Mysterium Iniquitatis of Sinful Man Aspiring into the Place of God," *The Scientific Monthly*, Vol. 80, No. 1 (Jan. 1955), 36. Also in *Collected Works of Warren S. McCulloch*, Vol. III, 985.
[31]Ibid, 38.

Wiener entered Tufts University when he was 11 years old, received a B.A. in mathematics at 14, and then became the youngest recipient of a Harvard Ph.D. at the age of 18. Still, Wiener's father would tell members of the press that his son was "not even exceptionally bright" and indeed, "lazy."[32] His parents also withheld information from him: Norbert Wiener was 15 before he found out he was Jewish.

After leaving Harvard, Wiener studied mathematical logic at Cambridge with Bertrand Russell and number theory with G. H. Hardy, differential equations with David Hilbert at Göttingen on the eve of the Great War, and philosophy with John Dewey at Columbia University. In 1919, he joined the faculty of the Massachusetts Institute of Technology.

In the period between the wars, Wiener pioneered in the fledgling fields of communication engineering and analog computing. He was involved with Vannevar Bush's analog-computing projects at MIT, and seems to have influenced Claude Elwood Shannon in the development of communication theory. During World War II, Wiener worked on systems to implement anti-aircraft fire. These systems incorporated a more complex form of prediction than previous techniques to anticipate the ways that the aircraft would try to avoid the missile being aimed at it. Wiener was particularly interested in the concept of feedback — getting information back to incrementally correct a process.

Norbert Wiener was *not* in attendance at the first historic meeting of physiologists, psychologists, and anthropologists who gathered at the Beekman Hotel on May 13, 1942, under the sponsorship of the Josiah Macy, Jr. Foundation to explore some interdisciplinary connections. Warren McCulloch was there as were the husband-and-wife anthropology team of Gregory Bateson and Margaret Mead. Wiener was present at the first postwar Macy conference entitled "The Feedback Mechanisms and Circular Causal Systems in Biology and the Social Sciences Meeting,"[33] as were Walter Pitts and John von Neumann, with everyone assimilating everyone else's work and examining how everything seemed to fit together.

In 1947, Norbert Wiener wrote a book bringing together some of the research that had been discussed at these conferences. He wanted a new word for studies that encompassed communication and feedback in machines, living things, and social structures. He chose the Greek word *cybernetics*, meaning *steersman*, or *helmsman*, or *pilot*. Essential to the job of steering a ship is the incorporation of feedback to compensate and correct for any drift off course. Wiener's book, published in 1948, became *Cybernetics: or Control and Communication in the Animal and the Machine*.

Time magazine proclaimed, "Once in a great while a scientific book is published that sets bells jangling wildly in a dozen different sciences. Such a book is

---

[32]Flo Conway and Jim Siegelman, *Dark Hero of the Information Age: In Search of Norbert Wiener, the Father of Cybernetics* (Basic Books, 2005), 21.

[33]Conway and Siegelman, *Dark Hero*, 155.

Cybernetics."[34] Read today, *Cybernetics* is an odd little book combining startling visionary prose with dense pages of mathematics. In the introduction, Wiener pays homage to the many people whose work he had assimilated, including Warren McCulloch, "who was interested in the study of the organization of the cortex of the brain," Alan Turing, "who is perhaps first among those who have studied the logical possibilities of the machine as an intellectual experiment," Walter Pitts, who "had been a student of Carnap at Chicago and had also been in contact with Professor Rashevsky and his school of biophysicists," as well as early computer pioneers "Dr. Aiken of Harvard, Dr. von Neumann of the Institute for Advanced Study, and Dr. Goldstine of the Eniac and Edvac machines at the University of Pennsylvania."[35]

Chapter 5 of *Cybernetics* is devoted to "Computing Machines and the Nervous System." Wiener compares the switching mechanisms of digital computers with the McCulloch and Pitts model of the brain:

> It is a noteworthy fact that the human and animal nervous systems, which are known to be capable of the work of a computation system, contain elements which are ideally suited to act as relays. These elements are the so-called *neurons* or nerve cells. While they show rather complicated properties under the influence of electrical currents, in their ordinary physiological action they conform very nearly to the "all-or-none" principle; that is, they are either at rest, or when they "fire" they go through a series of changes almost independent of the nature and intensity of the stimulus.[36]

Two chapters later, Wiener notes that "the realization that the brain and the computing machine have much in common may suggest new and valid approaches to psychopathology and even to psychiatrics."[37] Wiener was no blind technophile, however. He was profoundly concerned about the impact that this new science and technology would have on people, and wrote *The Human Use of Human Beings: Cybernetics and Society* (Houghton Mifflin, 1950) as a follow-up to his 1948 book.

Cybernetics became a focal point for wide-ranging research until late in 1951 when Wiener suddenly and without explanation severed all ties with Warren McCulloch and the group of cyberneticians who had formed around McCulloch's charismatic personality, including Pitts, who had been writing his Ph.D. thesis

---

[34]December 27, 1948 issue, quoted in Conway and Siegelman, *Dark Hero*, 182.

[35]Norbert Wiener, *Cybernetics: or Control and Communication in the Animal and the Machine* (John Wiley & Sons, 1948; second edition, MIT Press, 1961), 12, 13, 14, 15. Page numbers refer to the second edition.

[36]Wiener, *Cybernetics*, 120.

[37]Wiener, *Cybernetics*, 144.

under Wiener's supervision. Several explanations have been suggested for this split: One theory is that the emotionally damaged Wiener was unable to gauge the nuances of McCulloch's personality. Sometimes Wiener couldn't distinguish between McCulloch's recitation of facts and his wild speculations.[38] Another theory is that Wiener's wife, in jealously guarding her husband's reputation, had falsely told him that McCulloch's "boys" had seduced their daughter.[39]

Without the Wiener-McCulloch connection, cybernetics as a unified discipline suffered greatly. Among those personally affected by the rift, perhaps Walter Pitts took it hardest. He was emotionally devastated, destroyed his research and his Ph.D. thesis, and began a long slow decline. "He did not simply drink — as befitting a man of his talents, he synthesized novel analogues of barbiturates and opiates in the laboratory and experimented on himself by ingesting long-chain alcohols."[40] Walter Pitts died in 1969 at the age of 46 from bleeding esophageal varices, a problem often associated with chronic alcoholism.

Even without the split between Wiener and McCulloch, it's not certain that cybernetics would have survived. The concept of a broad interdisciplinary umbrella doesn't quite fit into American academia, where specialization is the key to success. Although there have been numerous attempts to revive the ideals of cybernetics, it lives on mostly linguistically in popular culture with words like cyborg (short for "cybernetic organism"), and the ubiquitous cyber- prefix in cyberspace, cybercafé, cyberpunk, and the oxymoronic cybersex. Even the use of these cyber- words has been diminishing in recent years in submission to the popular "e-" prefix.

The McCulloch and Pitts paper on the mathematical model of the neural network also served as a catalyst for John von Neumann, who was involved in the design of several seminal computer projects including the EDVAC (Electronic Discrete Variable Automatic Computer). In the *First Draft of a Report on the EDVAC* (dated June 30, 1945), von Neumann described the computer switching mechanism: "Every digital computing device contains certain relay like *elements*, with discrete equilibria. Such an element has two or more distinct states in which it can exist indefinitely."[41] Citing the McCulloch and Pitts paper, von Neumann wrote: "It is worth mentioning, that the neurons of the higher animals are definitely elements in the above sense."[42]

By the following year, von Neumann was exploring the connections between living beings and machines using a Greek word for a mechanism that exhibits

[38] Arbib, "Warren McCulloch's Search for the Logic of the Nervous System," 201–202.

[39] Conway and Siegelman, *Dark Hero*, 222–229.

[40] Smalheiser, "Walter Pitts," 223.

[41] John von Neumann, *First Draft of a Report on the EDVAC* (Moore School of Electrical Engineering, 1945), §4.1.

[42] Ibid, §4.2

living characteristics: *automaton*.[43] In a letter to Norbert Wiener, von Neumann wondered aloud how they had ambitiously come to study the human brain, surely the most complex of all natural or artificial automata:

> Our thoughts — I mean yours and Pitts' and mine — were so far mainly focused on the subject of neurology, and more specifically on the human nervous system, and there primarily on the central nervous system. Thus, in trying to understand the function of automata and the general principles govern-ing them, we selected for prompt action the most complicated object under the sun — literally . . . Our thinking — or at any rate mine — on the entire subject of automata would be much more muddled than it is, if these extremely bold efforts — with which I would like to put on one par the very un-neurological thesis of R. [sic] Turing — had not been made.[44]

To von Neumann, an automaton was anything with an input, output, and some kind of processing in the middle. In September 1948, he gave the lead presentation in a "Cerebral Mechanisms in Behavior" symposium at the California Institute of Technology. His talk (entitled "The General and Logical Theory of Automata") contains much comparison of the human brain and 1948-era computers in terms of size, speed, switches, and energy dissipation. He identified the need to develop a new kind of logic, and speculated about something that was to become one of von Neumann's major interests: self-reproducing automata.[45]

Wiener kidded von Neumann about the concept: "I am very much interested in what you have to say about the reproductive potentialities of the future. . . . It may be an opportunity for a new Kinsey report."[46] To von Neumann, self-reproducing automata were no laughing matter. He wondered whether there was some kind of unknown law that prohibited a machine from building a replica of itself. Even living things don't reproduce in this way (although DNA itself does) so the question presents some interesting ontological issues as well.

Increased research into the theory of automata and Turing Machines made possible the seminal book *Automata Studies* edited by founder of communications

---

[43] William Aspray, "The Scientific Conceptualization of Information: A Survey," *Annals of the History of Computing*, Vol. 7, No. 2 (April, 1985), 133.

[44] Letter of November 29, 1946, from Miklós Rédei, ed., *John von Neumann: Selected Letters* (American Mathematical Society, 2005), 278.

[45] John von Neumann, "The General and Logical Theory of Automata" in Lloyd A. Jeffress, *Cerebral Mechanisms in Behavior: The Hixon Symposium* (John Wiley & Sons, 1951), 1–41.

[46] Letter of August 10, 1949, quoted in Steve J. Heims, *John von Neumann and Norbert Wiener: From Mathematics to the Technologies of Life and Death* (MIT Press, 1980), 212.

theory Claude Elwood Shannon and artificial-intelligence pioneer and inventor of the Lisp programming language John McCarthy, and published by Princeton University Press in 1956. The book includes papers on automata by John von Neumann, Stephen Kleene, and artificial-intelligence pioneer Marvin Minsky (b. 1927), and some of the first papers on Turing Machines by Claude E. Shannon and Martin Davis.

As the Cold War of the early 1950s heated up, Norbert Wiener and John von Neumann found themselves at opposing political poles. Wiener was appalled by the use of nuclear weapons against the Japanese cities of Hiroshima and Nagasaki in the Second World War. He stopped taking government money for research and his writings increasingly focused on social concerns prompted by the rising use of technology in both war and peace. In contrast, the Cold War sparked John von Neumann's anti-communist tendencies and he became a strong advocate of nuclear weapons. In 1955, von Neumann discovered he had bone cancer. He was hospitalized in 1956 and died the following year at the age of 53. It's possible that the cancer was caused by exposure to radiation while witnessing atomic bomb tests.[47]

John von Neumann left behind an unfinished series of lectures that were published in 1958 as the book *The Computer and the Brain*. Ultimately unsatisfying, the book contains many tantalizing hints of what the completed version might have offered. A long unfinished manuscript on automata was edited and completed by Arthur W. Burks (1915–2008) and published in 1966 under the title *Theory of Self-Reproducing Automata*.

Early in his investigations into self-reproducing automata, von Neumann imagined a machine that might live in a big soup with spare parts floating around, and explored how the machine might assemble its duplicate from these parts. These types of automata became known as *kinematic* automata, and might be similar to what we commonly regard as robots.

In discussions with his friend Stanislaw Ulam (who was doing research into crystal growth), von Neumann decided to investigate instead a much simpler model called *cellular* automata.

Cellular automata are mathematical constructs that resemble a structure of cells. Cellular automata can potentially exist in various dimensions, but most studies have been restricted to a two-dimensional grid. Each cell in the grid is affected by its neighbors as if the cells are linked in a simple network. Through successive "moves" or "generations," cells change state according to certain rules. Simple rules for cellular automata can often lead to complex behavior. John von Neumann worked with cells that have 29 states, and proved that these can be implemented to form a Universal Turing Machine.[48]

[47] Heims, *John von Neumann and Norbert Wiener*, 369–371.

[48] William Aspray, *John von Neumann and the Origins of Modern Computing* (MIT Press, 1990), 203–204.

Cellular automata burst from their academic confines in 1970 when British mathematician John Horton Conway (b. 1937) designed a simple type of cellular automata that he called the Game of Life (not to be confused with the board game of the same name). The Game of Life automata have simple rules: In a two-dimensional grid resembling graph paper, a cell is either alive (filled) or dead (not filled). In each successive generation a cell potentially changes its state based on its eight immediate neighbors: If a live cell is surrounded by two or three live cells, it remains alive. If surrounded by only zero or one live cell, it dies of loneliness; surrounded by four or more live cells, it dies of overcrowding. A dead cell surrounded by exactly three live cells becomes alive as a result of an obscure form of reproduction.

Several of Martin Gardner's "Mathematical Games" columns in *Scientific American* popularized Conway's Game of Life,[49] and by 1974, *Time* magazine complained that "millions of dollars in valuable computer time may have already been wasted by the game's growing horde of fanatics."[50] Of course, in 1974 these were not *personal* computers, but corporate mainframes. Today the Game of Life is mostly played on personal computers, about which *Time* magazine would presumably be less frantic.

Despite the simple rules, Game of Life automata exhibit some very complex patterns. It is possible to create patterns that continuously spawn offspring, for example. Although it hardly seems possible, Turing Machines can be constructed from these cellular automata. The Game of Life is Turing complete.[51]

Also interested in cellular automata was German engineer Konrad Zuse (whose last name is pronounced "tsoo-za"). Zuse was born just two years and one day earlier than Alan Turing, and while Turing was writing his paper on computable numbers, Zuse was building a computer in his parent's apartment in Berlin.

In 1969, Zuse published a short, 74-page book entitled *Rechnender Raum* (translated as *Calculating Space*) that pioneered the field of "digital physics" — the interpretation of the workings and laws of the universe within a framework of computability.

Historically, the laws of physics had been assumed to be continuous. Quantities of distance, velocity, mass, and energy seem best described with real numbers and manipulated through differential equations. Some aspects of quantum theory instead suggest that the underlying structure of the universe might be discrete and digital in nature, and the continuous nature of the real world might be

---

[49] These columns on the Game of Life were later collected in Martin Gardner, *Wheels, Life, and Other Mathematical Amusements* (W. H. Freeman, 1983).

[50] Issue of January 21, 1974, quoted in William Poundstone, *The Recursive Universe: Cosmic Complexity and the Limits of Scientific Knowledge* (William Morrow, 1985), 24.

[51] Paul Rendell, "A Turing Machine in Conway's Game of Life," March 8, 2001, http://www.cs.ualberta.ca/~bulitko/F02/papers/tm_words.pdf. See also http://rendell-attic.org/gol/tm.htm.

only an illusion. "*Is nature digital, analog or hybrid?*" Zuse asked. "And is there essentially any justification in asking such a question?"[52] To explore physical laws in a digital manner, Zuse created "digital particles" that he manipulated with the rules of cellular automata. *Rechnender Raum* is a very tentative exploration into the potential of digital physics to model the universe, but it is nonetheless an ambitious step.

At first glance, it's hard to conceive of the universe as a massive computer. If we ignore the relatively insignificant life forms inhabiting at least one celestial object in the universe, there doesn't seem to be a lot of computational activity involved. Isn't the universe really just a lot of rocks flying around?

It might help to view the broader temporal picture. The current cosmological model indicates that the universe arose from the Big Bang 13.7 billion years ago, the Earth formed about 4.5 billion years ago, life on Earth first appeared about 3.7 billion years ago, early primates perhaps about 10 million years ago, and modern humans about 200,000 years ago. Certainly something's been happening that has resulted in increased complexity. Immediately following the Big Bang, the universe was completely uniform — the epitome of simplicity — and then more complex particles and eventually atoms and molecules began developing. This progression from the simple to the complex — presumably based on the relatively simple laws of the universe — is very reminiscent of cellular automata.

Computational models of the universe often owe as much to the communication theory of Claude Elwood Shannon and Norbert Wiener as they do to Turing. The use of the concept of entropy to measure information has forged a tight bond between communications and thermodynamics that has been the subject of several entertaining popular books over the past few years.[53] Maxwell's Demon, for example — that imaginary imp invented by James Clerk Maxwell (1831–1879) who can operate a door to separate gases into fast-moving molecules and slow-moving molecules and hence reduce entropy — turns out to be impossible because the demon is extracting *information* from the system.

American physicist John Archibald Wheeler (1911–2008) linked the existence of the universe to the human observation of it. We ask yes-no questions in these observations and receive information in answer. Wheeler's three-word description of this process is the indelibly catchy phrase "It from bit":

---

[52] Konrad Zuse, *Calculating Space*, translation of *Rechnender Raum* (MIT Technical Translation, 1970), 22 (page 16 in the German publication).

[53] Tom Siegried, *The Bit and the Pendulum: From Quantum Computing to M Theory — The New Physics of Information* (John Wiley & Sons, 2000). Hans Christian von Baeyer, *Information: The New Language of Science* (Harvard University Press, 2003). Charles Seife, *Decoding the Universe: How the New Science of Information is Explaining Everything in the Cosmos from Our Brains to Black Holes* (Viking, 2006).

It from bit symbolizes the idea that every item of the physical world has at bottom — at a very deep bottom, in most
instances — an immaterial source and explanation; that what
we call reality arises in the last analysis from the posing of yes-no
questions and the registering of equipment-evoked responses; in
short, that all things physical are information-theoretic in origin
and this is a **participatory universe**.[54]

While proposing a universe fabricated from information, Wheeler rejected the
concept of the universe as any type of machine because it "has to postulate
explicitly or implicitly, a supermachine, a scheme, a device, a miracle, which will
turn out universes in infinite variety and infinite number."[55]

Quite a different conception is that of David Deutsch (b. 1953), one of the
pioneers of quantum computing. Deutsch is a strong advocate of the "many worlds"
interpretation of quantum physics originated by American physicist Hugh Everett
(1930–1982). What we perceive as the paradoxes of the particle and wave duality
of quantum physics is actually interference from multiple worlds that branch off
with quantum events. The universe that we know is only one possible universe in
a complete *multiverse*.

In his 1997 book *The Fabric of Reality*, Deutsch sets out to explain the nature of
the universe through interweaving four strands:

- Epistemology as characterized by the Vienna-born philosopher of science
  Karl Popper (1902–1994);
- Quantum physics in the framework of the many-worlds interpretation of
  Hugh Everett;
- Evolution as described by English naturalist Charles Darwin (1909–1982)
  and British evolutionary biologist Richard Dawkins (b. 1941); and
- Computation as pioneered by Alan Turing.

Within a discussion about virtual reality generators, Deutsch develops what
he calls the *Turing principle*. At first, the Turing principle seems to be about
mechanisms performing computations: "*There exists an abstract universal computer
whose repertoire includes any computation that any physically possible object can
perform.*" Deutsch is actually identifying this computer as simulating every type
of physical process. He soon shows that these computations are equivalent
to generating a virtual-reality universe. Gradually the Turing principle evolves

[54]John Archibald Wheeler, "Information, Physics, Quantum: The Search for Links" (1989) in Anthony
J.G. Hey, ed., *Feynman and Computation: Exploring the Limits of Computers* (Perseus Books, 1999), 311.
[55]Ibid, 314 but here Wheeler quoted another paper he wrote from 1988.

to a much stronger version: "*It is possible to build a virtual-reality generator whose repertoire includes every physically possible environment,*"[56] which would certainly include the universe in which we live.

Self-described "quantum mechanic" and MIT professor of mechanical engineering Seth Lloyd (b. 1960) prefers to interpret quantum physics in terms of "weirdness" rather than multiple worlds, but he describes the universe and its parts in terms of computation and information — "*The Big Bang was also a Bit Bang.*" Lloyd rejects the idea of modeling the universe on a Turing Machine, however. "The universe is fundamentally quantum-mechanical, and conventional digital computers have a hard time simulating quantum-mechanical systems."[57] This is one reason why he finds the quantum computer more appropriate to the task.

> The universe is a physical system. Thus, it could be simulated efficiently by a quantum computer — one exactly the same size as the universe itself. Because the universe supports quantum computation and can be efficiently simulated by a quantum computer, the universe is neither more nor less computationally powerful than a universal quantum computer ... We can now give a precise answer to the question of whether the universe is a quantum computer in the technical sense. The answer is Yes. The universe is a quantum computer.[58]

One feature that quantum computers add to the conventional Turing Machine is the ability to generate true random numbers as a result of quantum processes.

Cellular automata have also reemerged as a model for the physical laws of the universe in the work of British physicist, mathematician, and creator of the Mathematica computer program Stephen Wolfram (b. 1959), culminating in the huge, ambitious, and copiously illustrated 2002 book *A New Kind of Science*. Wolfram was inspired in this quest by observing how cellular automata exhibit great complexity based on simple rules. He closely ties his automata to the universality of Turing Machines and describes how they can model physical processes. Wolfram does not introduce quantum mechanics into his system, but suggests he needn't because "it is my strong suspicion that the kinds of programs that I have discussed ... will actually in the end turn out to show many if not all the key features of quantum theory."[59]

---

[56]David Deutsch, *The Fabric of Reality* (Penguin Books, 1997), 132–135.

[57]Seth Lloyd, *Programming the Universe: A Quantum Computer Scientist Takes on the Cosmos* (Alfred A. Knopf, 2006), 46, 53.

[58]Ibid, 54–55.

[59]Stephen Wolfram, *A New Kind of Science* (Wolfram Media, 2002), 538.

In *A New Kind of Science*, Wolfram finds computational universality in so many manifestations that he defines a Principle of Computational Equivalence that

> introduces a new law of nature to the effect that no system can ever carry out explicit computations that are more sophisticated than those carried out by systems like cellular automata and Turing machines ... So what about computations that we perform abstractly with computers or in our brains? Can these perhaps be more sophisticated? Presumably they cannot, at least if we want actual results, and not just generalities. For if a computation is to be carried out explicitly, then it must ultimately be implemented as a physical process, and must therefore be subject to the same limitations as any such process.[60]

Once we become convinced that the universe is displaying no uncomputable characteristics (whether of conventional digital computers or quantum computers), then nothing that is part of the universe can be an exception to the rule. Life, for example, is part of a computable universe, as well as one of the most mysterious manifestations of life that we know — the human mind.

For centuries, philosophers, biologists, psychologists, and just plain folk have struggled with the nature of the human mind. While we often freely acknowledge that most of our bodily functions are mechanistic results of physical and chemical processes in our various organs, we're not quite ready to attribute the workings of the mind to similar mechanisms. The mind, we feel, is something special. Certainly the brain has *something* to do with the mind, but surely, we plead, it can't account for *everything* that goes on inside.

In Western culture, this belief is known as "mind/body dualism" and is most commonly associated with René Descartes (1596–1650) and particularly his *Meditationes de Prima Philosophia* of 1641. Descartes believed that most of our human bodies (and entire so-called lower animals) were basically machines, but that the mind operated quite differently.

In the 1940s, dualism began taking a beating. To neuroscientist and computer scientist Michael A. Arbib, McCulloch and Pitts had resolved the question in their 1943 paper on the neuron. The brain had a suitable structure for performing computation; hence McCulloch and Pitts "had shown that 'anything finite enough' that could be logically conceived could be done by a neural network. They had killed dualism."[61]

Several years later, philosopher Gilbert Ryle (1900–1976) took a swing at dualism in his book *The Concept of Mind* (1949), building a strong case without referring

---

[60] Ibid, 720, 721.
[61] Arbib, "Warren McCulloch's Search for the Logic of the Nervous System," 213.

to the McCulloch and Pitts paper. These days, dualism is certainly in eclipse. Most people who research the mind (either philosophically or neurobiologistically) do so from the perspective that the mind is solely a manifestation of the physical workings of the human body, in particular the nervous system and brain.

Perhaps not surprising, this rejection of dualism has coincided with an increased understanding of computation and algorithms. The Turing Machine was conceived as a model of a human computer performing a precisely defined algorithmic task, so this connection between machine and mind has existed from the very beginnings of automated computation. Perhaps not surprising as well is that one of the first people to explore the notion of artificial intelligence was Alan Turing himself, most famously in his 1950 *Mind* article "Computing Machinery and Intelligence," in which he invented what's now called the Turing Test.

Once dualism is abandoned, the mind must be viewed as a natural manifestation of the physical brain (along with the rest of the body) and not as a supernatural "something else." Despite our emotional reluctance, it becomes hard to avoid these conclusions: First, that the mind is basically a Turing Machine with both the capabilities and limitations of Turing Machines; and secondly, that it is theoretically possible to build an artificial mind.

As American philosopher Daniel Dennett (b. 1942) put it, "Alan Turing had the basic move that we could replace Kant's question of how it was possible for there to be thought, with an engineering question — let's think how can we make a thought come into existence."[62]

What seems to bother us most about the Turing Test — and indeed, any suggestion that the brain is a computer — is the nagging first-person voice inside our heads that we call "consciousness." Consciousness gives strength to our feelings of subjective autonomy and our belief in free will.

Consciousness is nonetheless elusive and slippery. Most of us would probably claim to have the interior monologue of consciousness going on continuously during our entire waking days, but by its very nature consciousness becomes invisible when it's not working. Most of us interact with other people under the assumption that they have similar consciousnesses as our own, and yet we can't be sure that they do, and we'd be at a loss to convince others of the existence of our own consciousness.

Determining how our brains manufacture self-awareness is what Australian philosopher David Chalmers (b. 1966) calls the "hard problem" of consciousness as opposed to the comparatively easy problems of how the brain interacts with our organs of sensory input and output.

The Turing Test — which challenges machines to fool humans into thinking they're smart — implicitly takes a behaviorist stance that it is unnecessary to know

---

[62]Daniel Dennett, interview in Susan Blackmore, *Conversations on Consciousness: What the Best Minds Think About the Brain, Free Will, and What it Means to be Human* (Oxford University Press, 2006), 81.

what's going on inside someone (or something) else's central processing unit to classify an entity as "intelligent." We're treating whatever we're conversing with as a "black box." This is how we ultimately interact with other human beings, because we can't prove that anyone else has consciousness. Yet even if we can't differentiate a machine from a human being, we seem to want very much to differentiate between the machine and ourselves.

Everything we think we know about computers tells us that they're really only following a set of rules. They don't know what they're doing the same way we humans do. This is the issue raised by the famous thought experiment of American philosophy professor John Searle (b. 1932) called the "Chinese room." A person who knows no Chinese nonetheless has a book that lets him respond to questions in Chinese with reasonable answers. This person might pass a Turing Test in Chinese with absolutely no understanding of the questions or answers.[63]

The big problem is that computers deal only with syntax, while people can handle semantics as well. To Searle, this means that a digital computer — no matter how sophisticated it becomes — will never understand what it's doing in the same way that a human can.

English mathematical physicist Roger Penrose (b. 1931) is also certain that the mind is more than just a computational organ. In his books *The Emperor's New Mind* (1989) and *Shadows of the Mind* (1994), Penrose asserts that consciousness is beyond computation, and speculates that some kind of quantum process in the brain performs non-algorithmic chores that transcend the capabilities of the Turing Machine.

Penrose finds Gödel's Incompleteness Theorem to be a particularly revealing problem. We as human beings understand the truth of the unprovable statement that Gödel derives, yet no computation can show that truth because it doesn't derive from the axioms. This is not a new observation: In their 1958 book *Gödel's Proof* (New York University Press), Ernest Nagel and James R. Newman found in Gödel's theorem a similar rejection of machine intelligence, as did philosopher John Randolph Lucas (b. 1929) in his famous 1961 essay on "Minds, Machines and Gödel."[64] These seem to be arguments that while machines can easily perform axiomatic mathematics, they can't perform metamathematics that require an understanding outside the axioms.

Daniel Dennett — who perhaps more than anyone else has combined a philosopher's thoughtfulness with a scientist's empiricism to fashion a portrait of the mind in fascinating books such as *Consciousness Explained* (1991) — thinks differently. Dennett has assimilated the concepts of computability and combined them with a

---

[63] John R. Searle, "Minds, Brains, and Programs," from *The Behavioral and Brain Sciences, Vol. 3* (Cambridge University Press, 1980). Republished in Douglas R. Hofstandter and Daniel Dennett, eds., *The Mind's I: Fantasies and Reflections on Self and Soul* (Basic, Books, 1981), 353–373.

[64] J. R. Lucas, "Minds, Machines and Gödel," *Philosophy*, Vol. 36, No. 137 (Apr.–Jul. 1961), 112–127.

solid understanding of evolution and a vast knowledge of modern neurobiological research. His vision of the brain and mind seem an unlikely medium for a Turing Machine: The brain is part of a nervous system that is itself part of a body; there can be no separation. Get a little excited about a train of thought, and the heart may pump a little faster to deliver more oxygen to the brain. Various drugs affect the brain in a variety of ways. The brain receives a barrage of stimuli from the eyes, ears, and other organs, and constantly interacts through the body with the real world.

The brain is not a linear processing system. It is a massively parallel decentralized system without even an area where it all "comes together" in one central "Cartesian theater" (as Dennett derisively calls the concept). Dennett suggests instead a "multiple drafts" model of the mind in which bits and pieces of sensory input, visual data, and words remain unfinished, sketchy, and incomplete. If the brain is a computer, it's not like a computer any rational engineer would design! It is truly a mess in there.

Moreover, what we think of as consciousness is a more serial activity riding on top of this parallel structure. Dennett posits,

> the hypothesis that human consciousness (1) is too recent an innovation to be hard-wired into the innate machinery, (2) is largely a product of cultural evolution that gets imparted to brains in early training, and (3) its successful installation is determined by myriad microsettings in the plasticity of the brain, which means that its functionally important features are very likely to be invisible to neuroanatomical scrutiny in spite of the extreme salience of the effects.[65]

Consciousness is, in some sense at least, "talking" to oneself, and that requires the cultural construct of language.

Certainly there would be little point in designing a computer to mimic the human mind. It would need to have a heavy amount of fancy input, and wouldn't even work satisfactorily without years of education and experience. Nonetheless, is it theoretically possible to construct a computer that can pass an unrestricted Turing Test (which Dennett believes to be a very difficult and just test) and would such a computer have consciousness? Dennett believes the answer to both questions is Yes.

Regardless of which mechanistic view of the brain you prefer, another chilling implication is that the machinery determines our decisions rather than the other way around. What's happened to free will?

The disappearance of free will in a mechanistic universe was really implied long ago by the discovery that strict deterministic laws govern the movement

---

[65]Daniel Dennett, *Consciousness Explained* (Back Bay Books, 1991), 219.

of every particle. Early in his book *Essai Philosophique sur les Probabilités* (1814) Pierre-Simon, Marquis de Laplace (1749–1827) wrote,

> Given for one instant an intelligence which could comprehend
> all the forces by which nature is animated and the respective
> situation of the beings who compose it — an intelligence suffi-
> ciently vast to submit these data to analysis — it would embrace
> in the same formula the movements of the greatest bodies of the
> universe and those of the lightest atom; for it, nothing would
> be uncertain and the future, as the past, would be present to its
> eyes.[66]

This concept is sometimes known as Laplace's Demon. It's hard to avoid the implication that the motion of every atom in the universe — including those atoms that make up the cells in our brains — became fixed at the time of the Big Bang, and these atoms have been bouncing around in the predetermined pattern ever since.

Of course, Laplace's Demon can't really exist. To store all the information required to track every particle in the universe would require a computer larger than the universe itself. The Heisenberg Uncertainty Principle tells us that we can't know both the location and momentum of elementary particles. Mathematically anticipating the outcome of these atomic collisions is classically known as the "many-body problem," and even the three-body problem is enough for major algorithmic headaches.

If the universe is truly a Turing Machine, and even if we could know the current "complete configuration" and could have a table of all the configurations that govern the machine, we could not predict where this universe is going without actually "running" the "program."

Undecidability is essentially free will. Seth Lloyd notes that the halting problem,

> foils not only conventional digital computers but any system
> capable of performing digital logic. Since colliding atoms intrin-
> sically perform digital logic, their long-term future is uncomput-
> able . . . The inscrutable nature of our choices when we exercise
> free will is a close analog of the halting problem: once we set a
> train of thought in motion, we do not know whether it will lead
> anywhere at all. Even it if does lead somewhere, we don't know
> where that somewhere is until we get there.[67]

---

[66]Pierre Simon, Marquis de Laplace, *A Philosophical Essay on Probabilities*, translated by Frederick Wilson Truscott and Frederick Lincoln Emory (John Wiley & Sons, 1902; Dover, 1995).
[67]Lloyd, *Programming the Universe*, 98, 36.

David Deutsch mulls over the possibilities that the brain is a "classical" non-quantum computer or a quantum one:

> It is often suggested that the brain may be a quantum computer, and that its intuitions, consciousness and problem-solving abilities might depend on quantum computations. This *could* be so, but I know of no evidence and no convincing argument that it is so. My bet is that the brain, considered as a computer, is a classical one.[68]

He then acknowledges that "the Turing explanation of computation seems to leave no room, even in principle, for any future explanation *in physical terms* of mental attributes such as consciousness and free will." Keep in mind, however, that in the many-worlds interpretation of quantum physics, worlds constantly split off, so that in this world you may choose to do one thing, while in another world, you're really choosing another. If that isn't free will, then what is? Deutsch concludes, "Turing's conception of computation seems less disconnected from human values, and is no obstacle to the understanding of human attributes like free will, provided it is understood in a multiverse context."[69]

When Stephen Wolfram began studying the complex structures that arise from cellular automata, he tried to find ways to predict the outcomes and perhaps make shortcuts through the generations. He could not, for "there can be no way to predict how the system will behave except by going through almost as many steps of computation as the evolution of the system itself... For many systems no systematic prediction can be done, so that there is no general way to shortcut their process of evolution ..." The inability to make predictions in effect gives freedom to the system to exercise free will, and Wolfram even provides a diagram of a "cellular automaton whose behavior seems to show an analog of free will."[70]

It's a consolation. Even if the universe and the human brain have as their foundations the simple rules and complex structure of a cellular automaton or a Turing Machine, we can't predict the future based simply on those rules. The future doesn't exist until the program runs the code.

Or, as Dr. Emmett Brown says to Marty McFly and Jennifer Parker at the conclusion of the "Back to the Future" trilogy[71], "It means your future hasn't been written yet. No one's has. Your future is whatever you make it. So make it a good one, both of you."

---

[68]Deutsch, *The Fabric of Reality*, 238.

[69]Ibid, 336, 339.

[70]Wolfram, *A New Kind of Science*, 739, 741, 750.

[71]Screenplay by Bob Gale, based on the story and characters by Gale and Robert Zemeckis.

18 The Long Sleep of Diophantus

Long after Alan Turing and Alonzo Church had proved that there can be no general decision procedure for first-order logic, the very first decision problem was still unresolved. This was the famous Tenth Problem listed by David Hilbert in his address to the International Congress of Mathematicians in 1900 as one of the challenges facing mathematicians of the twentieth century:

> 10. Determination of the Solvability of a Diophantine Equation
>
> Given a diophantine equation with any number of unknown quantities and with rational integral numerical coefficients: *To devise a process according to which it can be determined by a finite number of operations whether the equation is solvable in rational integers.*[1]

The algebra problems created by third-century Alexandrian mathematician Diophantus in his *Arithmetica* can always be expressed as polynomials with integer coefficients and multiple variables. Hilbert's Tenth Problem asked for a general process to show if a particular Diophantine equation has a solution in whole numbers.

Of course, after Gödel's Incompleteness Theorem and the undecidability results of Church and Turing, few mathematicians expected anyone to fulfill Hilbert's wish and actually "devise a process" to determine the solvability of Diophantine equations. Pretty much everyone expected a negative result — a proof that such a general process was impossible.

Many mathematicians were fascinated by the Tenth Problem, and at least one devoted almost her entire professional career to pursuing this elusive negative proof. This was Julia Robinson.

One of Julia Robinson's earliest memories was of arranging pebbles near a giant saguaro cactus near her home in Arizona.

[1]Ben H. Yandell, *The Honors Class: Hilbert's Problems and Their Solvers* (A. K. Peters, 2002), 406.

> I think that I have always had a basic liking for the natural num-
> bers. To me they are the one real thing. We can conceive of a
> chemistry that is different from ours, or a biology, but we cannot
> conceive of a different mathematics of numbers. What is proved
> about numbers will be a fact in any universe.[2]

Julia Robinson was born Julia Bowman in St. Louis in 1919. Her sister Constance
was two years older. When Julia was about 2, their mother died, and they were
sent to live with their grandmother near Phoenix. They were later joined by their
father with his new wife, and they moved to Point Loma on San Diego Bay.

When Julia was 9 years old, she came down with scarlet fever, and then
rheumatic fever, and eventually missed more than two years of school. To help her
catch up, her parents hired a tutor who brought Julia through the fifth through
eighth grades in one year.

> One day she told me that you could never carry the square root
> of 2 to a point where the decimal began to repeat. She knew
> that this fact had been proved, although she did not know how.
> I didn't see how anyone could prove such a thing and I went
> home and utilized my newly acquired skills at extracting square
> roots to check it but finally, late in the afternoon, gave up.[3]

Julia entered San Diego High School in 1933, the same year that mathematicians
began fleeing Göttingen and other German universities. Her childhood illnesses
had left her shy, quiet, and awkward, but also able to work alone with great
determination and patience.

As she progressed through the grades, eventually she became the only girl in her
class taking courses in mathematics and physics, and found herself getting the best
grades in those subjects as well. Her high school graduation present was a slide
rule, and in the fall of 1936, not yet 17 years old, she began attending San Diego
State College (now called San Diego State University) majoring in mathematics.
The tuition was $12 a semester and Julia expected she'd be a teacher. "At the time
I had no idea that such a thing as a mathematician (as opposed to a math teacher)
existed."[4]

---

[2]Constance Reid, *Julia: A Life in Mathematics* (Mathematical Association of America, 1996), 3. This
quotation is from the part of the book entitled "The Autobiography of Julia Robinson," which was
actually written by Constance Reid based on interviews with her sister. The Autobiography was
previously published in the book Constance Reid, *More Mathematical People* (Academic Press, 1990),
262–280.

[3]Constance Reid, *Julia: A Life in Mathematics*, 9.

[4]Ibid, 21.

In 1937, Simon & Schuster published the now-famous book *Men of Mathematics* by mathematician Edward Temple Bell (1883–1960). Reading it, Julia got her first insights into who mathematicians are and what they actually do. Despite its rather fanciful interpretations of history and personalities, *Men of Mathematics* was a real inspiration to Julia, as it has been for many budding mathematicians in the decades since.

In 1939, Julia left San Diego State College for the University of California at Berkeley, which at the time was building an impressive mathematics faculty. During her first year, her teacher in a class in number theory was Raphael M. Robinson, just about eight years older than Julia. "In the second semester there were only four students — I was again the only girl — and Raphael began to ask me to go on walks with him.... On one of our early walks, he introduced me to Gödel's results."[5]

Perhaps they spoke of other theorems as well, for Raphael Robinson and Julia Bowman were married in 1941. Due to a nepotism rule, Julia could not teach in the mathematics department at Berkeley, although she already had a job as a teaching assistant in the statistics department. (When she applied for that job, the personnel department asked what she did each day. She wrote, "Monday — tried to prove theorem, Tuesday — tried to prove theorem. Wednesday — tried to prove theorem, Thursday — tried to prove theorem, Friday — theorem false."[6])

Although Raphael and Julia Robinson wanted to raise a family, Julia's childhood illnesses had seriously weakened her heart. She had one miscarriage and their doctor strongly advised against her continuing to try to have children.[7]

In the academic year 1946–1947, Raphael was a visiting professor at Princeton University. He and Julia attended classes given by Alonzo Church, and heard Kurt Gödel lecture on the foundations of mathematics during the Princeton bicentennial.

Back in Berkeley, Julia Robinson studied under famed Polish-born logician Alfred Tarski (1902–1983), and received her Ph.D. in 1948. Even at that time her dissertation revealed "that her main field of interest lay on the borderline between logic and number theory."[8]

In 1948, Tarski got her working on a question peripherally connected to the problem that would dominate her life as a professional mathematician: Hilbert's Tenth Problem.

---

[5]Ibid, 31, 35.
[6]Ibid, 33.
[7]Ibid, 43.
[8]Constance Reid with Raphael M. Robinson, "Julia Bowman Robinson (1919–1985)," in *A Century of Mathematics in America*, Part III (American Mathematical Society, 1989), 410.

Like most mathematicians, Julia Robinson had no illusions that the Tenth Problem could have a solution that would have made Hilbert happy. As her first paper on Diophantine Equations[9] explained,

> Since there are many classical diophantine equations with one parameter for which no effective method is known to determine the solvability for an arbitrary value of the parameter, it is very unlikely that a decision procedure can be found. For example, no way is known to determine the values for which the diophantine system,
>
> $$x^2 + ay^2 = s^2, \qquad x^2 - ay^2 = t^2,$$
>
> is solvable. (This problem was first studied by the Arabs in the Middle Ages.)

Some mathematicians trying to get a handle on Diophantine equations approached the problem obliquely rather than head on. They defined a *Diophantine set* as the set of all solutions to a particular Diophantine equation. For example, the set of all even numbers is actually the set of whole number values x that are solutions to the following Diophantine equation:

$$x - 2y = 0$$

This equation has two variables, but the set is constructed from just the x values; if x and y are whole number solutions, then x is always even.

It's also possible to define a *Diophantine relation* among multiple variables. For example, suppose you want to express the relation x is less than y. The values x and y that satisfy this condition are solutions to the following Diophantine equation:

$$x - y + z + 1 = 0$$

Julia Robinson's paper didn't prove that certain sets and relations were Diophantine, but instead that certain sets and relations could be defined in terms of exponentiation — that is, x^y, where both x and y are variables.

The introduction of exponentiation into a discussion of Diophantine equations at first seems irrelevant. Exponentiation isn't allowed in Diophantine equations. A Diophantine equation can contain variables raised to whole number powers, but not a variable raised to a variable power.

Nevertheless, the paper showed that exponentiation was an important relationship because binomial coefficients, the factorial function, and the set of primes

---

[9] Julia Robinson, "Existential Definability in Arithmetic," *Transactions of the American Mathematical Society*, Vol. 72 (1952), 437–449. Also published in Julia Robinson, *The Collected Works of Julia Robinson*, ed Solomon Feferman (American Mathematical Society, 1996), 47–59.

could all be defined in terms of exponentiation. Was it possible that exponentiation was truly Diophantine because it could be defined as a Diophantine relation? That was not clear, but Julia Robinson's paper also proved that exponentiation could be defined in terms of any Diophantine relation that exhibited roughly exponential growth. No such Diophantine relation was known, but it seemed to her "very likely"[10] that one existed.

Strictly speaking, Fermat's Last Theorem (also known as Fermat's Great Theorem) is *not* a Diophantine equation:

$$x^n + y^n = z^n$$

Fermat's Theorem states that the equation is not solvable in whole numbers for any *n* greater than 2, which means that *n* is being treated as a variable. Replace *n* with any whole number greater than 2 and only then does it become a Diophantine equation. If exponentiation turned out to be a Diophantine relation, then Fermat's equation could actually be expressed as a normal Diophantine equation — albeit one *much* more complex than its common form.

Julia Robinson's paper was presented in 1950 to the International Congress of Mathematicians, held that year at Harvard. It was here that Julia Robinson first met Martin Davis.

Martin Davis had been bitten by the Tenth Problem bug while an undergraduate at City College in New York. Among the faculty in the mathematics department at CCNY was Emil Post, who had written that the Tenth Problem just "begs for an unsolvability proof."[11]

While a graduate student at Princeton, Davis found that he "couldn't stop myself from thinking about Hilbert's Tenth Problem. I thought it unlikely that I would get anywhere on such a difficult problem and tried without success to discipline myself to stay away from it," although his Ph.D. thesis did touch on the topic.

Martin Davis had just received his Ph.D. when he attended the International Congress, and Julia Robinson remembers Davis's reaction to her paper as rather mystified: "I remember that he said he didn't see how my work could help to solve Hilbert's problem, since it was just a series of examples. I said, well, I did what I could."[12] Davis later confessed: "It's been said that I told her that I doubted that her approach would get very far, surely one of the more foolish statements I've made in my life."[13]

Julia and her older sister Constance hadn't been close while growing up, but in 1950, Constance married Neil Dan Reid, a law student at the University of San Francisco. Now living nearby each other, the two sisters soon became friends. With

---

[10] Robinson, "Existential Definability in Arithmetic," 438.

[11] Martin Davis, Foreword to Yuri V. Matiyasevich, *Hilbert's Tenth Problem* (MIT Press, 1993), xiii.

[12] Reid, *Julia: A Life in Mathematics*, 61.

[13] Davis, Foreword to *Hilbert's Tenth Problem*, xiv.

encouragement from the Robinsons, Constance Reid wrote her first book *From Zero to Infinity* (Crowell, 1955). Following a pilgrimage by the sisters to Göttingen, Constance Reid wrote a biography of David Hilbert (1970) that I greatly relied on in Chapter 3 of this book. Constance Reid's later biographical subjects were Richard Courant (1976), Jerzy Neyman (1982), E. T. Bell (1993), as well as the tribute to her sister, *Julia: A Life in Mathematics* (1996).

In the summers of 1958, 1959, and 1960, Martin Davis had the opportunity to work with Hilary Putnam (b. 1926), known more as a philosopher than a mathematician, but skilled in both fields. In the summer of 1959, they began combining their work with Julia Robinson's methods. Eventually Davis and Putnam sent Julia Robinson a paper they had drafted. She improved some parts and all three collaborated on a new paper, "The Decision Problem for Exponential Diophantine Equations" published in 1961.[14]

As the title says, this paper was about *exponential* Diophantine equations, which are a variation of Diophantine equations where exponentiation is allowed in several forms: exponentiation either of one variable to the power of another, or a constant to a variable power, or a variable to a constant power (as in normal Diophantine equations). The second sentence of the Davis-Putnam-Robinson paper states the result of the proof that "there is no general algorithm for deciding whether or not an exponential Diophantine equation has a solution in positive integers."

A negative solution to Hilbert's Tenth Problem was now missing one crucial piece, which Davis referred to as "Julia Robinson's hypothesis."[15] This was the existence of a Diophantine relation of roughly exponential growth, which would then imply that exponentiation itself is a Diophantine relation, which would mean that exponential Diophantine equations can be expressed as normal Diophantine equations.

Throughout the 1960s, Julia Robinson was a lecturer in mathematics (and for one semester, philosophy) at Berkeley, occasionally working on and publishing on Hilbert's Tenth Problem. For a 1969 book *Studies in Number Theory*, she wrote a 40-page chapter that summed up the progress to that point, leaving open the one major question:

> Is the relation $r = s^t$ diophantine? If so, then every exponential diophantine equation could be replaced by an equivalent diophantine equation in more variables. Also, every recursively enumerable relation would be diophantine and hence Hilbert's

---

[14] Martin Davis, Hilary Putnam, and Julia Robinson, "The Decision Problem for Exponential Diophantine Equations," *Annals of Mathematics*, Vol. 74, No. 3 (November 1961), 425–436. Also in *The Collected Works of Julia Robinson*, 77–88.

[15] Davis, Foreword to *Hilbert's Tenth Problem*, xiii.

problem would be unsolvable. At present, we don't know the answer to this question.[16]

During the 1960s, Martin Davis taught at Rensselaer Polytechnic Institute and New York University, and often had occasion to lecture about Hilbert's Tenth Problem. If someone asked his predictions on its solvability or unsolvability, he had a ready answer: Like a prophet from the Hebrew Bible, Davis would pronounce, "I think that Julia Robinson's hypothesis is true, and it will be proved by a clever young Russian."[17]

Yuri Vladimirovich Matiyasevich was born in Leningrad in 1947, and attended high schools dedicated to mathematics and science. He went to Leningrad State University at the age of 17, and spoke at the 1966 International Congress of Mathematicians, held that year in Moscow. He received his Ph.D. in 1970 from the Leningrad Department of the Steklov Institute of Mathematics, known as LOMI.

Matiyasevich had first heard about Hilbert's Tenth Problem in 1965 when he was a sophomore at Leningrad State University. His advisor Sergei Maslov (1939–1981) told him to "Try to prove the algorithmic unsolvability of Diophantine equations. This problem is known as Hilbert's tenth problem, but that does not matter to you." He also recommended a course of action: "Unsolvability is nowadays usually proved by reducing a problem already known to be unsolvable to the problem whose unsolvability one needs to establish." What Maslov could not recommend was any literature on the subject, only that "there are some papers by American mathematicians about Hilbert's tenth problem, but you need not study them. ... So far the Americans have not succeeded, so their approach is most likely inadequate."[18]

After pursuing some unpromising approaches to the Tenth Problem for a few years, Matiyasevich's obsession became rather well known around the Leningrad State University campus. One professor would taunt him, "Have you proved the unsolvability of Hilbert's tenth problem? Not yet? But then you will not be able to graduate from the university!"[19] Matiyasevich finally decided to read the Americans' papers, including the crucial Davis-Putnam-Robinson paper of 1961.

Shortly after New Year's Day in 1970, Matiyasevich found a Diophantine relation involving Fibonacci numbers that satisfied Julia Robinson's hypothesis. He was 22 years old. He gave his first public lecture on the unsolvability of Hilbert's Tenth Problem toward the end of January, and word traveled around the world.

---

[16]Julia Robinson, "Diophantine Decision Problems," in W. J. LeVeque, ed., *Studies in Number Theory* (Mathematical Association of America, 1969), 107. Also in *Collected Works of Julia Robinson*, 176.

[17]Davis, Foreword to *Hilbert's Tenth Problem*, xiii.

[18]Yuri Matiyasevich, "My Collaboration with Julia Robinson," *The Mathematical Intelligencer*, Vol.14, No.4 (1992), 38–45. Reprinted in Reid, *Julia: A Life in Mathematics*, 99–116.

[19]Ibid.

Julia Robinson wrote to him, "If you really are 22, I am especially pleased to think that when I first made the conjecture you were a baby and I just had to wait for you to grow up!"[20]

Julia and Raphael Robinson went to Leningrad in 1971 to meet Yuri Matiyasevich and his wife. In the next several years, they collaborated by mail on a few papers on Diophantine equations.

Martin Davis wrote a popular article on the subject for *Scientific American*[21], and a more technical article[22] that became Appendix 2 when his classic book *Computability and Unsolvability* was republished by Dover Publications in 1982. In May 1974, the American Mathematical Society held a symposium in pure mathematics at Northern Illinois University focusing on the Hilbert problems. Davis, Matiyasevich, and Robinson presented a paper, "Diophantine Equations: Positive Aspects of a Negative Solution,"[23] in which they explored some promising outcomes of the proof.

With her prominent role in the resolution of Hilbert's Tenth Problem, Julia Robinson was now famous. In 1976, she was finally made a full professor at Berkeley and became the first female mathematician elected to the National Academy of Sciences. In 1982, she became the first female president of the American Mathematical Society, and the *Ladies Home Journal* included her in a list of the hundred most outstanding women in America.[24]

In 1983, Julia Robinson was awarded a MacArthur Fellowship (popularly known as the "genius grant") and donated part of the money anonymously to make possible the publication of the *Collected Works* of Kurt Gödel by Oxford University Press — books that are essential to anyone doing research in the field of mathematical logic and computability.

In 1984, Julia Robinson was diagnosed with leukemia, and she died the following year at the age of 65. Her husband Raphael Robinson died in 1995 at the age of 83.

Matiyasevich recently turned 60 years old, and Martin Davis will turn 80 years old in the year this book is published. Both are still very active in mathematics.

In 1993, Yuri Matiyasevich wrote a book entitled *Hilbert's Tenth Problem* that was quickly translated into English and published by MIT Press. Although the

---

[20]Reid, *Julia: A Life in Mathematics*, 73.

[21]Martin Davis and Reuben Hersh, "Hilbert's 10th Problem," *Scientific American*, Vol. 229, No. 5 (Nov. 1973), 84–91.

[22]Martin Davis, "Hilbert's Tenth Problem is Unsolvable," *The American Mathematical Monthly*, Vol. 80, No. 3 (Mar. 1973), 233–269.

[23]Martin Davis, Yuri Matijasevic, and Julia Robinson, "Hilbert's Tenth Problem. Diophantine Equations: Positive Aspects of a Negative Solution," in Felix E. Browder, ed., *Mathematical Developments Arising from Hilbert Problems* (American Mathematical Society, 1976), Vol. 2, 323–378. Also in *Collected Works of Julia Robinson*, 269–324.

[24]Reid, *Julia: A Life in Mathematics*, 81.

proof that Hilbert's Tenth Problem is unsolvable occupies the book's first hundred pages, Matiyasevich reworked the proof to be entirely self-contained and require almost no prior knowledge of the topics involved.

Turing Machines enter the proof in Chapter 5 of *Hilbert's Tenth Problem*. As a child of the computer age, Matiyasevich gives his machines names reminiscent of keywords in modern programming languages, and then illustrates their linkages with program-like statements. He proves that "Turing machines are incapable of deciding whether or not the equations belonging *to one particular family of Diophantine equations* have solutions, to say nothing of *arbitrary Diophantine equations*."[25]

The ancient riddle tells us that Diophantus was a boy for the sixth part of his life, acquired a beard after another twelfth, married after another seventh, bore a son five years later, and then saw his son die after reaching half the measure of his father's years. He then spent the last four years of his life assuaging his grief by writing a book of algebra problems.

Seventeen centuries later, Alan Turing died at very nearly the same age as Diophantus's son. He had built a tool of the imagination that continues to allow us to explore the capabilities and limitations of the human mind, and its logical and mathematical pursuits.

Both Diophantus and Turing left behind mysteries. Like human motivations, some Diophantine equations have solutions, some do not, and for many others, we'll just never know.

---

[25]Matiyasevich, *Hilbert's Tenth Problem*, 93.

Selected Bibliography

Web Resources

Alan Turing website maintained by Andrew Hodges, www.turing.org.uk
The Turing Archive for the History of Computing, www.AlanTuring.net
The Turing Digital Archive, www.turingarchive.org

Books

Ackermann, Wilhelm. *Solvable Cases of the Decision Problem*. North-Holland
Publishing Company, 1962.
Agar, John. *Turing and the Universal Machine: The Making of the Modern Computer*.
Icon Books, 2001.
Arbib, Michael A. *Brains, Machines, and Mathematics*. McGraw-Hill, 1964.
Aspray, William. *John von Neumann and the Origins of Modern Computing*. MIT
Press, 1990.
Beth, Evert W. *The Foundations of Mathematics: A Study in the Philosophy of Science*,
second edition. North-Holland, 1964; Harper & Row, 1966.
Boolos, George S., John P. Burgess, and Richard C. Jeffrey. *Computability and
Logic*, fourth edition. Cambridge University Press, 2002.
Börger, Egon, Erich Grädel, and Yuri Gurevich. *The Classical Decision Problem*.
Springer, 1997, 2001.
Boyer, Carl B. *A History of Mathematics*, second edition revised by Uta C.
Merzbach. John Wiley & Sons, 1989.
Cantor, Georg. *Contributions to the Founding of the Theory of Transfinite Numbers*,
translated and with an introduction by Philip E. B. Jourdain. Open Court,
1915; Dover, 1955.
Carpenter, B. E. and R. W. Doran. *A. M. Turing's ACE Report of 1946 and Other
Papers*. MIT Press, 1986.
Ceruzzi, Paul E. *A History of Modern Computing*, second edition. MIT Press, 2003.
Ceruzzi, Paul E. *Reckoners: The Prehistory of the Digital Computer, from Relays to the
Stored Program Concept, 1935–1945*. Greenwood Press, 1983.

Chaitin, Gregory. *Meta Math! The Quest for Omega*. Vintage Books, 2005.

Chaitin, Gregory. *Thinking about Gödel and Turing: Essays on Complexity, 1970-2007*. World Scientific, 2007.

Church, Alonzo. *The Calculi of Lambda-Conversion*. Princeton University Press, 1941.

Church, Alonzo. *Introduction to Mathematical Logic*. Princeton University Press, 1956.

Clark, Andy and Peter Millican, eds. *Connectionism, Concepts, and Folk Psychology: The Legacy of Alan Turing*, Vol. 2. Clarendon Press, 1996.

Conway, Flo and Jim Siegelman. *Dark Hero of the Information Age: In Search of Norbert Wiener, the Father of Cybernetics*. Basic Books, 2005.

Copeland, B. Jack. *Alan Turing's Automatic Computing Engine*. Oxford University Press, 2005.

Copeland, B. Jack. *The Essential Turing*. Oxford University Press, 2004.

Dauben, Joseph Warren. *Georg Cantor: His Mathematics and Philosophy of the Infinite*. Princeton University Press, 1979.

Davis, Martin. *Computability and Unsolvability*. McGraw-Hill, 1958. Enlarged edition, Dover, 1982.

Davis, Martin. *The Universal Computer: The Road from Leibniz to Turing*. W. W. Norton, 2000. Published in paperback under the title *Engines of Logic: Mathematicians and the Origin of the Computer*.

Davis, Martin, ed. *The Undecidable: Basic Paper on Undecidable Propositions, Unsolvable Problems and Computable Functions*. Raven Press, 1965.

Dawson, John W. Jr. *Logical Dilemmas: The Life and Work of Kurt Gödel*. A. K. Peters, 1997.

DeLong, Howard. *A Profile of Mathematical Logic*. Addison-Wesley, 1970; Dover, 2004.

Dennett, Daniel. *Consciousness Explained*. Back Bay Books, 1991.

Devlin, Keith. *Mathematics: The New Golden Age*. Penguin, 1988.

Enderton, Herbert B. *A Mathematical Introduction to Logic*, second edition. Harcourt, 2001.

Epstein, Richard L. and Walter A. Carnielli. *Computability: Computable Functions, Logic, and the Foundations of Mathematics*, second edition. Wadsworth, 2000.

Eves, Howard. *Foundations and Fundamental Concepts of Mathematics*, third edition. PWS-Kent, 1990; Dover, 1997.

Ewald, William. *From Kant to Hilbert: A Source Book in the Foundations of Mathematics*, in two volumes. Clarendon Press, 1996.

Franzén, Torkel. *Gödel's Theorem: An Incomplete Guide to Its Use and Abuse*. A. K. Peters, 2005.

Gödel, Kurt. *Collected Works, Volume I: Publications 1929–1936*, edited by Solomon Feferman et. al. Oxford University Press, 1986.

Gödel, Kurt. *Collected Works, Volume II: Publications 1938–1974*, edited by Solomon Feferman et. al. Oxford University Press, 1990.

Gödel, Kurt. *Collected Works, Volume III: Unpublished Essays and Lectures*, edited by Solomon Feferman et. al. Oxford University Press, 1995.

Goldstein, Rebecca. *Incompleteness: The Proof and Paradox of Kurt Gödel*. W. W. Norton, 2005.

Goldstern, Martin and Haim Judah. *The Incompleteness Phenomenon: A New Course in Mathematical Logic*. A. K. Peters, 1995.

Grattan-Guiness, I. *The Search for Mathematical Roots, 1870–1940: Logics, Set Theories and the Foundations of Mathematics from Cantor through Russell to Gödel*. Princeton University Press, 2000.

Gray, Jack and Keith Thrower. *How the Turing Bombe Smashed the Enigma Code*. Speedwell, 2001.

Heath, Sir Thomas L. *Diophantus of Alexandria: A Study in the History of Greek Algebra*, second edition. Cambridge University Press, 1910; Dover, 1964.

Heims, Steve J. *John von Neumann and Norbert Wiener: From Mathematics to the Technologies of Life and Death*. MIT Press, 1980.

Herkin, Rolf, ed. *The Universal Turing Machine: A Half-Century Introduction*. Oxford University Press, 1988. Second edition, Springer-Verlag, 1995.

Hilbert, David and Wilhelm Ackermann. *Grundzüge der Theoretischen Logik*. Springer, 1928. Second edition, Springer, 1938; Dover, 1946.

Hilbert, David and Wilhelm Ackermann. *Principles of Mathematical Logic* (translation of the second German edition of *Grundzüge der Theoretischen Logik*). Chelsea, 1950.

Hodges, Andrew. *Alan Turing: The Enigma*. Simon & Schuster, 1983.

Hodges, Andrew. *Turing: A Natural Philosopher*. Phoenix, 1997.

Hofstadter, Douglas R. *Gödel, Escher, Bach: an Eternal Golden Braid*. Basic Books, 1979.

Hunter, Geoffrey. *Metalogic: An Introduction to the Metatheory of Standard First Order Logic*. University of California Press, 1971.

Kleene, Stephen Cole. *Introduction to Metamathematics*. Van Nostrand, 1952.

Kleene, Stephen Cole. *Mathematical Logic*. John Wiley & Sons, 1967; Dover, 2002.

Kline, Morris. *Mathematics: The Loss of Certainty*. Oxford University Press, 1980.

Kneale, William and Martha Kneale. *The Development of Logic*. Clarendon Press, 1962.

Leavitt, David. *The Man Who Knew Too Much: Alan Turing and the Invention of the Computer*. W. W. Norton, 2006.

Levin, Janna. *A Madman Dreams of Turing Machines*. Alfred A. Knopf, 2006.

Lewis, C. I. *A Survey of Symbolic Logic*. Univesity of California Press, 1918; Dover, 1960.

Mancosu, Paolo. *From Brouwer to Hilbert: The Debate on the Foundations of Mathematics in the 1920s.* Oxford University Press, 1998.

Matiyasevich, Yuri M. *Hilbert's Tenth Problem.* MIT Press, 1993.

Mendelson, Elliott. *Introduction to Mathematical Logic*, fourth edition. Chapman & Hall, 1997.

Millican, Peter and Andy Clark, eds. *Machines and Thought: The Legacy of Alan Turing*, Vol. 1. Clarendon Press, 1996.

Niven, Ivan. *Numbers: Rational and Irrational.* Mathematical Association of America, 1961.

Ore, Oystein. *Number Theory and Its History.* McGraw-Hill, 1948; Dover, 1988.

Peano, Giuseppe. *Selected Works of Giuseppe Peano*, translated and edited by Hubert C. Kennedy. George Allen & Unwin, 1973.

Penrose, Roger. *The Emperor's New Mind: Concerning Computers, Minds, and the Laws of Physics.* Oxford University Press, 1989.

Petzold, Charles. *Code: The Hidden Language of Computer Hardware and Software.* Microsoft Press, 1999.

Phillips, Esther R., ed. *Studies in the History of Mathematics (MAA Studies in Mathematics, Volume 26).* Mathematical Association of America, 1987.

Prager, John. *On Turing.* Wadsworth, 2001.

Quine, Willard Van Orman. *Mathematical Logic*, revised edition. Harvard University Press, 1951, 1981.

Reid, Constance. *Hilbert.* Springer-Verlag, 1970, 1996.

Reid, Constance. *Julia: A Life in Mathematics.* Mathematical Association of America, 1996.

Robinson, Julia. *The Collected Works of Julia Robinson*, edited by Solomon Feferman. American Mathematical Society, 1996.

Russell, Bertrand. *Introduction to Mathematical Philosophy*, second edition. George Allen & Unwin, 1920; Dover, 1993.

Russell, Bertrand. *The Principles of Mathematics.* Cambridge University Press, 1903. W. W. Norton, 1938.

Shanker, S. G., ed. *Gödel's Theorem in Focus.* Routledge, 1988.

Sipser, Michael. *Introduction to the Theory of Computation.* PWS, 1997.

Teuscher, Christof, ed. *Alan Turing: Life and Legacy of a Great Thinker.* Springer, 2004.

Tiles, Mary. *The Philosophy of Set Theory: An Historical Introduction to Cantor's Paradise.* Basil Blackwell, 1989; Dover, 2004.

Turing, A. M. *Collected Works of A. M. Turing: Mathematical Logic*, edited by R. O. Gandy and C. E. M. Yates. Elsevier, 2001.

Turing, A. M. *Collected Works of A. M. Turing: Mechanical Intelligence*, edited by D. C. Ince. North-Holland, 1992.

Turing, A. M. *Collected Works of A. M. Turing: Morphogenesis*, edited by P. T. Saunders. North-Holland, 1992.

Turing, A. M. *Collected Works of A. M. Turing: Pure Mathematics*, edited by J. L. Britton. North-Holland, 1992.

van Atten, Mark. *On Brouwer*. Wadsworth, 2004.

van Heijenoort, Jean. *From Frege to Gödel: A Source Book in Mathematical Logic, 1879–1931*. Harvard University Press, 1967.

von Neumann, John. *The Computer and the Brain*. Yale University Press, 1958.

Wang, Hao. *Popular Lectures on Mathematical Logic*. Van Nostrand Reinhold, 1981; Dover, 1993.

Wang, Hao. *Reflections on Kurt Gödel*. MIT Press, 1987.

Whitehead, Alfred North and Bertrand Russell. *Principia Mathematics to *56*. Cambridge University Press, 1962.

Whitemore, Hugh. *Breaking the Code*. Fireside Theatre, 1987.

Wiener, Norbert. *Cybernetics, or Control and Communication in the Animal and the Machine*. John Wiley & Sons, 1948. Second edition, MIT Press, 1961.

Wilder, Raymond L. *Introduction to the Foundations of Mathematics*. John Wiley & Sons, 1952.

Wolfram, Stephen. *A New Kind of Science*. Wolfram Media, 2002.

Yates, David M. *Turing's Legacy: A History of Computing at the National Physical Laboratory 1945–1995*. Science Museum (London), 1997.

Index